CHRISTIAN ATTITUDES TOWARD THE JEWS IN THE MIDDLE AGES

Anna Komnene and Her Times
edited by Thalia Gouma-Peterson

William Langland's Piers Plowman
A Book of Essays
edited by Kathleen M. Hewett-Smith

The Poetic Edda
Essays on Old Norse Mythology
edited by Paul Acker and Carolyne Larrington

Regional Cuisines of Medieval Europe
A Book of Essays
edited by Melitta Weiss Adamson

The Italian Novella
edited by Gloria Allaire

Christine de Pizan
A Casebook
edited by Barbara K. Altman and Deborah L. McGrady

Violence in Medieval Courtly Literature
A Casebook
edited by Albrecht Classen

Medieval Rhetoric
A Casebook
edited by Scott D. Troyan

Christian Attitudes toward the Jews in the Middle Ages
A Casebook
edited by Michael Frassetto

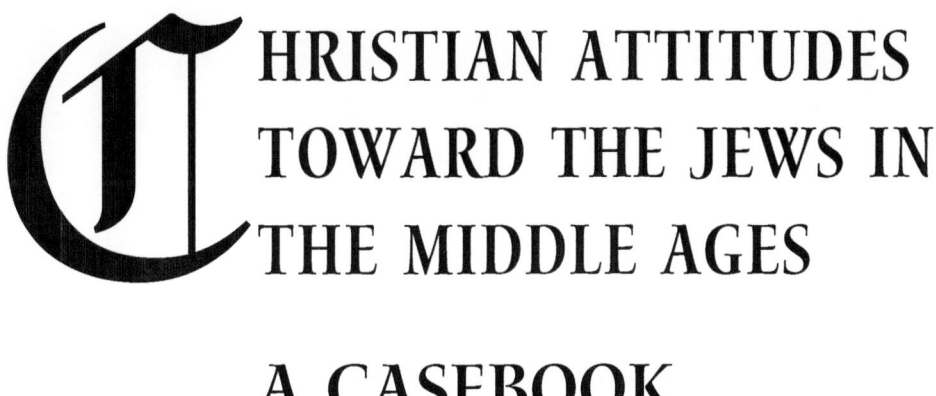

CHRISTIAN ATTITUDES TOWARD THE JEWS IN THE MIDDLE AGES

A CASEBOOK

EDITED BY
MICHAEL FRASSETTO

Routledge
Taylor & Francis Group
New York   London

Routledge is an imprint of the
Taylor & Francis Group, an informa business

Routledge
Taylor & Francis Group
711 Third Avenue
New York, NY 10017

Routledge
Taylor & Francis Group
2 Park Square
Milton Park, Abingdon
Oxon OX14 4RN

© 2007 by Taylor & Francis Group, LLC

First issued in paperback 2013

Routledge is an imprint of Taylor & Francis Group, an Informa business

International Standard Book Number-13: 978-0-415-97827-9 (Hardcover)

International Standard Book Number-13: 978-0-415-54262-3 (Softcover)

Library of Congress Cataloging-in-Publication Data

Christian attitudes toward the Jews in the Middle Ages : a casebook / edited by
   Michael Frassetto.
       p. cm. -- (Routledge medieval casebooks ; v. 37)
     ISBN 0-415-97827-0 (hardback : alk. paper)
     1. Christianity and other religions--Judaism. 2. Judaism--Relations--Christianity.
3. Antisemitism--History--To 1500. 4. Judaism--Controversial literature--History and
criticism. I. Frassetto, Michael.

BM535.C5244 2006
261.2'00902--dc22   2006022435

Visit the Taylor & Francis Web site at
http://www.taylorandfrancis.com

and the Routledge Web site at
http://www.routledge-ny.com

Contents

Acknowledgments

As this volume could not have emerged without the hard work and patience of many people, I would like to take this opportunity to thank them for bringing to this volume what value it may have. I would like to thank the contributors for their commitment to the project and for making my job as editor all the more pleasant. Several of the chapters first appeared at the 2003 meeting of the American Historical Association in Chicago, and I would like to thank the organizers of the conference for providing the opportunity to present some of the ideas that appear herein. I offer special thanks to R. I. Moore, the respondent at that session whose comments were most helpful in the revision of those conference papers. The anonymous reviewer for Routledge offered much valuable advice and pointed out a number of editorial infelicities. The editors and production staff at Routledge also were most helpful throughout. And, as ever, I am most thankful for the support of Jill and Olivia, without whom this volume could not have been completed.

Abbreviations

Ademar: Ademar of Chabannes, *Chronicon*, vol. 129 of the CCCM, ed. Richard Landes and Georges Pon (Turnhout: Brepols, 1999)

Chazan: Robert Chazan, *European Jewry and the First Crusade* (Berkeley: University of California Press, 1987)

CCCM: Corpus Christianorum Continuatio Mediaevalis (Turnhout: Brepols, 1947–)

Cohen: Jeremy Cohen, *Living Letters of the Law: Ideas of the Jew in Medieval Christianity* (Berkeley: University of California Press, 1999)

Glaber: John France, ed. and trans., *Rodvlfi Glabri Historiarum Libri Quinque: Rodulfus Glaber the Five Books of the Histories* (Oxford: Clarendon Press, 1989)

Moore: R. I. Moore, *The Formation of a Persecuting Society: Power and Deviance in Western Europe, 950–1250* (Oxford: Blackwell, 1987)

PL: *Patrologiae cursus completes, series Latina*, ed. J. P. Migne and continuators (Paris: Migne, 1852–1904)

Poliakov: Léon Poliakov, *The History of Anti-Semitism: From the Time of Christ to the Court of the Jews*, trans. Richard Howard (London: Elek Books, 1965)

Roth: Cecil Roth, *History of the Jews in England,* 3d ed. (Oxford: Oxford University Press, 1964)

Signer and Van Engen: Michael Signer and John Van Engen, eds., *Jews and Christians in Twelfth Century Europe* (Notre Dame, IN: University of Notre Dame Press, 2001)

Stow: Kenneth R. Stow, *Alienated Minority: The Jews of Medieval Latin Europe* (Cambridge, MA: Harvard University Press, 1992)

Witness to Witchcraft: Jeremy Cohen, ed., *From Witness to Witchcraft: Jews and Judaism in Medieval Christian Thought* (Wiesbaden: Harrassowitz, 1996)

Introduction: Christians and Jews in the Middle Ages

Michael Frassetto

The history of Jewish and Christian relations in the Middle Ages has traditionally been seen as one of the gradual erosion of Jewish liberty and independence and the segregation and submission of the Jews. From a state of acceptance and integration during the early Middle Ages, the Jews were ultimately forced onto the margins of society, where they were often harassed and intimidated by the Christian rulers of church and state. The progressive disenfranchisement of the Jews and diminution of their social status was accompanied by the changing theological and anthropological understanding of the Jews. This process yielded the topos of the Jew as something less than human, marked by distinct physical characteristics, and, at its worst, as the minion of the devil. By the end of the Middle Ages, many of the stereotypes of the Jews that would become the commonplaces of modern anti-Semitism were already in place, as was the tradition of segregating Jews from Christian society.

During the early Middle Ages, however, the status of the Jews and Christian attitudes toward them did not demonstrate the animosity they would in the later Middle Ages.[1] Due in part to the prevailing theological understanding of the Jews as providing witness to the truth of Christianity, the Jews stood in relatively good position and found themselves a full part of society.[2] Early medieval attitudes were also influenced by the legacy of antiquity and the tradition of Roman law, which afforded the Jews special protections that secured Jewish religious and cultural identity.[3] Although imperial legislation imposed increasing restrictions on the Jews after the conversion of Constantine in the early fourth century, as did ecclesiastical decrees, the Jews continued to enjoy relative peace and prosperity in European society. Indeed, repeated conciliar enactments in the fifth and sixth centuries restricted the social intercourse between Christians and Jews, suggesting that Jews and Christians had frequent contact and were even intermarrying.[4] Moreover, as Leonard Glick argues, "the most hostile legislation against a category of persons may reflect resentment of their social and economic status."[5] There is evidence demonstrating the good relations that existed between Christians and Jews, who were clearly integrated into the community. The Jews spoke the common language of the time as translations of Hebrew texts into the vernacular illustrate, and many Jews adopted Christian names or Latinized Hebrew names.[6] Good relations are confirmed by the writings of the Frankish bishop Gregory of Tours and, especially, by Pope Gregory the Great, who forbade the forced conversion of Jews and demanded that restitution be paid for damage done to synagogues.[7]

Good relations between Christians and Jews continued throughout the Carolingian age and are most notably revealed in the favorable treatment accorded the Jews by Louis the Pious. But even before his reign, Carolingian rulers treated the Jews of their realm well. Pippin the Short, the first of the Carolingian kings, allowed the Jews of newly conquered territory the right to keep control of hereditary property as well as the right to employ Christian workers.[8] Charlemagne recognized the religious traditions of the Jews and encouraged their commercial activities. During his reign, there is evidence of successful Jewish landowners and merchants who were involved in local and long-distance trade and, on one occasion, served in an official imperial embassy.[9] Even greater success was had during the reign of Charlemagne's son Louis, who appointed Jews to government positions and created an imperial administrator to oversee the affairs of the Jews and to ensure that they were not mistreated. Jewish commerce was protected by imperial legislation, and Jews were granted rights and privileges in accord with Christian members of the empire and could even proselytize openly.[10] This favorable treatment, however, led to a reaction from the ranks of the bishops, most notably Agobard of Lyons, who wrote several treatises denouncing the Jews and the privileges they had been granted.[11] Other Carolingian ecclesiastics made anti-Jewish proposals, including placing limitations on Jewish synagogue building and office holding as well as removing Jewish children from their homes.[12] None of these ideas was accepted by Carolingian rulers, and even Agobard accepted the Augustinian tradition of Jewish witness.

A turning point in the history of Jewish–Christian relations, and the beginning of the medieval antisemitic tradition, however, occurred at the end of the eleventh century, and crusader violence against the Jews in the Rhineland is the signal of the imminent deterioration of Jewish and Christian relations and the place of the Jew in European society.[13] Although incidents of persecution and hostility to the Jews may have taken place before 1096, it was from the late eleventh century that an ongoing tradition of hatred of the Jews began to develop. Indeed, at the very moment that medieval society began a period of political and economic expansion and cultural rebirth, the place of the Jew became increasingly circumscribed, and the Jews faced ever greater animosity. The contributions of the Jews to society as a whole are said to have decreased, and their social and economic opportunities were progressively restricted. Legal restrictions on the Jews were increased, and regulations concerning dress, movement, and work were imposed on them. The social and political repression reached an extreme when the Jews were expelled from England in 1290 and from France in 1306. In this increasingly restrictive environment, it should come as no surprise that the worst allegations of Jewish antisocial tendencies were devised, including the notorious blood libel and allegations that the Jews poisoned the wells. This more intense and institutionalized hostility toward the Jews has been seen not only as a distinct phenomenon but also as part of a hardening of attitudes against all marginal groups in medieval society.[14]

Christian attitudes toward the Jews, therefore, underwent a profound and dramatic change during the eleventh, twelfth, and thirteenth centuries, even though the exact moment of the so-called origins of medieval antisemitism remains obscure. In a variety of sources and circumstances throughout England and the Continent in this period, Christians came to reevaluate their relationship with their Jewish neighbors and developed a new understanding of the Jews. Although the general trend was one that contributed to the demonization of the Jew, Christian attitudes evolved in a complex and nuanced fashion and did not always express the hostility that formed the basis of medieval and modern antisemitism. It is the purpose of the essays that follow to chart this development and to examine Christian attitudes toward the Jews in the Middle Ages and the changing relationship between these heirs of Abraham.

Patricia Skinner, in a wide-ranging survey of the relations between Jews and Christians in early medieval Italy, confirms the traditional understanding of Jewish–Christian contacts by exploring that history in a region not usually addressed by scholars. Although the documentation is sufficiently dense, Skinner argues that a consistent picture of relations cannot be drawn and suggests that no precise image appears because contact between Jews and Christians was common and not worthy of note before the eleventh century. The next several essays concentrate on developments of the eleventh century, a pivotal period in the history of the relationship between Christians and Jews, and confirm the important transformation in relations that will take shape in the coming generations, which is alluded to at the close of Skinner's opening chapter. Although sometimes the extent of the transformation has been overstated, the period clearly revealed the gradual worsening of relations between the members of the faiths. And the century is marked by particularly dramatic manifestations of Christian hostility toward the Jews at both the beginning and the end of the century.

The events of 1096 are particularly well known, but developments during the opening decade of the eleventh century are perhaps as significant if not as well known as those at the end of the century. The first chapters, therefore, concentrate on Christian attitudes toward the Jews in the early eleventh century and seek to demonstrate the importance of this period in the evolution of Christian animosity toward the Jews. The pivotal event in the evolution of anti-Jewish attitudes was the destruction of the Holy Sepulcher by the Fatimid caliph al-Hakim in 1009. As the chapters by Daniel Callahan, Phyllis Jestice, and Michael Frassetto demonstrate, the Western Christian reaction to this event was most dramatic indeed. In his examination of one of the sermons of Ademar of Chabannes, Daniel Callahan argues that Ademar fit the assault on the church into broader patterns of millennialism and increasing devotion to the cross and the *Inventio Crucis* tradition; these various elements thus contributed to rising hostility toward the Jews. The destruction of the Holy Sepulcher, for Phyllis Jestice, was critical to the rise of animosity toward the Jews, but she looks beyond the works of Ademar to consider the broader reaction of Western society to the event. Drawing from sources in southern France and the empire, Jestice charts the rise of animosity toward the Jews stimulated by the event. She also draws from sources in the eastern Mediterranean to help explain al-Hakim's motivations, before returning to Christian sources to argue that the severity of the reaction was motivated, in part, by Jewish polemic against Christians. Although addressing the destruction of the church in my essay, I compare the emerging stereotype of the Jews with the image of heretics drawn by Ademar and Rodulphus Glaber and argue that the similarities between Jews and heretics identified by the two Christian writers contributed to the harsh reactions against both Jews and heretics in the early eleventh century.

The developments around the year 1000 prefigured the terrible events at the end of the century, which opened a period of increasing animosity toward the Jews that was sometimes balanced by the recognition of shared values and ideals. One of the most dramatic manifestations of hostility toward the Jews in the Middle Ages occurred when crusaders on their way to the Holy Lands attacked the Jews in a number of towns. In his essay, Matthew Gabrielle examines the actions of the crusaders and their leader Emicho of Flonheim, placing them and their assault on the Jews in the context of the Last Emperor and the general apocalyptic expectations that were part of the First Crusade. Although the transition to the twelfth century was heralded by one of the worst examples of anti-Jewish violence in the Middle Ages, it was also a time in which both Jews and Christians experienced a cultural renaissance. As both Constant Mews and Alex Novikoff demonstrate, although attitudes toward the Jews were hardening, there was some interest in Jewish ideas and a shared approach to certain religious matters. For Mews, Peter Abelard clearly recognized the superiority of Christianity to Judaism but was interested in what the Jews had to say and appreciated the Jews' zeal for their faith. Novikoff, too, demonstrates the growing intolerance of Christianity toward Judaism in the twelfth century, but in his study of the works of Abelard, Petrus Alfonsi, and Yehuda Halevi he reveals the shared interests of Jewish and Christian intellectuals and polemicists. Moreover, as Thomas Renna argues in "The Jews and the Golden Legend," hostility toward the Jews coexisted with a more positive understanding of the role of the Jews in salvation history. Although negative stereotypes abound in hagiographic literature, the Jews, Renna notes, also provide positive examples for Christians by their devotion to God and willingness to convert to Christianity. In this way, the Jews testify to the greatness of God.

Despite a degree of ambivalence or even respect toward Jewish traditions and the Jews, a more ominous trend appeared alongside that represented by Abelard and some hagiographical works. Indeed in a variety of texts composed beginning in the twelfth century and in various events beginning in that same period the clear lines of medieval antisemitism were being drawn. The growing hostility toward the Jews and the stereotypes associated with this hostility are revealed, according to Maureen Boulton, in a number of Anglo-Norman texts. Certainly, these texts very clearly demonstrate the increasing virulence of Christian attitudes toward the Jews in the twelfth and thirteenth centuries; the Jews evolved from being seen as simply blind to the truth of Christ to being understood as violent and deserving of punishment not only for killing Christ, according to these texts, but also because they murdered Christian boys. This hardening of attitudes in England can also be seen in the open violence against them and the growing animosity toward Jews shared by all levels of society, as John Hosler shows. As a result of Jewish wealth, Christian devotion to Jesus, and other social and religious concerns the English during the reign of King Henry II developed an increasingly hostile attitude toward the Jews, which exploded in persecutions of the Jews following Henry's death.

The increased hostility toward the Jews that was manifest as early as the eleventh century gained further expression in texts of the late thirteenth and fourteenth centuries. Although, as the works of Abelard and others in the twelfth century reveal, the evolution of anti-Jewish attitudes in medieval Europe was not a smooth, continuous process; by the end of the Middle Ages a distinctly anti-Judaic, even antisemitic, perspective came to dominate Christian thinking toward the Jews. In both theological and popular religious treatises, the Jews were denigrated and demonized. In the works of John Duns Scotus animosity toward the Jews is especially prevalent. Although, as Nancy Turner argues, Scotus revered the Law of the Hebrew Scriptures and recognized the validity of circumcision in the Law, he denounced biblical Jews as violent and deicides. He advocated the forced conversion of Jewish adults and children and declared that a small number of Jews should be placed on an island so that they could practice their faith until the Last Judgment but that all others should be forced to convert.

The seeming paradox in Scotus's attitude toward the Jews — veneration of the Hebrew Scriptures but hostility toward contemporary Jews — demonstrates medieval Christianity's own attitude toward the Jews. Medieval writers from the eleventh to the fourteenth century very clearly voiced a persistent and vehement opposition to the Jews and the Jewish faith that has been understood both to foreshadow modern anti-Semitism and to reveal the interconnection of violence and tolerance in the Middle Ages.[15] At the same time, however, other writers revealed a more open and positive understanding of Jews and Judaism.[16] It is the purpose of this volume to explore medieval Christian attitudes toward the Jews in both their positive and negative aspects.

Notes

1. For a thorough survey of the history of the Jews in the early Middle Ages, see Bernard Bachrach, *Early Medieval Jewish Policy in Western Europe* (Minneapolis: University of Minnesota Press, 1977). For the briefer treatments see Poliakov, 17–37; Leonard B. Glick, *Abraham's Heirs: Jews and Christians in Medieval Europe* (Syracuse, NY: Syracuse University Press, 1999), 26–76. For a contrary view, see Stow, 6–101.
2. On the doctrine of witness see Cohen. See also Paula Fredriksen, "*Secundum Carnem*: History and Israel in the Theology of St. Augustine," in *The Limits of Ancient Christianity: Essays on Late Antique Thought and Culture in Honor of R. A. Markus*, ed. William E. Klingshirn and Mark Vessey (Ann Arbor: University of Michigan Press, 1999), 26–41.
3. R. I. Moore, *The Formation of a Persecuting Society: Power and Deviance in Western Europe, 950–1250* (Oxford: Blackwell, 1987); Moore, 27–28.
4. Glick, *Abraham's Heirs*, 35.
5. Ibid.
6. Bernhard Blumenkranz, *Juifs et Chrétiens dans le Monde Occidental, 430–1096* (Paris: Moutons, 1960), 9.
7. Glick, *Abraham's Heirs*, 38–39. See also Cohen, *Living Letters of the Law*, 73–94, for a thorough examination of Gregory the Great's relations with the Jews.
8. Glick, *Abraham's Heirs*, 49.
9. Ibid., 50–51; Poliakov, 29.
10. Glick, *Abraham's Heirs*, 51–53.
11. Cohen, 123–45; Glick, *Abraham's Heirs*, 53–56; Poliakov, 29–32.
12. Moore, 28–29.
13. Much has been written on this topic, and the theme is also reflected in the pages following. See, especially, Chazan; Jonathan Riley-Smith, "The First Crusade and the Persecution of the Jews," in *Persecution and Toleration*, ed. W. J. Sheils (Oxford: Blackwell, 1984), 51–72. See also Cohen, "A 1096 Complex? Constructing the First Crusade in Jewish Historical Memory, Medieval and Modern," in Signer and Van Engen, 9–26; Glick, *Abraham's Heirs*, 58–110; D. Malkiel, "Jewish–Christian Relations in Europe, 840–1096," *Journal of Medieval History* 29 (2003): 55–83; Poliakov, 3–56; Stow, "Conversion, Apostasy, and Apprehensiveness: Emicho of Flonheim and the Fear of the Jews in the Twelfth Century," *Speculum* 76 (2001): 911–33.
14. Moore.
15. David Nirenberg, *Communities of Violence: Persecution of Minorities in the Middle Ages* (Princeton: Princeton University Press, 1996).
16. Robert E. Lerner, *The Feast of Abraham: Medieval Millenarians and the Jews* (Philadelphia: University of Pennsylvania Press, 2001) is an important study of the more positive relations between Jews and Christians in the later Middle Ages.

1

Conflicting Accounts
Negotiating a Jewish Space in Medieval Southern Italy, c. 800–1150 CE

Patricia Skinner

At that time, when the earthly princes were fighting to increase their prosperity, God, who is the creator of all kings and princes, continued his work. A young man called Achilles was fooled by the perversity of the Jews in this way: that he did not believe that the Son of God was made flesh in the virgin Mary or appeared visibly in this world. And it happened this way that the same Achilles believed he could chase the Jews from their evil beliefs and their bad faith; but the Jews chased him from the true Christian Faith. He offered honey, and the Jews gave him poison. The Christian begged the Jews to believe in the Son of God, and the Jews admonished the Christian to let the Son be, and to believe only in the Father. And of these things the Christian spoke to them through his mouth, but the Jews touched his heart. And the Christian, returning home several times, manifested his thoughts to his spiritual father. He was warned, and often informed by the priest's preaching. All the same, in the way that a dog returns and eats his vomit, so his soul returned to error; and he fought with himself just as men out of duty fight battles [et se combat entre soi meismes, et come de doi home fait bataille]. Every time the malice of the Jewish usurpation defeated the devotion of the true Faith, the miserable man tried to banish these thoughts from his mind, which was lost and moved through Faith and conscience; but the devil had tied him up with the arguments of the Jews. The obscurity of so many doubts lasted a long time. But this illness which wonder [?mire] did not know how to heal, was healed by God. What these matters have to do with the prince is that this Christian was one of his followers and ministers, who with arms had served God faithfully. In all ways the heretical thoughts did not empty themselves from his mind. But one day, having closed the door and being alone in the church, he felt his conscience moved, and did not approach but remained far away from the altar. And with this word he asked for God's help. And this reply came to him: "You, what do you want? And yours the heart from which nothing can escape!" [And he replied] "You know my intention, and I cannot conceal it from you. I would like to believe in you just as the holy church teaches and I would like to put into effect what the holy baptism promised me. The ancient error has attacked me, and the savagery of the Jews has wrecked my thoughts [m'a navrée la moie pensée]. And having been purged of the purity of the Christian faith, the poisonous sweetness of the Jews' words has made everything dirty and ugly. O piteous Jesus Christ, help my illness with the medicine of health! So that I might not perish, whom you bought with your precious blood, help me with your right hand!" And then, when he had said these things, the image of Jesus Christ descended to where he was, and came to where this young man was, and comforted him with these words: "Know that I am the perfect God and perfect man." And he returned to his correct Christian faith and belief, and thus the young man was outside all error and heresy. But now let us leave off speaking of these matters and return to the history which we had left.[1]

This story of a Christian boy led astray by the perversity of the Jews, set in Salerno and recounted in the Cassinese monk Amatus's history of the Norman takeover of southern Italy, forms a good starting point for a chapter that takes conflicting accounts and negotiated relationships in medieval southern Italy as its twin themes. Written around 1086, but inserted within a book of Amatus's history purporting to relate to the middle years of the eleventh century, the story will have resonance for students of Jewish medieval history in other parts of Europe. For a researcher on the history of southern Italy, however, the overt hostility of Amatus's account, albeit written by a monastic author, seems discordant when set in the context of Jewish–Christian relations in central-southern Italy. By situating Amatus's story, we can ask whether it represented a more widely held attitude toward the southern Italian Jews than has hitherto been realized.

We are not short of evidence for a Jewish presence in southern Italy: In fact, almost every genre of written text is represented in the corpus of material available to the historian. From the Jewish inhabitants of and visitors to the region, we have the eleventh-century author Ahimaaz ben Paltiel's *Scroll of Genealogies* and the itinerary of Benjamin of Tudela (written c. 1165), letters of medieval Jewish traders preserved in the Genizah or document store of Fustat (Old Cairo), and numerous epitaphs commemorating individual community members. The Christian sources are similarly rich, including narrative histories, hagiography, and charters recording property transactions. Indeed, the ongoing project to produce volumes of documents relating to the Jewish communities of Italy suggests that the process of documentation is still paramount and that analysis is still some way in the future.[2] So how did Jews and Christians relate to each other in medieval southern Italy, and how can the historian reconstruct the day-to-day negotiations that took place between the two communities in this region? This chapter uses both Jewish and Christian narrative and documentary sources to compare textual traditions surrounding the Jews of southern Italy between the ninth and twelfth centuries. We are likely neither ever to write a genuinely complete social history of the Jewish communities in this region nor to reach the real life hinted at by the texts, notwithstanding the richness of our sources here. Nevertheless, a critical analysis of the texts can suggest the ways Jewish–Christian relations subtly changed during our period.

The population of medieval southern Italy is often portrayed as one of the most ethnically and religiously diverse in Europe, at least until the twelfth century. In fact, Ahimaaz's *Scroll* has been used extensively as evidence of that diversity.[3] We know from both Christian and Jewish sources that the Jewish communities of the South were numerous and, for the most part, enjoyed good relations with their non-Jewish neighbors. They were also, as is well known, in regular contact with Jews and non-Jews in other parts of the Mediterranean, as attested by the *Scroll* and the rich contents of the Cairo Genizah.[4] The only evidence of tension comes in the form of outside interventions (for example, Byzantine persecutions and Arab attacks, both of which were episodic in their nature) and from Christian hagiography, whose portrayal of Jews is often shaped by genre rather than the realities of life on the ground. In particular, the sharpness of discourse over Jewish medical practice suggests that the latter was held in high regard by both Jewish and Christian consumers.[5]

We know that Jews colonized southern Italy very early on, and the relative abundance of evidence about their presence has led to considerable scholarly interest. However, despite several local studies in the nineteenth century, and the surveys by Cecil Roth and Nicola Ferorelli,[6] drawing on these and on nineteenth- and early twentieth-century publications of more primary sources, more recent work on Mediterranean Jewry has been curiously silent on the communities of the Mezzogiorno, whereas the work of specialists on the region has had relatively little impact on wider discussions.[7] Yet it is telling that the first two chapters of Cecil Roth's *History of the Jews of Italy*, dealing with the first millennium CE, focus on substantially more southern than northern Italian cases, with significant Jewish settlements at Naples and Venosa in the sixth century and the North described as a "blank" at this time. This is reflected in the epigraphic evidence collected by David Noy: Of 192 Jewish inscriptions surviving from Italy excluding the city of Rome, over 140 are from southern Italian or Sicilian contexts (including 75 from the catacombs of Venosa), justifying Cesare Colafemmina's earlier assertion that surviving inscriptions from the medieval period are sufficiently numerous to warrant a full-scale project to publish a *Corpus*.[8] The inscriptions, however, only document communities — they cannot tell us much about Jewish–non-Jewish relations beyond the fact that several survive in the fabric of later buildings, suggesting that Jewish burial sites were not always respected by their neighbors.

This vacuum in part reflects the survival of evidence for early medieval Italian life generally. The letters of Pope Gregory I, for instance, deal primarily with southern Italian issues because that was where the papacy held extensive property requiring active management. Some twenty-five of Gregory's letters deal with Jewish subjects, and of these seventeen relate to southern Italy,[9] and offer further insight into Jewish–non-Jewish relations at this time. They articulate very clearly the church's stance on Jews: Though there was a hope that Jews would see the error of their faith and convert (for which they received financial incentives and protection[10]), they were neither permitted to disrupt Christian life nor to assume any position that might enable them to influence others to convert to Judaism.[11] In return they were to be left alone and not disturbed in turn. Overzealous bishops seem to have been a problem: The bishop of Palermo seized the Jews' synagogues, books, and vessels, and Gregory wrote to both him and the local rector, ordering the restitution of everything. The bishop of Naples was ordered not to prevent the Jews from celebrating their festivals.[12] However, Jewish disturbance of Christian life was not tolerated. Thus, the bishop of Terracina, initially chastised by Gregory for twice moving the Jews from their chosen place of worship, was helped in his action by two other bishops under Gregory's direction when it was found that the Jews' singing was disturbing a nearby church.[13]

Gregory's letters suggest a widespread distribution of Jewish communities throughout the South. By the ninth century most cities and smaller towns appear to have had their Jewish enclaves, and Ahimaaz's *Scroll* conveys a strong sense of the vitality of southern Italian Jewry in this period.[14] The political divisions of the peninsula meant that some Jews lived under Lombard rule (e.g., in the principalities of Benevento and Salerno and, by the tenth century, Capua), whereas those further south in Puglia and Calabria were subject to the Byzantine emperor. Sicily had fallen to the Arabs in the ninth century, but it is clear from later evidence — primarily the Cairo Genizah — that the Jews here flourished under Muslim rule. The most peaceful region for Jewish settlers, however, appears to have been that controlled by Lombards. Here, there seems to have been relative security against the Arab raids of the ninth and tenth centuries — unlike the Byzantine regions further south, we do not hear of major displacements of Jews in Arab sacks, although arguments from silence are dangerous.

Further south, the Fatimid sack of Oria in 925 led to the scholar Shabbetai, known as "Donnolo" or "little master," being taken captive as a boy: He appears later documented in the *vita* of St Nilus of Rossano in Calabria.[15] This *vita* is notable among the collection of Greek saints' lives from the South for its overtly hostile stance against Donnolo and in another story of the Jews of Bisignano, where the principle of one Christian life being worth seven Jewish ones is expressed.[16] As I outline later, the intensity of hostility may directly reflect the confidence of Jews in this region, but it also signals the failure of successive imperial persecutions. These took place in 872–73, which might plausibly be linked to the Byzantine emperor Basil's campaign against the Muslims of Bari in 871 (did his attack on unbelievers get out of hand?), and, more seriously, in 932–44, when emperor Romanus I issued a decree demanding the conversion of all Jews to Christianity. This prompted attacks on the Jews at Bari and the burning of Jewish books in Bari and Oria.[17] The latter community was dispersed. Evidence for this upheaval comes in a letter from the community of Bari to the Jewish physician Hasdai ibn-Shaprut, courtier at Cordoba to the caliph Harun al-Rashid.[18] Thereafter until the Norman conquest, these communities lived under nominal Byzantine sovereignty, but their exact relationship with the local representatives of Byzantine rule is unclear; the city of Bari, certainly, rebelled against the Byzantines in the early eleventh century.[19] Such events were within living memory when Nilus's hagiographer set down his story, and the failure of the conversion campaign is clearly signalled by the fact that on a local level Jews lived alongside and did business with their non-Jewish neighbors in the Byzantine South. In Taranto, the Jew Theophylact is seen in 1033 and 1039 buying vineyards and other land. The boundary clause of the latter transaction mentions the *plantarium* of the Jews, suggesting that Theophylact was unexceptional in owning land here.[20]

Within the Lombard-ruled regions, Jews are more regularly documented but do not appear to have owned landed property. Whether this was from choice or compulsion is unclear. Certainly the city of Salerno had such a sufficiently large Jewish community that the area in which they lived became known as the *iudaica* by the early eleventh century.[21] It seems that the Salernitan princes' church of St. Mary owned the land here and leased out plots to Jews to build houses.[22] Alternative ways of exploiting the plots was not permitted, to judge from a dispute in 1004. Judex the Jew son of Juda the doctor had apparently only used part of his plot to build a house and was told to return the leftover land to the church in return for a cash sum.[23] A well was leased to a group of eight Jews, possibly community representatives, in 1031.[24] The *iudaica* is still documented in the twelfth century, but by this time non-Jewish tenants were documented, suggesting perhaps that the density of Jewish occupation had dwindled.[25]

Is it possible to see any change in Christian–Jewish relations in southern Italy between the ninth and twelfth centuries? Apart from the overt hostility of Amatus, and the Greek hagiographers, there is insufficient evidence in the Christian narrative sources to judge, and the situation is shown as even worse when examining Jewish authors. Ahimaaz's *Scroll* offers some evidence of his family's rise to prominence as servants of non-Jewish rulers but is largely focused on their place within the Jewish world; the Spanish traveller Benjamin of Tudela's *Itinerary* mentions the difficulties faced by Jews living in Constantinople, but his account of the southern Italian communities focuses entirely on their leading members and gives brief descriptions of the places they inhabit. This sense of separateness should of course not be surprising, for keeping apart was one of the central tenets of Jewish law. The Jewish narrative sources had little interest in the surrounding Gentile communities, and their ideological purpose shapes their picture. As scholars have remarked, the Italo-Ashkenazic texts such as Ahimaaz's and the *Sefer*

Yosippon, a ninth–tenth century account of Jewish antiquity, were concerned to present the Jewish people as a holy community of hasidim or righteous saints. Thus, "a clear cultural boundary existed between themselves and Christians," which did not require further comment.[26] Robert Bonfil goes further, reading in Ahimaaz a "deep contempt for the Byzantine world."[27]

By contrast, Christian writers might have a much greater interest in the non-Christian communities of the South, shaped by the demands of genre. Greek hagiography from the Byzantine South is a case in point — the sharpness with which the hagiographer treats the Jews in the *vita* of St. Nilus was designed to reassure Christians whose faith might be shaken by their vulnerability in the face of Muslim attacks. Such isolated accounts, however, are not sufficient on which to argue for continuity or change in attitudes toward the Jews.

The charter evidence, however, may provide an unexpected indicator of how attitudes toward the Jews may have changed with the arrival of the Normans from the mid-eleventh century. Charters are, of course, no less problematic as sources than chronicles and other narratives. The concern of the charter was to record the transaction being made, not to give an account of the social relations that had brought the transaction into being. Nevertheless, it is precisely this lack of interest that may render charters more reliable mirrors of social relations at the time they were made, and these individual pieces can be built into a rich and informative picture. Two major types of charter exist: those in which Jewish individuals are seen and those in which the Jewish community of a particular center is treated as a collectivity. Some of the individual cases already have been discussed to show how individuals and small groups of Jews interacted with their Christian neighbors to obtain land and housing. The Jewish community as a collectivity will be far more familiar to scholars of northern Europe, and it is striking that evidence of rulers treating it as such becomes overt only after the Norman conquest. It is worth asking, therefore, whether the Normans were responsible for a change of attitude toward and treatment of the Jews of southern Italy.

Straightaway it must be acknowledged that some Jewish communities may well have existed in a relationship of direct dependence on the local ruler earlier: In 1041 Prince Guaimarius IV of Salerno granted some Jewish families in Capua to his relative Grimoald.[28] After the Norman conquest of Salerno and the South by Robert Guiscard, however, such transactions become strikingly frequent. Robert's Lombard bride, Duchess Sichelgaita, received revenues from the Jews of Bari as part of her dowry, and she granted them to its archbishop in 1086.[29] Three years later, she granted the taxes (*redditis*) of the Jews of Palermo to the bishop there, Alcherius, reserving five-sixth of the income to herself during her lifetime.[30] Salerno's Jews passed under the protection of the local archbishop in 1090,[31] and in 1093 Robert Guiscard's brother, Count Roger I of Sicily, confirmed to the church of Melfi the Jews of the city.[32] Thus, as Norman rule expanded, by the end of eleventh century it had created explicit evidence of Jewish communities enjoying the protection of the Hauteville family or their local representative and Jewish activities contributing to the ruler's financial well-being. In the twelfth century, some of these documents provide an insight into the economic value of Jewish communities and the types of trade in which they were engaged: The Jews of Gaeta paid taxes on their dyeing, salt extraction, and olive oil pressing to the short-lived civic authorities in 1129,[33] and Leo the Jew and his family were handed over with the dyework of *Bibone* to the abbey of St Trinity at Mileto in Calabria by King Roger in 1136.[34]

Taken as a whole, we can see that the Jewish communities of southern Italy were subject to regulation, which may have become more intrusive as the Normans sought to establish their credentials as rulers, but alongside this are isolated signs of increased repression: In 1062 the Jews were expelled from Benevento.[35] How does Amatus of Montecassino's anti-Jewish tale, with which this chapter opened, reflect these trends? One possibility with which we must first deal, given the late provenance of the manuscript in which it survives, is that the story does not belong to the eleventh century at all. The youth of the wayward Christian might bring to mind the rash of ritual murder stories flourishing in Europe a century later,[36] whereas the reference to Achilles's frequent discussions with the Jews has more than a little of the disputation genre, again of a later period. Both strands, the forced link with the preceding and successive chapters ("What this has to do with the prince is that...") and the fact that Amatus's history survives only in a fourteenth-century French translation all serve to raise the suspicion that the story of Achilles (a name unheard of in contemporary charters) is a later interpolation into the eleventh-century text. Certainly Ferorelli identifies a change in attitudes toward the Jews in southern Italy in the thirteenth century, with an accusation of desecrating a crucifix at Trani in 1260 and violence in Naples at the same, accompanied by increased pressure from the church for Jews to convert.[37] Perhaps this was the point at which Amatus's history gained its anti-Jewish digression, but unless other texts are discovered we cannot know for sure.

The other possibility, then, is to take the story at face value and to seek reasons for its inclusion in the contemporary eleventh-century context. The theme of conversion is, I think, the central issue: Here was a Christian soul in danger from persuasive Jewish arguments. Might we read this as a cautionary tale provoked precisely by the regular interaction between Christians and Jews in and around Salerno? The church had offered long-standing protection to Jews provided that they did not proselytize or try to expand their religious activities (e.g., by building new synagogues). Yet we know that conversions to Judaism did take place. Indeed, that of archbishop Andrea of Bari, circumcised in Constantinople around 1066, must have reverberated throughout the Christian communities of the South.[38] Could Amatus's account provide an early reaction to the anxiety and doubt that some Christians felt when living in day-to-day contact with their Jewish neighbors? Is there a connection between this and the fact that Jews of

Salerno were placed under the archbishop's direct patronage in 1090? And is this a localized phenomenon, or should it be seen as part of a wider importation of ideas about Jews brought in by the new Norman rulers? (Duke Robert had, after all, given the Jews of Bari, another flourishing community, to his wife.) I have suggested elsewhere that the unease provoked by the Norman arrival may have contributed in 1054 to Ahimaaz deciding to write down his family's history for posterity and thus preserving its memory in a period when oral memory may have become ruptured by the displacement of his family members.[39] But perhaps the unease was felt on both sides: Amatus's work, as I have discussed elsewhere, owed much to Robert and Sichelgaita's patronage;[40] perhaps his inclusion of the story was intended to highlight a perceived threat to Christian rule in the confident, well-established Jews of the South, in the hope it might please his patrons, Robert and Sichelgaita, and encourage a more regulatory stance.

To run this argument a little further, we might consider the world from which the Normans came and think about the situation of the Jews there. The archetype of a ruler controlling Jewish communities in a state of dependence is that of Duke William of Normandy and his transfer of Jews to England after 1066. William Chester Jordan points to a hardening of Jewish regulation as a means of securing uncertain successions in France and signalling the new king's legitimacy.[41] Both of these ideas — dependence and regulation — may have been influential on the Norman adventurers to the South when they came up against the wealthy and confident Jews of southern Italy: By adopting protection as a strategy of rule, they not only signalled a legitimacy of sorts, alongside other strategies such as intermarriage with local dynasties, but at the same time secured an important economic asset. Were the Jews of the South punished for their proselytising? Colafemmina certainly links the destruction of the Barese synagogue and its replacement with the church of SS Silvester and Leo to Andrea's conversion.[42] If the coming of the Normans did lead to a change in Jewish–Christian relations, it would be one of the very few areas in which their arrival had an impact on the social life of the South and illustrates how studying the history of the Jewish minority might challenge the generally accepted view that the Norman takeover was one of continuity rather than change.

How did the Jews react? Unfortunately, we have no Jewish voices to guide us through the late eleventh and early twelfth centuries, and this in itself may be telling. Once the Normans became established, and the new regime established over the Jewish communities, the twelfth century seems to have been a golden age for southern Italian Jewish culture. Certainly Puglia became famous throughout Europe for the richness and density of its Jewish culture, to the extent that the twelfth-century French rabbi Yacob ben Meir Tam could comment, "From Bari comes forth the Law, and the word of God from Otranto."[43] The itinerary of Benjamin of Tudela confirms this impression of the continued flourishing of Jews across the South in the twelfth century. From Rome he went to Capua, clearly a center of learning, to Pozzuoli, Naples, Salerno, where he comments on the medical school and the presence of 600 Jews,[44] to Amalfi, Benevento, Melfi, Ascoli, the "great and beautiful" city of Trani, Bari, which was deserted, having been laid waste in 1156, to Taranto, Brindisi, and Otranto. On his return journey he stopped in Messina and found 1,500 Jews, by far the largest Italian figure, in Palermo. Even taking into account the fact that Benjamin was conveying a sense of the relative size of each community rather than taking a systematic head count, it is still clear that he met the great majority of Italian Jews in the South.[45]

At this point, it might be suggested, the history of the Jews of southern Italy looks much more similar to that of other Jewish communities in Europe, with royal protection taking the place of a looser relationship between the Jews and their local rulers. The tighter regulation of Jewish transactions by central authorities might be indicated by a drop in Cairo Geniza letters relating to southern Italy and Sicily, with the twelfth century noted as a turning point by Goitein.[46] If the Norman kings were imposing more regulation on the economic transactions of Jewish merchants, this may have led to their bypassing the kingdom. Within southern Italy, the relationship of increased dependence on the ruler would eventually leave the Jews more vulnerable to persecution, as elsewhere in Europe. It is striking that as northern Italy developed local polities in the form of city-states in the twelfth and thirteenth centuries, it was to these that Jews gravitated,[47] and it is entirely possible that the more obvious commercial opportunities available may have in fact masked a growing disaffection with the centralizing Norman state.

In conclusion, despite its relative density, the evidence from southern Italy is still too sparse to trace a consistently held attitude toward the Jews on the part of their neighbors. Perhaps the lack of comment on the subject, outside hagiographic sources, is an indicator of how commonplace and unremarkable Jewish–Christian interactions were in this region up until the eleventh century. The arrival of the Normans may have upset this equilibrium, causing both sides to reevaluate how they viewed the other and, more importantly, how they accommodated the newcomers. This resulted in the production of texts whose overall tone is more openly hostile to the Jewish minority. Yet such texts speak also of insecurity on the part of their Christian writers, perhaps shaken by the high-profile conversion of Andreas of Bari and by a need on the part of the clerical community to see real progress being made in controlling the threat within their midst. It is no coincidence that many Jewish communities found themselves directly ruled not by the Norman leaders but by the ecclesiastical authorities to which the rulers granted them. This relationship represented protection of sorts, but at a high price.

Notes

1. Vincenzo de Bartholomaeis, ed., *Storia de' Normanni di Amato di Montecassino*, Fonti per la Storia d'Italia 76 (Rome: Tipografia del Senato, 1935), 104–6.
2. Cesare Colafemmina, "Insediamenti e condizione degli ebrei nell'Italia meridionale e insulare," in *Gli Ebrei nell'alto medievo, Settimane di Studio del Centro Italiano di Studi sull'alto Medioevo* 26 (Spoleto: Presso la sede del Centro, 1980), 197–227, is rather limited in scope despite its title and is a good example of the tendency to document rather than to analyze. Shlomo Simonsohn, ed., *The Jews in Sicily, I: 383–1300 (A Documentary History of the Jews in Italy, XIII)* (Leiden: Brill, 1997). The *Italia Judaica* series (see note 4) complements the document collections but extends beyond the medieval period and has not as yet examined the South in detail. See, however, *Italia Judaica V: gli ebrei in Sicilia sin all'espulsione del 1492* (Rome: Pubblicazioni degli Archivi di Stato, Saggi 35, Ministero per i beni culturali e ambientali/Ufficio centrale per i beni archivistici, 1995).
3. Stephen D. Benin, "Jews, Muslims and Christians in Byzantine Italy," in Benjamin H. Hary, John Hayes, and Fred Astren, eds., *Judaism and Islam: Boundaries, Communication and Interaction* (Leiden: Brill, 2000), 27–35, is almost entirely based on Ahimaaz's work.
4. Shelomo D. Goitein, "Sicily and Southern Italy in the Cairo Geniza documents," *Archivio Storico per la Sicilia Orientale* 67 (1971): 9–33, is an excellent introduction to the material and is only partly supplemented by Moshe Gil, "The Jews in Sicily under Muslim rule, in the light of the Geniza documents," in *Italia Judaica I: Atti del I convegno internationale, Bari, 18–22 maggio 1981* (Rome: Ministero per i Beni Culturali e Ambienti: pubblicazioni degli Archivi di Stato, saggi 2, 1983). See also Eliyahu Ashtor, "Gli ebrei nel commercio mediterraneo nell'alto medioevo (sec. X–XI)," in *Gli Ebrei nell'alto Medioevo*, 401–64.
5. See Patricia Skinner, "A Cure for a Sinner: Sickness and Healthcare in Medieval Southern Italy," in *The Community, the Family and the Saint: Patterns of Power in Early Medieval Europe*, ed. Joyce Hill and Mary Swan (Turnhout: Brepols, 1998), 279–309.
6. Cecil Roth, *The History of the Jews of Italy* (Philadelphia: Jewish Publication Society of America, 1946); see also Nicola Ferorelli, *Gli Ebrei nell'Italia Meridionale* (Bologna: Forni, 1915). Earlier work Roth might have consulted, despite bemoaning the lack of English-language studies, includes Herbert M. Adler, "The Jews in Southern Italy," *Jewish Quarterly Review* 14 (1902): 111–15.
7. The state of play for medieval Italy as a whole was outlined in 1981 by Shlomo Simonsohn, "Lo stato attuale della ricerca storica sugli ebrei in Italia," in *Italia Judaica I*, 29–37. At that stage he described an explosion of interest in Jewish history (citing *Gli Ebrei nell'alto medioevo* [note 2] as an example of the trend), but the past twenty-five years have not seen this interest influence broader studies. For example, Benjamin Arbel, ed., *Intercultural Contacts in the Medieval Mediterranean* (Portland, OR: F. Cass, 1996), has only a chapter on twelfth- to fourteenth-century Genoa and nothing earlier or southern in focus; Signer and van Engen has only a passing reference to southern Italy.

8. David Noy, *Jewish Inscriptions of Western Europe I: Italy (excluding the city of Rome), Spain and Gaul* (Cambridge: Cambridge University Press, 1993); Colafemmina, "Archeologia ed epigrafia ebraica nell'Italia meridionale" in *Italia Judaica I*, 199–210.

9. Dag Norberg, ed., *S. Gregori Magni Registrum Epistularum, Libri I–VII*, and *S. Gregori Magni Registrum Epistularum, Libri VIII–XIV* (Corpus Christianum Series Latina, 140 and 140A, Turnhout: Brepols, 1982). The southern Italian letters are book I, 42, 34, 66, 69; II, 45, 50; III, 37; IV, 31; V, 7; VI, 29; VII, 41; VIII, 23, 25; IX, 38, 40, 105; XIII, 13.

10. Protection: ibid., I, 69; II, 50; VIII, 23. Financial support: ibid., IV, 31; V, 7.

11. Jewish ownership of Christian slaves was regularly condemned: ibid., III, 37; IX, 105. A *nefas* Jew buying the church vessels of the church of Venafro had to return them without compensation: ibid., I, 66. A remarkable case was brought to Gregory's attention in 593 involving the *sceleratissimus* Jew Nasas setting up a fake altar to St. Elias in Sicily, but no detail is given: ibid., III, 37.

12. Palermo: ibid., VIII, 25; IX, 38. Naples: ibid., XIII, 13.

13. Ibid., I, 34; II, 45.

14. Marcus Salzmann, trans., *The Chronicle of Ahimaaz* (New York: Columbia University Press, 1924); a brief and rather dismissive treatment of Ahimaaz's work is in Roth, *History*, 50–51; on Ahimaaz as a family historian, see Skinner, "Gender, Memory and Jewish Identity: Reading a Family History from Southern Italy," *Early Medieval Europe* 13 (2005): 277–98.

15. Andrew Sharf, *The Universe of Shabbetai Donnolo* (Warminster: Aris and Phillips, 1976) is the standard work on Shabbetai; see also Robert Bonfil, "Can Medieval Storytelling Help Understand Midrash?" in *The Midrashic Imagination: Jewish Exegesis, Thought and History*, ed. Michael Fishbane (New York: State University of New York Press, 1993), 228–54, at 228 where the brief life of Shabbetai in the *Sefer Hasidim* is discussed.

16. Joannes Stilting, et al., eds., *Vita Sancti Nili Abbatis, AA.SS. Sept.VII* (Antwerp: B. A. Vander Plassche, 1760), vii 50 and v 35, respectively.

17. Sharf, *Byzantine Jewry from Justinian to the Fourth Crusade* (London: Schocken Books, 1971), 95–100.

18. Jacob Mann, *Texts and Studies in Jewish History and Literature, I* (Cincinnati: Hebrew Union College Press, 1931); Umberto Cassuto, "Un lettera ebraica del secolo X," *Giornale della Società Asiatica Italiana* 29 (1917), 97–110; Elkan Nathan Adler, "Un document sur l'histoire des juifs en Italie," *Revue Études Juifs* 67 (1914): 40–43.

19. Ferorelli, *Gli ebrei*, 33, reports the intriguing suggestion that Melo of Bari's family may have been of Jewish ancestry, linking the rebellion to the persecutions against Jews. Such speculation has no substantiation in the documentation, however.

20. Francesco Trinchera, ed., *Syllabus Graecarum Membranarum* (Naples: Typis Josephi Caetano, 1865), docs. 26, 31.

21. Huguette Taviani-Carozzi, *La principauté lombarde de Salerne* (Rome: Ecole Française, 1991), 355–56; note 83 discusses the documents and related bibliography. See also Skinner, *Health and Medicine in Early Medieval Southern Italy* (Leiden: Brill, 1997), 81–82.

22. See, for example, Michele Morcaldi, Mauro Schiani, and Sylvano de Stefano, et al., eds., *Codex Diplomaticus Cavensis* (Milan: P. Piaazi, 1873–93), IV, docs. 567, 651.

23. Ibid., doc. 567.

24. Ibid., V, doc. 841.

25. Riccardo Filangieri di Candida, ed., *Codice Diplomatico Amalfitano*, I (Naples: Stab. tip. S. Morano, 1917), doc. 183 (1172); Jole Mazzoleni and Renate Orefice, eds., *Il Codice Perris: Cartulario Amalfitano*, I (Amalfi: Centro di cultura e storia amalfitana, 1985), doc. 155 (1174).

26. Ivan G. Marcus, "History, Story and Collective Memory: Narrativity in Early Ashkenazic Culture," *Prooftexts* 10 (1990): 383.

27. Bonfil, "Medieval Storytelling," 241.

28. Giovanni Mongelli, ed., *Abbazia di Montevergine: Regesto delle Pergamene*, I (Rome: Ufficio centrale degli archivi di Stato, 1956), 33, doc. 47. Taviani-Carozzi, *Principauté*, I, 448–49, nevertheless points up the "nouvelles formes de dependence" that this document may represent.

29. Giovanni Battista Nitto de Rossi and Francesco Nitti di Vito, eds., *Codice Diplomatico Barese*, I–II (Bari: V. Vecchi, 1897–99), doc. 30: "especially those in the area *sinagoge*."

30. Bartolomeo and Giuseppe Lagumina, eds., *Documenti per servire alla storia di Sicilia I, 6: Codice Diplomatico dei Giudei di Sicilia I* (Palermo: Tip. di M. Amenta, 1884), 9, doc. 12.

31. Graham A. Loud, *The Age of Robert Guiscard: Southern Italy and the Norman Conquest* (London: Longman, 2000), 264.

32. Angelo Mercati, "Le pergamene di Melfi all'Archivio Segreto Vaticano," *Miscellanea Giovanni Mercati*, 5 (Vatican City: Città del Vaticano, 1946), 303, doc. 9.

33. *Codex Diplomaticus Cajetanus*, II (Montecassino: Typis Archicoenobii Montis Cassino, 1891), 240, doc. 317.

34. Carl-Richard Brühl, ed., *Codex Diplomaticus Regni Siciliae, II.i: Rogerii II Regis Diplomata Latina* (Köln: Böhlau, 1987), doc. 42. Another gift by Roger, of a tenth of the revenue of the Jewish dyeworks, was confirmed to the archbishop of Rossano by Empress Constance and her son Frederick II in 1198: Walter Holzmann, "Papst-, Kaiser- und normannen Urkunden aus Unteritalien II: S. Giovanni di Fiore, Erzbistum Rossano, Bistum Bova, S. Elia Carbone," *QFIAB* 36 (1956): 24.

35. Moore, 32.

36. Sophia Menache, "Faith, Myth and Politics: The Stereotype of the Jews and Their Expulsion from England and France," *Jewish Quarterly Review* 75 (1985): 353–54, summarizes those in England.

37. Ferorelli's pessimism was not wholly shared by Cassuto, who suggests that the peaceful burial and surviving epitaph of Adoniyyah b. Baruk in the Jewish cemetery at Trani in 1290 is evidence that the anti-Jewish measures within the Kingdom of Naples in this period were not universal: Umberto Cassuto, "Iscrizioni ebraiche a Trani," *Rivista degli Studi Orientali* 13 (1931–32): 172–80.

38. Bernhard Blumenkranz, "La conversion au judaisme d'André archevéque de Bari," *Journal of Jewish Studies* 14 (1963): 33–36; see also Norman Golb, "Notes on the Conversion of European Christians to Judaism in the Eleventh Century," *Journal of Jewish Studies* 16 (1965): 69–74. Colafemmina, "L'itinerario pugliese," 88, suggests that Andrea's example might have inspired the Norman priest John of Oppido to convert in 1102. For an extended discussion of both men see Joshua Prawer, "The Autobiography of Obadyah the Norman, a Convert to Judaism at the Time of the First Crusade," in *Studies in Medieval History and Literature,* ed. Isadore Twersky (Cambridge, MA: Harvard University Press, 1979), 110–34; see also Shelomo D. Goitein, *A Mediterranean Society: the Jewish Communities of the World as Portrayed by the Documents of the Cairo Genizah II: The Community* (Los Angeles: University of California Press, 1971), 308–9.
39. Skinner, "Gender, Memory and Jewish Identity."
40. Skinner, "'Halt! Be men!' Sikelgaita of Salerno, Gender and the Norman Conquest of Southern Italy," *Gender and History* 12 (2000): 622–41.
41. For Jews in Normandy and France see Golb, *The Jews in Medieval Normandy* (New York: Cambridge University Press, 1998); William Jordan, *The French Monarchy and the Jews* (Philadelphia: University of Pennsylvania Press, 1989).
42. Colafemmina, "L'itinerario pugliese," 88.
43. Roth, *History*, 61, from Rabbi Tam's *Sefer ha-Yashar.* Bonfil, "Mito, retorica, storia: saggio sul 'Rotolo di Ahima'az'" in Robert Bonfil, *Tra due mondi: cultura ebraica e cultura cristiana nel medioevo* (Naples: Liguori, 1996), 100, suggests that Rabbi Tam was drawing attention to the lively independence of Italo-Jewish culture, with Palestinian customs persisting alongside the dominant Babylonian tradition.
44. Skinner, *Health and Medicine* looks at the early intersection of Jews and medicine in the territory of Salerno.
45. In fairness, Benjamin's itinerary took him to more places in the South; only Genoa, Pisa, and Lucca feature in his northern journey, but without wishing to run a circular argument it might be suggested that the prospect of meeting substantial numbers of Jews influenced his choice of route: Marcus Nathan Adler, ed. and trans., *The Itinerary of Benjamin of Tudela* (London: H. Frowde, 1907). See also Colafemmina, "L'itinerario pugliese di Beniamino da Tudela," *Archivio Storico Pugliese* 28 (1975): 81–100.
46. Goitein, "Sicily and Southern Italy," 16.
47. Despite Roth's earlier pessimism, the North is not entirely a blank: Vittore Colorni, "Gli Ebrei nei territori Italiani a nord di Roma dal 568 agli inizi del secolo XIII," in *Gli Ebrei nell'Alto Medioevo,* 241–307, provides an overview with extensive bibliography. In common with earlier approaches, however, it focuses on Jewish intellectual life rather than their social history.

2

The Cross, the Jews, and the Destruction of the Church of the Holy Sepulcher in the Writings of Ademar of Chabannes[1]

Daniel F. Callahan

In autumn 1009 the Church of the Holy Sepulcher in Jerusalem was destroyed on the orders of the caliph of Cairo al-Hakim. When word of this destruction of the most holy structure in Christendom, with its tomb of Christ and remains of the True Cross, reached the West, the reaction was immediate and intense. The Aquitanian chronicler Ademar of Chabannes, writing in the 1020s, says that the tomb of the Lord was smashed by the Jews and the Saracens because the Jews of the West and the Saracens of Spain had sent letters to the East accusing the Christians of ordering armies of the West to attack eastern Saracens. Then, aroused to fury, Hakim, or, as Ademar called him, the Nebuchadnezzar of Babylon — the name of Cairo in the West during the Middle Ages — made a law that required all Christians in his lands to become Muslims or to face execution. Few, according to Ademar, remained true to their Christian beliefs, except most prominently the patriarch of Jerusalem, who was executed after various tortures. Then Hakim destroyed many churches — especially the basilica of the tomb of Christ, which was demolished to its foundation — crushing the stones as much as they could and then setting fire to what remained. But when the church in Bethlehem was miraculously preserved, as was the monastery of Mount Sinai, and plague and famine lasting three years killed 90,000 Saracens and Jews, Hakim had a change of heart. He and his people did penance, and he ordered the Church of the Holy Sepulcher rebuilt because they were deeply terrified.[2]

Another important chronicler of West Frankish developments of this period, Rodulfus Glaber, also has much material on the Western reaction to the Church of the Holy Sepulcher or, as he calls it, the Temple, a popular name for the church in Jerusalem.[3] His description offers many additional details to Ademar's but in general does not essentially contradict it. Glaber specifically blames the Jews of Orleans for sending the message to the caliph that resulted in the destruction of the Church of the Holy Sepulcher. He states, "A little while after the Temple had been destroyed it became quite clear that the wickedness of the Jews had brought about this great disaster. Once they knew this, all the Christians throughout the whole world decided unanimously to drive the Jews from their lands and cities. They became the object of universal hatred; they were driven from the cities, some were put to the sword, others were drowned in rivers, and many found other deaths; some even took their own lives in diverse ways. So it was that after this very proper vengeance had been taken, very few of them were to be found in the Roman world."[4] Glaber goes on to state that after this initial explosion of anti-Judaism had occurred, relative order was restored. He writes,

> The dispersed and wandering Jews who had survived this affliction remained hidden in distant and secret places until five years after the destruction of the Temple, when a few began to reappear in the cities. For it was proper, although ultimately to their confusion, that some of them should survive for the future to serve as witnesses of their own perfidy, or testimony to the blood of Christ which they had shed. That is why, we believe, thanks to the disposition of divine providence, the fury of the Christian people against them cooled. In that same year, by divine clemency, the mother of that prince, the ruler of Cairo, a truly Christian woman called Maria, began with well-dressed square stones to rebuild the Temple of Christ, which had been destroyed by the command of her son...Then an incredible multitude of men from all over the world came exultantly to Jerusalem bearing countless gifts for the restoration of the house of God.[5]

Now where does one begin to demythologize the accounts of these two chroniclers? It is not the purpose of this chapter to do that, although Hakim's decision to destroy the church in Jerusalem may have been the result of his disapproval of the so-called miracle of the new fire, which occurred each year on Holy Saturday and which was found to be the result of human intervention.[6] On the other hand, it may have been the action of a mentally unstable ruler who seems to have considered himself divine.[7] Whatever the case, there is little likelihood that he acted in response to warnings from Jews in western Europe. As for a so-called army of the West, Pope Sergius IV in 1010 did indeed call for such a force, but it was the result of the destruction of the Church of the Holy Sepulcher and not the cause of the Hakim's actions there.[8] Moreover, the magnitude of the Christian attack on the Jews in the West was clearly exaggerated by Glaber and Ademar, as both Richard Landes and I have indicated in the past decade.[9]

Yet it is clear that the destruction of the church in Jerusalem that housed the remains of the True Cross did contribute directly to the changing Christian attitude in the West toward the Jews. This chapter draws on material in my forthcoming book, *The Making of a Millennial Pilgrim: Jerusalem and the Cross in the Life and Writings of Ademar of Chabannes,* which examines this question in much greater depth and considers briefly only one of Ademar's sermons to see what it tells us about the connection between the Cross and the rise of Western anti-Judaism at this particular time in the first third of the eleventh century.

That Ademar is so valuable a source for this material should not be surprising. A monk of Saint-Cybard of Angoulême, he lived between 989 and 1034 and probably is best known for his chronicle and his role as the orchestrator of the campaign to have St. Martial of Limoges recognized as an apostle in the late 1020s.[10] His failure to gain this recognition resulted in a great outpouring of writings he completed before leaving on a pilgrimage to Jerusalem in 1033. His many manuscripts, the largest surviving collection from the hand of any one individual from the early Middle Ages, bear witness to his wide-ranging interests in sacred history and his knowledge of the scriptures and the writings of the church fathers. They testify to his keen sense, shared with Rodulfus Glaber, that he was living in the end time and that the presence of the devil and his minions — the antichrist and the heretics, including the Jews — was evident everywhere.[11]

Much of his writing remains unedited. Especially important are his many sermons, particularly those in Latin Manuscript 2469 at the Bibliotheque Nationale in Paris and in Latin Manuscript 1664 in the Deutsche Staatsbibliothek in Berlin, works now being edited by Michael Frassetto and me for the Ademar collection in the Corpus Christianorum.[12] The sermon to be considered in this piece is one of the forty-six in the Paris manuscript and is by far the longest in the collection, with a length for which Ademar apologizes.

This item, running from folio 38v to 50v, is a rambling, disjointed work written to commemorate the dedication of the church of St. Peter in Limoges, a structure that supposedly could trace its foundation to Duke Stephen, the purported ruler of Gaul in the first century at the time of the mission of the "apostle" Martial. The church is celebrated as the resting place of the remains of St. Martial and thus is a place of extraordinary sanctity. At the center of the sermon, and what makes it so pertinent to this essay, is the theme of the connection between Jerusalem and Limoges: Jerusalem, with the Cross and Resurrection; and Limoges, where the fruits of Christ's salvific actions were supposedly first tasted in transalpine Europe. Much space is devoted to a comparison of the Old Testament temple in Jerusalem and the Church of St. Peter in Limoges, one with the ark of the covenant, the other with the tomb of St. Martial. The opulent decoration of the temple allows Ademar to write about the comparable decoration of the church in Limoges and the value of Christian decorations in general, especially the use of gold, silver, and jewels to honor the cross to emphasize its precious quality.[13]

Cross imagery is interwoven throughout the piece, and he draws on the example of St. Helena, the mother of Constantine and finder of the True Cross in the Inventio Crucis legend, in giving honor to the sacred wood.[14] Although Ademar does not present the full legend of the finding of the Cross by Constantine's mother in the 320s, an account found in many manuscripts of the early Middle Ages, his sermon presupposes a knowledge of it to appreciate fully its usage in this sermon.[15] The presentation begins with the image of Zacheus the publican standing in a tree and searching for the sight of Christ on his way to Jerusalem (Luke 19). Ademar, using the Inventio Crucis legend, establishes a parallel between Zacheus climbing the tree to see Christ and the history of the wood of the cross.[16] In the legend Zacheus is the grandfather of Judas Cyriacus, who led Helena to the place where the True Cross was buried. Zacheus in the Cross legend and in that of St. Martial was related to Joseph of Arimathea, who helped the latter bury Christ and the Cross.[17] Before Zacheus died, he told his son where the Cross was placed. The son, in turn, later tells his son, Judas Cyriacus, where the Cross can be found.

Throughout the sermon, following the intense anti-Judaism of the Inventio Crucis legend of the late fourth and early fifth century when it was written, Ademar condemns the Jews for crucifying Christ. He states, "At the time of Tiberius our Lord suffered from the Jews..." The Jews are "...a most base people who derided the humanity of the Lord on the Cross." Next, using Matthew 27, he quotes the Jews as saying, "Take him, take him, crucify him and let his blood be over us and over our sons."[18] He presents the Cross as a scandal to the Jews.[19] They were responsible for fastening the humanity of Christ to the wood. He praises Zacheus for saving the sacred wood for future generations because the "malignantes Judei" would not destroy it by blades or fire.[20]

In this piece Ademar also emphasizes the need to glorify the cross with gold and silver.[21] This is the way the Cross will appear in the last days, supremely decorated, the glorious vexillum that will mark the ultimate triumph of Christ the King, the Omega Cross that will precede the ultimate appearance of the Lord.[22] He rejoices, "Then the mystery of the Cross will shine, with the devil prostrated by the victory and the world will be raised up."[23] As I pointed out in my *Journal of Ecclesiastical History* article on anti-Judaism, there was clearly a connection in Ademar's mind and in the minds of many of his contemporaries between the devil and the Antichrist, on the one hand, and the actions of the Jews and Muslims and the appearance of other heretics in the West, which revealed the growing wickedness of the period.[24]

Although Ademar does have some positive images of Jews, especially of Christ the king of the Jews and his apostles, particularly Peter, Paul, and Martial, his depiction is essentially strongly negative. Peter and Martial were cast out by the Jews of Judea.[25] Martial suffered from the attacks of the Jews, as did St. Paul, who was accused by them and then went to Rome.[26] As he says in the sermon, all of this preceded the Roman destruction of Jerusalem after the wicked rule of the Herods.[27]

Yet the Inventio Crucis material had existed throughout the early Middle Ages and most certainly would have been drawn on for earlier sermon material.

Why did this material become so incendiary in the early eleventh century? Surely the destruction of the Church of the Holy Sepulcher is central. This destruction took on added meaning for those who had visited Jerusalem and the sites of the Holy Land. For them, the holiest spot for the West had become a visible reality. Moreover, the number of pilgrims continued to grow in the tenth and eleventh centuries with thousands going forth, as Glaber states.[28] This movement was greatly assisted by the opening of a land route through Hungary about the year 1000 with the conversion of King Stephen and his people. Ademar's writings in general greatly reflect this interest in the holy pilgrimage. The sermon just examined is an excellent example, for it mentions individuals like St. Paul and the Queen of Sheba going to the holy city.[29] To be sure, such an interest is hardly surprising during the Benedictine centuries when a liturgical civilization flourished and the Psalms with their many references to Jerusalem served as a central prayer. Psalm 136:5–9 demonstrates this longing clearly:

> If I forget thee, O Jerusalem, let my right hand be forgotten. May my tongue cleave to my palate if I do not remember thee, if I place not Jerusalem ahead of my joy. Remember, O Lord, the children of Edom, the day of Jerusalem, when they said, "Raze it, raze it down to its foundations!" O daughter of Babylon you destroyer, happy the man who shall repay the evil you have done us! Happy the man who shall seize and smash your little ones against the rock!

Thus the destruction of the central structure of the Holy City, the new temple, by the ruler of Babylon in 1009 was bound to bring such words to mind and to generate immense anger.

Compounding this animosity was the fact that millennial fears were growing. One sign of the presence of the Antichrist was that he would rebuild the temple.[30] So it hardly should be surprising that Hakim's destruction of the temple and reports that he was rebuilding the structure called the temple would cause the West to become aroused. As Glaber notes, his mother, Maria, was behind the rebuilding effort.[31] The fact that the ruler of Babylon, who considered himself divine and had a mother named Maria, was rebuilding the temple in Jerusalem caused many, as Glaber comments, to go forth to the Holy City to face the Antichrist.[32]

The rise of anti-Judaism at this moment is also increased by another factor. Christianity is a bipolar religion with both incarnational, or alpha, and transcendental, or omega, poles ever present. Generally one pole is rising, and the other falling, as one sees in the ascendance of the incarnational in the twelfth and thirteenth centuries. Rarely is there a balance. Even more rarely do both poles ascend at the same time, as is the case in the late tenth and early eleventh centuries when both alpha and omega currents were running strongly. Caught in the middle were the Jews, attacked as killers of Christ and supporters of the Antichrist. And the eyes of the West were on Jerusalem where God had dwelled and to which he was about to return. How could not the attention of the West be focused on the destruction of the most sacred site of the most sacred city, the center of the center of the earth? All had been predicted and now was occurring.

Yet although the moment passed, its powerful influences remained. Continuing work on the origins of the Crusades confirms Herbert Cowdrey's view on the central role of Jerusalem in the development of holy war.[33] The destruction of the Church of the Holy Sepulcher and the remains of the True Cross there and the resulting attacks on the Jews of the West will not be forgotten. The persecution of the Jews as the crucifiers of Christ will resume and intensify in the wake of the First Crusade, when the West found the leadership and resources to undertake such a campaign.

Moreover, the connection between the Cross and the Jews has continued to create serious problems throughout the development of Western civilization. The controversy over the presence of crosses placed at Auschwitz during the past thirty years is just one reminder, as James Carroll pointed out in his recent book *Constantine's Sword,* of how poisonous the issue remains in Jewish–Christian relations.[34] No matter how many times Pope John Paul II apologized for the past actions of Christians toward Jews, the issue would remain. The reverberations of the destruction of the Church of the Holy Sepucher continue to be felt almost a millennium later.

Notes

1. This article was originally delivered as a paper at the American Historical Association annual meeting in January 2003 in a session on anti-Judaism organized by Michael Frassetto. I wish to express my gratitude to the other members of the session — R. I. Moore, Matthew Gabriele, and Michael Frassetto — and to the audience in attendance for their valuable comments. Biblical quotations come from the Vulgate.

2. Ademar, 3:47, 166–67; Ademar of Chabannes, *Commemoratio Abbatum Basilice S. Martialis,* in *Chroniques de Saint-Martial de Limoges,* ed. H. Duplès-Agier (Paris: Mme Ve. J. Renouard, 1874), 6.

3. Glaber, esp. 3:7.24, 132–37. As Eusebius indicated in his life of Constantine, the construction of this extraordinary new building by Constantine was inspired by God. He compares this inspiration to that given to David and Solomon for the building of the temple to house the ark of the covenant. The message is that the old temple is gone and has been replaced by the new, just as Christianity has triumphed over Judaism. This transfer of identity from the Jewish temple to the Christian is also evident in the fourth-century feast of the presentation of the Christ child in the temple was especially commemorated at the new temple, the Church of the Holy Sepulcher, as Egeria specifically mentioned in her account of her visit to Jerusalem. These are but several of the numerous examples that could be cited from the Patristic period of the early identification of this very special Christian church with the temple. For more on this material, see Joshua Prawer, "Jerusalem in the Christian and Jewish Perspectives of the Early Middle Ages," in *Settimane di Studio del Centro Italiano di Studi sull' Alto Medioevo* (Spoleto, 1980), esp. 317–30. A revised version of this

piece appears in Joshua Prawer and Haggai Ben-Shammai, eds., *The History of Jerusalem: The Early Muslim Period, 638–1099* (New York: New York University Press, 1996), 311–48.

4. Glaber, 3:7.24, 135.

5. Ibid., 3.7.25, 136–37.

6. Marius Canard, "Destruction de l'Église de la Résurrection," *Byzantion* 35 (1965): 16–43.

7. On al-Hakim, see Wolfgang Felix, *Byzanz und die islamische Welt im früheren 11. Jahrhundert* (Vienna: Verlag der Österreichischen Akademie der Wissenschaften, 1981), 57.

8. On the call of Pope Sergius IV, see Hans Martin Schaller, "Zur Kreuzzugsenzyklika Papst Sergius IV," in *Papsttum, Kirche und Recht im Mittelalter: Festschrift für Horst Fuhrmann zum 65 Geburtstag*, ed. Hubert Mordek (Tübingen: M. Niemeyer, 1991), 135–52.

9. Richard Landes, "The Massacres of 1010: On the Origins of Popular Anti-Jewish Violence in Western Europe," in *Witness to Witchcraft*, 79–112; Daniel Callahan, "Ademar of Chabannes, Millennial Fears and the Development of Western Anti-Judaism," *Journal of Ecclesiastical History* 46 (1995): 19–35.

10. On the campaign to have Martial recognized as an apostle, see Callahan, "The Sermons of Ademar of Chabannes and the Cult of St. Martial of Limoges," *Revue Bénédictine* 86, nos. 3–4 (1976): 251–95; Landes, *Relics, Apocalypse and the Deceits of History: Ademar of Chabannes, 989–1034* (Cambridge, MA: Harvard University Press, 1995), esp. part 3 on the apostolic controversy.

11. See most recently Michael Frassetto, "Heretics, Antichrists, and the Year 1000: Apocalyptic Expectations in the Writings of Ademar of Chabannes," in *The Year 1000: Religious and Social Response to the Turning of the First Millennium*, ed. Michael Frassetto (New York: Palgrave, 2002), 73–84; Callahan, "The Tau Cross in the Writings of Ademar of Chabannes," in Frassetto, *Year 1000*, 63–71.

12. The collection under the general editorship of Pascale Bourgain is expected to consist of an edition in five volumes of all of his principal writings.

13. B.N., Ms. Lat. 2469, esp. fols. 40v–42r. For example, on 42r, "Cum igitur sub veteri tempore Moises et Salomon, Iudas etiam Machabeus qui ornavit faciem templi coronis aureis, in novo quoque Marcialis apostolus templum Dei non absque multo decore auri legantur exornasse quis tantorum patrum auctoritatem contempnendam dicat? Quis non videat auctoritatem plurimam esse tam veteris quam novi instrumenti ecclesiam Dei ornandam foris in oculis carnalium non sine argenti et auri venustate?"

14. For example, B.N., Ms. Lat. 2469, fols. 49v–50v.

15. On the legend, see Stephan Borgehammar, *How the Cross Was Found: From Event to Medieval Legend* (Stockholm: Almqvist and Wiksell International, 1991), esp. 145–95, appendix.

16. B.N., Ms. Lat. 2469, fol. 49v. "Porro autem nequorundam questio de Zacheo publicano praetereat in discussa si ut fertur a quibusdam hic iste est Zacheus qui crucem Domini in eo loco ubi eam postea regina Helena invenit propter devotionem abscondit sciendum est quod hoc non videtur a laudis misterio vacare quod arborem ascendit ad videndum Dominum. Nec sine divino nutu fortasse actum videtur quod qui lignum arboris subierat ut Dominum videret lignum etiam crucis sub terra abscondit ut quandoque dominicae passionis triumphus revelaretur."

17. B.N., Ms. Lat. 2469, fol. 48v. For example, "Ait quippe historiographus ipsius libri eo articulo temporis quo eximiae indolis adolescens Marcialis iubente Salvatore a Petro baptizatus est Zacheum et Ioseph qui postea Dominum sepelivit multosque alios Iudeorum baptizatos."

18. B.N., Ms. Lat. 2469, fol. 45v: "Tempore Tiberii Dominus noster Ihesus Christus passus est a Iudeis octavo decimo eiusdem Caesaris anno." Fol. 41v: "Qui Noe maledictione filii Cam qui patris turpitudinem nunciavit populum Iudaicum qui humanitatem Domini derisit in cruce blasphemans et caput movens praemonstravit. Benedictione autem duorum filiorum Sem et Iafed credentium et gentibus et Iudeis populos figuravit. Nec in amaritudinem vitis alienae ille per Cham designatus populus sibi adoptabat clamans, 'Tolle, tolle, crucifige eum, sanguis eius super nos et super filios nostros.'"

19. B.N., Ms. Lat. 2469, fol. 41v: "Unde crucifixus Iudeis quidem scandalum gentibus autem stultitia est nobis autem Dei virtus et Dei sapientia."

20. B.N., Ms. Lat. 2469, fol. 49v: "Quod si forte ille devotus publicanus in illo tumultu qui a Iudeis in passione Domini agebatur crucem Domini abscondere curavit ut generationibus futuris esset in salutem utque passionis Domini teste fieret saeculo praeciosum lignum neve malignantes Iudei ipsam crucem vel ferro vel igne penitus abolerent non minima laude in saecula dignus est."

21. B.N., Ms. Lat. 2469, fols. 40v–41r. There is much material on this theme in these folios. For example, 41r: "Scitote, o aemuli, cruces argenteas et aureas nequaquam esse signa Mercurii, Dianae et Veneris, sed esse triumphum Domini nostri Ihesu Christi qui per signum crucis triumphavit Iovem, Saturnem et sola omnia idola daemonum sed etiam omnes ipsos daemones."

22. B.N., Ms. Lat. 2469, fol. 42r. On the adornment of the cross, "Cruces siquidem in ecclesia argento et auro ac gemmis decorari constat ab ipsis apostolis primum fuisse traditum…Nam et ecclesia quotiescumque vexilla in itinere depraecantium precedere ante crucis signa solent victoriam bellicosam Christi quae per crucem de hoste superbo celebrata est oculis nostris reducit. Tum namque quasi quodammodo ante victoriae populum victoriosi regis vexilla praeferuntur."

23. B.N., Ms. Lat. 2469, fols. 42v: "Tum crucis fulget misterium cuius victoria diabolus prostratus mundus erectus est."

24. Callahan, "Ademar," 29–30.

25. B.N., Ms. Lat. 2469, 44v: "Quippe Marcialis aliique apostolorum tum temporis a Hierusalem abfuisse intelliguntur occupati ad praedicandum per alias urbes Iudeae. Legitur enim eo quod antequam venisset in Aquitaniam Marcialis et praesens esset cum Petro rogante Petro eodem Marcialis idem praedicabat incessanter verbum Dei. Neque enim apostoli in triennio a passione Domini dispersi sunt passim per provintias sed diu apud Iudeam manserunt quousque Iudeis eos abicientibus nec recipientibus verbum apostoli ad gentes transmigrarent."

26. B.N., Ms. Lat. 2469, 45v: "Neronis vero imperii anno secundo Paulus apostolus primitus venit Romam ea de causa qua accusatus a Iudeis Caesarem appellavit iunctusque illuc missus est a festo praeside Iudeae."

27. B.N., Ms. Lat. 2469, 45v: "Porro quadragesimo secundo anno a passione Domini, hoc est quarto Vespasiani, Hierosolim a Vespasiano et Tito funditus eversa est." On the wickedness of the Herods, see esp. fols. 45r–46r.

28. Glaber, 4:6.18, 198–201.

29. B.N., Ms. Lat. 2469, 44v.: "Hinc Paulus apostolus narrat se post annos tres a sua conversione venisse Hierosolimam videre Petrum et mansisse apud eum diebus quindecim non ut ab eo disceret evangelium sed ut ei honorem deferret tamquam principi apostolorum." Ibid., 48r: "Ecce ipse Paulus de se ipso testimonium perhibet dicens venisse se Hierosolimam videre Petrum et alium apostolorum neminem vidisse nisi Iacobum fratrem Domini qui episcopus erat Hierosolimorum…Sicut regina Saba venit videre Salomonem quem numquam viderat sicut Haerodes in passione Dominum videre cupiebat quem numquam viderat sicut gentiles quem numquam viderant Dominum videre quaerebant dicentes Philippo."

30. On the antichrist rebuilding the temple, see Richard Emmerson, *Antichrist in the Middle Ages: A Study of Medieval Apocalypticism, Art, and Literature* (Seattle: University of Washington Press, 1981), 42, 77, 91.

31. Glaber, 3:7.25, 136–37.

32. Glaber, 4:6.21, 204–5. The actual rebuilding of the temple may have begun under al-Hakim, who died in 1021, but the large-scale rebuilding was not undertaken until a treaty between al-Hakim's son Daher and the Byzantine emperor Romanus III was signed and was not completed until the middle of the century after a period of great support by Emperor Constantine Monomachus in the 1040s. The Constantinian basilica was not rebuilt — only that portion of the structure called the rotunda, which housed the tomb and possibly some relics of the True Cross.

33. H. E. J. Cowdrey, "Pope Urban II's Preaching of the First Crusade," *History* 55 (1970): 177–88.

34. James Carroll, *Constantine's Sword* (Boston: Houghton Mifflin, 2001), esp. 3–12.

3

A Great Jewish Conspiracy? Worsening Jewish–Christian Relations and the Destruction of the Holy Sepulcher

Phyllis G. Jestice

In the year 1009, the Fatimid caliph Abu 'Ali al-Mansur al-Hakim ordered the destruction of the Church of the Holy Sepulcher in Jerusalem. Demolition work started on September 28, 1009, aimed not only against the church itself but also the convent beside it, although the destruction does not appear to have been particularly thorough. This event is pertinent to the subject of this volume because of a peculiar rumor that circulated at least in the kingdom of France in the first half of the eleventh century: that this attack on the holiest point of the Christian cosmos had been instigated by the Jews. Two near-contemporary chroniclers, Rodulfus Glaber and Ademar of Chabannes, both tell the story, varying in details but both firm in placing the ultimate blame on a Jewish plot — specifically, a conspiracy by the Jews of France to convince al-Hakim that the Christians were a threat and could best be countered with an attack on the Holy Sepulcher. This story is an important, though enigmatic, piece of evidence for historians studying the rise of anti-Semitism in Western Europe in the period before the First Crusade. The tale appears as one of a number of negative statements about Jews in eleventh-century Christian sources and specifically occurs in the context of a series of violent attacks on Jews that took place in the years 1007 to 1012. But these accounts of a great Jewish plot against the heart of Christianity, the most spectacular in their claims, have been the least studied of these extant texts for what they can reveal of Jewish–Christian interactions and attitudes in a period of worsening relations.

Several theories have been presented to account for the new antisemitism of the early eleventh century. Were the persecutions of Jews that occurred in this period the first signs of a new period of Christian enthusiasm, inspired by apocalyptic fears and hopes, as Richard Landes has argued?[1] Or were they the work of Christian princes and prelates who were increasingly fearful of dissidents, whether Jewish or Christian, according to the formulation of R. I. Moore and Robert Chazan?[2] A surprising gap in scholarly writing appears on this question, though. There has been a strong tendency to look completely to the Christian world — whether religious or political — and not at all to Judaism when attempting to explain the rise of antisemitism in the eleventh century. Certainly I do not mean to suggest that the Jews were asking for it or that they were responsible for their fate; the Christians who persecuted and killed large numbers of Jews starting in the early eleventh century must surely bear the lion's share of blame. But were the Jews of the time completely passive victims, nonprovocative and desiring nothing but to live in peace with their Christian neighbors, the victims of new forces for which the Christian communities were solely responsible?

The case of Rodulfus's and Ademar's tale of a Jewish plot again the Holy Sepulcher is a useful angle from which to approach this issue. A largely unasked question is whether this tale of Jewish involvement in a plot to destroy the holiest place in Christendom could have any basis in fact — whether at the literal level or as revelatory of the mutually antagonistic relations between Jews and Christians of the time. It is this last question that this chapter seeks to explore. It focuses on the account of the great Jewish conspiracy given by Rodulfus Glaber in Book III of his *Histories*, written in c. 1040, rather than that of Ademar. Ademar's account seems by far the less historical of the two, telling how the caliph's troops were driven from Bethlehem and St. Catherine's, Mt. Sinai, by miracles, how al-Hakim performed terrified penance for his evil and restored the Holy Sepulcher, how "all the land of the Saracens" suffered a devastating famine, and how the overly proud caliph was caught by his enemies and disemboweled.[3] Rodulfus's account is much less reliant on the Bible and leaves out the supernatural element completely. Though it seems unlikely that the Jews of France did indeed have anything to do with the destruction, I argue that Rodulfus's account is not merely the product of Christian paranoia. Instead it was, from an eleventh-century perspective, a plausible explanation, making excellent sense in light of current attitudes in France and what really is known of the destruction of the church.

To begin with the story, Rodulfus places the events of the Jewish conspiracy in the context of the massive rise in pilgrimage to Jerusalem that began when the conversion of Stephen of Hungary opened the overland route to the Holy Land. Great crowds were flocking to Jerusalem, Rodulfus tells us, to the point that the devil got worried. So he decided that something had to be done to dampen Christian ardor and turned to his "accustomed instruments, the Jews" to do his dirty work. At that time the Jews of Orleans were numerous, "arrogant," and "insolent," we are told. They decided that the best way to harm Christians was through the medium of a message to the Fatimid caliph of Egypt, al-Hakim, whom Rodulfus calls the "prince of Babylon," as was standard in medieval historiography. The Fatimids controlled the city of Jerusalem at the time. A letter from the French Jews, hidden in a hollowed-out staff and carried by a Jew masquerading as a pilgrim, urged the caliph to destroy the Holy Sepulcher, warning that if he did not take action the Christians would soon take over the whole Fatimid realm. Al-Hakim believed the warning and at least partially destroyed the church. But word soon spread of the Jewish role in this perfidy. Jews became universally hated and were driven from the cities of France; many were killed, and some committed suicide, all while the bishops said that Christians should not associate with these enemies of the faith.[4]

A first important point to note is that Rodulfus puts very little blame for the catastrophe on the man who ordered it, Caliph al-Hakim. The caliph is portrayed as gullible rather than ill-intentioned toward Christianity, and Rodulfus indeed notes that the caliph's Christian mother almost immediately started rebuilding the church.[5] As a point of historical fact, al-Hakim did not just suddenly decide to destroy Christendom's greatest shrine out of the blue. This event should instead be seen in the context of al-Hakim's general anti-Christian policy. The Fatimids had been very liberal in their treatment of both Jews and Christians, employing many non-Muslim officials, marrying non-Muslims, and providing generous legal protection to both churches and synagogues. But al-Hakim launched a major persecution against these non-Muslim *dhimmis* — at first only affecting Christians but in time including Jews — that lasted through most of his reign.[6] If Rodulfus knew of this more general persecution, however, he gave no sign of it, nor does he issue a blanket condemnation of Islam, unlike Ademar, for whom the persecution includes forcible conversions to Islam and divine retribution visited on the caliph. Instead, Rodulfus seems rather more approving than otherwise of the Muslim rulers of the East. He was interested in Muslims, providing the first northern European account of Islam and the first mention of Muhammad by name in a Western Christian source.[7] For Rodulfus, the evil Jews who plotted the destruction of the sepulcher were tools of the devil, not of the Muslims.

Allan Cutler and Helen Cutler have suggested that an important reason for Christian dislike of Jews in the eleventh century is that they were perceived as being pro-Muslim. Certainly there is a clear trail of such association. Already in the 630s several persecutions of Jews sprang up because they were viewed as Muslim collaborators. Closer to our period, the eleventh-century *vita* of Archbishop Theodard of Narbonne tells that the Jews betrayed the city of Toulouse to the Arabs — probably mixing up the facts of the actual Jewish betrayal of Marseilles in c. 848).[8] Cutler and Cutler also point out that many of the Jews in Western lands in the early eleventh century would have been immigrants from the Islamic world and were most likely Arabized in customs and clothing.[9] No sense of this emerges from the pages of Rodulfus's or Ademar's accounts, however. Neither historian even suggests that the Jews, in their conspiracy to destroy the Church of the Holy Sepulcher, so much as used the international trade connections that would have provided a visible ground for suspicion. Instead, Rodulfus created the image of the evil message bearer disguised as a Christian pilgrim, as if in complete ignorance of the fact that Jews did in fact engage in trade with the Islamic world.

Equation of Jews and Muslims in Christian minds therefore seems to be a dead end as an explanation for the tale of the great conspiracy. What seems to have happened for Rodulfus was rather a transference than an equation, rewriting a tale he heard to explain the calamity in such a way as to put the blame on the Jews. Oddly, non-Western sources also suggest that the destruction of the church was the result of a plot — but not a Jewish one. Here several non-Western chronicles come to our aid. Two twelfth- and thirteenth-century Arabic chronicles, written by al-Qalanisi and al-Djawzi, both tell of the attack on the shrine, drawing on a common eleventh-century source. Their accounts both assert that al-Hakim's anger against the tomb of the prophet Jesus — one should remember that Jesus is venerated in Islam as well as in Christianity — was provoked by hearing a report of fraudulent practices by the clerics there. Specifically, the chroniclers place the blame on the priests of the Holy Sepulcher for their manipulation of the so-called miracle of the holy fire.

The annual spontaneous, miraculous lighting of the lamp at the Holy Sepulcher every Easter is one of the most controversial miracles of the modern world. This spectacular occurrence is attested as early as the ninth century and seems to have been accepted without question in the Christian world; Rodulfus even includes an account of the miracle he heard from a bishop who saw it while on pilgrimage in a later section of his *Histories*, telling of a Muslim who received miraculous punishment for mocking it.[10] A Muslim, tolerating Christianity as an inferior version of his own religion, would indeed have been likely to mock and certainly would have been dubious of the purported miracle. Al-Qalanisi and al-Djawzi both tell that the caliph's anger was provoked by the fire miracle. The Syriac chronicler Bar Hebraeus adds more compelling details: that "a certain man" who hated the Christians told al-Hakim about the fraudulent nature of the annual lamp lighting.[11] Anger at supposedly fraudulent priests cheating gullible pilgrims — and their Muslim neighbors — is indeed a plausible explanation for al-Hakim's vendetta against the tomb of Christ.

It is at this point that likely historical events and Rodulfus's tale of Jewish conspiracies come close to one another. Although al-Hakim had been persecuting Christians for years, before 1009 he had not moved against the great holy places of Palestine. It is likely that a particular event touched off the destruction, and perceived evidence of false, hypocritical Christian behavior would have filled the bill nicely. But who could the certain man who hated Christians have been? To be an effective slander, the report had to come from somebody in a position to know the inner secrets of the Church of the Holy Sepulcher. So the certain man of Eastern sources is very unlikely to have been a Jew. Indeed, Severas ibn Muqaffa in his *History of the Patriarchs of Alexandria* asserts that the evil informant was a Christian monk named John, whose ambitions were frustrated by the patriarch of Jerusalem and who gained his revenge by going to the caliph with calumnies against the patriarch. Severas tells that the patriarch was arrested and the destruction of the church was ordered, suggesting that the calumnies involved some sort of dirty work at the Holy Sepulcher.[12] Interestingly, Ademar preserves a mention of the patriarch's death, which he regards as martyrdom plain and simple.[13]

This brings us back to Rodulfus's tale, where a similar call to action by people who hated Christians is voiced in a more concrete form. In Rodulfus's version, the messenger tells the caliph that the Christians will soon take over all his domains unless he launches a preemptive strike by destroying the holiest place of Christendom. Rodulfus shows no knowledge of any report of Christian abuses, although his explanation of what convinced the caliph is very weak. One must suspect that whomever the informer was — Jew, Christian, or Muslim — he must have told the caliph something new rather than just saying, "Look at all the Christian pilgrims who have been annoying us lately." Surely the Fatimid caliphs could not have been completely ignorant of political conditions in Europe and the improbability of a Christian attack.

Were the Christians of Europe a threat? It has recently been argued that Pope Sergius IV's crusade encyclical of 1010, in which he calls for an armed expedition to avenge the destruction of the sepulcher, was in fact a contemporary document rather than the later forgery that it has often been dismissed as.[14] But if this is indeed the case, the pontiff was indulging in some seriously wishful thinking. Even if the document was published, it caused barely a ripple in European society of the time. The unreformed papacy of the early eleventh century did not have the necessary moral prestige to launch a crusade, and apparently nobody was interested — which sheds an interesting light on just how important Urban II's plenary indulgence was in getting the crusades under way at the end of the century.

Certainly pilgrimage was picking up rapidly in the early years of the eleventh century, and Rodulfus describes a massive flocking of the European population to the Holy Land. As so often, though, we are confronted with medieval people's sweeping and maddeningly vague use of numbers. How many people make up a mass? It is unlikely in the extreme that enough pilgrims came from the West to have been perceived as any sort of a threat to the Fatimid caliphate in 1009. The thousands-strong pilgrimages of mid-century were still in the future.

Thus, it appears highly unlikely that the Fatimid caliph could have had any realistic fears of European invasion as early as 1009. Nor does it appear to have been the case that our French chroniclers perceived the Jews of their region as natural allies of the Muslims. Why, then, was this accusation of secret conniving to harm Christianity levied against the Jews? To attempt an answer, one must focus on events in Western Europe, the source of these odd rumors, rather than on what actually occurred in the Near East.

Rodulfus's and Ademar's tale of a Jewish conspiracy against Christendom appear in a context of growing Christian–Jewish antagonism around the turn of the millennium, a series of events for which Rodulfus and Ademar are the best, but not the only, sources. There is general agreement that a series of attacks on Jews occurred between 1007 and 1012, accompanied by a number of edicts pressuring Jews to convert. Many Jews chose exile, but there is also evidence of some martyrdom, the earliest cases in the Ashkenazic Jewish tradition.[15] There are even hints in the sources that some Jews accepted baptism under threat, including the children of great rabbis of the age, such as a son of Rabbi Gershom Meor Ha Golah.[16]

The Western European evidence, sparse as it is, provides valuable clues that can help provide a rational explanation of how Rodulfus and Ademar came up with their tale of Jewish plotting. The written sources, when closely examined, do not bear out the notion of a great conspiracy. But they do reveal a pattern, not just of Christian antagonism toward Jews but of Jewish antagonism toward Christians.

A first glaring point is that accounts of the 1007–1012 atrocities against Jews include an element of popular Christian outrage against the Jews involved rather than being imposed by rulers while the larger Christian community remained largely indifferent. For example, both Rodulfus and Ademar tell how in 1010 King Robert of France commanded the Jews in his territories to convert or die. This is confirmed by the Jewish chronicler known as the Hebrew Anonymous, if indeed the events he describes in the year 4767 (A.D. 1007) are misdated and describe the same events as those discussed by Rodulfus and Ademar.[17] This chronicler adds that King Robert acted on the insistence of his advisors. But this source also points out that there was a massacre of Jews, a term suggesting undisciplined slaughter by a Christian mob rather than soldiers acting at a king's command.[18] Both Jewish and Christian accounts of the aftermath of the royal edict tell of Jewish collective suicides. Surely anyone who had the opportunity to go into voluntary exile instead of dying would have done so, which again suggests that the danger came upon the Jews involved without warning rather than as part of a royal plan being implemented and prefaced by an edict that gave an ultimatum. The Hebrew Anonymous further suggests that the official policy did allow some time before the Jews would be forced to convert or die, reporting that in Normandy the Jews came up with the idea of appealing to the pope for help. They sent Jacob bar Yekutiel to Rome and did indeed obtain the services of a papal legate who persuaded Duke Richard to spare the Jews.[19] Thus, since it is confirmed from several sources that massacres occurred, they provide strong evidence of popular rather than merely official hatred of the Jews.

It is in this category of popular hatred that one must include an incident Ademar related about events in Toulouse from sometime around the year 1020. A custom appeared about that time of publicly denouncing Judaism on Easter Sunday, driving home the point by striking a Jew on the face outside the church. This was clearly more than just a symbolic gesture, and passions could be engaged, since in the year Ademar mentions the ceremony the striker was so vigorous that he knocked the poor Jew's eye out, and the victim died of his injuries.[20] It seems clear from such accounts that popular Christian hatred of Jews was on the rise. Again, historians have come up with several explanations, ranging from perception of the Jews as an economic threat to changes within Christianity.

A second element to note is the number of eleventh-century authors who linked Jews with heretics, often referring to them in the same phrase and complaining about them as if the two groups were the same. I believe that this equation of heretics and Jews provides a valuable clue to explain why the Jews were blamed for the destruction of the Holy Sepulcher and, more generally, why the persecution of Jews took root in this period. This *heretic = Jew* formulation, or at least an association of the two by proximity, appears widely on the continent. For example, the author of the German *Annales Quedlinburgensis* tells, under the year 1012, that Emperor Henry II expelled the Jews from the city of Mainz for a short time. The phraseology is telling: "The king expelled the Jews from Mainz; and also the insanity of certain heretics was refuted."[21] It is improbable that, as has been suggested, the reason for the expulsion was because a priest converted to Judaism; the timing is wrong for the notorious conversion of the cleric Wecelinus to whom the story has sometimes been linked. Nor is it very likely that the event was connected with the destruction of the Holy Sepulcher, as others have argued, since it seems to have been limited to a single German city — albeit probably the largest Jewish community in Germany at the time — and the banishment was rescinded the next year.[22] Why does the chronicler speak of Jews and heretics in the same breath? That seems to be the key to understanding the attitude that could create a tale of conspiratorial Jews attacking the greatest center of Christian pilgrimage: that for some reason Jews and heretics were becoming connected in the popular mind and that both were reacting against such features of Christian religiosity as pilgrimage.

The early eleventh century saw the first real awareness of popular heresy in medieval Europe, manifest on a scale sufficient to worry both bishops and secular rulers and to find a prominent place in both Ademar's and Rodulfus's chronicles. We will probably never know for certain what these heretics believed — if indeed they shared common doctrines at all, which seems unlikely. Chroniclers, groping for insulting terms, label them as *Manichaeans* or *Arians*, sometimes even using the terms interchangeably for the same group. It is clear, at least, that these depraved figures were not Jews. None seem to have rejected trinitarian theology. They seem, however, to have followed a Jewish line in some way in their preaching — an attitude toward the Christian society around them that had at some level a parallel to Judaism.

Occasional conversions to Judaism appear in the records of early medieval Europe. Apostasy seems to have been on an upswing in the early years of the eleventh century, however, even though social and legal impediments to conversion were enormous. For example, a letter written c. 1011 tells of a Christian who converted to Judaism and found it expedient to flee to Damascus. But even then he was pursued, and a serious effort was made to bring him back. So he went on to Jerusalem and found himself persecuted by the Christians there; he intended at the time the letter was written to go on to Egypt, with the hope of picking up the threads of his life.[23]

One of the great *causes célebres* of the early eleventh century was the conversion to Judaism of a man named Wecelinus, a cleric in the service of Duke Conrad. Not only did Wecelinus apostatize, probably in the year 1005 or 1006; he also wrote a treatise against Christianity. Emperor Henry II was so outraged that he ordered one of his own clerics to compose a rebuttal. An account appears in Alpert of Metz's *De diversitate temporum*, written sometime before 1025, who reports that Wecelinus eventually converted back to Christianity.[24] But why did he leave his birth religion in the first place?

Judaism clearly exercised a deep, if forbidden, fascination on some people, perhaps, as the case of Wecelinus suggests, especially people inclined to think deeply about their faith instead of simply accepting what they were told at face value. A person surely would not take such a radical step as apostasy — or heresy — lightly. A hagiographical work written in c. 1012, Constantine's *vita* of Bishop Adalbero II of Metz, hints at that attraction for contemporaries. The author tells how the bishop worked assiduously against those who drank the "pestilential wine of the Jews,"[25] which suggests both how tasty Jewish teaching might have been and that some Christians came to it voluntarily. Constantine also reports that Bishop Adalbero constantly hoped to convert Jews to Christianity.[26]

Clearly, mainstream ecclesiastical authorities felt threatened when Christians listened to Jews. This seems to imply that more Christians were doing so than had at any time since the triumph of Catholic Christianity in the fourth century. In part, this can be explained by the greater visibility of Jews in Western Europe by the early eleventh century. Peter Damian might hopefully suggest that the Jews "have now nearly vanished from the earth," a sentiment echoed in Rodulfus's *Histories* when he speaks of massive attacks on Jews after the Holy Sepulcher plot was "uncovered."[27] In reality, though, as urban life gained vitality in the tenth century a number of Jewish communities were established, providing the first Jewish presence in many areas of Europe. By the year 1000 there were especially large settlements at Troyes and Rheims, but new communities appeared in many other areas.[28] There is evidence of synagogues in at least twenty French towns in the eleventh century,[29] which further suggests a lively, and visible, Jewish spiritual life. Most scholars agree that the Jewish communities of France and Germany produced an atmosphere of intellectual ferment parallel to that of Christians in the same period, although little of the material produced is still extant.[30]

By c. 1000, Leonard Glick argues, the Jewish society of Western Europe had undergone a transformation, making them at a fundamental level religious rather than secular communities. The role of the rabbi had become the central determinant of community life, to the point that Western European Jews probably accepted the authority of their religious leaders more than at any other time in the history of Judaism. Rabbinic scholarship assumed a central position, and rabbinic pronouncements on proper behavior exerted a very strong control over the Jewish populace. It was an age of great Jewish intellectuals who were also leaders of their communities. Of these, the greatest was certainly Gershom ben Judah of Mainz (c. 960–c. 1028), who won the resounding soubriquet Light of the Exile. He was part of a considerable group known as the "learned men of Lotharingia," who were not just solitary scholars but played a very active role in the daily Jewish life of these young settlements.[31] It seems too great a coincidence to be mere chance that the Jews of Mainz were expelled at a time when Judaism's greatest Talmudic scholar was head of the community there.

These Jewish scholars were not friendly to Christianity, especially the outward observances of Christianity taking root in their own time. Gershom ben Judah is credited with founding rabbinic studies in northern Europe. He was, however, building on a Jewish turn toward observance that had begun at least a generation before his time. Taitz describes the process as a growing "self-consciousness and independence," pointing to a new emphasis on Talmudic studies as well as the emergence of liturgical poetry composed by European Jews in the tenth century.[32] Schools developed in a number of locations; the most famous was Gershom's school at Mainz, but it was clearly not the first, since he had studied Torah and Talmud at a Western European school.[33] These schools trained rabbis, who in turn emphasized the letter of the Law to their communities. As a responsum attributed to Rabbi Eleazar put it, "In our locality there are disciples, sages who hold to the Torah, the prohibited and the permitted, and who know how to distinguish good from its opposite."[34]

Part of the teaching of such schools was a far sharper critique of Christianity than had been the norm, and in general Jewish hatred toward Christianity skyrocketed in the course of the eleventh century. This is hardly surprising, in light of rising Christian persecution of Jews — legend tells that a son and maybe even the wife of Gershom ben Judah were forcibly baptized,[35] which would give an edge to any rabbi's relations with his Christian neighbors. But this upswing of Jewish hatred was not just a reaction. Instead, an influential body of rabbinic opinion argued more generally that Christians were the deadly enemies of God, not just because they persecuted the true worshippers of God but also because they were idolaters. Avraham Grossman cogently argues that the eleventh century saw a deep intellectual and emotional rejection of Christianity because Jews condemned the Christians as idol worshippers.[36]

It has been the habit to put all the blame for deteriorating Jewish–Christian relations in the eleventh century on the Christians. Surely, those who used force against Jews must bear much more blame in the matter than their victims. There are, however, tantalizing hints that the Jews may have baited Christians. The context was a major shift in Christian religiosity taking place at the time. As a number of studies have pointed out, the years around the turn of the millennium saw a refocusing of Christian piety toward the concrete and physical, encouraging worshippers to visualize as clearly as possible holy people and events in a highly charged emotive atmosphere. This new religiosity appears in the form of a new obsession with physicality — large carved holy figures, relics, an emphasis on the real presence of Christ in the Eucharist, and of course the longing to be physically present at the sites of Christ's passion that enters Rodulfus's story of the destruction of the Holy Sepulcher.

A series of firsts fall in this period, all of which must have appeared repugnant and ludicrous to a pious Jew — and to judge from the reports of heretics, also to a significant number of Christians. Rodulfus tells that in the early years of the eleventh century the relics of "many saints" were discovered, starting in Sens but spreading to other areas. He proclaims enthusiastically that all of these newly uncovered relics attracted large numbers of pilgrims, even from Italy and beyond.[37] Ademar confirms the high popularity of pilgrimage to saints' shrines, telling under the year 1010 that when the monastery of St. John of Angely displayed the head of John the Baptist, "all of Aquitaine and Gaul, Italy, and Spain" went to venerate it.[38]

A closer link to Rodulfus's tale of the destruction of the Holy Sepulcher is the large number of idolatrous new fashions in worshipping Christ. Christian communities began to reenact the events of Jesus' passion and resurrection, including parading a figure of Christ on a donkey around town, first attested in the *vita* of Ulrich of Augsburg, dating from c. 980.[39] The same practice appears as far away as Essen, where it seems to have been established by Abbess Matilda (r. 973–1011), suggesting widespread diffusion. Matilda was also responsible for commissioning a golden statue of the Virgin Mary, which seems to have been carried around in processions, making that and other holy images impossible to ignore by those who disliked this development.[40] As attested by the English *Regularis Concordia* of c. 970, communities also began the process of formally depositing in a tomb and then resurrecting a Christ substitute — either a cross or a host — as the centerpiece of Holy Week celebrations.[41]

There was also a striking increase in veneration of the cross. Cross-shaped reliquaries came into fashion shortly after the year 1000, and placement of a cross on altars began to spread at the turn of the millennium. Even more blatantly idolatrous, in the early years of the second millennium more and more of them included the modeled body of Christ, abstract symbolism giving way to more concrete and emotive representation.[42] The new-style crucifixes were prominent as never before: processional crosses and monumental crucifixes of both wood and bronze spreading throughout Western Europe.[43]

The use of crucifixes to inspire lay spirituality would certainly have helped people to visualize holy events, but the exaggerated veneration they received seems at times to have crossed the line into idolatry by any definition, much less that of an observant Jew. A synod held at Arras in 1025 felt it necessary to explain the adoration of the crucifix, pointing out firmly that the wooden object was not receiving veneration but rather that it was honored because "that visible image arouses the interior mind of the person," making it possible for Christ's passion and death to be "inscribed in the membrane of the heart."[44] That is doubtless how trained theologians saw the matter. For others, though, the distinction between symbolism and reality could become very fuzzy. Accounts proliferated of weeping, gesturing, nodding figures of the crucified Christ, in which Jesus seems to have been regarded as every bit as truly present in his cult statue as any Babylonian deity had been. For example, Rodulfus tells of a portent in St. Peter's monastery at Orleans in 988. In the middle of the monastery was a "banner of the cross" (*crucis uexillum*) with an image of the suffering savior. This figure was seen to weep for several days, clearly foretelling the great fire that raged through the city soon afterward. Of course a great crowd came to see the miraculous figure, and it is hard to imagine that the spectators did not worship that crucifix as in some way embodying Christ.[45] Similar stories can be found in chronicles and the *vitae* of saints of the eleventh century in a variety of contexts, suggesting the popularity of this close identification of the image with the living God.

Such images would have been even more potent if they contained a relic. The Gero Crucifix of c. 970, the oldest extant Western crucifix that depicts Christ dead on the cross, contained relics in the back of its head. The nature of those relics is not known, but the wooden crucifix of Ringelheim, dating from c. 1000, had a chip of stone from the Holy Sepulcher enclosed in the head of the figure, specially brought from Rome by Bernward of Hildesheim.[46] Relics from the Holy Sepulcher were the greatest on Earth, and pilgrims were bringing them home in large numbers

The new fashion in Christian art in Western Europe explains why Jews and Christian heretics were so often yoked together in the extant sources. It was not as simple a matter as heretics adopting elements of Judaism. Instead, both heretics and Jews seem to have been reacting against the novel images of the age. What heretics are reported as doing can, thanks to this equation in the minds of their critics, suggest what the Jews were also doing at the same time.

A theme running through accounts of early eleventh-century heresy is that the heretics were attacking this newly popular religious art. In other words, they seem to have been attacking what they perceived to be idolatry. For example, iconoclasm is a prominent issue in Rodulfus's account of the heretic Leutard, active in c. 1000. After sending his wife away, Leutard's first act was to go to his church in the diocese of Châlons and break the crucifix there, or as Rodulfus terms it, "the cross and image of the savior." Leutard won a popular following, convincing people that he had acted because of a special revelation from God[47] — at least that is how Rodulfus explains the business. It is unlikely, though, that Leutard's audience would have needed much in the way of special revelation to explain the breakage. Certainly in sixteenth-century Europe fanatical minorities were easily persuaded to commit iconoclasm when a reformer made the case that holy images were idolatrous, and by that time they had a tradition of such images that went back half a millennium. In the case of eleventh-century iconoclasts, the presence of large-scale venerated images would not have been hallowed by custom.[48] Similarly, the heretic Gundulf, active in Liège and Arras in 1025, rejected the veneration of images along with other physical manifestations of Christian religiosity.[49] Ademar reports that Manichaeans were going around Aquitaine "seducing people" a few years after the destruction of the Holy Sepulcher. But they were an odd sort of Manichaeans. They did not denounce the physical, corporeal world as evil, as a product of an evil god, as in Manichaean theology. But Ademar's mistake can be excused because these heretics did at least reject the use of things as holy, proclaiming that the altar was only a hunk of stone and the cross only a piece of wood.[50] In other words, these Christian dissidents were arguing that such objects were not fit objects of devotion. These seem to have been protesters against idolatry rather than against Manichaeans.

It was not just ignorant folk, unable to appreciate the sublime symbolism of Christian art, who rejected the extreme realism of early eleventh-century Christianity. A crisis was provoked at the monastery of St-Pierre-le-Vif in Sens in 1025 when the theologian Odorannus was accused of heresy by several monks. Specifically, they denounced him for saying that God does not have physical reality. Odorannus put up a spirited defense, responding that his attackers were anthropomorphizing heretics.[51] In other words, by the theological standards that were coming into prominence at the time, he was sounding a lot like a Jew, but he would have seen himself as a good, old-fashioned Christian.

Ademar states specifically in a sermon that the new heretics were "like the Jews," going on to report a particular blasphemy — that these heretics and Jews were asserting that Christians honor wood and an idol rather than the cross of Christ.[52] Thus, yet again the heretics being equated with Jews in the popular mind were marked by their anti-idolatry tendencies. Again, the linkage between the two groups suggests that, like the heretics in question, at least some Jews had been outspoken in their mockery of Christian image fixation. Ademar's is a telling statement, suggesting an atmosphere of Jewish mockery that could have been seriously annoying to the average pious Christian and perhaps might even have helped inspire the iconoclasm of some heretics.

There are several hints in the sources that the Jews derided this newfangled Christian religiosity. Ademar reports that a 1020 earthquake and great storm in Rome had a singular cause: A Jew told the pope that at the time the earth shook, a group of Jews in the synagogue were entertaining themselves by deriding a crucifix. The pope, Benedict VIII, had the malefactors beheaded, after which the wind fell silent.[53] This tale both confirms belief in the supernatural power of crucifixes by mainstream Christians and shows that Jewish attacks on such images were regarded as plausible. There is also a suggestion of Jewish desecration of Christian images behind an odd story of Le Mans in 992. A Jewish source reports that the Jew Sehok ben Esther converted to Christianity, was naturally treated as an apostate by the Jewish community, and decided to avenge himself. So he made a little man-shaped figure and put it into the ark of the synagogue and then went to the count and told him that the Jews had made this image and pierced it regularly to kill him by black magic. Naturally the count was annoyed, although apparently he was suspicious enough of Sehok's claims that he ordered the Jews to submit to trial by combat (the Jews claimed that they were exempt from that sort of ordeal). The Jewish chronicle seems to refer to an earlier incident, which Chazan suggests might have been an alleged desecration of Christian images.[54] Whether they actually physically harmed Christian images or not, it seems clear that the issue of Christian idolatry came up in Jewish circles. In 1040, Peter Damian wrote a treatise against the Jews, citing as a reason their calumnies and "insults," again suggesting an atmosphere of mockery.[55]

It would be hard to imagine a member of a minority population deriding a central tenet of Christianity, at least in public. Mockery of idolatry, though, may have received a sympathetic hearing from some Christians, as the evidence of Christian heresy suggests. And indeed Jewish sources allude to rising indignation against the Christians as idolators. Although the late eleventh-century Jewish scholar Rashi declared that the Christians were not idol worshippers, popular Jewish opinion was another matter. For example, Rabbi Gershom ben Judah also pronounced that Christians were not true idolators. But the context was a specific question of whether it was proper to keep priests' clothing as pledges for loans, since after all the garments were worn while "singing to their idols."[56] Clearly, the questioner thought the Christians were idolators, even if the rabbi did not.

The other major point at which Jews and heretics appear to have joined in condemnation of Christian idolatry was in their response to the triumph of the doctrine of the Real Presence: that Christ is actually physically present in the eucharistic bread and wine. Once again, this trend in Christianity was a recent development. Although suggested by patristic writers such as Ambrose and vigorously argued by Paschasius Radbertus in the ninth century, it only took true root in the latter years of the tenth century.[57] By the early years of the eleventh century, it was already a risky matter for a Christian to deny the Real Presence.[58] A rash of treatises, usually titled *De corpore et sanguine domini*, appeared, defending the corporeal presence of Christ with a ferocity that suggests they were written in reaction to a strong opposition. And this opposition seems to have been both Christian and Jewish, and at least sometimes to have taken the form of mockery of the doctrine as ludicrous and contrary to nature. In the polemic against Christians who did not believe in the doctrine, it is clear that mockery was an important element, with these heretics taking a position that Humbert of Silva Candida in the next generation labeled as *stercorian*. This literally means *excrement* and refers to assertions that Christ cannot be corporeally present in the eucharistic elements because of what happens to bread and wine when they pass through the human digestive system. A reaction to this view is already present in Heriger of Lobbes's (d. 1007) eucharistic treatise, which in turn relies on an earlier anti-stercorian work.[59] Heriger specifically takes a stand against heretics who say that the Eucharist passes through the human digestive system.[60] Such stercorian mockery is, however, a logical response to a perception that ordinary material things, like consecrated bread, are receiving a level of worship that should by right be limited to the divine.

Such an environment within the Christian population of Europe sheds a suggestive light on the anti-Jewish polemic in Gezo of Tortona's treatise on the Eucharist, written in c. 981. Gezo includes what may be the earliest tale of a Jew trying to steal a consecrated host from a church with the intent of dishonoring it. This story is normally treated as pure fiction, as a sign of Christian paranoia rather than Jewish reality. However, in light of stories of both Jews and Christians mocking the new fashion in Christian idolatry, both Jews and Christians harming crucifixes and other holy images, and Christian skeptics rudely deriding the realist opinion of the Eucharist with scatological imagery, we need to revisit this account and consider that it may have a basis in truth.

Gezo seems to be afraid that Jews will come into churches and mock the Eucharist, a scenario it is hard to imagine anyone inventing out of whole cloth without some basis in fact. He orders that churchmen should be particularly careful not to let Jews profane the sacrament or even to cross the threshold of a church, warning that these "most evil and most damned of all human beings" might detract the sacrament, as their leader the devil does. Gezo goes on to tell a story of how a Jew came into a church during mass. He wanted to receive a consecrated host, intending to "throw it on a dung heap." But when the host was placed in his mouth it burned and proved to be impossible to swallow or spit out until the saintly bishop administering the sacrament prayed over the by-now repentant Jew.[61]

Was this Jew a stercorian? The intention not just to destroy the host but to throw it out with the manure suggests mockery very much like that of the Christian stercorian heretics. That the same accusations are levied against both Jews and Christians — and that Jews and heretics are so often equated in the extant sources — raises a strong suspicion that at least some events like that which Gezo describes were actually occurring. Both Jews and heretics had the same stimuli around them — extreme veneration of the eucharistic elements — and if one body of evidence is to be accepted, then there is no good reason to reject the other. In both cases, the key factor is disbelief and repugnance at the thought of venerating a physical thing as if it were God, in this case the eucharistic host. In the case of Gezo's Jew, he soon received conclusive confirmation that the host was indeed Jesus Christ in the flesh. Thoroughly cowed by his unpleasant experience, he was baptized and went to mass, where as he watched the ceremony he saw the body of a man being torn apart on the altar. Gezo tells that the bishop rejoiced at the Jew's consternation: It was proof that the Jew had received grace, since he was able to discern the underlying Real Presence.[62] The story has close parallels to the weeping and moving crucifixes discussed previously: In both cases the physical object proves that it contains the divine, highlighting this element of mainstream Christian belief.

The trail of sources from the early eleventh century is sparse, but sufficient evidence exists to argue that Jews were active in their mockery of Christian holy objects. Whether or not they ever took the risky step of actually assaulting them, it seems clear that at least some Jews derided the crucifixes, relics, cult statues, consecrated hosts, and so on of their Christian neighbors as evidence of a repugnant resurgence of idolatry. It seems unlikely that heretics were learning their lessons from the Jews any more than that Jews were learning how best to criticize Christianity from the heretics. Despite the linkage of perfidious Jews and depraved heretics in the sources[63] no specific connection has been discovered, and it seems unlikely that the small Jewish communities ever had much direct contact with Christian heretics. Both, however, had a common ground in their reaction to the new physicality of the incoming millennium, with its exaggerated veneration of holy images and objects.

This brings us at long last back to Rodulfus Glaber's account of the destruction of the Church of the Holy Sepulcher. We do not have specific condemnations of pilgrimage by heretics, although some of those denounced as heretics seem to have set themselves against ecclesiastical rituals as a whole. But what sort of effect must the worshipping of chips of rock purportedly from the Holy Sepulcher, as well as other great finds from the Holy Land, have had on people who condemned and destroyed crucifixes and denounced the turn from symbolism to realism? It seems very likely that, under these circumstances, some Jews — and heretics — also made fun of the streams of devout pilgrims so avidly described by Rodulfus.

What, then, lay behind this story of a Jewish conspiracy to harm the holiest place of Christianity? I would like to suggest that the most significant element behind such a denunciation was that Jews were seen as willing to do anything they could to destroy a Christian holy place because they were perceived as mockers of holy things rather than as detractors of the theology of Christianity. Jews mocked central Christian teachings, for example in the *Toldot Yeshu* (Generations of Jesus), a popular anti-Christian polemic probably written in the ninth century, which tells that Jesus was the bastard son of a Roman soldier and used magic to perform his miracles.[64] But there is no evidence in eleventh-century sources that the Christians knew of these scurrilous tales. The only point at which Jews would have felt safe enough to engage in public mockery, the evidence of eleventh-century heretics suggests, would have been on a matter that was a novelty and not approved by all of the Christians themselves: worship of images, reverence paid to bits of bread, and visits to empty tombs among them. The new practices of eleventh-century piety were apparently accepted enthusiastically by the majority of Christians, but only at the price of resentment and derision by sectors of the population. This tension exacerbated the worsening relations between Jews and the majority population of Western Europe. The existence of such an environment of iconoclasm and mockery of the extremely visible, in-your-face new Christian religiosity goes a long way toward explaining why two French historians could have come to believe in a great Jewish conspiracy to destroy the Church of the Holy Sepulcher.

Notes

1. Richard Landes, "The Massacres of 1010: On the Origins of Popular Anti-Jewish Violence in Western Europe," in *Witness to Witchcraft*, 95–96.
2. Moore, 123; Chazan, 35.
3. Adémar de Chabannes, *Chronique*, ed. Jules Chavanon (Paris: Alphonse Picard, 1897), 3:47, 167–71.
4. Glaber, 3:24, 132–34.
5. Ibid., 3:25, 136.
6. Wolfgang Felix, *Byzanz und die islamische Welt im früheren 11. Jahrhundert* (Vienna: Verlag der Österreichischen Akademie der Wissenschaften, 1987), 58.
7. Glaber, 1:9, 20.
8. Allan H. Cutler and Helen E. Cutler, *The Jew as Ally of the Muslim* (Notre Dame: University of Notre Dame Press, 1986), 91.
9. Cutler and Cutler, *Jew as Ally*, 93–94.
10. Glaber, 4:19, 203.
11. Marius Canard, "La destruction de l'Eglise de la Résurrection par le calife Hakim et l'histoire de la descent du feu sacré," *Byzantion* 35 (1955); reprint in *Byzance et les musulmans du Proche Orient* (London: Variorum Reprints, 1973), 17–18.
12. Canard, "Destruction de l'Eglise," 17.
13. Ademar, 3:47, 170.
14. Hans Martin Schaller, "Zur Kreuzzugsenzyklika Papst Sergius IV," in *Papsttum, Kirche und Recht im Mittelalter: Festschrift für Horst Fuhrmann* (Tübingen: Max Niemeyer Verlag, 1991), 135–53.
15. Chazan, 13.
16. Avraham Grossman, "The Cultural and Social Background of Jewish Martyrdom in Germany in 1096," in *Juden und Christen zur Zeit der Kreuzzüge*, ed. Alfred Haverkamp (Sigmaringen: Jan Thorbecke Verlag, 1999), 75.
17. Landes, "Massacres of 1010," 89–90.
18. For the evidence of the Hebrew Anonymous, see ibid.
19. Landes suggests that the Jewish appeal to the pope for protection may be a fourteenth-century forgery; see Landes, "Massacres of 1010," 81. See also Grossman, "Cultural and Social Background," 74.
20. Ademar, 3:52, 175; See also Moore, 32–33.

21. *Annales Quedlinburgensis*, MGH SS 3: (a. 1012), 81. "Expulsio Iudaeorum facta est a rege in Moguntia; sed et quorundam haereticorum refutata est insania."
22. See Norman Roth, ed., *Medieval Jewish Civilization: An Encyclopedia* (London: Routledge, 2002), 249.
23. Roth, *Medieval Jewish Civilization*, 199.
24. Alpertus Mettensis, *De diversitate temporum*, ed. Hans van Rij and Anna S. Abulafia (Amsterdam: Verloren, 1980), I.7, 16–18; Abulafia, "An Eleventh-Century Exchange of Letters between a Christian and a Jew," *Journal of Medieval History* 7 (1981): 153.
25. Constantinus, *Vita Adalberonis II. Mettensis episcopi*, MGH SS 4: (6) 661.
26. Ibid., (9) 661.
27. Peter Damian, *Die Briefe des Petrus Damiani*, ed. Kurt Reindel, MGH: Briefe der deutschen Kaiserzeit 4 (Munich: MGH, 1983), (letter #1) 1: 66; Glaber, III, 24, 134.
28. Roth, *Medieval Jewish Civilization*, 144.
29. Emily Taitz, *The Jews of Medieval France: The Community of Champagne* (Westport, CT: Greenwood Press, 1994), 63–64.
30. Chazan, 17.
31. Leonard B. Glick, *Abraham's Heirs: Jews and Christians in Medieval Europe* (Syracuse: Syracuse University Press, 1999), 67–68.
32. Taitz, *Jews of Medieval France*, 53–54.
33. Ibid., 54.
34. This text appears in the *Teshuvot Rashi*. Cited in Taitz, *Jews of Medieval France*, 81.
35. Roth, *Medieval Jewish Civilization*, 304–5.
36. Grossman, "Cultural and Social Background," 77.
37. Glaber, 3:19, 126.
38. Ademar, 3:56, 180. Herrmann-Mascard's analysis places this passage into a larger context of growing pilgrimage enthusiasm at the time. See Nicole Herrmann-Mascard, *Les reliques des saints. Formation coutumière d'un droit* (Paris: Editions Klincksieck, 1975), esp. 212.
39. Gerhard von Augsburg, *Vita sancti Uodalrici*, ed. and trans. Walter Berschin and Angelika Häse (Heidelberg: Universitätsverlag C. Winter, 1993), 1:4, 124. Mayr-Harting suggests that the Augsburg Palm Sunday effigy was probably a painting on wood, rather than the three-dimensional rolling figures of Jesus on the donkey that were popular in the later Middle Ages. Henry Mayr-Harting, *Ottonian Book Illumination: An Historical Study* (London: Harvey Miller, 1999), 122.
40. Hagen Keller, "Ritual, Symbolik und Visualisierung in der Kultur des ottonischen Reiches," *Frühmittelalterliche Studien* 35 (2001): 43.
41. *Regularis Concordia Anglicae Nationis Monachorum Sanctimonialiumque*, ed. and trans. Thomas Symons (London: Thomas Nelson, 1953), IV.46, 44–45.
42. Robert Deshman, "The Exalted Servant: The Ruler Theology of the Prayerbook of Charles the Bald," *Viator* 11 (1980): 390, points out that it was rare for an altar cross to have a corpus on it before 1000.
43. See Johannes Fried, "Endzeiterwartung um die Jahrtausendwende," *Deutsches Archiv* 45 (1989): 450–53; Sylvain Gouguenheim, *Les fausses terreurs de l'an mil* (Paris: Picard, 1999), 193; Keller, "Ritual, Symbolik und Visualisierung," 45.
44. Joannes Mansi, *Sacrorum conciliorum nova et amplissima collectio* (reprint ed. Graz: Akademische Druck- u. Verlagsanstalt, 1960), vol. 19, 455.
45. Glaber, 2:8, 64.

46. Mayr-Harting, *Ottonian Book Illumination*, 100.
47. Glaber, 2:11, 90.
48. Étienne Delaruelle has already suggested that Leutard's heresy was a reaction to his society's new emphasis on the iconography of the crucifix. See *La piété populaire au moyen âge* (Turin: Bottega d'Erasmo, 1975), 37.
49. Malcolm Lambert, *Medieval Heresy: Popular Movements from Bogomil to Hus* (New York: Holmes and Meier, 1976), 27.
50. Ademar, 3:69, 194.
51. Robert-Henri Bautier, "L'hérésie d'Orléans et le movement intellectuel au début du XIe siècle. Documents et hypothèses," in *Enseignement et vie intellectuelle (XIe-XVIe siècle): Actes du 95e congrès national des societés savantes* (Paris: Bibliothèque Nationale, 1975), 83.
52. Ademar, cited in Michael Frassetto, "The Sermons of Ademar of Chabannes and the Letter of Heribert. New Sources Concerning the Origins of Medieval Heresy," *Revue Bénedictine* 109 (1999): 334.
53. Ademar, 3:52, 175. See also Gouguenheim, *Les fausses terreurs*, 160.
54. Chazan, 34–35. See also Taitz, *Jews of Medieval France,* 52.
55. Peter Damian, *Die Briefe*, 1: 66.
56. Roth, *Medieval Jewish Civilization*, 152.
57. Charles R. Shrader, "The False Attribution of an Eucharistic Tract to Gerbert of Aurillac," *Mediaeval Studies* 35 (1973): 178–79.
58. See, for example, Bautier, "L'hérésie d'Orléans," 85.
59. Joseph Lebon, "Sur le doctrine eucharistique d'Hériger de Lobbes," in *Studie Mediaevalia in honorem admodum reverendi patris Raymundi Josephi Martin* (Bruges: De Tempel, 1949), 71. The term *stercorian* first appears in Humbert of Silva Candida, *Contra Nicetam*, PL 143: (22) 993, in which Humbert refers to his opponent as "perfidious stercorian."
60. Heriger of Lobbes, *De corpore et sanguine domini*, PL 139: (9) 187–88.
61. Gezo abbas Dertonensis, *Liber de corpore et sanguine domini*, PL 137: (39) 390.
62. Gezo abbas Dertonensis, *Liber de corpore*, (42) 394–95.
63. For example, in Petrus Damiani Letter 35, 1: 338.
64. Roth, *Medieval Jewish Civilization*, 532.

4

Heretics and Jews in the Early Eleventh Century
The Writings of Rodulfus Glaber and Ademar of Chabannes

Michael Frassetto

The twelfth century has long been recognized as a time of momentous change in European society, a period in which the essential institutions of high medieval civilization emerged.[2] A period of renaissance and dramatic institutional growth, the twelfth century has also been recognized as the period in which the medieval church redefined its relations with heretics and Jews. Indeed, it was at this point that the church developed both a negative stereotype of the Jews that laid the foundation for medieval antisemitism and an aggressive stance toward religious dissent that was based on the diabolical image of the heretic.[3] Although these attitudes were fully formalized in the twelfth century, they were foreshadowed in the works of ecclesiastics writing in the early eleventh century. Faced with religious dissidents for the first time in some 500 years, church leaders responded quickly and forcefully to the appearance of heretics.[4] They saw them not as advocates of simpler or more ascetic religious belief and practice but as part of a widespread conspiracy intended to undermine the very foundations of the church. Moreover, for some contemporaries the heretics were not alone in their assault on Christian society but were aided by the Jews, the age-old religious rivals of all Christians. At the very moment that churchmen were forced to respond to heretics, whom they identified as tools of the devil, they developed a diabolical image of the Jews that would form the core of later medieval and modern antisemitism. This chapter examines the treatment of Jews and heretics in the writings of the early eleventh century and suggests that response of orthodox clergy to the reappearance of heresy contributed to the creation of an increasingly negative stereotype of the Jews.

The association of the birth of heresy in the eleventh century and the declining image of the Jews is most evident in the writings of a monk of St. Martial of Limoges named Ademar of Chabannes and the Burgundian monk Rodulfus Glaber.[5] The work of history that Ademar wrote and revised in the course of the 1020s and that Rodulfus wrote from sometime before 1030 until c. 1046, along with Ademar's collection of sermons written in the late 1020s and early 1030s, reveals the reaction of two orthodox clerics to the reappearance of popular religious dissent.[6] In their histories, both monks identify a number of episodes of heresy in the late tenth and early eleventh centuries, and they also note the harsh reaction of the official church to the appearance of heresy. For Rodulfus, heresy first appeared in learned form shortly before the turn of the millennium when Vilgard of Ravenna, a grammarian who held that Virgil and other classical writers should be believed in all things, was active.[7] Vilgard taught other things contrary to the faith, according to the Burgundian monk Glaber, and was condemned by the bishop of the city. Vilgard was also part of a widespread heresy that reached Sardinia and Spain before it was exterminated by the authorities. Heresy emerged again for Glaber in the diocese of Châlons-sur-Marne around the year 1000, when the peasant Leutard of Vertus spread a number of unorthodox teachings.[8] While resting in the fields one day, Leutard's body was entered by a swarm of bees that stung him and convinced him "to do things impossible to men."[9] He then returned home, dismissed his wife, and went to the local church, where he smashed the crucifix and told the local peasants it was not necessary to pay tithes.[10] Leutard, like Vilgard, met an unfortunate end. The bishop investigated and exposed the errors of Leutard, who then committed suicide by throwing himself down a well. Heresy next appeared for Glaber at Orleans in 1022, the best known and best documented of the episodes of the early eleventh century, when an Italian woman, who was possessed by the devil, converted members of the clergy and laity to her error.[11] The heretics at Orleans, led by Heribert and Lisioius, would not return to the true faith, despite efforts to correct them, and were ultimately burned. Finally, Glaber reported on the heresy at Monteforte in 1028, observing that "[the nobles] there were so tainted by an evil heresy that they would rather have suffered a cruel death than allow themselves any return to the saving faith of Christ the Lord."[12] He notes further that the heretics at Monteforte made "vain sacrifices" just like the Jews.[13] The sect at Monteforte was described further as devil worshippers who were captured by the local lord and bishop and burned to death when they refused to be recalled from their madness (*insania*).[14]

Ademar, writing slightly earlier than his contemporary, recorded in his history several other incidents of heresy in his native Aquitaine and elsewhere in France in the opening decades of the eleventh century. According to the monk of St. Martial, heresy first broke out in Aquitaine in 1018, when *Manichaeans* appeared seducing the people, faking chastity, and rejecting the power of the cross, baptism, and all sane doctrine.[15] And in an earlier draft of the history, he noted that the heretics rejected the cross, the honor of the saints, and the Redeemer of the world and turned many people from the faith.[16] Like his Burgundian contemporary, the monk of Limoges also addressed the heresy at Orleans, but in slightly different terms. The canons at Orleans, according to Ademar, were deceived by a certain rustic from Perigord who possessed a powder made from the bones of dead boys that made anyone with whom he shared it (*posset communicare*) a Manichaean.[17] The heretics of Orleans appeared more religious than others but adored the devil, who appeared to them as an angel of light, and rejected Christ and indulged in shameful acts. These heretics, or messengers of Antichrist, appeared at the same time in Toulouse and elsewhere and were destroyed just as they were burned at Orleans. He makes a final reference to heresy near the end of his history, when he describes a peace council in 1028 at which Duke William V and the bishops of Aquitaine resolved to eliminate heresy. Indeed, like Glaber, Ademar depicted a violent reaction to heretics who were identified as messengers of Antichrist or minions of the devil and appeared to the two monks as part of a broad movement intended to undermine the faith.

The heretics described by Ademar and Glaber shared a number of characteristics, beyond their alleged diabolical nature, which raised doubts about the central teachings of the faith. Although Rodulfus provides few specific details about the heretics in his history, he does offer important suggestions about their belief and states that each outbreak of heresy is part of a broader movement. He says explicitly that Leutard smashed the crucifix in the local church and thus attacked one of the basic symbols of the faith. In his account of the heresy at Orleans, Glaber indulges in an elaborate defense of orthodox teaching on the Trinity, which includes commentary on the true nature of Christ. His view that the heretics were part of a widespread movement rejecting orthodox teachings is confirmed by Ademar's history, which offers fuller details concerning the beliefs of the heretics and their rejection of "all sane doctrine." The Limousin monk's use of the term *Manichaean* to refer to the heretics of Aquitaine and Orleans suggests that he understood them to have held the same set of beliefs, which included the rejection of Catholic teachings on the sacraments. This use of the term *Manichaean* and the allegation that the heresy at Orleans was inspired by a rustic from Perigord suggests further that Ademar understood heresy to be a widespread movement. Moreover, Ademar's Manichaeans recall Leutard in their rejection of the cross and Glaber's heretics of Orleans in their repudiation of the Redeemer of the world. And in each episode of heresy, whether reported by Ademar or Glaber, the sectaries' refusal to repudiate their beliefs only reinforced doubts about Catholic doctrine at a time in which church teachings on the sacraments, the nature of Christ, and related matters were being redefined by orthodox churchmen.[18]

The force of those doubts, perhaps, and the lingering threat of heresy are revealed in Ademar's sermons, which were written in the late 1020s and early 1030s and demonstrate his continued concern with the emergence of heresy.

Indeed, it is in the sermons that Ademar provides one of the most complete pictures of religious dissent in the early eleventh century. The contemporary perception that heresy was part of a diabolical conspiracy against the church is reinforced in Ademar's sermons. The heretics, according to Ademar at the end of his sermon on the Lord's Prayer and the mass, are precursors of Antichrist who "secretly rise among us and deny baptism, the mass, the cross, [and] the church."[19] In his sermon on the Eucharist, Ademar repeats his account of the powder made from human bones, noting that those who receive this powder are made oblivious of God and that "neither preaching, nor terror, nor love will bring them back to the holy Catholic church."[20] In other sermons, he notes the zeal the heretics have for spreading their pollution against the faith and associates them with antichrists and pseudo-apostles.[21] Indeed, in one sermon he compares the apostles, who witnessed Christ in the flesh, with the heretics who opposed God and are witnesses of Antichrist (*testes Antichristi*); in another, he notes that the Antichrist and his messengers seek the destruction of all Christians.[22] Ademar not only identifies the hostile intent and diabolical nature of the heretics but places them outside the community of the saved and associates them with the other enemies of the faith, including pagans, Saracens, and, most notably, Jews.[23]

Ademar's concerns in the sermons were not limited to demonizing the heretics and placing them outside the congregation of the saved but included the description and repudiation of their teachings. Although his description of their beliefs remains controversial, Ademar, like Glaber and other contemporaries, believed the heretics of the day advocated a sophisticated and fully developed alternative to the doctrines of the church.[24] In three distinct but related areas, the heretics offered a doctrinal challenge to the church. As indicated throughout the sermons, the heretics of the early eleventh century rejected Catholic teaching on the sacraments, including the Eucharist. Their denial of the Eucharist was already described in Ademar's history, and his account of the powder of human bones in both the history and sermons may have been a parody of the practices of the heretics.[25] In other parts of the sermons, Ademar offers more explicit testimony concerning the heretics' rejection of the Eucharist. Most notably, in his sermon on the Eucharist, Ademar warns of heretics who assert that communion at the altar offers nothing. These heretics, who are full of the devil and seek to lead Christians to damnation, also reject baptism and the cross. He cites the passage from the Gospel of John against these heretics, asserting that only through the Eucharist can anyone come to eternal life. He complements this passage with a long discussion in defense of the sacraments of the Eucharist and baptism and asserts the necessity of the sacraments for salvation against the errors of the heretics.[26] In a later sermon, he again cites John and compares the heretics with the Jews, who once rejected Christ in the flesh. Now, Ademar says, heretics and other unbelievers murmur against the faith in their hearts and do not believe in the mystery of the Eucharist.[27] His attention to the Eucharist and the heretics' denial of it led

Ademar to describe a number of miracles believed to demonstrate the truth that the literal body and blood of Jesus Christ were manifest in the sacrament of the bread and wine.[28]

The heretics also rejected the church's teaching on the nature of Christ at the time when the church began to emphasize his humanity and as Ademar and others also stressed the presence of Christ's human flesh in the Eucharist.[29] Indeed, although Glaber offers little discussion on the exact nature of the heretics he describes, he provides a long defense of the teachings on Christ and the Trinity and notes that rejection of these teachings "is the origin of all the heresies and perverse sects which exist all over the globe."[30] Ademar's defense of the church's teachings on the nature of Christ confirms Glaber's concerns and suggests that the monk of Limoges understood it to be one of the fundamental errors of the heretics both in his day and throughout the history of the church. Because he saw heresy as part of an ongoing diabolical conspiracy against the faith, Ademar denounced the Christological errors of the precursors of the contemporary heretics. In his sermon on the Catholic faith, Ademar opposed the beliefs of Apollonarian and other heretics who merged the two natures of Christ into one or denied his human nature with the Catholic teaching that Christ was true God and true man in one.[31]

Ademar's concerns, however, were not merely historical, as his denunciation of the Saracens indicates. In the sermon on the Catholic faith, he criticizes the errors of Saracen heretics who claim to accept God but do not accept the Incarnation and assert that God cannot die.[32] He then provides the Catholic counterpoint to the errors of the Saracens. Further evidence that the matter of the nature of Christ was a contemporary concern appears in another passage from this sermon where Ademar proclaims Christ perfect God and perfect man; this is followed by a warning not to discuss the mysteries of the Trinity before the laity who would misunderstand and fall into blasphemy.[33] Failing to heed his own warning, Ademar wrote in the sermon on the Eucharist, which is much concerned with heresy and orthodoxy, that true Christians believe that Jesus suffered according to his flesh and that his crucifixion was a victory over the devil.[34] In a passage from the *In Sermo Sindo* he argued that Christ's sacrifice on the cross, like the sacrifice of his body and blood at the altar, offers salvation to true Christians but not to heretics, Jews, and others who do not accept baptism in Christ.[35] Clearly, the heretics of Aquitaine who rejected the Redeemer of the world were not among the saved for Ademar, and their denial of church teaching inspired his concerns about and defense of that teaching.

One further concern for Ademar was the heretics' refusal to honor the cross, which both he and Glaber mentioned in their histories. In three separate passages from the sermon *De Eucharistia*, Ademar warns of heretics who refuse to adore the image of the cross and notes that those who deny the cross are "full of the devil and messengers of Antichrist."[36] For the heretics, the cross was an idol of wood or silver or gold and not the true Cross of Christ, which alone is worthy of adoration. In response to their accusations that the cross is an idol, Ademar argues that true Christians do not prostrate themselves before an idol, but instead they honor and adore Christ, who is depicted on the image.[37] Moreover, he argues that the cross is a symbol of power. It serves to confuse and confound the devil, and it is the sign of Christ's perpetual glory and provides defense and security for all men and angels.[38] The cross will also appear in the heavens as witness to Christ's victory when he comes to judge the living and the dead at the end of time.[39] And thus, as he did with the Eucharist and nature of the person of Christ, Ademar responded to the heretics of Aquitaine by denouncing their errors and promoting church teachings.

Ademar and Rodulfus Glaber were clearly concerned about the sudden reappearance of heresy, which challenged the fundamental tenets of the faith. Their concerns over matters of orthodoxy and the diabolical attack on it mounted by the heretics were paralleled by their interest in the Jews, who also challenged the validity of orthodox teaching and suffered for it. Just as both monks depicted heretics as servants of the devil who rejected the core of Christian teaching, they developed an image of contemporary Jews who were in league with the devil to destroy the church. This image revealed Christian Europe's changing attitude toward the Jews and was the precursor of the full-blown antisemitic depiction of the diabolical and murderous Jew of the later Middle Ages.

This new attitude toward the Jews is readily apparent in the histories of the two monks, and it is also in the histories that the connection between the heretics is made. Glaber explicitly states that the heretics of Monteforte made "vain sacrifices" like the Jews and in another passage speaks of the "wicked customs of the Jews."[40] There is also an implicit connection made between the Jews and heretics in the history when Glaber treats in consecutive passages the destruction of the temple in Jerusalem and the heresy of Orleans. The proximity of the two passages suggests that Glaber recognized the mutual threat posed to the church by its enemies, heretics and Jews. Although he does not link Jews and heretics as clearly as the Burgundian monk did, Ademar reveals the deteriorating image of the Jews in his history. In several passages of the work, he demonstrates Jewish hostility toward the church and its symbols as well as growing Christian animosity toward the Jews.[41] In the year 1010, according to the Limousin monk, Alduin, bishop of Limoges, forced the Jews of the city to convert or leave. Christian doctors debated with the Jews over the meaning of Scripture, and three or four Jews converted. The majority, however, refused to convert, and some even committed suicide rather than to accept baptism.[42] This steadfast devotion to their faith in the face of persecution surely struck contemporary Christian observers and most likely raised doubts about the devotion to their own faith, especially when compared with Christian lack of resolve.[43] Further violence against Jews occurred in c. 1018, according to Ademar's history, when the annual ritual slap (*colapham Judeorum*)

was administered by Hugh, the chaplain of Aimery, the viscount of Rochech-
ouart.[44] The force of the blow was so severe that the victim's eyes burst from his
head, and he died almost immediately. Although the reason for the performance
of this ritual is not stated, its occurrence at Easter suggests that is was punishment
for the murder of Christ by the Jews and thus brings to mind the stereotype of the
Jews as deicides.[45] The connection in Ademar's mind of the incident in 1018 and
the murder of Christ is reinforced by his description of events in Rome, which
preceded the account of the slap. Following a terrible storm and an earthquake in
Rome during Lent, it was discovered that the Jews had been mocking the cross in
their synagogues as the natural disasters were occurring.[46] This incident recalls
the desecration and repudiation of the cross by contemporary heretics, and it also
suggests that the Jews were not merely insulting Christian symbols but were reen-
acting the murder of Christ.[47] Like the heretics of the early eleventh century, the
Jews were depicted as the enemies of the faith bent on its destruction.

The belief that the Jews, like the heretics, were part of a broader conspiracy
bent on the destruction of Christendom is most clearly demonstrated in the histories of the two monks in their description of the events of 1009 and 1010 and the
demolition of the Church of the Holy Sepulcher. According to both Ademar and
Glaber, the Jews sent a letter to al-Hakim informing him that Christian soldiers
were preparing to conquer his kingdom. Glaber explains that the letter, which
was sent by the Jews of Orleans, instructed al-Hakim that he should destroy the
Holy Sepulcher to prevent the invasion of Christian soldiers.[48] Ademar's version
contains no such reference to the destruction of the church, but it does note that
the emir was so enraged upon learning of the alleged plans of the Christians
that he persecuted the Christians and destroyed churches in his realm. So severe
was the persecution that the majority of Christians, unlike the Jews of Aquitaine,
quickly converted to Islam. Indeed, according to Ademar, the actions of the Jews
followed the forced conversions and persecution of Hilduin and may have been
the result of that persecution. Moreover, al-Hakim was clearly an antichrist figure
for Ademar, and the alleged alliance between al-Hakim and the Jews neatly fit
into the developing Antichrist legend in which the Jews, who rejected Jesus as the
messiah, would flock to the Antichrist and form part of his effort to destroy the
faith.[49] The alleged contact with al-Hakim also fit in with the medieval belief in
the alliance between Jews and Muslims, who were seen by Ademar and others
as heretics, and further reinforced the notion of a widespread conspiracy against
Christendom and its faith.[50]

Once again, however, Ademar's sermons demonstrate the growing animosity
toward and deteriorating image of the Jews in the early eleventh century. At the
very least, the sermons reveal the perception that the Jews were in league with
diabolical and heretical forces opposed to the faith. In several of the sermons in
the Berlin manuscript, Ademar links the Jews with heretics and other enemies. In
the sermon on the Eucharist, he asserts that "the congregation of Jews, pagans,

Saracens, and all heretics" is in opposition to the congregation of believers of the true faith.[51] In another piece in the Berlin collection, he declares that the Christian faith is the destruction of "Jews and Saracens and pagans and heretics and antichrists and devils."[52] The Jews, along with Saracens, pagans, heretics, and antichrists, stand in opposition to God, according to Ademar in his sermon on the mass.[53] And belief in the Jewish opposition to God and alliance with heretics and other forces of evil is reinforced in the sermons where Ademar contends that the Jews will accept the Antichrist as their messiah.[54] Their acceptance of the Antichrist, therefore, would include the Jews in the diabolical conspiracy against humanity and would put them in league with the heretics, Ademar's messengers of Antichrist.

Ademar further established the association of the Jews and heretics by portraying the Jews as rejecting the very teachings that the heretics did. As he did in regard to the heretics, Ademar identified three fundamental critiques of Christian teachings that the Jews made and that involved the Eucharist, the person of Christ, and the cross. In his sermon to a church synod Ademar emphasizes the importance of the Eucharist and subscribes to the notion of the real presence in the host. As noted already, he describes several eucharistic miracles in this sermon in defense of orthodox teaching against the heretics. And just as he responded to the heretics, Ademar addressed the matter of Jewish denial of the true nature of the Eucharist. In one telling passage, he asserts that the heretics are the new Jews because of their denial of the Eucharist. In this sermon, following a passage concerning manna the ancient Hebrews received in the desert, Ademar argues that the true bread from heaven is Christ and uses the Gospel of John as his proof text for this claim. He then notes that just as the Jews once asked how Jesus could offer his flesh as a sacrifice, so do the heretics reject the true mystery of the sacrifice at the altar. Later in the sermon, in his defense of the miracle at the altar he notes that the sacrifice at the altar is only for those who believe in Christ and not for Jews, heretics, or pagans.[55] Moreover, throughout the sermons Ademar suggests that the Jews continue to reject the truth of the sacrifice of Christ and the eucharistic sacrifice and that they do so despite the teachings in the Hebrew Scriptures. He cites the sacrifices of Abel, Abraham, and Melchisedech as precedents for the eucharistic sacrifice and that of Jesus and, therefore, as evidence from the Hebrew Scriptures to prove Christian teachings.[56] The Jews, thus, err on two levels in that they reject the truth taught by the church and by their own scriptures. The willful rejection of scriptural truth would become a commonplace of the medieval antisemitic tradition, and it was tantamount to heresy.[57]

The repudiation of their own scriptural tradition, according to Ademar, led the Jews, like the Manichaeans of Aquitaine, into another heresy: the denial of Jesus Christ. At several points throughout the sermons, Ademar emphasizes this denial. In one of the early sermons in the Berlin collection, he compares the Jews with the heretics, who maintain that Jesus was not conceived by the power of the

Holy Spirit and thus deny his divinity.[58] Moreover, he draws a distinction between contemporary and biblical Jews, asserting that all "just Jews" before the advent of Christ recognized the truth that the messiah would be born of a virgin and would suffer and be resurrected.[59] His understanding that the ancient Hebrews would recognize the messiah when he came is set in stark contrast to later Jews who deny the truth of the Hebrew Scriptures. The Jews, according to Ademar, have numerous references in their holy books to the truth but refuse to accept the teachings of the prophets concerning the Incarnation and resurrection of Christ.[60] Consequently, their refusal to accept the truth led to the crucifixion; although the Jews at the time of the Incarnation knew the truth, they killed him. In fact, Ademar argues in what would be one of the main themes of medieval antisemitism that because the Jews knew who Jesus truly was they killed him, committing the greatest of crimes and preparing the way for further crimes against the Christian faith and its followers.[61] The Jews' murder of Jesus and their refusal to accept him as the Christ also means that they will accept the Antichrist as their messiah.[62] Ademar, therefore, again associates Jews and heretics, the messengers of Antichrist, and again asserts the diabolical nature of the Jews.

Jewish attitudes toward the Eucharist and Christ, as well as the belief that they killed Christ, can be associated, as with the heretics, with the rejection of the cross. Indeed, Ademar reveals the growing importance of the cross as the greatest Christian symbol as well as the symbol of the newly developing image of the human Christ and the Christ of the Last Judgment in his writings at the same time that it was being rejected by heretics in Aquitaine and elsewhere.[63] In his sermon on the Eucharist, Ademar provides a defense of the power of the cross and attacks the heretics and Jews who blaspheme it and accuse Christians of adoring an idol of wood. Moreover, he prefaces these remarks by citing the Gospel of John, in which the Jews call for the crucifixion, and defending the power of the cross against the devil and the enemies of the faith.[64] Ademar, however, does not claim merely that the Jews rejected the cross but that they continue to desecrate it just as they once killed Christ. In a passage that recalls his discussion from the history of Jewish abuse of the cross in Rome, Ademar describes Jewish violence against the cross. The Jews allegedly struck the figure on the cross with lance blows, wounding it and causing a miraculous flow of blood and water from its side just as Christ bled on the cross.[65] As with so many of his other attitudes concerning the Jews, Ademar's allegation that the Jews actively destroyed Christian symbols was part of the emerging medieval antisemitic tradition.[66]

The writings of Ademar and Glaber reveal, therefore, a fundamental shift in medieval Christian patterns of thinking concerning the Jews, which can be associated with the church's response to the appearance of religious dissidents. Just as the heretics challenged the fundamental teaching of the church, according to these two monks, so did the Jews. The sudden appearance of heresy after centuries of dormancy led to a rather dramatic response by the church, including the burning of heretics at Orleans. The church also exhibited an increasingly hostile tone toward the Jews, whose denial of church teachings was perceived as being similar to the heretics' rejection of church teaching. The aggressive response to heresy, chronicled by both Ademar and Glaber, and the identification of heretics as minions of the devil influenced developing attitudes toward the Jews, who were now implicated in the great diabolical conspiracy against the faith. Although long recognized as rivals of the faith, the Jews assume a more sinister role in the writings of Ademar and Glaber that is manifest in Jewish rejection of the Eucharist, Christ, and the cross. The rejection of these teachings and related characteristics that Ademar, especially, and Glaber associate with the Jews would become commonplaces of later medieval stereotypes of the Jews, and thus the foundation of medieval antisemitism, and persecution of the other, is found not in the twelfth century, but the eleventh.

Notes

1. A version of this article was originally presented at the American Historical Association annual meeting in January 2003 in a session on anti-Judaism that Daniel Callahan and I organized. I wish to express my thanks to the other members of session — R. I. Moore, Daniel Callahan, and Matthew Gabriele — for their comments on this essay.
2. On the importance of the twelfth century see the classic statement of Charles H. Haskins, *The Renaissance of the Twelfth Century* (Cambridge, MA: Harvard University Press, 1927). See also R. W. Southern, *The Making of the Middle Ages* (New Haven, CT: Yale University Press, 1953); and, more recently, R. I. Moore, *The First European Revolution, c. 970–1215* (Oxford: Blackwell, 2000).
3. The classic statement of this, of course, is Moore. See also Robert Chazan, "The Deteriorating Image of the Jews — Twelfth and Thirteenth Centuries," in *Christendom and Its Discontents*, ed. Scott L. Waugh and Peter Diehl (Cambridge: Cambridge University Press, 1996), 220–33; Chazan, *Medieval Stereotypes and Modern Antisemitism* (Berkeley: University of California Press, 1997); Signer and Van Engen. I follow the convention of Chazan, *Medieval Stereotypes*; Gavin Langmuir, *History, Religion, and Antisemitism* (New York: I. B. Tauris and Co. Ltd, 1990); Langmuir, *Toward a Definition of Antisemitism* (Los Angeles and Berkeley: University of California Press, 1990); and others in the use of *antisemitism* to describe anti-Jewish sentiments in the period beginning c. 1000. Although clearly distinct from modern, biological anti-Semitism, medieval attitudes provide modern anti-Jewish attitudes with a variety of stereotypes and, after 1000, are fundamentally irrational. For a general introduction to the development of medieval anti-Jewish attitudes, see also Poliakov, 3–95; *Witness to Witchcraft*; Diana Wood, ed., *Christianity and Judaism* (Oxford: Blackwell, 1992).
4. See Antoine Dondaine, "L'Origine de l'hérésie médiévale," *Rivista di storia della chiesa in Italia* 6 (1952): 43–78; R. Gorre, *Die ersten Ketzer im 11. Jahrhundert: Religiöse Eiferer — Soziale Rebellen?* Konstanzer Dissertationen 3 (Constance: W. Hartung-Gorre, 1985); Malcolm Lambert, *Medieval Heresy: Popular Movements from the Gregorian Reform to the Reformation*, 3d ed. (Oxford: Blackwell, 2002),

1–40; Moore, *The Origins of European Dissent*, rev. ed. (Oxford: Blackwell, 1985), 1–45; Claire Taylor, "The Letter of Heribert of Périgord as a Source for Dualist Heresy in the Society of early Eleventh Century Aquitaine," *Journal of Medieval History* 26 (2000): 313–39; Taylor, *Heresy in Medieval France: Dualism in Aquitaine and the Agenais, 1000–1249* (Woodbridge: Boydell Press, 2005), 55–138 for discussion of the revival of heresy after c. 1000.

5. For the life and career of Ademar, see Richard Landes, *Relics, Apocalypse, and the Deceits of History: Ademar of Chabannes, 898–1034* (Cambridge, MA: Harvard University Press, 1995); Robert Lee Wolff, "How the News Was Brought from Byzantium to Angoulême; or, The Pursuit of a Hare in an Oxcart," *Byzantine and Modern Greek Studies* 4 (1979): 162–209. Ademar's extensive literary corpus has been considered in Daniel Callahan, "The Sermons of Ademar of Chabannes and the Cult of St. Martial of Limoges," *Revue Bénédictine* 83 (1976): 251–95; Callahan, "The Problem of the *Filioque* and the Letter from the Pilgrim Monks of the Mount of Olives to Pope Leo III and Charlemagne: Still Another Ademar Forgery?" *Revue Bénédictine* 102 (1992): 75–134; Leopold Delisle, "Notice sur les manuscrits originaux d'Adèmar de Chabannes," *Notice et extraits de la Bibliothèque Nationale* 35 (1895): 241–355; Michael Frassetto, "The Sermons of Ademar of Chabannes and the Origins of Medieval Heresy" (Ph.D. dissertation, University of Delaware, 1993). For Rodulfus, see Glaber, "Introduction," xix–cv; Paul Dutton, "Raoul Glaber's 'De Divina Quaternitate': An Unnoticed Reading of Eriugena's Translation of the *Ambigua* of Maximus the Confessor," *Mediaeval Studies* 42 (1980): 431–53; John France, "Rodulfus Glaber and the Cluniacs," *Journal of Ecclesiastical History* 39 (1988): 497–507; Dominique Iogna-Prat, "Raoul Glaber et l'historiographie clunisienne," *Studi medievali* 3d ser. 26 (1985): 437–72.

6. On the dating of the history of Ademar, see Landes, *Relics,* 131–78; Ademar, xi–c. For the dating of Glaber, see Glaber, "Introduction," xix–cv.

7. Glaber, 2:12.23, 92–93: "Ipso quoque tempore non impar apud Rauennam exortum est malum. Quidam igitur Vilgardus dictus, studio artis gramatice magis asiduus quam frequens, sicut Italicis mos semper fuit artes negligere ceteras, illam sectari...Ad ultimum uero hereticus est repertus atque a pontifice ipsius urbis Petro dampnatus. Plures etiam per Italiam tunc huius pestiferi dogmatis sunt reperti, qui et ipsi aut gladiis aut incendiis perierunt. Ex Sardinia quoque insula, que his plurimum habundare solet, ipso tempore aliqui egressi, partem populi in Hispania corrumpentes, et ipsi a uiris catholicis exterminati sunt." See also Moore, *Origins,* 23–24.

8. Glaber, 2:11.22, 88–91: "Extitit circa finem millesmi anni homo plebeius in Galiis apud uicum Virtutis uocabulo, in pago Catalonico, Leutardus nomine, qui, ut finis rei probauit, Satane legatus credi potuit." For further discussion on Leutard see Lambert, *Medieval Heresy,* 35–36; Brian Stock, *The Implications of Literacy: Written Language and Models of Interpretation in the Eleventh and Twelfth Centuries* (Princeton, NJ: Princeton University Press, 1983), 101–6.

9. Ibid., 90: "...et multa hominibus impossibilia precipere ut faceret."

10. Ibid.: "Tandem fatigatus exurgens uenit domum, dimittensque uxorem quasi ex precepto euuanvangelico fecit divortium. Egressus autem uelut oraturus, intrans ecclesiam, arripiensque crucem et Saluatoris imaginem contruit...Nam decimas

dare dicebat esse omnimodis superfluum et inane. Et sicut hereses cetere, ut cautius decipiant, Scripturis se diuinis, quibus etiam contrarie sunt, palliant, ita et iste dicebat prophetas ex parte narrasse utilia, ex parte non credenda."

11. Ibid., 3:8.26–31, 138–51. This is one of the most widely discussed episodes among modern historians. On the heresy see, especially, R. H. Bautier, "L'hérésie d'Orléans et le mouvement intellectuelle au début du XIe siècle," in *Actes du 95e Congrès National des Sociétés Savantes (Reims, 1970)*; *Section philologique et historique* (Paris: Bibliothèque nationale, 1975) I, 63–88; for an important corrective, see Lambert, *Medieval Heresy*, 14–21. See also Moore, *Origins*, 25–30; Stock, *Implications of Literacy*, 106–20.

12. Glaber, 4:2.5, 176: "Castrum igitur erat per idem tempus in gente Longobardorum, quod, ut erat, uocabatur Mons uidelicet Fortis, plenum etiam ex nobilioribus eiusdem gentis. Hos nempe cunctos ita maculauerat prauitas ante erat illis crudelis morte finiri quam ab illa quoquo modo possent ad saluberrimam Christi Domini fidem reouocari." The translation is by the volume's editor, John France, 177. For fuller consideration see Arthur Siegel, "Italian Society and the Origins of Eleventh-Century Western Heresy," in *Heresy and the Persecuting Society: Essays on the Work of R.I. Moore*, ed. Michael Frassetto (Leiden: Brill, 2006), 43–72; and Moore, *Origins*, 23–24.

13. Glaber, 4:2.5, 176: "...cum Iudeis inepta sacrificia litare nitebantur."

14. Ibid., 176–78.

15. Ademar, 3:49, 170: "Pauco post tempore per Aquitaniam exorti sunt manichei, seducents plebem, negantes baptismum sanctum et crucis virtutem, et quidquid sane doctrine est, abstinentes a cibis quasi monachi et castitatem simulantes, sed inter se ipsos omnem luxuriam exercentes; quippe ut nuncii Antichristi, multos a fide exorbitare fecerunt."

16. Ibid., 13: "E vestigio exorti sunt per Aquitaniam Manichei, seducentes promiscuum populum a vertitate ad errorem. Suadebant negare baptismum, signum sanctae crucis, ecclesiam, et ipsum redemptorem seculi, honorem sanctorum Dei, coniugia laegitima, aesum carnium, unde et multos simplices averterunt a fide." See also Landes, "Between Aristocracy and Heresy: Popular Participation in the Limousin Peace of God, 944–1033," in *The Peace of God: Social Violence and Religious Response in France around the Year 1000*, ed. Thomas Head and Landes (Ithaca, NY: Cornell University Press, 1992), 207–13.

17. Ademar, 3:59, 180: "Eo tempore decem ex canonicis Sanctae Crucis Aurelianis, qui videbantur aliis religiosiores, probati sunt esse manichei...Nam ipsi decepti a quodam rustico Petragoricensi, qui se dicebat facere virtutes, et pulverem ex mortuis pueris secum deferebat, de quo si quem posset communicare, mox manicheum faciebat, adorabant diabolum, qui primo eis in Etyopis, deinde angeli lucis figuratione apparebat, et eis multum cotidie argentum deferebat."

18. For the transformation of doctrine in the early eleventh century see Southern, *Making of the Middle Ages*, 235–57; Tennyson J. Wellman, "Apocalyptic Concerns and Mariological Tactics in Eleventh-Century France," *The Year 1000: Religious and Social Response to the Turning of the First Millennium,* ed. Frassetto (New York: Palgrave, 2002), 133–63; Phyllis G. Jestice, "A New Fashion in Imitating Christ: Changing Spiritual Perspectives around the Year 1000," in Frassetto, *Year 1000,* 165–85.

19. D.S. MS. Lat Phillipps, 1664, fol. 114v: "Dicere habemus vobis de aliis rebus quae pertinent ad sinodum et de haereticis qui modo latenter inter nos surgunt qui negant baptismum, missam, crucem, ecclesiam, qui praecursores Antichristi sunt." A similar comment is found on fol. 160v.

20. Ibid., fol. 75r: "Solent enim quidam ex eis portare secum pulvere de ossibus mortuorum hominum, et quasi propter medicinam aliquibus rusticis in cibo aut potu de ipso pulvere ministrant, de quo pulvere, si quis aliquid sumpserit, statim obliviscitur vertiatem Dei, et in amentia versus fit eorum similis. Et ita seductus in desperationem cadit, ut nec praedicatione neque terrore neque amore nullatenus ad sanctam Catholicam ecclesiam redeat ultra."

21. Ibid., fol. 90v. Similarly, on fol. 71v, he contends that anyone who rejects the creed is a "filius perditionis et haereticus."

22. Ibid., fols. 117r, 100v.

23. Ibid., fols. 74v, 83v, 96v, 97r.

24. On the history and historiography of heresy of the early eleventh century, see Moore, "The Origins of Medieval Heresy," *History* 183 (1970): 21–36; Heinrich Fichtanau, *Heretics and Scholars in the High Middle Ages, 1000–1200*, trans. Denise A. Kaiser (University Park: Pennsylvania State University Press, 1998), 13–57; Lambert, *Medieval Heresy*, 3–40; J. B. Russell, "Some Interpretations of the Origins of Medieval Heresy," *Mediaeval Studies* 25 (1963): 26–53; Taylor, "Dualist Heresy in Aquitaine and the Agenais, c. 1000–c. 1249" (Ph.D. dissertation, University of Nottingham, 1999), 66–111. For a more general treatment of the study of heresy see Peter Biller, "The Historiography of Medieval Heresy in the USA and Great Britain, 1945–92," in *The Waldenses, 1170–1530,* ed. Peter Biller (Aldershot: Variorum, 2001), 25–47.

25. On the use of parody in the accounts of heresy see Taylor, "Letter of Héribert," 338–43.

26. D.S. MS. Lat Phillipps, 1664, fols. 74v–75r.

27. Ibid., fols. 107v–108r: "Sicut Iudei murmurabant nec credebant de hoc quia dicebant Dominus, 'Ergo sum panis qui de caelo descendi.' [John 6:41] et irati dicebant 'Quomodo potest hic nobis carnem suam dare ad manducandum?' [John 6:52] ita nunc haeretici et hi qui in fide Christiani non credunt murmurant et causantur in cordibus suis non credentes tam magnum esse misterium sacrificium Christanorum."

28. Ibid., fols. 103r–103v: On miracles associated with the Eucharist, see Benedicta Ward, *Miracles and the Medieval Mind*, rev. ed. (Philadelphia: University of Pennsylvania Press, 1987), 13–18.

29. Ademar's support for the apostolicity of St. Martial and attention to the apostolic period is, perhaps, an indication of the growing interest in the human Christ.

30. Glaber, 3:7.30, 148–49.

31. D.S. MS. Lat Phillipps, 1664, fols. 94r, 96v.

32. Ibid., fol. 91v: "Sed multi Sarraceni sunt qui dicunt se credere in sanctam Trinitatem, sed non credunt incarnationem Domini. Et dicunt qui Dominus non potuit mori. Et nos similiter dicimus, quia Dominus non potuit morit, sed Filius Dei incarnatus secundum carnem mortuus est non secundum divinitatem. Et illi qui dicunt quia Deus non potuit accipere carnem humanitatis nostrae omnes prophetae qui de incarnatione Domini prophetaverunt mendaces ostendunt." For Ademar's view of Saracens as heretics see my "The Saracen as Heretic in the Sermons of Ademar of Chabannes," in *Western Views of Islam in Medieval and Early Modern Europe:*

Perception of Other, ed. David R. Blanks and Michael Frassetto (New York: St. Martin's Press, 1999), 83–96; Callahan, "Ademar of Chabannes, Millenial Fears and the Development of Western Anti-Judaism," *Journal of Ecclesiastical History* 46 (1995): 28–30.

33. D.S. MS. Lat Phillipps, 1664, fol. 94r.
34. Ibid., fol. 72v.
35. Ibid., fol. 106v: "Et sicut Dominus non pro omnibus sed pro multis, hoc est pro eis qui in eum credituri erant et ante crediderant in remissionem peccatorum in cruce occisus est, ita in altare corpus et sanguis Domini non pro Iudeis, non pro haereticis, non pro paganis, hoc est non pro omnibus, sed pro multis, hoc est pro his qui baptismum Christi susceperunt."
36. Ibid., fols. 72v, 73r, 75v.
37. Ibid., fol. 73r: "Nos itaque ante crucem ligneam, sive auream, sive alterius materiae prostrati non adoramus creaturam sed creatorem cuius signum et victoriam videtur crux. Et ante imaginem crucifixi prostrati non dicimus adoramus te imago auream aut lignea aut argentea, sed dicimus adoramus te Christo et benedicimus tibi."
38. Ibid.: "Ideo ubicumque diabolus signum crucis senserit fieri vel etiam nominari confusus contremiscit qui mors Christi victoria mundi est crux Christi gloriam perpetua defensio et triumphus Christianorum securitas hominum et angelorum est."
39. Ibid., fol. 72v: "Nam et in die quando iudicabit Dominus mundum apparebit signum crucis in caelo in testimonio victoriae Christi et gloriae sanctae ecclesiae suae." See also Glaber, 3:4.20, 128–29.
40. Glaber, 4:2.4, 176–77: "Colebant enim idola more paganorum ac cum Iudeis inepta sacrificia litare nitebantur." See also Callahan, "Development of Western Anti-Judaism," 29.
41. See also Callahan, "Heretics and Jews in the Writings of Ademar of Chabennes and the Origins of Medieval Anti-Semitism," *Church History* 71 (2002): 1–15; Adriann Bredero, "The Role of Theology in the Vilification of the Jews in the Late Middle Ages," in *Christendom and Christianity in the Middle Ages* (Grand Rapids, MI: Wm. B. Eerdmans Publishing Co., 1994), 207–18; and Callahan, "Development of Western Anti-Judaism," 19–35. See following for discussion of Christian readiness to convert in the face of persecution.
42. Ademar, 3:47, 166: "Ipso anno Alduinus episcopus Judeos Lemovice ad baptismum compulit, lege prolata ut aut christiani essent aut de civitate recederent, et per unum mensem doctores divinos jussit disputare cum Judeis, ut eos ex suis libris recincerent; et tres vel quatuor Judei christiani facti sunt, cetera autem multitudo per alias civitas diffugere cum uxoribus et liberis festinavit. Quidam etiam seipsos ferro jugulaverunt, nolentes baptismum suscipere."
43. For discussion of Jewish and Christian response to the massacres of 1095 see Chazan, *God, Humanity, and History: The Hebrew First Crusade Narratives* (Berkeley: University of California Press, 2000), which suggests possible insights into how Christians might respond to this episode of suicide and refusal to convert.
44. Ademar, 3:53, 171: "Quo tempore Ugo, capellanus Aimerici vicecomitis Rocacardensis, cum eodem seniore suo Tolose in Pascha adfuit, et colaphum Judeorum, sicut illic omni Pascha semper moris est, imposuit, et cerebrum illico et oculos ex capite perfido ad terram effudit; qui Judeus statim mortuus, a sinagoga Judeorum de basilica Sancti Stephani elatus, sepulturae datus est." See also Callahan, "Development of Western Anti-Judaism," 24–25; Moore, 32–33.

45. Chazan, *Medieval Stereotypes*, 13–14, 69–70, notes the importance of the image of Jews as Christ killers in the medieval view.

46. Ademar, 3:52, 171: "His diebus in Parasceve, post crucem adoratam, Roma terra motu et nimio turbine periclitata est. Et confestim quidam Judeoarum de schola grecia intimavit domno papae quia ea hora deludebat sinagoga Judeorum Crucifixi figuram. Quod Benedictus papa sollicite inquirens et comperiens, mox auctores sceleris capitali sententia dampnavit. Quibus decollatis, furor ventorum cessavit." See also Callahan, "Development of Western Anti-Judaism," 24; Moore, 31–34. For a general discussion of host and image desecration see Joshua Trachtenberg, *The Devil and the Jews: The Medieval Conception of the Jew and Its Relation to Modern Anti-Semitism* (Philadelphia: Jewish Publication Society, 1988), 109–23.

47. Trachtenberg, *Devil and the Jews,* 118–21, esp. 120 where the incident at Rome is noted.

48. Once again there is an implicit connection between the Jews and heretics in Glaber's account. The section on al-Hakim is followed by Glaber's report on the heresy of Orleans, and it is not inconceivable that Glaber meant to imply that some connection between the Jews and heretics of Orleans existed.

49. On the antichrist legend see Bernard McGinn, *Antichrist: Two Thousand Years of the Human Fascination with Evil* (San Francisco: HarperCollins, 1994), 57–113; Richard K. Emerson, *Antichrist in the Middle Ages: A Study of Medieval Apocalypticism, Art, and Literature* (Seattle: University of Washington Press, 1981); Adso of Montier en Der, *Libellus de Antichriste* 45 (Turnhout: Brepols, 1976). For the relationship of Jews and Muslims see Cutler and Cutler, *The Jew as Ally of the Muslim: Medieval Roots of Anti-Semitism* (Notre Dame, IN: University of Notre Dame Press, 1986). For Ademar's understanding of this relationship see Callahan, "Development of Western Anti-Judaism," 19–35; Frassetto, "Saracen as Heretic," 83–96; Landes, "The Fear of an Apocalyptic Year 1000: Augustinian History, Medieval and Modern," *Speculum* 75 (2000): 118–23.

50. Frassetto, "Saracen as Heretic," 83–96. For more general treatments of medieval attitudes toward Islam see Norman Daniel, *Islam and the West: The Making of an Image* (Oxford: Oneworld Publications, 1993); R. W. Southern, *Western Views of Islam in the Middle Ages*, 2d printing (Cambridge, MA: Harvard University Press, 1978).

51. D.S. MS. Lat Phillipps, 1664, fol. 74v: "...inter congregationem Christianorum qui veriter fidem credunt et inter congregationem Iudeorum, paganorum, Sarracenorum, et omnium haereticorum."

52. Ibid., fol. 97r: "In capite concilii primum debetis audire de fide Catholica quod est principalitas est virtus nostra et tocius Christiani imperii salus et Iudeorum atque Sarracenorum et paganorum et haereticorum et Antichristi et diaboli et inferni destructio et confusio."

53. Ibid., fol. 102v: "[E]t ipse diabolus qui Deo contrarius est et ipsi impii homines Iudei, Sarraceni, pagani, haeretici qui Deo contrari sunt."

54. Ibid., fol. 91v.

55. Ibid., fol. 106v.

56. Ibid., fol. 109v: "Sicut Melchisedech in tempore Abrahae optulit in sacrificium panem et vinum ita vos sacerdotes cotidie in pane et vino offertis Christum Ihesum. Ille agnus Abel et ille filius Abrahae et ille panis et vinum Melchisedech significabant quod est modo verum corpus est sanguinem Domini in altari. Et sicut sunt illa

tria sacrificia acceptabilia habuit agnum et hominem et panem et vinum quia significabant venturum Dominum Ihesum Christum filius eius qui pro nobis passus est et quem cotidie immolamus in altari ita acceptabile habet hoc sanctum sacrificium panis et vini et aquae in altari quia verum corpus et sanguis filii eius est. Et sicut homines principes illam non quam valde diligunt claro aspectu et placabili aspicere volunt ita Deus pater de caelesti sua sede et maiestate supra ista sacramenta panis et vini et aquae propitio vultu ac sereno hoc est placabilis et clemens aspicit."

57. For the implications of Jewish rejection of scriptural truth, see Cohen, 212; Gavin Langmuir, *History, Religion, and Antisemitism* (London: I. B. Tauris and Co. Ltd, 1990), 284–88; Trachtenberg, *Devil and the Jews*, 15–18. Ademar notes that the Jews reject the truth of their own holy book earlier in the sermons when he wrote, "Iudei tam in suis libris inveniunt trintatem atque ascensionem Domini in omnia quae de Domino Ihesus Christo credimus ipsi inveniunt praedicta a prophetis in suis libris sed non credunt quia non praedestinati ad vitam aeternam." D.S. MS. Lat Phillipps, 1664, fol. 84v.

58. D.S. MS. Lat Phillipps, 1664, fols. 72r–72v: "Credimus quia redemptor noster non est conceptus de Ioseph sicut Iudei et haeretici blasphemant sed de spiritu sancto id es per administrationem et virtutem spiritus sancti."

59. Ibid., fol. 74v: "Nam David et omnis iusti Iudei qui ante adventum Domini fuerent recte crediderunt in sanctam trinitatem quia credebant in filium Dei quod quando cumque nasciturus esset de virgine et passurus et moriturus et resurrecturus sicut nos credimus et scimus quia iam ista in eo competa sunt."

60. Ibid., fol. 83v: "Iudei tam in suis libris inveniunt trinitatem se credere nolunt sicut nativitatem et resurrectionem atque ascensionem Domini et omna quae de Domino Ihesu Christo credimus ipsi inveniunt praedicta a prophetis in suis libris sed non credunt quia non sunt praedestinati ad vitam aeternam. Innumera sunt testimonia in libris Iudeorum de trinitate quia unus est Deus et Deus trinitas sit sed unum nunc dicamus." And fol. 91v: "Et sicut nos salvi sumus quia credimus iam esse facta incarnationem Domini ita antiqui iusti salvifacti sunt quia credebant incarnationem Domini venturam et passionem et mortem resurrectionem quoque et ascensionem. Et Iudei ideo non credunt quia incarnationem Domini quam legunt in prophetis pronunciatam non credunt adhuc factam sed expectavit futuram. Et tamen Iudei illo tempore quo incarnatio Domini facta est cognoverunt et locum et tempus ipsum esse per prophetas praedictum." See Trachtenberg, *Devil and the Jews*, 14–18, for discussion of Jewish rejection of their Scriptures.

61. Ibid., fol. 89r, and elsewhere in the sermons in his discussion of the life of St. Martial, Ademar emphasizes the idea of the Jews as killers of Christ. As noted previously, Ademar represents the growing interest in the human Christ, and the rejection of Christian emphasis on the incarnation by heretics and Jews reinforced Christian doubt, which in turn reinforced hostility toward heretics and Jews. See Chazan, *Medieval Stereotypes*, 88–94; Jeremy Cohen, "The Jews as Killers of Christ in the Latin Tradition, from Augustine to the Friars," *Traditio* 39 (1983): 3–27. For further discussion on Ademar and the Jews as Christ killers see Callahan, "Heretics and Jews," 12–15.

62. D.S. MS. Lat Phillipps, 1664, fol. 91v: "Iudei adhuc expectant incarnationem eius venturam ideo quia propter peccatum quo occiderunt Dominum nostrum excetati sunt et ira Dei est super illos et pro Christo Antichristo recipient."

63. This complex image of the cross and Christ as Alpha and Omega can be seen in the vision Ademar had in the year 1010 in which a weeping Christ appears in the night-time sky the color of fire and blood on the cross. Ademar, 3:46, 165–66.

64. D.S. MS. Lat Phillipps, 1664, fol. 73v.

65. Ibid., fol. 73r: "Et quem multocies Iudei zelantes imagines crucifixi...lanceis vulnerarunt et sanguine et aqua ex eis profluit tamquam quondam ex latere Domini." See Callahan, "Development of Western Anti-Judaism," 24.

66. Trachtenberg, *Devil and the Jews*, 109–23.

5

Against the Enemies of Christ
The Role of Count Emicho in the Anti-Jewish Violence of the First Crusade[1]

Matthew Gabriele

By late July 1096, the Jews of the Rhineland had virtually ceased to exist. An army gathering at Speyer to take part in the First Crusade attacked the Jews there on May 3, 1096, but the bishop dispersed the Jews to the surrounding communities, and the incident was quickly put down. The crusaders then moved on to Worms (May 18) followed by Mainz (May 25–29) where the protests of those bishops fell on deaf ears and both Jewish communities were destroyed, with most of the Jews either being murdered or committing ritual suicide, although some accepted baptism in exchange for their lives. Emboldened by their success at Mainz, the army then moved north — deliberately away from the Holy Land.[2] Splitting up, one group arrived at Cologne in June and early July, whereas the others were directed toward the Moselle Valley and Trier and Metz, arriving in June and early July as well. According to the Hebrew chronicler Solomon bar Simson, only a few Jews were killed at Trier, whereas the majority were forcibly baptized. Twenty-two were killed, and the rest converted at Metz.[3] When the other half of the crusading army reached Cologne, they found that the bishop had dispersed the Jews from the city, much as the bishop of Speyer had done. Nevertheless, virtually all of the Jews in the surrounding villages were found and either were converted or killed. After Metz and Cologne, the two crusading armies turned finally toward the Holy Land.[4]

Much has been written on this series of events, its causes, and especially the role of its supposed leader, Count Emicho of Flonheim.[5] One source in particular, the Jewish chronicler Solomon bar Simson, offers a very distinct portrait of Emicho, writing that he was spurred to the crusade by a vision of an apostle branding him and promising him a crown in "Italian Greece" and victory over his foes.[6] The value of this vision for this study lies in the Jewish chronicler's clear familiarity with the messianic pretensions of the Christian Last Emperor legend.[7] As Hannes Möhring convincingly argues, Simson's account of Emicho's vision was likely derived from Benzo of Alba's interpretation of the Last Emperor legend for, in a letter written in the 1080s to Emperor Henry IV, Benzo urged Henry to journey to the East, be crowned at Constantinople, and conquer the Holy Land after defeating all of God's enemies.[8] The similarities between the two accounts are self-evident.

Based primarily on Simson's account, several historians, such as Paul Alphandéry, Norman Cohn, and Joshua Prawer, have seen the attacks and forcible conversions of the Jews as stemming from the apocalyptic pretensions of the crusading army. Count Emicho, they continue, thought himself to be the messianic Last Emperor who would call the pagans to baptism during the drama of the Last Days.[9] Jonathan Riley-Smith was one of the first to link Emicho's vision as described by Solomon bar Simson to Benzo of Alba's apocalyptic letter to the emperor Henry IV. Riley-Smith, however, attaches a caveat to this observation by suggesting that any apocalyptic feelings the army may have had were of secondary importance, being subsumed within the idea of feud or vengeance against the supposed killers of Christ.[10] Benjamin Z. Kedar also accepts the likely millennial motives of the Rhenish crusading army as a whole but rejects the centrality of Emicho to the project. For Kedar, the attacks on the Jews in 1096 arose out of a "streak of popular spirituality that led some Christians of the Rhineland to believe that it was their duty to baptize the offspring of the Jews even against their will."[11]

A recent article in *Speculum* by Kenneth Stow goes even further than Kedar regarding Emicho and seeks to fully disentangle him from the persecutions specifically and from apocalypticism from the crusading army more generally.[12] Stow wants to separate the literary Emicho from the historical, suggesting that most of the man we see in modern studies, including his messianic pretensions, is no more than a literary construct — no more than so much smoke and mirrors.[13] Stow argues that Emicho was only physically present during the attacks at Mainz and did not journey down the Rhine to the other persecutions. Instead, he immediately left for the Holy Land only to have his army destroyed in Hungary. Since Emicho was so unsuccessful, Solomon bar Simson's well-known report about Emicho's vision was thus intended as no more than a mockery of his spectacular failure.[14]

What Emicho represented to the Christian chroniclers, Stow continues, was a subversion of crusading virtue and established clerical authority. As such, the clerics who narrated the First Crusade demonized Emicho. The forcible conversions, most of which by and large ended in apostasy, fueled the fears of an increasingly powerful clergy about both its own power and the Jewish social presence. This led to a literary reaction against the Rhenish crusaders.[15] Clerics like Albert of Aachen worried that these Jews were not truly baptized, as these baptisms were not performed by priests, nor were the Jews allowed a sufficient reflective time to ensure the sincerity of their conversion.[16]

Reviewing the evidence, though, there is no indication whatsoever that the crusading armies who attacked the Jewish settlements along the Rhine were bereft of clerics or that the baptisms were carried out by laypersons. The crusade attracted a large number of clerics from all over Western Europe, and it seems unwise to propose that this particular army was any exception. Furthermore, the conversions of the Jews may not have even been forced. Conversion at the point of a sword had a strong Carolingian precedent that continued in the Rhineland through the eleventh century.[17] In this region, the "margins of permissible coercion [to baptism] could be very wide indeed" during this period, with the paradigm of baptism or expulsion not uncommon between 930 and 1060.[18]

Most importantly, Emicho was not simply a straw man. On the contrary, he played an absolutely vital role in the anti-Jewish violence that accompanied the First Crusade. The Rhenish crusading army, fed by apocalyptic ideas from the numerous itinerant preachers who sprang up after Urban's call, converged on the cities of the Rhine determined to combat the enemies of Christ. In the emotionally and religiously charged period between Easter and Pentecost 1096,[19] they found the Jewish communities and tried to eradicate them — through conversion or massacre. Emicho emerged as their leader in this apocalyptic drama that was predicated on two things: the final conversion of the Jews and the emergence of a powerful leader who would lead a united Christendom to Jerusalem as its conqueror. This was a drama predicated on Emicho as the apocalyptic Last Emperor.

As Kedar has shown, it seems very clear that "for many of the early crusaders...the forcible christianization of Jews constituted a major goal" of their endeavor.[20] This predilection toward evangelism is understandable since it was an integral feature of early Christianity and continued to be so throughout the Middle Ages. But note that these missionary efforts were often specifically motivated by eschatology — perhaps not surprising, given the prevalence of imminent apocalypticism in the early Middle Ages.[21] Paul wrote that both the Gentiles and Jews would be converted before the end of time, and this assertion had not been lost on his early medieval readers.[22] St. Patrick justified his missionary efforts by quoting Acts 2:17 and Matthew 24:14, two passages that explicitly refer to the Last Days.[23] Bede spoke of "two very certain indicators of the approach of the Day of Judgment, namely the conversion of the Jewish people, and the reign and persecution of Antichrist."[24]

But why were these missionary efforts toward the Jews matched with violence? There had been incidents of anti-Jewish violence in the West before 1096 — most notably in 1010 at Limoges and Orleans — but never on the scale that would be seen at the end of the century.[25] 1096 was unprecedented. Why did the Christians resort to slaughter when their efforts at conversion failed? For the answer to this, we must turn to another strand of medieval apocalyptic tradition — one built on a zero-sum logic, which allows, and in fact necessitates, unsuccessful efforts at conversion to become massacres — that of the Last Emperor.

Both original sources of the Last Emperor legend — the Latin Tiburtine Sibyl and the Pseudo-Methodius — are replete with martial imagery and state that the Last Emperor will make the whole world Christian before the Last Judgment.[26] Composed in reaction to the Muslim invasions of the Byzantine Empire in the seventh century, the legend had arrived in the West within 100 years and survives in over 140 manuscripts dating from between the eighth and twelfth centuries.[27] Promising vengeance for the vanquished, the legend, by its very nature, is a violent prophecy that promises peace only after the destruction of Christ's enemies.[28] Most importantly, however, this legend also affords the Christian community an active role in the apocalyptic drama.[29] With the Last Emperor at their head, Christians are called on to fight against the enemies of Christ — be they Gog and Magog or servants of the Antichrist. Because it attests to the creation of a new, wholly Christian society, the Last Emperor legend places the Jews outside of the traditional Augustinian paradigm, which said that they were a necessary component of a Christian society, with their exile from Jerusalem and subservient status attesting to the truth of the Christian version of sacred history.

Moreover, the Jews played an especially nefarious role in some eschatological thinking. Isidore of Seville suggested that anyone outside the church and the unity of faith — be they pagan, Jew, Muslim, heretic, or whatever — was the Antichrist spoken of in 2 Thessalonians and 1 John.[30] Agobard of Lyons defined this more closely and explicitly argued in a letter to Louis the Pious that the Jews were, in fact, antichrists one and all.[31] Adso of Montier-en-Der, almost certainly drawing on Bede, notes in his hugely popular tract on the antichrist that he will be born of the Jews and that they will flock to his service.[32] An eleventh-century reworking of the Tiburtine Sibyl records that the Last Emperor will bring the whole world to Christianity — by the sword if necessary. The Jews, however, will be the most obstinate and the final group to come to the Lord before the end.[33] The Pseudo-Alcuin, which is a late eleventh-century reworking of Adso's *De ortu et tempore Antichristi*, echoes the Tiburtine Sibyl in asserting the necessity of the Jews' conversion before the end could occur.[34]

Finally, it should be noted that there was little distinction made between Jews and Muslims during the eleventh century.[35] Both were considered minions of the devil and servants of the Antichrist and as such often were thought to be in league with one another. Ademar of Chabannes and Rodulfus Glaber, for example, both wrote that the European Jews were ultimately responsible for the destruction of the Holy Sepulcher by the Caliph al-Hakim in 1009 — egging their Muslim cohorts on in letters sent to the Holy Land.[36] The rhetoric explicitly deployed against the Muslims in the run-up to the First Crusade, which may have been present in Urban's speech, could thus be rather easily expanded to include the Jews. For instance, Robert of Reims recorded that Urban spoke of an accursed race that was circumcising Christians in Jerusalem.[37] It would not do to overlook one enemy in pursuit of another during the final march to the East. The Jews were either to be converted or destroyed.

But was apocalypticism a factor in motivating these men to go on crusade? This was the main thesis of Paul Alphandéry's posthumously published book,[38] but Bernard McGinn's highly influential 1978 article titled *"Iter sancti Sepulchri*: The Piety of the First Crusaders" argued just the opposite, saying that the "late eleventh century was not a time of widespread fear of the end of the world."[39] Though there may have been some apocalyptic sentiment present in popular preaching of the crusade, McGinn concluded that the squabbling between emperor and pope at the time precluded the sort of messianic apocalypticism to be found in the Last Emperor legend in a papally sponsored event.[40] Nonetheless, the vast majority of the other scholars does not go as far as either Alphandéry or McGinn and appears to agree that any millennial sentiment, if any, among the crusading armies was confined to the poorer elements.

Carl Erdmann had earlier suggested the importance of the Last Emperor legend to the origins of the First Crusade but placed its ideological foundations squarely on the shoulders of the reform papacy. The crusade was intended, essentially, as an exercise to aid the Eastern Church and to unite it with the West under the banner of the papacy — a co-optation of the lay nobility by the church.[41] As noted already, Jonathan Riley-Smith proposed that there likely was some eschatological feeling among the Rhenish crusaders before the crusade, but this was more true for Emicho personally than the rest of the army. Any overt apocalypticism that existed in the other armies was likely confined to the poor and did not exert a strong effect on the army as a whole.[42]

Norman Cohn's *The Pursuit of the Millennium* focused on the messianic apocalypticism of the poor during the Middle Ages and as such saw the locus of this messianic sentiment in the first wave of armies that left Europe — those of the "Peasants' Crusade."[43] Apocalypticism in other armies was either insignificant or absent. André Vauchez recently argued that the crusade attempted to use popular apocalyptic feeling to motivate people to take up the cross but sought to transform a belief in the imminent end (apocalypticism and millennialism) into an allegory for reform and penance (eschatology) — synthesizing, in a way, Cohn and Erdmann. But, Vauchez continues, the crusade had the unforeseen consequence of creating a climate of "here and now" among the poorer classes, which was manifest in the attacks on the Jewish communities along the Rhine.[44]

Jean Flori and Hannes Möhring support Cohn and Alphandéry generally in saying that apocalypticism was alive and well throughout the eleventh century.[45] Yet, although apocalypticism existed, it was not universal. Both seek to limit Alphandéry's claims, with Flori doing so by proposing a dialectical model to properly understand the crusade. Urban's crusade was more aristocratic and political and was embodied in the baronial armies. This crusade may have had individuals influenced by eschatology but it was not widespread. There was, however, also a more popular crusade, embodied in the followers of Peter the Hermit and those along the Rhine, which was rooted in ideas of vengeance, as Riley-Smith suggested, and eschatology and was possibly linked to older ideas of anti-Judaism like that of 1010.[46] For these popular preachers, "it sufficed to 'dream' on words like Jerusalem, Charlemagne, Sepulcher, infidels or enemies of Christ, that the Pope in all probability must have said in his initial sermon" for them to arrive at their own vengeful and eschatological sermons.[47] It was therefore this unofficial crusade that led to the attacks along the Rhine.

It should be noted that these scholars are at least implicitly — and some-times rather explicitly — making the Peasants' Crusade a distinct entity from the papally sanctioned First Crusade. They are suggesting that the Peasants' Crusade was inspired by different factors and was composed of a different sort of person. It was to this Peasants' Crusade that apocalyptic sentiment was confined. Pope Urban II and the better-known leaders of the crusading armies are thus, in some sense, exonerated from the troublesome sentiments that apocalypticism seems to have excited. They were too well versed on Augustine to subscribe to the thought that they could predict the time of the end.[48] These massacres, it seems, were all the fault of irresponsible popular preachers and a senseless rabble. But that would be wrong.

To begin with, this understanding of that part of the First Crusade more com-monly known as the Peasants' Crusade does not account for much recent scholar-ship. The Rhenish crusaders were not simply a murderous barbarian horde, and Emicho was not "a noble fighting alongside rabble."[49] Riley-Smith and Flori con-clusively argue against just such an interpretation. The armies that assembled along the Rhine did possess a large popular element but were also comprised of many notables and professional soldiers, such as Emicho, likely in similar percentages to the armies of the "Baronial Crusade."[50] They may have left at a different time from the proper crusading armies and been subject to a different set of preachers urging them to go, but they were inspired to the same task by the same general set of ideas. The actions of the Rhenish crusaders, including their attacks on the Jews, were very much a part of the First Crusade — not some unfortunate byproduct.[51]

More importantly, the very ideas inherent in *crusade* seem almost necessar-ily apocalyptic. Too much of the argument against an apocalyptic influence on the calling of the crusade has been influenced by modernist historians reacting against the "Terrors of the Year 1000" argument of the Romantics. These "Terrors of the Year 1000" have been effectively denounced by the modernists, and it is widely accepted that apocalyptic belief around the year 1000 was initially overstated — and too much made of the trembling fear with which one was thought to await the end. People did not, it seems, run about all willy-nilly in terror of the imminent apocalypse.[52] But this modernist historiographical reaction swung the pendulum too far to the opposite side, and some scholars have gone so far as to argue that apocalypticism all but disappeared around the millennium and only sprang up again, almost *ex nihilo*, with Joachim of Fiore in the late twelfth century.[53]

Though Augustine had rejected millennialism generally and the ability of man to predict the end specifically, evidence for apocalyptic concern in the early Middle Ages abounds.[54] For example, in tracing the sources of Adso of Montier-en-Der's tract on the Antichrist, Daniel Verhelst has compiled a rather lengthy list of late antique and early medieval apocalyptic writings stretching from the New Testament through to the late Carolingians.[55] As a way of explaining this acknowledged proliferation of apocalyptic sentiment despite Augustine's warnings, McGinn suggests that the Augustinian "rejection of predictiveness may paradoxically have allowed the end-time anxiety a more pervasive, if necessarily somewhat diffuse, power." McGinn further differentiates between *psychological* (believing the last events to be under way) and *predictive* (putting a specific date for the end forward) apocalyptic imminence, suggesting that with Augustine having rejected predictive apocalypticism, psychological apocalypticism became all the more common.[56] Moreover, the lack of overt apocalyptic evidence from the period in question may actually stem from a problem in modern assumptions about the discourse. The modernists may have been quite right in rejecting the "Terrors of the Year 1000," for Richard Landes suggests that apocalyptic expectation in the early Middle Ages was not simply an early form of nihilism but could rather be creative. One should therefore think more of galvanizing hopes rather than paralyzing fears when dealing with the issue.[57]

This is not to suggest that early medieval man lived in a constant state of heightened tension about the imminence of the Last Days, nor is it to suggest that all political or cultural developments during the Middle Ages generally — and the tenth and eleventh centuries specifically — can be traced to some sort of apocalyptic feeling. That would be far too reductionist. Yet the inhabitants of the Middle Ages were constantly conscious that the end was approaching and were always aware of events that might be significant indicators that the Last Days were at hand.[58] People knew enough of the relevant sacred texts to recognize certain signs when they occurred, and they were able to immediately draw on a stock of cultural referents about the end of the world to help them understand what appeared to be unfolding around them. Not every war, earthquake, flood, or plague would be viewed as apocalyptic but would be "viewed as signs of the imminent end only when there is a compelling rhetorical stimulus to interpret them as such."[59] Perhaps it would therefore be best to think of the continuation of apocalyptic feeling in the West throughout the Middle Ages as always simmering below the surface and only erupting through into the historical record and the popular consciousness at key moments — either because of the advent of specific dates or a conjunction of events. These eruptions, in turn, could spur some portion of the population into action.[60]

Thus, in peculiar political or cultural situations, even relatively common ideas or actions — such as pilgrimage, penance, and warfare against pagans — can take on profoundly different meanings.[61] Urban may have drawn on such familiar themes in calling the crusade, yet if, as seems so very likely, he saw the recapture of Jerusalem and possibly the reunification of the Eastern and Western churches as the ultimate goals of a divinely inspired band of armed pilgrims, then how could apocalypticism not have been a factor in his thinking? Apocalyptic ideas in conjunction with just such an expedition were at the very least in the air, for only a little more than twenty years previously Gregory VII had styled his proposed expedition to the East in a manner similar to Benzo of Alba's apocalyptic pseudo-Sibylline prophecy.[62] Urban, when he received the call from Emperor Alexius at the Council of Piacenza, likely dreamed of Jerusalem as the ultimate goal of his expedition. The enemy at hand — clearly believed to be agents of the devil by the end of the eleventh century — the goal, Jerusalem — the terrestrial city often conflated with the heavenly, constantly evoked as the patrimony of Christ that the crusaders were rightfully retaking and site of the drama of the Last Days — the return to a united, Frankish ideal of Christendom among the crusading armies, including the likely evocation of Charlemagne[63] at Clermont, all point to the inherent apocalypticism of the enterprise at its inception. Urban's speech at Clermont may not have been as explicitly apocalyptic and tied to the imminent arrival of the Antichrist as reported by Guibert of Nogent, but one cannot summarily dismiss the sentiments expressed therein.[64]

It should be noted here that both Flori and Möhring, like Alphandéry before them, believe that Emicho claimed to be the Last Emperor and that at least some in his army believed him. Flori claims that Emicho was playing on the credulity of the masses to gain power for himself, and although he does warn against mono-causality, Möhring suggests much the same: that Emicho was trying to exploit the space between the residents of the towns and bishops to increase his own political power.[65] Flori and Möhring are right in pointing out the possible political subtext of Emicho and his army's actions, yet the problem with their analysis exists in that, in a sense, Flori and Möhring's argument tends to portray Emicho as little more than a cynical con man. This more functionalist argument is also too reductionist in its dismissal of the power of ideas as a motivating factor to action.

One may argue that the deployment of such terms as *antichrist* and *Last Emperor* may simply be "mere rhetoric," but rhetoric contains and conveys meaning and influences action. After all, humans "find their being within language; they are, to that extent, constrained by it."[66] In other words, language and the ideas contained therein can make people do things. Both Robert Chazan and Jeremy Cohen argue that the attacks on the Jews were carried out because of "ideas and ideals,"[67] and David Nirenberg recently demonstrates with regard to interfaith relations in late medieval Aragon — and specifically when considering the place of the Jews in medieval Christian society — that normal interaction between social groups is often, if not exclusively, predicated on a particular idealization of the relationship between the two groups. Incidents of violence develop directly from, and are extensions of, simple transgressions of the customary restraints governing these idealized relationships.[68] The line in the sand between violence and tolerance, in other words, was not very hard to cross. People in the central Middle Ages understood what the elision of terms like *antichrist, Charlemagne, Franks, enemies of Christ,* and *Jerusalem* meant. As Flori writes, it would suffice simply to dream on such terms — as Urban, his audience, and the preachers that followed undoubtedly did — to arrive at a multitude of apocalyptic implications.[69]

Although dreaming on such terms as described previously clearly proved catastrophic for the Jews of the Rhineland, the anti-Jewish violence was "neither general nor wide-ranging."[70] Other than the incidents clearly attributable to Emicho and the armies of the Rhineland (i.e., Speyer, Worms, Mainz, Cologne and the surrounding communities, Trier, and Metz), there is a general report of violence perpetrated by an army supposedly led by the priests Folkmar and Gottschalk, as well as specific reports of trouble at Monieux, Rouen, Regensburg, and Prague. All of these, however, seem to have been either isolated events or derive from problematic accounts. For example, Ekkehard of Aura notes that a breakaway force from Peter the Hermit's army, led by the priests Folkmar and Gottschalk, either massacred the Jewish communities they encountered or forced them into the church.[71] Albert of Aachen partially corroborates Ekkehard's account in describing a similar rogue element of Peter's army, led only by Gottschalk this time, that rampages across the countryside out of avarice before being destroyed in Hungary. Albert, however, significantly does not mention any sort of attacks on the Jews.[72] The weight of the evidence, and the primacy of Albert as a source, led Chazan to conclude that Peter the Hermit and his army may have extorted money and forcibly baptized the Jews of Regensburg, but they "did no damage [violence] whatsoever to the Jews of Trier or…to the other Jewish communities they encountered."[73] This particular out-of-control element of Peter's army may have been just that: rampaging across the countryside, looting whatever they found along the way.

The incidents at Rouen and Monieux perhaps do testify to a more widespread anti-Jewish sentiment in western Francia at this time, but the accounts are tendentious and, if they did occur, may have been spontaneous, isolated incidents.[74] The reports concerning Prague are, again, also rather vague and may have even been carried out by elements of Emicho's army. Of the two Latin accounts, Cosmas of Prague does not mention any specific dates or names, and the anonymous Saxon annalist clearly implies that Emicho's army is responsible for those attacks as well as all the others.[75] All of these inconsistencies led Chazan to note that the available Christian sources point exclusively to one crusading group for attacks on the Jews during the First Crusade: the army of Count Emicho. The Hebrew sources do much the same. In fact, "by emphasizing so intensely the actions of Count

Emicho, the *Mainz Anonymous* [for example] seems to be pointing to the depth and uniqueness of his anti-Jewish animus."[76]

No source, Christian or Jewish, seems to doubt the central role played by Emicho in the tragic series of events, but there is no consensus as to when he took command of the army. The violence against the Jews may have begun at Speyer, but it is unclear if Emicho had joined the army by then. The Mainz Anonymous mentioned his presence at both Speyer and Mainz, whereas Solomon bar Simson said that Emicho only arrived late at the siege at Mainz.[77] The Christian sources are not terribly helpful in this respect, aside from noting that Emicho was from the Rhineland and played a central role in all of the persecutions.

Being from Flonheim, which is west of Mainz, Emicho would likely have met up with the crusaders there to travel down the Main to the Danube and into the Balkans.[78] Thus, it seems plausible to suggest that he would not have been present during the attacks on the Jews at Speyer and Worms. This seems to militate against Emicho's role in the attacks on the Jews, but Emicho's arrival on the scene at Mainz could explain the more organized way this attack was carried out and why the archbishop of Mainz was so spectacularly unsuccessful in his attempts to save the Jews.

At Mainz, the attack on the Jews there was particularly successful. The scale of the violence was so great because the Jewish community at Mainz was one of the largest, if not the largest, in Europe at the time, because a significant number of Jews committed ritual suicide to avoid what might befall them if they fell into the hands of the crusaders. Yet, from all accounts, Archbishop Ruthard of Mainz acted vigorously to save the Jews, bringing them into his palace and repeatedly negotiating with Emicho and his army.

So why did this end up as a repeat of Worms and not of Speyer? Is it the fault of the bishops? Chazan, for one, does not doubt the sincerity of the bishop of Worms and archbishop of Mainz in their attempts to save their Jews.[79] It is interesting to note, however, that the bishop of Worms is not mentioned in either of the Jewish sources, whereas Archbishop Ruthard of Mainz and his attempts to save the Jews are mentioned repeatedly in both sources. This may be a narrative choice to enhance the drama of the events at Mainz or simply the result of a lack of information, but it also could be evidence of a less than wholehearted defense of the Jews by the bishop of Worms.

If this latter possibility is the case, it would explain why Mainz is treated so differently in the Jewish sources: simply because it was so different. The ecclesiastical authorities at both Speyer and Mainz worked to save the Jews in their towns. The archbishop of Mainz failed because he encountered "a further and most potent source of anti-Jewish violence... — a crusading army ideologically committed to the annihilation of Jews."[80] These crusaders, already dreaming on the apocalyptic implications of the crusade since Speyer, found a true focal point for their messianic apocalypticism in Emicho. His success in eliminating the Jews at Mainz may well have been its own proof of the truth of his claims and may have been enough to silence any doubters. After all, since at least the Carolingian age victory in battle had displayed the rightness of one's cause.[81]

This is not to suggest that Archbishop Ruthard believed Emicho to have been the Last Emperor, but it would explain why his resistance seems so ineffectual and why the residents of virtually every city the crusaders entered joined them in attacking the Jews. It is important to remember that the crusading army met very little overt resistance. The inhabitants of Speyer initially aided the crusaders but were quickly cowed by the actions of the bishop. The inhabitants of Mainz conversely seem to have resisted the crusaders at first but later aided in the persecutions.[82] At Cologne, Trier, and Metz there seems to have been wholehearted support for the crusaders.[83] There is no mention of resistance by the local nobility; many were likely crusaders themselves. Although the episcopal authorities in the towns they entered may have attempted to protect the Jews of their cities, this does not, as has so often been implied in reference to the Peasants' Crusade, represent an essential divide between high and low culture during the central Middle Ages, with the heaving masses placed in stark relief against the forces of order in the bishops. The clerics who were assuredly part of Emicho's army appeared to have no problem believing that the Last Days were at hand and that the Jews should be eliminated. Galvanized by the arrival of Emicho and even more convinced that the Last Days had begun, the crusaders marched through the towns of the Rhineland attacking the enemies of Christ, the Last Emperor at their head.

Emicho, by all accounts, was a powerful Rhenish noble, and the call to crusade clearly affected him deeply. Little is directly known about him,[84] but he was, by Albert of Aachen's account, *potentissimus* and therefore likely well known in the region. He claimed a divine calling to this enterprise, and it was believed that he had been emblazoned with a celestial cross.[85] Ekkehard of Aura does not offer specifics as to the nature of this calling but clearly shows its influence on events when he writes, "There arose in those days a certain military man, a count of those lands around the Rhine named Emicho, formerly a very infamous tyrant, then however by divine revelations, it was said, called to this sort of religious profession [crusade (or conversion of the Jews?)] like another Saul, took control of 12,000 crusaders; who were led through the cities of the Rhine, Main, and Danube, and wherever they found the accursed Jews, because of Christian zeal they either killed them all or tried to force them into the bosom of the church."[86] The mention of Saul in this context has excited some scholarly comment. Riley-Smith and Stow take this reference to the leader of Israel to mean that Ekkehard possibly thought Emicho to have been unstable.[87] Ekkehard, however, was not referring to that Saul. He was referring to the man who changed his name from Saul after his conversion on the road to Damascus. Ekkehard was referring to Paul.[88]

This passage is solely laudatory in tone. The Jews are accursed (*execrabilem*), and the crusaders are fired by Christian zeal (*zelo christianitatis*). What is more, Emicho was formerly a tyrant but underwent a conversion with the call to crusade and became Paul — a champion of Christendom. Further, Ekkehard is likely paralleling Paul's prophecy on the pre-apocalyptic conversion of the Jews with Emicho's actual forcible conversions.[89]

Far from creating Emicho as an arch villain as Stow had earlier suggested, this more positive reading is consistent with the other Latin chronicles that discuss Emicho. The sexual sins of Emicho's army — not the army's actions toward the Jews — are almost universally blamed for the army's destruction before reaching Constantinople.[90] Frutolf of Michelsberg notes that Emicho was a *vir militarus* and that a spirit of fornication overcame his army in Hungary and led to its destruction.[91] Ekkehard and the anonymous Saxon Annalist do much the same: blaming the fornication of the army for destroying them in Hungary.[92] The *Annales sancti Disibodi* does not mention Emicho specifically but concurs in blaming the destruction of that army in Hungary on its illicit sexuality, not on its depredations of the Jewish communities.[93]

Even Albert of Aachen, whom Stow primarily uses to prove contemporary ecclesiastical displeasure with Emicho, was more ambiguous toward the Rhenish count than might first be thought. Before describing the massacres, Albert suggests that God may have been the one who inspired the crusaders to attack the Jews.[94] Moreover, when he arrives on the scene at Mainz, Emicho is described as *nobilis* and *potentissimus* in the region. He and the other leaders of the army are *viri militari actione illustres*.[95] When his army is finally destroyed, it is because of their fornication and because they attacked the Jews out of avarice for their money. That the crusaders forced the Jews to accept baptism is only added at the end, almost as an afterthought.[96] In this sense, the standard scholarly reading of Albert's critique of the forcible conversions is rather tautological. Emicho's army failed, so God, and Albert, must not have approved of the army's avarice in their forcible baptisms of the Jews. Perhaps if the army were not so plagued by avarice and fornication, Albert thought that Emicho and his army would have made it to the East. Consequently, it seems "far-fetched...to present Albert...as claiming that the defeat in Hungary was perceived by most good Christians as a divine punishment of the Jews' murderers."[97]

Unsurprisingly, the Jewish chronicles are much more critical of Emicho. This, of course, makes Solomon bar Simson's account of Emicho's vision problematic. Again, Simson said that Emicho embarked on the crusade because he had a vision of an apostle branding him and promising him a crown in "Italian Greece" and victory over his foes.[98] Unlike Ekkehard, Simson was quite specific in reporting the nature of Emicho's vision, which appears to have been drawn from Benzo of Alba's apocalyptic letter to Emperor Henry IV. Summoned and promised a crown directly by the divine, Emicho would journey to the East and defeat all his enemies and, by implication, all the enemies of Christ. This vision, in all of its promised glory, may be a mockery of the eventual failure of Emicho and his army in Hungary, since Simson well knew that Emicho was neither crowned nor victorious over all his enemies. More importantly though, Simson's account reveals that, as a Jew, he nonetheless understood something of Christian spiritual trends, specifically the Last Emperor legend — awareness of which was apparently present in the crusading army and undoubtedly current in papal and imperial circles for at least twenty years previously, since the reign of Pope Gregory VII. Simson understood that Emicho was a false messiah. There is scarcely a more damning charge in Jewish — or Christian — spiritual thought than that. Thus, the fact that Emicho and his army were annihilated by an army of fellow Christians in Hungary makes his mocking relation of Emicho's vision all the more ironic. Here was a man and an army who believed they were to defeat all the enemies of Christendom brought low by fellow Christians.

No period in history — least of all the modern world — has been a stranger to the sudden, cataclysmic breakdown in peaceful relations between social groups. In the early Middle Ages, though relations between Christians and Jews may have been theologically problematic even at the best of times, relations between the two groups were by and large at least superficially peaceful in practice. This all broke down in the Rhineland during spring and early summer 1096. Whatever Urban said at Clermont in November 1095 struck a chord with all segments of society. Though the call was not universally heeded, large numbers of the poor, the nobility, and all manner of churchmen decided to undertake this armed pilgrimage to Jerusalem. Each group that made, or attempted to make, this journey likely did so for a number of different reasons. The thing that united them all, however, was that they all sought to fight against the enemies of Christ and to reclaim the Holy City for Christendom.

To ascribe an apocalyptic motivation to Urban or the Rhenish crusaders is not intended to be reductionist. There was no one cause of the crusades.[99] Apocalypticism, however, is a thread woven through the very fabric of the Middle Ages. Apocalyptic prophecies "deeply affected political attitudes. For medieval people the stupendous drama of the Last Days was not a phantasy about some remote and indefinite future but a prophecy which is infallible and which at almost any given moment was felt to be on the point of fulfillment."[100] Apocalypticism, as Cohn suggests in this quotation, constantly touched all parts of life in the Middle Ages. Certainly, there were periods of both heightened tension and profound indifference, but the genie, as it were, could never be put back in the bottle.

The crusading army that formed throughout the Rhineland was, as is true of every other crusading army, undoubtedly composed of representatives of every social stratum, each with different reasons for journeying to the East. But as all the armies did, they generally began to coalesce around a particular interpretation of the call to crusade. And Brian Stock's idea of a textual community seems particularly relevant in understanding the impact of the specific ideas that shaped the army that attacked the Jewish communities along the Rhine.[101]

Stock argues that certain groups form around a particular text or set of texts and use these texts to justify their actions — making the hermeneutic leap from "what the text says" to "what they think it means." This common understanding "provides the foundation for changing thought and behaviour."[102] In this case, the text was a series of sermons.

In 1096, the itinerant preachers who traveled through the Rhine valley dreaming on the key words of Urban's call brought their distinctive reading of the crusade to those they found. The crusaders consequently coalesced around these preachers, Emicho, and a particular set of texts dealing with the Last Emperor — probably related to, as Riley-Smith and Möhring suggested, Benzo of Alba's letter to Henry IV. The prophecies contained therein guided their subsequent actions and the Rhenish crusaders subsequently behaved much as the heretical and reformist groups that Stock uses as his case studies. They actively recruited those they met, convinced — by these texts and those that carried them — that theirs was the correct interpretation of the contemporary situation.

The struggle was framed in the minds of the Rhenish crusaders as being of historic, even cosmic, importance.[103] Their particular interpretation led them to believe that they had been called to participate in the last, zero-sum battle between good and evil, where victory or defeat had to be absolute. These apocalyptic prophecies necessitated the final elimination of Christ's enemies, by conversion or the sword.[104] The violence against the Jews may have been generated at Speyer, inspired by the nexus of these apocalyptic sentiments, but it coalesced at Mainz, where this particular army found their leader in Emicho. But these crusaders were not so unique; such sentiments likely could be found in many of the other crusading armies, with Urban and other preachers conflating key words with definite apocalyptic connotations.[105] The Rhenish crusaders' attacks on the Jews cannot be considered an aberration but rather an integral part of this particular army's involvement in the First Crusade, in which their prophesied victory at Jerusalem was a critical stage in the final drama of the Last Days.

Notes

1. Earlier versions of this essay were presented in October 2002 at the Institute of Historical Research in London and in January 2003 at the Conference of the American Historical Association in Chicago. I wish to thank the participants at the seminar and session, respectively, and especially Theo Riches, Daniel F. Callahan, and Jay Rubenstein, for their thoughtful comments and suggestions.
2. Cologne may have been a preliminary or alternate assembly point for crusaders coming from northern Germany or France, from which they would travel upstream toward the Main, and Mainz. This would explain why Emicho's band was joined by more crusaders — who presumably had not left for Mainz yet — once they reached Cologne.

3. Solomon bar Simson, *Chronicle,* in *The Jews and the Crusaders: The Hebrew Chronicles of the First and Second Crusades,* trans. Shlomo Eidelberg (Madison: University of Wisconsin Press, 1977), 62–67.

4. The chronology presented previously is generally agreed on by all scholars of these events. The preceding paragraph specifically follows the chronology assembled in Jonathan Riley-Smith, "The First Crusade and the Persecution of the Jews," *Studies in Church History* 21 (1984): 51–52.

5. See the marvelous historiographical surveys by Benjamin Z. Kedar, "The Forcible Baptisms of 1096: History and Historiography," in *Forschungen zur Reichs-, Papst- und Landesgeschichte: Peter Herde zum 65. Geburstag von Freunden, Schülern und Kollegen dargebracht,* ed. Karl Borchardt und Enno Bünz, v. 1 (Stuttgart: Hieresmann, 1998), 187–200; Kedar, "Crusade Historians and the Massacres of 1096," *Jewish History* 12:2 (1998): 11–31.

6. Simson, *Chronicle,* 28. *Italian Greece* likely refers to Byzantium.

7. On the messianism of the Last Emperor legend more generally, see Paul J. Alexander, "The Medieval Legend of the Last Roman Emperor and its Messianic Origin," *Journal of Warburg and Courtald Institutes* 41 (1978): 1–15.

8. Hannes Möhring, *Der Weltkaiser der Endzeit: Entstehung, Wandel und Wirkung einer tausendjährigen Weissagung* (Stuttgart: Thorbecke, 2000), 165.

9. Kedar, "Forcible Baptisms," 195.

10. Ibid., 196.

11. Ibid., 199.

12. Kenneth Stow, "Conversion, Apostasy, and Apprehensiveness: Emicho of Flonheim and the Fear of the Jews in the Twelfth Century," *Speculum* 76 (2001): 911–33.

13. Ibid., 913.

14. Stow further downplays Emicho's role in the persecutions by arguing that the attacks on the Jews of Mainz were unplanned, spontaneous events. Ibid., 915–17. Friedrich Lotter agrees with Stow on Emicho only being at Mainz, whereas Hannes Möhring argues that Emicho was actually at Speyer but not at Mainz. Nonetheless, these four scholars all agree that the majority of the violence against the Jews was led by other notables in the Rhenish contingent. See Lotter, "'Tod oder Taufe': Das Problem der Zwangstaufen während des Ersten Kreuzzugs," in *Juden und Christen zur Zeit der Kreuzzüge,* ed. Alfred Haverkamp (Sigmaringen: Jan Thorbecke Verlag, 1999), 112–13; Möhring, "Graf Emicho und die Judenverfolgungen von 1096: Für Harald Zimmermann zum 65: Geburtstag," *Rheinische Vierjahrsblätter* 56 (1992): 105–8.

15. Stow, "Conversion," 912.

16. Ibid., 926, 931.

17. On Carolingian missionary practices, see Richard E. Sullivan, "Carolingian Missionary Theories," in Richard E. Sullivan, *Christian Missionary Activity in the Early Middle Ages,* I (Brookfield, VT: Variorum, 1994), 273–95.

18. Kedar, "Forcible Baptisms," 196–97; also the historiographical sketch in David Malkiel, "Jewish–Christian Relations in Europe, 840–1096," *Journal of Medieval History* 29 (2003): 64–82.

19. On the significance of the timing of the attacks, see Rudolf Hiestand, "Juden und Christen in der Kreuzzugspropaganda und bei den Kreuzzugspredigern," in *Juden und Christen zur Zeit der Kreuzzüge,* ed. Alfred Haverkamp (Sigmaringen: Jan Thorbecke Verlag, 1999), 207. On the significance of Pentecost to apocalyptic thinking in another context, see Matthew Gabriele, "Otto III, Charlemagne, and

Pentecost 1000 AD: A Reconsideration Using Diplomatic Evidence," in *The Year 1000: Religious and Social Response to the Turning of the First Millennium*, ed. Michael Frassetto (New York: Palgrave, 2002), 111–32.

20. Kedar, "Forcible Baptisms," 187–88.

21. Bernard McGinn, "The End of the World and the Beginning of Christendom," in *Apocalyptic Theory and the Ends of the World*, ed. Marcus Bull (Oxford: Blackwell, 1995), 58. *Imminent* should be understood as believing that the Last Days are at hand.

22. Romans 11:25–27.

23. "In the last days — the Lord declares — I shall pour out my Spirit on all humanity," and "This good news of the kingdom will be proclaimed to the whole world as evidence to the nations. And then the end will come," respectively. Mark 13:10 expresses similar sentiments. All quotations from the Bible are taken from *The New Jerusalem Bible* (London: Doubleday, 1985). On St. Patrick, see McGinn, "End of the World," 66.

24. Bede, *The Reckoning of Time*, trans. Faith Wallis (Liverpool: Liverpool University Press, 1999), 241–42.

25. On the persecutions of 1010, see Landes, "The Massacres of 1010: On the Origins of Anti-Jewish Violence in Western Europe," in *Witness to Witchcraft*, 79–112; Daniel F. Callahan, "Ademar of Chabannes, Millennial Fears and the Development of Western Anti-Judaism," *Journal of Ecclesiastical History* 46 (1995): 19–35. See also Malkiel, "Jewish–Christian," 55–83.

26. Both texts had been in circulation in the West since at least the early eighth century, although the Tiburtine Sibyl only gained widespread popularity in the eleventh century. See Paul J. Alexander, "Byzantium and the Migration of Literary Works and Motifs: The Legend of the Last Roman Emperor," in Paul Alexander, *Religious and Political History and Thought in the Byzantine Empire* XII (London: Variorum, 1978), 61; Anke Holdenried, "The *Sibylla Tiburtina* and Its Medieval Audience: Interpretation and Diffusion of the Latin Text" (Ph.D. diss., University College, London, 1998), 124. Translations of the relevant texts can be found in Bernard McGinn, *Visions of the End: Apocalyptic Traditions in the Middle Ages* (New York: Columbia University Press, 1979), 49–50, 75–76, respectively. The Latin can be found in Ernst Sackur, *Sibyllinische Texte und Forschungen* (Halle: M. Niemeyer, 1898), 177–87, 59–96, respectively.

27. This includes fifty-seven manuscripts of Adso's *De ortu et tempore Antichristi* (which is derived directly from the Pseudo-Methodius), forty-two of the Pseudo-Methodius, and forty-two of the Tiburtine Sibyl. See the manuscript summaries of the different versions of Adso's treatise in Verhelst, ed., *De ortu et tempore*; also Marc Laureys and Daniel Verhelst, "Pseudo-Methodius, *Revelationes*: Textgeschichte und kritische Edition: Ein Leuven-Groninger Forschungsprojekt," in *The Use and Abuse of Eschatology in the Middle Ages*, ed. Werner Verbeke, Daniel Verhelst, and Andries Welkenhuysen (Leuven: Leuven University Press, 1988), 112–36; Holdenried, "*Sibylla Tiburtina*," 120–24.

28. Alexander, "Medieval Legend," 2.

29. McGinn, *Visions*, 72.

30. "Omnes enim, qui exeunt de Ecclesia et ab unitate fidei praeciduntur, et ipsi Antichristi sunt." Isidore of Seville, *Etymologiae*, ed. José Oroz Reta and Manuel-A. Marcos Casquero (Madrid: Editorial Católica, 1982), 722.

31. "Quis enim est mendax, nisi is, qui negat quoniam Iesus non est Christus? Hic est Antichristus, qui negat Patrem et Filium. Omnis qui negat Filium, nec Patrem habet; qui confitetur Filium, et Patrem habet. [1 John 2:22–23] Ex quibus verbis evidentissime declaratur non solum mendaces, sed et Antichristos esse Iudeos, qui, eam negant Filium, frustra confitentur Patrem; non autem confitentes Filium, nec Patrem habere merentur." Agobard of Lyons, *De Iudaicis Superstitionibus et Erroribus (ad Ludovicum)*, in *Opera Omnia*, ed. L. van Acker, CCCM 52: 214.

32. Adso of Montier-en-Der, *De ortu et tempore Antichristo*, ed. D. Verhelst, in CCCM, 45:23, 27–28. "Sicut ergo auctores nostri dicunt, Antichristus ex populo Iudeorum nascetur, de tribu scilicet Dan, ...Nam, sicut supra diximus, in ciuitate Babilonie natus, Hierosolimam ueniens, circumcidet se, dicens Iudeis: Ego sum Christus uobis repromisus, qui ad salutem uestram ueni, ut uos, qui dispersi estis, congregem et defendam. Tunc confluent ad eum omnes Iudei, estimantes Deum suscipere, sed suscipient diabolum."

33. The Sibyl interestingly linked the conversion of the Jews with an oft-quoted (in early medieval pilgrim narratives) passage from Isaiah. "Iudei convertentur ad Dominum, et erit ab omnibus sepulchrum eius gloriosum." Sackur, *Sibyllinische Texte*, 185. Cf. Isaiah 11:10: "in die illa radix Iesse qui stat in sugnum populorum ipsum gentes deprecabuntur et erit sepulchrum eius gloriosum." Taken from *Biblia Sacra: Iuxta Vulgatum Versionem* (Stuttgart: Deutsche Bibelgesellschaft, 1994). On the phrase's use in pilgrim accounts, see, for example in reference to the large German pilgrimage of 1064–65, *Annales Altahenses Maiores*, MGH: SSrG, ed. Edmund LB ab Oefele, vol. 4 (Hannover: impensis bibliopolii Hahniani, 1891), 66. On the reworking of the Sibyl in the eleventh century, see McGinn, *Visions*, 43–44.

34. Pseudo-Alcuin, *Vita antichristi ad Carolum Magnum*, in *De ortu et tempore Antichristi*, ed. D Verhelst, CCCM, 45, 125. "Omnes ergo insulas et civitates paganorum devastabit et universa idolorum templa destruet et omnes paganos ad baptismum convocabit, et per omnia templa crux Christi dirigetur. Iudei quoque tunc convertentur ad Dominum."

35. Riley-Smith, "Persecution of the Jews," 67; Jean Flori, "Une ou plusieurs 'première croisade'? Le message d'Urbain II et les plus anciens pogroms d'Occident," *Revue Historique* 285 (1991): 17; Allan Harris Cutler and Helen Elmquist Cutler, *The Jew as Ally of the Muslim: Medieval Roots of Anti-Semitism* (Notre Dame, IN: University of Notre Dame Press, 1986).

36. Ademar of Chabannes, *Chronicon*, ed. R. Landes and P. Bourgain, CCCM 129: 10; Glaber, 133–35.

37. Robert of Reims, *Historia Iherosolimitana*, RHC: Occ., vol. 3, 727. "Gens regni Persarum, gens extranea, gens prorsus a Deo aliena,...terras illorum Christianorum invaserit, ferro, rapinis, incendio depopulaverit,...Altaria suis foeditatibus inquinata subvertunt, Christianos cicumcidunt, cruoremque circumcisionis aut super altaria fundunt aut in vasis baptisterii immergunt."

38. Paul Alphandéry, and Alphonse Dupront, *La Chrétienité et l'Idée de Croisade*, 2 vols. (Paris: A. Michel, 1954–59).

39. McGinn, "*Iter sancti Sepulchri*: The Piety of the First Crusaders," in *The Walter Prescott Webb Memorial Lectures: Essays on Medieval Civilization*, ed. Bede Karl Lackner and Kenneth Roy Philip (Austin: University of Texas Press, 1978), 47.

40. McGinn, *"Iter sancti Sepulchri,"* 47–48. This represents, to my mind, a far too literal reading of the Last Emperor legend: one that would have been rejected by the majority of medieval readers familiar, as they were, with numerous other hermeneutic techniques. On a more allegorical medieval interpretation of the legend, see Gabriele, "Asleep at the Wheel? Messianism and Charlemagne's Passivity in the Oxford *Chanson de Roland,"* *Nottingham Medieval Studies* 43 (2003): 46–72; Gabriele, "Otto III, Charlemagne," 118–22.

41. Carl Erdmann, *The Origin of the Idea of the Crusade,* trans. Marshall W. Baldwin and Walter Goffart (Princeton, NJ: Princeton University Press, 1977). Hans Eberhard Mayer generally concurs with Erdmann's conclusions but concedes that the crusade may have been later hijacked by the participants, and Jerusalem made the explicit goal during the march to the East. See Mayer, *The Crusades,* trans. John Gillingham (New York: Oxford University Press, 1972).

42. Riley-Smith, "Persecution of the Jews," 61; Riley-Smith, *The First Crusade and the Idea of Crusading* (Philadelphia: University of Pennsylvania Press, 1986), 35. More recently, however, he seems to have disavowed even this slightly millenarian leaning, especially as it relates to the attacks on the Jews. See Riley-Smith, "Christian Violence and the Crusades," in *Religious Violence between Christians and Jews: Medieval Roots, Modern Perspectives,* ed. Anna Sapir Abulafia (New York: Palgrave, 2002), 8–11.

43. Norman Cohn, *The Pursuit of the Millennium: Revolutionary Millenarians and Mystical Anarchists of the Middle Ages* (Oxford: Oxford University Press, 1970), 64–75. More recently, Sylvia Schein follows Cohn's conclusions very closely in Schein, "Die Kreuzzüge als volkstümlich-messianische Bewegungen," *Deutsches Archiv für Erforschung des Mittelalters* 47 (1991): 119–37.

44. André Vauchez, "Les Composantes Eschatologiques de l'Idée de Croisade," in *Le concile de Clermont de 1095 et l'appel à la Croisade: Actes du colloque universitaire international de Clermont-Ferrand (23–25 Juin 1995) organisé et publié avec le concours du conseil régional d'Auvergne* (Rome: Ecole française de Rome, Palais Farnèse, 1997), 233–43.

45. Flori, *Pierre l'Ermite et la Première Croisade* (Paris: Fayard, 1999), 276–77; Möhring, *Weltkaiser der Endzeit,* 166–67.

46. Robert Chazan suggests something similar in his term *ideational deviation.* Chazan believes that the message from Urban was distorted by popular preachers along the Rhine, which led directly to the assaults against the Jews. See Flori, "Une ou plusieurs," 26; Chazan, 61.

47. Flori, "Une ou plusieurs," 22.

48. For an argument against the pervasive power of Augustinian teaching on the Apocalypse, see Landes, "The Fear of an Apocalyptic Year 1000: Augustinian Historiography, Medieval and Modern," *Speculum* 75 (2000): 97–145.

49. The quotation is from Stow, "Conversion," 918. Stow, however, is not alone in this view. See, for example, Chazan, *European Jewry,* 113. See also McGinn, *"Iter Sancti Sepulchri,"* 48, which is highly influential.

50. Riley-Smith, "Persecution of the Jews," 56; Riley-Smith, *First Crusade,* 51; Flori, *Pierre l'Ermite,* 263.

51. Schein, "Die Kreuzzüge," 127.

52. See the modernist historiographic survey in Daniel Milo, "L'An Mil: Un problème d'historiographie moderne," *History and Theory* 27 (1988): 261–81; and more recently a reconceptualization in Edward Peters, "Mutations, Adjustments, Terrors, Historians, and the Year 1000," in Frassetto, *Year 1000*, 9–28.

53. A particularly egregious example is Sylvain Gouguenheim, *Les fausses terreurs de l'an mil* (Paris: Picard, 1999). Gouguenheim's conclusions, as far as I can tell, stem particularly from a desire to read his sources far too literally. See a response in Johannes Fried, "Die Endzeit Fest im Griff des Positivismus? Zur Auseinandersetzung mit Sylvain Gouguenheim," *Historische Zeitschrift*, 275 (2002): 281–321.

54. On Augustine, see the summary in Landes, "Lest the Millennium," 156–60. Landes notes that Augustine was not too successful even in his own time, as one of his own disciples, Quodvultdeus of Carthage, wrote that the time of the Antichrist was at hand. See Landes, "Fear of an Apocalyptic Year," 97–145.

55. Daniel Verhelst, "La Préhistoire des Conceptions d'Adson concernant l'Antichrist," *Recherches de Théologie Ancienne et Médiévale* 40 (1973): 52–103. Adso composed his tract in the mid-tenth century.

56. McGinn, "End of the World," 63 (see also 60–63).

57. Landes, "Fear of an Apocalyptic Year," 101–2; similarly expressed in McGinn, "End of the World," 58–89.

58. A particularly popular Web site that charts the nearness of the apocalypse in our own time is the "Rapture Index." Constantly updated, it can be found at http://www.raptureready.com/rap2.html. As a point of fact, the indicator was at "fasten your seat belt" from late September 2001 until late 2003.

59. Rachel Fulton, *From Judgment to Passion: Devotion to Christ and the Virgin Mary, 800–1200* (New York: Columbia University Press, 2002), 75.

60. This is more or less the weak thesis that began with Henri Focillon and Johannes Fried. See the summary in Peters, "Mutations, Adjustments," 18–21.

61. Keith Michael Baker, *Inventing the French Revolution: Essays on French Political Culture in the Eighteenth Century* (Cambridge: Cambridge University Press, 1990), 5.

62. H. E. J. Cowdrey, "Pope Gregory VII's 'Crusading' Plans of 1074," in *Outremer: Studies in the History of the Crusading Kingdom of Jerusalem*, ed. B. Z. Kedar, H. E. Mayer, and R. C. Smail (Jerusalem: Yad Izhak Ben-Zvi Institute, 1982), 38–40. On Gregory VII and the apocalypticism more generally, see Karl Josef Benz, "Eschatologie und Politik bei Gregor VII.," *Studi Gregoriani* 14 (1991): 1–20. Note that the future Urban II served under Gregory VII as cardinal bishop of Ostia.

63. The inclusion of Charlemagne in this list of apocalyptic signs may seem rather peculiar, but he was commonly associated with the Last Emperor legend by the late eleventh century. See, for example, Robert Folz, *Le Souvenir et la Légende de Charlemagne dans l'Empire germanique médiéval* (Paris: Les Belles Lettres, 1950), especially 71–74; Gabriele, "Asleep at the Wheel?," 46–72; Gabriele, "Imperator Christianorum: Charlemagne and the East, 814–1100" (Ph.D. diss., University of California, Berkeley, 2005).

64. See Guibert of Nogent, *Gesta Dei per Francos, in The Deeds of God through the Franks: A Translation of Guibert de Nogent's Gesta Dei per Francos*, ed. Robert Levine (Rochester, NY: Boydell Press, 1997), 42–45; and Penny J. Cole's comments on Guibert in Cole, *The Preaching of the Crusades to the Holy Land, 1095–1270* (Cambridge, MA: Harvard University Press, 1991), 19–27. In light of the previous

comments, Guibert's reconstruction of Urban's speech is not as grotesque as Norman Housley has suggested in Housley, "Jerusalem and the Development of the
Crusade Idea, 1099–1128," in *The Horns of Hattin*, Kedar (London: Variorum,
1992), 29.

65. Flori, *Pierre l'Ermite*, 280–81; Möhring, "Graf Emicho," 109–11.
66. Baker, *Inventing*, 6.
67. The phrase is in Chazan, 64; cf. Jeremy Cohen, "Christian Theology and Anti-
    Jewish Violence in the Middle Ages: Connections and Disjunctions," in *Religious
    Violence between Christians and Jews: Medieval Roots, Modern Perspectives*, ed.
    Anna Sapir Abulafia (New York: Palgrave, 2002): 46–47.
68. David Nirenberg, *Communities of Violence: Persecution of Minorities in the Mid-
    dle Ages* (Princeton: Princeton University Press, 1996), especially 200–30.
69. See n. 46.
70. Chazan, *First Crusade*, 62–63.
71. "Primi namque Petrum quendam monachum sequentes, ad XV estimati, per Ger-
    maniam indeque per Baioariam atque Pannoniam pacifice transiebant…; aliique ad
    XII per Saxoniam atque Boemiam a quodam presbitero Folcmaro, itemque nonnulli
    a Gotescalco presbitero per orientalem Franciam ducti sunt. Qui et ipsi nefandis-
    simas Iudeorum reliquias, ut vere intestinos hostes ecclesie, per civitates quas tran-
    sibant aut omnino delebant aut ad baptismatis refugium compellebant…." Ekkehard
    of Aura, *Chronica: Recensio I*, in *Frutolfs und Ekkehards Chroniken und die Ano-
    nyme Kaiserchronik*, ed. Franz-Josef Schmale and Irene Schmale-Ott (Darmstadt:
    Wissenschaftliche Buchgesellschaft, 1972), 124. Frutolf of Michelsberg, on whose
    chronicle Ekkehard's is based, also reports this event. Frutolf, however, is more
    critical of the whole endeavor, noting that many called Peter the Hermit a hypocrite
    later and equivocating about whether Folkmar and Gottschalk's attacks on the Jews
    were inspired by God or not. "Primi namque Petrum quendam monachum sequen-
    tes, quem tamen postea multi hypocritam fuisse dicebant,… [Then, after Folkmar
    and Gottschalk's actions are described,] Quod quo Dei iudicio actum sit aut qualiter
    ei placuerit, ipsi relinquendum erit." Frutolf of Michelsberg, *Chronica*, in *Frutolfs
    und Ekkehards Chroniken*, 106–8.
72. Albert of Aachen, *Historia Iherosolimitana*, in "The Historia Iherosolimitana of
    Albert of Aachen: A Critical Edition," ed. Susan Beatrice Edgington (Ph.D. dis-
    sertation, University of London, 1991), 121–25.
73. Chazan, *God, Humanity, and History: The Hebrew First Crusade Narratives*
    (Berkeley: University of California Press, 2000), 115. If Peter's army did in fact
    attack the Jewish communities they encountered, the lack of violence may testify to
    the fact that they confined themselves to the more traditional baptism-or-expulsion
    paradigm Kedar previously highlighted. See n. 17.
74. On Monieux, see Norman Golb, "New Light on the Persecution of French Jews at
    the Time of the First Crusade," *Proceedings of the American Academy for Jewish
    Research* 34 (1966): 1–63; and the criticism of Golb's conclusions in Chazan, *First
    Crusade*, 311, n. 24. Guibert's account concerning Rouen offers no specific dates
    but does allude to the time of the crusade, though it may be 1095 or 1101. Nar-
    ratively, the passage seems to function primarily to explain the presence of, and
    Guibert's connection with, a former Jew as a monk at the monastery of Fly. On

Rouen, see Guibert of Nogent, *De vita sua*, in *Self and Society in Medieval France: The Memoirs of Abbot Guibert of Nogent (1064?–c. 1125)*, trans. C. C. Swinton Bland, ed. John F. Benton (New York: Harper & Row, 1970), 134–35.

75. Cosmas of Prague, *Chronica Boemorum*, MGH: Scriptores, 6: 103; *Annalista Saxo*, MGH: Scriptores, 6: 729. Although he is unclear as to its exact participants, Chazan does say, "Rather clearly…the attack was carried out by a crusader contingent making its way eastward in organized fashion." Chazan, "Anti-Jewish Violence of 1096: Perpetrators and Dynamics," in Abulafia, *Religious Violence,* 30.

76. Chazan, *God, Humanity*, 134.

77. Simson, *Chronicle*, 28; Mainz Anonymous, *The Narrative of the Old Persecutions*, in *The Jews and the Crusaders: The Hebrew Chronicles of the First and Second Crusades*, trans. Shlomo Eidelberg (Madison: University of Wisconsin Press, 1977), 101, 107.

78. See n. 1.

79. See Chazan, *God, Humanity*, 32.

80. Chazan, "Anti-Jewish Violence of 1096," 27.

81. See Flori, *Pierre l'Ermite*, 271–75.

82. Did this have something to do with the arrival of Emicho?

83. Though he comes to different conclusions as to the causes of this anti-Jewish violence, Chazan also argues for the town-dwellers' support for and participation in the attacks on the Jews in all the cities involved. He even argues that the residents of Cologne initiated the violence there, perhaps in anticipation of Emicho's arriving army. See Chazan, "Anti-Jewish Violence of 1096," 25–26, 33. It should be noted here that Worms seems to be a slightly problematic case. Although the Mainz Anonymous suggests that the Jews of the town were rather gleefully betrayed by their Christian counterparts from the start, the fact that many of the Jews felt comfortable under the Christian residents' protection (rather than in the bishop's palace) suggests that they may have — at least initially — been more sympathetic toward the Jews than otherwise portrayed. Mainz Anonymous, *Narrative of the Old Persecutions*, 101–2; cf. Simson, *Chronicle*, 23.

84. The collection of charters for the city of Mainz, for instance, lists approximately twenty to twenty-five Count Emichos as witnesses in the time period that would roughly correspond to our Emicho's lifetime. Most, however, simply say "Emicho comes," or some variation thereof. See *Die Urkunden bis zum Tode Erzbischof Adalberts I (1137)*, ed. Manfred Stimming, vol. 1, *Mainzer Urkundenbuch* (Darmstadt: Verlag des Historischen Vereins für Hessen, 1932).

85. The import of these revelations, reported by both Christian and Jewish sources, should not be underestimated. Revelations, as any scholar of the First Crusade will attest, were relatively common and immensely important during the march. With reference to this fact and its relation to Emicho, see Riley-Smith, "Persecution of the Jews," 59–60.

86. "Surrexit etiam diebus ipsis quidam vir militaris, comes tamen partium illarum, que circa Renum sunt, Emicho nomine, dudum tyrannica conversatione nimis infamis, tunc vero velut alter Saulus revelationibus, ut fatebatur, divinis in huiusmodi religionem advocatus, fere XII signatorum sibimet usurpans ducatum; qui nimirum per civitates Reni, Moeni quoque Danubii deducti execrabilem Iudeorum quocumque repertam plebam zelo christianitatis etiam in hoc deservientes aut omnino delere

aut etiam intra ecclesie satagebant compellere sinum." Ekkehard, *Chronica: Recensio I*, 146. A similar passage, minus the reference to Saul, can also be found in *Annalista Saxo*, 729.

87. Riley-Smith, "Persecution of the Jews," 61; repeated in Riley-Smith, *First Crusade*, 34; Stow, "Conversion," 916–17, and esp. n. 19.

88. Noted by the editors without comment in Ekkehard, *Chronica: Recensio I*, 147, n. 66.

89. My thanks to Callahan for bringing this parallel to my attention.

90. This is, of course, a common trope in monastic writing about armies, especially about the crusade. See, for example, the summary in James A Brundage, "Prostitution, Miscegenation and Sexual Purity in the First Crusade," in *Crusade and Settlement*, ed. Peter W. Edbury (Cardiff, Wales: University College Cardiff Press, 1985), 58.

91. Frutolf, *Chronica*, 108.

92. Ekkehard, *Chronica: Recensio I*, 126, 146; *Annalista Saxo*, 730.

93. *Annales sancti Disibodi*, MGH: Scriptores, 17: 16.

94. Kedar, "Crusade Historians," 20.

95. Albert of Aachen, *Historia Iherosolimitana*, 126, 128, respectively.

96. "Hic mane Domini contra peregrinos esse creditur, qui nimis inmundiciis et fornicario concubitu in conspectu eius peccauerunt, et exules Iudeos licet Christo contrarios, pecunie auaricia magis quam pro iusticia Dei graui cede mactauerant, cum iustus iudex Deus sit, et neminem inuitum aut coactum ad iugum fidei Catholice iubeat uenire." Albert of Aachen, *Historia Iherosolimitana*, 132.

97. Kedar, "Crusade Historians," 20.

98. Simson, *Chronicle*, 28.

99. See Riley-Smith, *The First Crusaders, 1095–1131* (Cambridge: Cambridge University Press, 1997). Riley-Smith, in this work, does not consider apocalypticism to have been a significant motivating factor.

100. Cohn, *Pursuit*, 35.

101. On textual communities, see Brian Stock, *The Implications of Literacy: Written Language and Models of Interpretation in the Eleventh and Twelfth Centuries* (Princeton, NJ: Princeton University Press, 1983), especially 88–240.

102. Stock, *Implications of Literacy*, 522.

103. Chazan, "From the First Crusade to the Second: Evolving Perceptions of the Christian-Jewish Conflict," in Signer and Van Engen, 58.

104. Flori argues for the crusade itself as a war of conversion — their predicted victory at Jerusalem being a testament to the truth of Christianity. Flori, *Pierre l'Ermite*, 271.

105. On the apocalypticism in Godfrey of Bouillon's army, for example, see ibid., 278–79.

6

Abelard and Heloise on Jews and *Hebraica Veritas*

Constant J. Mews

In any account of relationships between Jews and Christians in twelfth-century Europe, Peter Abelard's description of the situation of a Jew in his *Collationes*, also known as the *Dialogue of a Philosopher with a Jew and a Christian,* is frequently quoted as unusually vivid in its insight:[1]

> Whoever thinks that we shall receive no reward for continuing to bear so much suffering through our loyalty to God must imagine that God is extremely cruel. Indeed, there is no people which has ever been known or even believed to have suffered so much for God — we have borne so much for him without cease, and it should be granted that there can be no rust of sin which is not burnt up in the furnace of this affliction. Dispersed among all the nations, without a king or earthy ruler, are we not alone encumbered with such taxes that almost every day we pay an intolerable ransom for our wretched lives? Indeed, we are thought by everyone to be worthy of such hatred and contempt, that whoever does us any injury believes it to be the height of justice and a supreme sacrifice offered to God. For they say that the disaster of our being made such captives would not have occurred unless God hated us enormously, and both pagans and Christians reckon whatever savagery they inflict on us as being done justly in revenge. The pagans, indeed, remembering the conquests by which we first took over their land and the long-lasting persecutions with which we then wore them down and wiped them out, count whatever they do to us as deserved revenge; whilst the Christians seem to have greater cause for persecuting us, since (as they say) we killed their God...Sleep itself, which more than anything cherishes and restores human nature in relaxation fills us with such disturbing anxiety, that even when we sleep we may think of nothing but the danger of being murdered. Nowhere but heaven may we enter safely, and even our own homes are places of danger for us. When we travel to anywhere in the neighborhood, we must pay a high price to a guide in whom we have little trust.[1]

This passage has traditionally been interpreted as evidence that Abelard represents a rare voice of tolerance in Latin Europe in the twelfth century. It also reinforces a very negative image of the situation of Jews in twelfth-century France. More recently, Anna Sapir Abulafia has argued that Abelard still sees Judaism as inferior to Christianity in a philosophical as well as a religious sense, as part of her broader argument that the twelfth century witnessed a broader "Christianization" of reason and thus an intellectual marginalization of Jews.[2] Does Abelard's apparently sympathetic presentation of the Jew conceal greater sympathy for the philosopher and the Christian? Just as we need to respect the rhetorically constructed character of the philosopher in the *Collationes*, so we need to exercise caution with his image of a learned Jew.[3] To do justice to the complexity of Abelard's attitudes, we need to consider the broader evolution of his thinking, both about Jews and the *Hebraica veritas* on which the Old Testament was based. We also need to explore Heloise's position on these same issues as well as the great variety of attitudes toward Jews held by Abelard's contemporaries in twelfth-century France.[4]

Christian–Jewish Relations in the Kingdom of France, 1100–1180

As Gérard Nahon observes, Abelard's negative account of the economic difficulties endured by Jews fits awkwardly with an image of relative prosperity enjoyed by French Jews in the twelfth century, at least immediately prior to their expulsion from the royal domain by the newly crowned Philip Augustus in 1182.[5] In Paris, Abelard could not have avoided coming into physical contact with the Jewish community living in the *vicus Iudaeorum*, centered around the *rue aux juifs,* connecting the Petit Pont on the left bank to the Grand Pont on the right. On its western side stood the area dominated by the royal palace, whereas on the other stood the Notre Dame Cathedral and the cathedral cloister. A synagogue stood almost at the center of the Ile de la Cité until 1182, when Philip Augustus (1180–1223) had the Jews evicted from the royal domain and it was given to the cathedral as a parish church.[6] References in charters to an important bakery (*furnus*) in the *vicus Iudaeorum* suggest the importance of these ovens to the life of the city, likely to have been an important focus of day-to-day life in the city.[7]

The notion that 1096 provided a radical turning point in Christian attitudes toward Jews throughout Latin Europe has come under criticism from a number of historians for not appreciating that the violence occurring in that year in Worms, Mainz, and Cologne was not representative of the broader experience of European Jewry, even though the attacks provided a fulcrum for subsequent Jewish historiography.[8] Though there had been an isolated outbreak of violence in 1096 against Jews at Rouen, in Normandy, the construction of a new synagogue in the twelfth century testifies to their prosperity.[9] The support that Count John of Soissons gave to its local Jewish community provoked Guibert of Nogent to create a wild fantasy about the count's supposed pro-Jewish sympathies and to compose a treatise in 1111, *De incarnatione contra Iudaeos*. This does not mean, however, that Guibert's treatise can be taken as representing dominant Christian attitudes.[10] For the most part, Jewish communities in the kingdom of France, as well as in the county of Champagne, were spared the unusual violence that occurred in the Rhineland in 1096 and recurred fifty years later at the time of the Second Crusade. There was certainly suspicion between two communities who tended to live apart from each other. There was also awareness of the benefits that interaction — both commercial and intellectual — could bring.

This sense of suspicion, combined with official toleration, is well illustrated by Suger's account of how a contingent of Jews dependent on the Abbey of Saint Denis (on whom Suger relied for financial support) solemnly presented Pope Innocent II with a scroll of the Law, when the pope came to celebrate the liturgy of Maundy Thursday in 1131. The pope replied with the prayer, "May almighty God take away the veil from your hearts." Even if Suger describes this deputation as "the blind synagogue," the pope was duty bound to accept their offering.[11] Fifty years later, Rigord, a monk of the same abbey, created a much greater caricature when he explained that by 1180 the Jews had become so rich that they owned almost half the city and often had Christian servants. Even if Rigord exaggerated their wealth, it is clear that the Parisian Jewish community, fined by Philip Augustus in 1180 and expelled from the royal domain in 1182 (to return again in 1198), had achieved a significant place within French society.[12]

Though hostile voices against Jews were certainly raised in France throughout the twelfth century, this did not prevent intellectual debate and interaction from taking place between some clerics and rabbis. Aryeh Graboïs and Beryl Smalley both point out a number of references to scholarly discussions between Christian intellectuals, interested in the *Hebraica veritas* of the Bible, and their Jewish counterparts.[13] In the eleventh century, Sigo (1055–1070), abbot of Saint Florent at Saumur (Anjou), used his knowledge of both Greek and Hebrew to correct the title of the Latin Bible.[14] In the same spirit, Stephen Harding, abbot of Cîteaux, 1109–1134, approached Jewish rabbis to help him correct the text of the Bible, in particular the books of Kings, by listening to them explain its Hebrew meaning in French. He was troubled by the fact that the Latin translation Christians used had passages not found in the Hebrew text.[15] The great fame of teachers like Rashi of Troyes (1040–1105) in commenting on the Bible and the Talmud undoubtedly prompted Christian exegetes to attempt to create their own gloss on the Bible and to find rationally persuasive arguments for Christian belief. St. Anselm reports the argument of Roscelin of Compiègne: "The pagans [i.e. Muslims] defend their Law, the Jews defend their Law, therefore we Christians must defend our faith."[16] Soon after his conversion to Christianity at Huesca in 1106 Petrus Alfonsi composed his *Dialogi contra Iudaeos*, in which he juxtaposed the figure of Moses, representing the old Law, with that of Petrus, voice of the new dispensation.[17] Gilbert Crispin similarly constructs a reasoned dialogue between a Jew and a Christian.[18] Both treatises clearly argue for the supremacy of Christian belief but do so by creating the image of rational dialogue between two figures who share a common heritage.

Such attitudes coexisted with a more suspicious and adversarial attitude toward Jews that became more pronounced at the time of the calling of a second crusade in 1145 by Pope Eugenius III. Targeting Jews provided an easy way of distracting attention from internal criticisms being directed against the church as an institution as well as of potentially raising funds for a military expedition. In his *Adversus Iudaeorum inveteratam duritiem*, perhaps planned shortly before the crusade, Peter the Venerable adopted a harsh line against what he called the obstinacy of the Jews. His treatise, originally structured as a traditional refutation of Jewish belief, developed into an aggressive assault on Jewish obstinacy.[19] He questioned whether the Jews are rational human beings, as they do not recognize the majesty of Christ. Though Alfonsi had ridiculed the rationality of many Jewish beliefs through a dialogue he invented between the figure of Moses and Petrus, Peter the Venerable went much further in abandoning the genre of dialogue and instead established a generalized image of Jews as uniformly obstinate.

The abbot of Cluny completed this diatribe at about the same time as he sent a letter to Louis VII of France, urging him to take over the financial assets of the Jews, which he considered to be gained by fraud, to help pay for the military expedition. The abbot of Cluny vilified Jews as "far worse than the Saracens, they blaspheme without impunity Christ and all Christian sacraments…God does not want them to be completely killed or completely extinguished, but to be kept in great torment and great shame, like the fratricide Cain, with a life worse than death."[20] They deserve the punishment they suffer because of their responsibility in killing Christ. Such invective could easily be taken to a more extreme direction. Bernard of Clairvaux, then in close contact with the abbot of Cluny about the need to promote the crusade, was obliged to warn against a certain monk by the name of Rudolf, who was promoting the killing of Jews.[21] Bernard's efforts in this respect earned the gratitude of Ephraim of Bonn, who commented that Bernard "spoke raucously, as is their manner" but proclaimed that anyone who kills a Jew "harms Jesus himself."[22] Bernard of Clairvaux and Suger of Saint Denis represented an older generation of Christian preachers for whom *Judaei* were spiritually blind but should be tolerated within society. Only with the III Lateran Council in 1179 did anti-Jewish legislation begin to get inscribed into the teaching of the church, with prohibitions against Jews employing Christian servants and the testimony of Jews against Christians being offered in a court of law — rulings extended far more widely at the IV Lateran Council in 1215.[23]

When Abelard wrote his *Collationes*, most likely in the period 1129–32, the ecclesiastical campaign against Jews, supported by Philip Augustus for his own reasons, was a long way in the future. Abelard voiced sympathy for the way Jews were harassed, perhaps out of a sense of self-identification with his suffering, but it should not be read as a literally accurate description of their situation. His comments about the fear under which they lived may have had more relevance in smaller communities than to the situation of Jews in big cities like Paris, Rheims, or Troyes. When Abelard wrote the *Historia calamitatum* in around 1132, he recalled that a few years earlier he had felt himself under such hostility from ecclesiastical authorities that he even contemplated going to live in Muslim territory, where he felt that he would be left in peace if he simply paid a financial tribute.[24] Abelard voiced sympathy for the Jew in the *Collationes* in part to rebuke Christians who refused to recognize the common ground shared by Jews, Christians, and philosophers by virtue of their common commitment to natural law. It was a perspective very different from that which Peter the Venerable would develop in the mid-1140s, when fear of attacks on Christendom had gained new urgency.

The Jews in Abelard's Early Theological Writing

When in 1119 to 1120 Abelard composed the first version of his treatise on the Trinity, the *Theologia Summi boni*, he developed the theme that the Supreme Good, known by Jews and Christians as God, had been glimpsed in its triune nature by philosophers and prophets alike. He opens his discussion of biblical testimony about the Trinity with a point that had never been made by any of the fathers of the church: The word *Deus* in the opening verse of Genesis was in fact a Latin translation of a Hebrew word, the plural *Heloym*, meaning gods.[25] Though Jerome had given much emphasis to *Hebraica veritas* — far more so than Augustine — he had never offered this linguistic detail.

This argument that the plural *Heloym* reveals God's trinitarian nature had been raised by Alfonsi in *Dialogi contra Iudaeos*, in which he had sought to affirm the truth of Christian belief through a reasoned critique of the arguments of Moses.[26] Rashi (1040–1105), the great rabbi of Troyes, had rejected this argument of the heretics in favor of the Trinity.[27] Whether Abelard absorbed this linguistic insight from Alfonsi or from some other source, his comment about *Heloym* — the only such reference in his treatise to the *Hebraica veritas* of scripture — indicates that his early attitude toward the Jews was shaped by conventional anti-Jewish apologetics.

After making these comments about the Hebrew truth of scripture, Abelard attacked the Jews for not appreciating references in scripture to the Word of God and the Holy Spirit. He added a section titled *Invectio in Iudaeos*, which leads into the major section of the first book, about the testimony of philosophers about God's nature.[28] Though he suggested that both prophets, by which he included Moses, and philosophers constitute two walls to the body of the church, he gave much greater attention to the latter. In the *Theologia Summi boni*, his sense of the superiority of philosophical testimony led him to make a remark unusually explicit in its declaration:

> Thus Christ the Lord, agreeing greatly with the words of philosophers, called himself God the Son more than the Word, when he said "Father, enlighten your Son," not only because the philosophers distinguished this mode of generation more clearly than prophets, but also because he knew that this faith would develop greatly among the gentiles, if it was commended by the authority of their own learned people, namely the philosophers. In times of a rough people, this faith had to be hidden by the prophets; in the time of the philosophers, however, with the increase of zeal for investigating truth, understanding of the Creator grew at the same time as teaching about created things.[29]

Abelard did not repeat this claim about the superior insight of the philosophers in later versions of the *Theologia*.

In the *Theologia Christiana*, written after his initial treatise had been burned at the Council of Soissons, in 1121, Abelard gave more attention to supplying testimonies based on scripture. Though he slightly extended his original *Invectio in Iudaeos*, the focus of his assault is not Jews, but Christians who refuse to recognize the validity of using dialectic and secular learning to deepen their understanding of the divine nature.[30] A small change he made to a brief comment in the *Theologia Summi boni* about King Nebuchadnezzar witnessing an image of the Trinity in the fiery furnace reflects his desire to give a more balanced presentation of scriptural and philosophical authority. Abelard at this point suggested that Nebuchadnezar and Dindimus, the mythical Indian king, together with Kings David and Solomon, constituted the four wheels of the chariot of the Most High God.[31] The image of a chariot, based on both biblical and nonbiblical figures, suggests an effort to emphasize parity between scriptural and philosophical testimony more than in the original version of his treatise.

The *Collationes*

Though scholars have often assigned the *Collationes* to Abelard's final years at Cluny, no strong arguments support such a claim, even more so if the Council of Sens, as I have argued, is dated to May 25, 1141, rather than to June 2, 1140.[32] Certainly, it must have been written after the *Theologia Christiana*, completed by 1123 to 1125, as it makes explicit reference to its second book.[33] Abelard seemed to use the original version of the *Theologia Christiana* as his source for quoting a combination of certain passages from Augustine, before he modified this passage in the recension of the *Theologia Christiana* that serves as a draft for the *Theologia Scholarium*, composed in the early 1130s.[34] Abelard also referred back to part of his discussion of the Supreme Good in the *Collationes* in his commentary on the *Hexaemeron*, which he composed perhaps in the mid-1130s at the request of

Heloise.[35] Although I once suggested that the *Collationes* might have been written around 1126 to 1127, I am now inclined to support the judgment of Marenbon that it was most likely produced between 1127 and 1132.[36] The parallels between its discussion of circumcision and sermons of Abelard, delivered to the Paraclete in its early years that dealt with circumcision, suggest that he may have been working on the *Collationes* at about the same time. In the *Collationes*, Abelard moved away from the trinitarian concerns of the *Theologia Christiana* to explore the common ground in the ethical teaching of the Jew, the philosopher, and the Christian. In the *Collationes* Abelard laid out ethical arguments that he developed more fully in both his commentary on Romans and in his *Scito teipsum*, probably before embarking on transforming the *Theologia Christiana* into the *Theologia Scholarium*. In the first of its two dialogues, Abelard demonstrated a new degree of sympathy with the arguments of the philosophically minded Jew, even though he did not feel that the observances of the Law are necessarily binding on all people.

What makes this dialogue so different from earlier Jewish–Christian dialogues is the privileged role given to the philosopher as the figure who articulates arguments critical of those who do not understand what they believe. Compared to the consciously polemical tone of the *Dialogi* of Alfonsi or of the *Disputatio* between a Jew and a Christian of Gilbert Crispin — also widely diffused in the twelfth century — Abelard's presentation is significantly different. By having both the Jew and the Christian dialogue with a philosopher, Abelard emphasized the importance of recognizing good points on both sides of a debate rather than on contrasting the weakness of the Jewish argument with the rightness of the Christian perspective. Abelard had the philosopher acknowledge that the biggest influence on people's faith is the way they are raised by their parents. He was appalled by the way that so many people "judge everyone who appears to be different from them in faith to be outside God's mercy and, condemning all others, claim that they alone are blessed."[37] Abelard was no longer interested in proving the triune nature of God against the Jews. Rather, his interest was in exploring the common ground shared by the Jew and the philosopher in their reflection on what constitutes an ethical life. When he first composed his treatise on the Trinity in 1120, he was idealistically focused on the ancient philosophers as superior to the Jewish prophets in the quality of their perception of the supreme good. In the *Collationes*, he still maintained his idealism about the importance of philosophical reason in defining the essence of Christian truth, but he had a more nuanced awareness of how the Jew, the philosopher, and the Christian all strive toward the same goal.

Abelard used the discussion between the Jew and the philosopher to reflect on the meaning and purpose of the Law, without engaging in any of the conventional polemic about the Jew's failure to acknowledge the Trinity or the divinity of Christ, which was standard in polemical Jewish–Christian dialogues. During the 1120s he was concerned with philosophical and theological questions, but not to any large extent with scripture or Jewish tradition. After his early attempt to comment on the prophet Ezekiel at Laon, he steered away from scriptural commentary. At his school at the Paraclete, he was able to take for granted that his students had a common formation in the liberal arts. Becoming an abbot at Saint Gildas in 1127, and even more through transferring possession of the oratory at the Paraclete to Heloise, Abelard was obliged to become more familiar with scripture. The *Collationes* represents a precious moment in his intellectual evolution as he came to terms, at a theoretical level at least, with the relationship among Jewish, Christian, and philosophical traditions.

Abelard depicted the Jew presenting what he sees as the intention behind the written Law, namely to restrain human wickedness.[38] The philosopher recognizes the legitimacy of this role but focuses on the authority of the natural law, "which consists in loving God and one's neighbor."[39] Picking up on a Pauline theme, but argued through the authority of reason rather than of scripture, the philosopher points out the example of patriarchs who were guided only by natural law. Abelard quoted scripture to resist a narrow-minded interpretation of Judaism, which implies that God only favors the Jews, as in 3 Kings [= 1 Kings] 8:41–43: "Since it is promised that the prayers of foreigners, whatever they concern, will be granted, and you hold that they even fear God as you do, who among them should despair of salvation when it has been written: 'Blessed is the man who fears the Lord,' and again 'Nothing is lacking for those who fear God?'"[40]

The defense that the Jew puts forward of the written Law recalls the explanation that Abelard provides for the practice of circumcision in his early sermons for the Paraclete. The observances of the Law are explained in sociological terms, as established to preserve the identity of the Jewish people, against being absorbed by others.[41] Circumcision thus has a moral function, particularly appropriate because the man now shares in the pain by which women are afflicted when they give birth. Because the woman sinned first, before the man, she precedes him in punishment.[42] The essence of the written Law is identical to that of the natural law: the injunction to love God and one's neighbor.[43] This simple claim, not present in the dialogues of Alfonsi or Crispin, effectively challenges traditional Christian antitheses (going back to St. Paul) between the letter of the Law and the spirit of the Gospel.

The philosopher, by contrast, makes the case that the works of faith do not matter as much as the intention behind them, the same position Heloise argued so strongly in her third letter about the relationship between outward observance and inner disposition. As Abelard maintained in his sermon on circumcision, many virtuous figures in the Old Testament did not carry out all the observances of the Law. Although he couched the argument in terms of observance of the Law, the issue under debate is not Judaism but the relationship between outer duty and inner intention. Written law may have its place, but, as the philosopher argues, natural law can suffice for salvation.[44] Circumcision becomes a metaphor for any form of outward religious observance. The philosopher emerges as an interpreter of Jewish law, who reminds the Jew of the example of both Abraham and Job, the virtuous pagan. Abelard already anticipated in *Theologia Christiana* these themes of how Jews and non-Jews can respect the Word of God, but without the detailed discussion of how the Jews live out their faith in practice. The philosopher repeats a comment of Ovid that Abelard reported in the *Theologia Christiana:* "We always desire what is forbidden and wish for what we are denied."[45] Ovid understood as much as St. Paul that creating a legal prohibition could easily encourage occasion for sin. Abelard did not dissect the character of sin in depth here; rather, his concern was with the character of religious observance, which might often — as in the case of circumcision — have a practical function, namely, to encourage friendship and fellowship among the Jews.[46] Again, Abelard develops these thoughts more concisely in his sermons. Here the strands of argument are separated out, some elements developed by the Jew and others by the philosopher. Rather than engage in a commentary on the books of the Old Testament, Abelard used this dialogue as a way of debating an ethical dilemma. The dialogue provides a way of finding a deeper reason behind the precepts found in scripture, but one compatible with philosophical enquiry.

The goal of the Law, as expounded by the Jew, is the perfect love of God and neighbor, the same goal as that of the natural philosopher. Abelard's dialogue is not so much a comparison of two religious traditions, as an interpretation of the true meaning of Jewish scripture, offered through the insights of both the Jew and the philosopher. Religious observance was enjoined on the Jews to help them not be corrupted by unbelievers, but its true goal is simply the development of the love of God and of one's neighbor, in which true virtue consists.[47] The philosopher's criticism of the Jewish claim that circumcision is enjoined on those excluded from the Law is a way for Abelard to highlight for a Christian audience his sense of the inherent limitations of any religious observance. The decisive argument in this first dialogue is given to the philosopher, who argues — by quoting scripture — that God longs more for the sacrifice of a contrite heart than for external religious observance. He explains that what the Law calls unclean, whether it be the nocturnal emission of seed by a man, or a woman's menstrual flow, has nothing to do with impurities of the soul, "which we properly call sins." This argument recalls Heloise's own critique of the relationship between religious observance and the ethics of the inner person. Abelard used the philosopher to develop the argument that guilt is brought about by true contrition of heart, so that "the guilt of a perverse will, through which someone sins," is remitted. Whether this is presented as a legitimate Christian position is left for the reader to consider.

The Commentary on Romans and the *Commentarius Cantabrigiensis*

In many ways, the arguments laid out in the first of the two dialogues in the *Collationes* lay the foundations for the more thorough exposition presented by Abelard in his commentary on St. Paul's Epistle to the Romans. Here, St. Paul provided a classic definition of the Christian perspective on the Jews through his arguments about why Christians did not need to follow all the observances of the Law. In conventional Christian rhetoric, particularly as shaped by Augustine, the epistle provided a *locus classicus* for arguing that the Jews had been blind not to recognize Christ and that they failed to respond to the grace God had offered them. This epistle also most neatly crystallized a Christian sense that humanity had been bound in sin: "Since sin entered the world through one man, and through sin death, thus death has spread through the whole human race because everyone had sinned" (Romans 5:12). It was easy to read St. Paul as implying that the Jews in particular were responsible for transmitting this sense of sin and that redemption came only in the person of Christ. If Abelard was to emerge as a credible Christian theologian, he needed to respond for himself to the message of St. Paul.

The crux of Abelard's message in his commentary is to argue that it was a misreading of St. Paul to claim that the devil exercised control over humanity by some legitimate right over humanity. Rejecting the notion that one simple act of Adam meant that all who succeeded Adam were equally sinful, he interprets St. Paul as saying that humanity inherited his punishment rather than his actual sinfulness. Humanity was thus not intrinsically culpable — as the case of so many good and upright people in scripture testified, whether or not they observed the written Law — although certain individuals certainly had followed a perverted will.[48] It was not the death of Jesus that brought forgiveness of sins, as manifest by what Jesus said to Mary Magdalene and the paralytic. Rather, it was the love manifested by God in taking human nature and binding humanity to himself more closely through Christ's life and his passion.[49] Abelard thus emphasized the intrinsic capacity of humanity to pursue good and the importance of responding to divine grace through an act of the will. Christ redeems humanity through the example of his redeeming love rather than simply by the sacrificial death of a perfect God-man standing in the place of corrupt humanity. Repeating the argument given by the Jew in the *Collationes*, circumcision is of value as an outward sign of commitment to God in the same way as baptism. With both Jewish ritual observances and Christian sacraments, Abelard reserved the right to insist that outward conformity is no guarantee of spiritual health. Abelard applied to the Pauline discussion an essentially very simple message that the essence of the Law lies in love of neighbor and love of God while distancing himself from an Augustinian sense of humanity as totally corrupted by original sin and thus totally dependent on grace. Abelard acknowledges that though we need divine grace, we must exercise our free will to choose it.[50]

Abelard took this argument even further in *Scito teipsum*, in which he argued that those who crucified Christ were not guilty of sin if they were not acting out of contempt for God and were acting out of a noble motive.[51] Though they rightly incurred temporal punishment, their ignorance excuses them from fault. Though Abelard does not explicitly say that he was talking about Jews, the implication of his argument is that they were not automatically guilty of killing Christ. He did not deny that they sinned but argued, "They would have sinned more gravely in fault if they had spared them against their own conscience."[52]

Much less well known as a record of Abelard's interpretation of St. Paul is the *Commentarius Cantabrigiensis*, preserved in a single manuscript (Cambridge, Trinity College B.I.39).[53] Not only does it repeat all his major arguments about the Epistle to the Romans, paraphrasing patristic and scriptural quotations rather than quoting them exactly, but it also provides his reading of all the Pauline epistles, including Hebrews. Landgraf argued that its author was reliant on the oral teaching or *lectura* of Abelard on all the letters of St. Paul.[54] It certainly does seem to be a verbatim record, perhaps written up from notes, of lectures he gave on the entire Pauline corpus. In the commentary on Romans, the teaching is presented in the first person, as if taken down firsthand. Thus the argument of *Commentarius Cantabrigiensis,* in which Abelard rejected the argument of that Christ came to free man from some legitimate yoke to the devil, is repeated in very similar words, although in a less elegant way: "But we say that these people said little, or rather completely nothing."[55] Abelard was referred to with great frequency as the *philosophus*, or simply by *inquit* in comments on all of the epistles.[56] Though it is impossible to be certain at what points a disciple may be developing his master's teaching, the *Commentarius Cantabrigiensis* provides no evident divergence from any of Abelard's distinctive teachings. The one major difference from his commentary on Romans is that it is frequently more forthright in its remarks about abuses in the contemporary church. Thus, in a remark on Hebrews 5:13 ("Anyone who is still living on milk cannot digest the doctrine of righteousness because he is still a baby"), the commentator added, "It is as if it clearly is about the abbot of Clairvaux, who pursued that wonderful grace of speaking and instructing others by the spirit of God rather than by subtlety of intellect."[57] There are frequent rebukes of the false religion of bishops and monks, as in comments on the letter to the Philippians, about people "who struggle to sit at the right hand of the Pope" and abbots being more concerned to be administered to, than to serve others.[58]

In its comment on Philippians 2:1 ("If our life in Christ means anything to you, if love can persuade us at all..."), there is an explicit allusion to Heloise. The passage is not easy to understand, as it is a report of a spoken conversation, told in a very informal way: "Thus, when the abbess of the Paraclete was persuading her virgins to fear for their sins, saying: 'Look, because I do not die only in myself if I sin, but my death threatens each of you, if you sin; for God's sake take care for yourselves and for myself that I do not die in you.' One of them, responding well, said: 'Lady, although it was not for God's sake, at least we shall stay in our commitment for your sake.' Thus the apostle asked that they persevere in what they were for love of himself."[59] To explain how Paul was so devoted to the Philippians that he urged them to stay loyal out of love for himself, the commentator offers a conversation from the Paraclete. Its meaning is not fully clear, but it seems to turn on Heloise implying that her presence in the community is necessary to avoid them falling into sin. To this, another nun quips that although their commitment was not for God's sake (*etiamsi propter Deum non esset*), they were there because of her. It is a remarkable declaration of honesty in the cloister, which parallels the comment of Heloise that she was in the religious life out of love of Abelard rather than out of love for God. This seems to be a report transmitted by Abelard, perhaps having heard it from Heloise or having himself been at the Paraclete.

A little further on in the same commentary on Philippians 2:14 ("Do everything without grumbling"), the speaker laments that many people cleave to God out of fear of punishment or hope of some benefit rather than for God's sake alone:

> Just as last year, when a very great famine threatened the poor throughout his land, count Theobald, who daily looked after more than ten thousand poor people, urged that they should be looked after and instructed his knights and penitents to each look after a number of the poor according to their means. For many people in that war developed against the hunger of poor people were duplicitous, since they did this more by fear of the prince, lest they lose their possessions than out of a pure intention towards God.[60]

The reference to Count Theobald of Blois and Champagne (1125–1152) potentially provides a means of dating the commentary, if this particular famine could be identified.[61] The point of the story, about doing good out of self-interest, is completely consistent with ideas of Abelard, who seems to be its source. Peter the Chanter reports a similar story about Count Theobald wishing the rich to have compassion for the poor in his *Summa de sacramentis et animae consiliis* and another story about how Theobald's compassion for the poor was so great because he demonstrated tears of compunction.[62] In *Carmen ad Astralabium* Abelard spoke briefly of the moral ambiguity of gifts that were the result of plunder, in relation to Count Theobald, also reported — although in a different way — by Peter the Chanter as told by Abelard.[63] Abelard waxed eloquent about the goodness of Theobald to rebuke the selfishness of his knights, a revealing indication of Abelard's political loyalties. When Louis VII came to the throne, Abelard may have left Paris to go to the Paraclete, in the territory of the Count of Champagne, who embarked on fresh hostilities against the king shortly after 1141.

This emphasis on purity of intention and caustic criticism of those who operate out of self-interest is also evident in what Abelard, as reported in the *Commentarius Cantabrigiensis*, has to say about Jews. As in his written commentary on Romans, Abelard took for granted the Pauline use of *Iudaei* to refer to those who follow the written Law. With less caution than in the written commentary, he argued that circumcision has the same efficacy as baptism, which he did not think automatically confers salvation.[64] Baptism is superior to circumcision because it applies to women as much as to men. Circumcision, however, is a response to lust. Abelard's theme here is the same as in the written commentary, but his imagery is more frank: "In a boy it happens that it is equally beautiful to see his genitals as his face; but after he gains in years and feels lust, shame starts to show itself and something else is seen, so that whatever is born from that limb, we remember is born in sin."[65] This comment about male development may relate to his wider argument that an infant is without sin or fault.[66] Circumcision was a response to a particularly male tendency to lust. The core commands of the Law, which made one righteous, did not relate to sexual behavior but to love of God and neighbor, applying to Jews and Gentiles alike. Expounding St. Paul, he repeats the trope that Jews were generally too concerned with outward rules.[67] Abelard's criticism, however, is not so much against Jews as against all those driven by a desire for correctness and personal reward than out of selflessness. This he saw as the true message of St. Paul, when he criticized St. Peter for wishing to retain circumcision as the first of the sacraments.[68] Abraham is a true model of righteousness for us all to follow.

A small comment made by the disciple indicates that Abelard was interested in obtaining the opinion of other Jews: "The Jews, often asked by the philosopher, say that this blessing (made to Abraham) cannot be assigned to carnal Isaac, through whom or through whose seed, the gentiles were uprooted rather than receive any blessing." He used their comment to justify the Christian claim that the promise refers to the coming of Christ.[69] That Abelard has some basic knowledge of Hebrew grammar is revealed in a comment, not found in his commentary, about the lack of a substantive verb in Hebrew grammar, which might explain certain phrases by St. Paul, like "through one man."[70] Abelard's argument is that Paul is not saying that sinfulness has been transmitted through Adam — only punishment for sin. Sometimes God uses something that might seem very bad, like the crime of Judas, for the good of all.[71]

Much more devastating than his critique of Jewish observance of the Law are the criticisms he directed against his fellow Christians: "We find that none of the apostles served him apart from the women who ministered to him, one of whom, namely Mary Magdalene, anointed his feet. But our abbots sit at table and do not serve in the example of Christ, rather he is served by them splendidly by those who eat all the good things of the earth and wish to have the daily food for charity."[72] Bishops similarly are criticized for being more concerned with money than care of souls.[73] Following St. Paul, he recognized that some individual Jews were quite wicked, like Annas and Caiphas, but he insisted that the Christian attitude to Jews is one of concord, unlike the Saracens, who nurture old hatreds against Jews.[74]

Though the commentary never identifies him by name, the voice of the philosopher whose teaching is recorded in the *Commentarius Cantabrigiensis* is distinctively that of Abelard, who was much more openly critical of ecclesiastical authority here than in his written commentary on Romans. In comments made on Ephesians 6:1–4 about relationships between parents and children, he contrasted Christian practice with that of Jewish families by going back to the example of the parents of Susannah, whom Jerome had reported as educating their daughter in the Law of Moses:

> On the contrary, *Bring them up in discipline*. Hence it is that the Jews can much reprove us, as blessed Jerome says on that place, where it is said about Susannah: And her parents, since they were just, educated their daughter according to the Law of Moses; because Christians, if they educate their sons, do not do this for God, but for money, so that a brother, if he is a cleric, will help his father, mother and other brothers. For they say that a cleric is without heir, and whatever he has will belong to us and the other brothers. It will be sufficient for him to have a black cloak in which he may go to church and a surplice. The Jews, however, by zeal for God and love of the Law, turn whatever sons they have to letters, so that each may understand the law of God. About whom, when the apostle says, "my request to God is for salvation for them, he adds: I will give them a testimony because they have great fervor for God, although not according to knowledge. For a Jew, however poor, although he may have ten sons, sends them all to be educated not because of money, like the Christians, but in order to understand the Law of God, and not only sons, but also daughters.[75]

Abelard draws on the same passage of Jerome's commentary on Daniel to make exactly the same point in a sermon on Susannah he gave at the Paraclete: "The Jewish people, still greatly fervent in zeal for sacred letters in the very shadows of blindness, show up not a little our (that is Christian) negligence. They embrace the Law with such enthusiasm that any of them, no matter how poor, however many sons he has, allows no one to be ignorant of divine letters."[76]

In the sermon, delivered perhaps no later than the mid-1130s, Abelard emphasized Jewish zeal for learning but did not pick up the point implicit in Jerome's commentary: Good Jewish parents educated daughters as much as sons. He also has stronger words about the blindness of Jews. In the *Commentarius Cantabrigiensis* his account is much fuller, emphasizing educating daughters as well as sons, and speaks only of Jewish incompleteness in knowledge rather than of "the shadows of blindness." There can be little doubt that the person praising Jewish love of education is Abelard.

Heloise and the *Hebraica Veritas*

Abelard was not alone in his enthusiasm for *Hebraica veritas*. In his Letter 9, addressed to the nuns of the Paraclete — and possibly a continuation of his Rule — Abelard quotes extensively from Jerome's letters to holy women to urge the nuns of the Paraclete to devote themselves to the study of scripture.[77] He considered that the saying of Jerome, "Love the knowledge of Scriptures and you will not love the sin of the flesh," has particular relevance given the weakness of their flesh.[78] Not only did Abelard single out Jerome's account of how Paula became fluent in Greek and Hebrew, but he also urged them to learn from Heloise's competence in these same languages so that they could settle debates about the meaning of scripture: "You have a mother skilled in these three languages, [so] you should go on to perfection in these studies, so that, whatever dispute arises about the different translations, you may bring the examination to a conclusion...Nor do you need a long journey or great expense to learn these languages as the blessed Jerome did, since in your abbess, as I have said, you have a mother equal to this study."[79] Further in the letter, he repeated this claim about Heloise: "You have authority [*magisterium*] in a mother which can suffice for all purposes; that is, as much as an example of the virtues as for instruction in letters, not only in Latin but even in Hebrew and Greek; she alone in this age seems to have achieved that skill in three languages, which is proclaimed by everyone as a grace uniquely in blessed Jerome, but is greatly commended by him in the venerable women mentioned above."[80]

Heloise's knowledge of Hebrew is also mentioned by the chronicler, William Godell, who provides an unusually detailed account of Abelard's career, including the information that he founded the Paraclete *ex epistolari auctoritate*. He reported that Heloise was learned in both Latin and Hebrew (*litteris tam hebraicis quam latinis adprime eruditam*).[81] This information about Heloise's competence in Latin and Hebrew was then repeated by subsequent chroniclers, although not with all the detail given by Godell.[82] Peter the Venerable alluded to Heloise's knowledge of Hebrew when he commented in his letter to her that "the name Deborah, as your learning knows, means bee in the Hebrew language."[83] Though Peter's knowledge of the Hebrew meaning of *Debborah*, derived most likely from Jerome's *Liber interpretationis hebraicum,* was not in itself particularly profound, he was aware that Heloise would understand the allusion.[84]

That Heloise was particularly interested in understanding the meaning of the Hebrew text of scripture is evident from the forty-two *Problemata* she sent Abelard, all of which concern the meaning of difficult passages in the Old and New Testaments. Abelard was not able to draw extensively on any knowledge of the original Hebrew or Greek text. His technique was nonetheless philological in that he sought to determine the meaning of the original words behind their apparent diversity.[85] Though some of Heloise's questions concern the nature of the Law established by Moses, and its deeper function, a number relate to passages in the first book of Kings about Anna and her son, Samuel. In particular, she asked about how we can reconcile God's promises to raise a faithful priest and a faithful household (I Kings [= I Samuel] 2:35–36) when it was common opinion that Samuel was a Levite rather than a priest — information she would have derived from Jerome. Also, why did God demand the offering of a silver coin and piece of bread when these were not offerings required in the Law?[86] In his reply to this question, Abelard reported that he had heard a certain *Hebraeus* explain that the silver coin was the means to obtain redemption from the priest and that the piece of bread was an offering of the poor.[87] Abelard's information is not detailed, but it shows that he was quite prepared to approach a rabbi to resolve an inconsistency in scripture not addressed by any of the church fathers. There is no knowledge that Abelard had any profound knowledge of Hebrew, apart from a remark in the *Commentarius Cantabrigiensis* about Hebrew lacking a substantive verb. Heloise may have gained what knowledge she had of Hebrew from a learned Jew, perhaps from some in the region of Troyes, where there were significant Jewish communities. Prominent teachers there included Rashi's son-in-law, Meïr ben Samuel, and his eldest children, Samuel (Rachbam), Isaac (Rivbam), and Jacob (Rabenou Tam, c. 1100–1171).[88]

The interest of both Abelard and Heloise in the *Hebraica veritas* is also evident in their decision to replace the term *quotidianum* in the Lord's Prayer (Luke 11:3) with *supersubstantialem*, the term used in the version offered by Matthew 6:11. Abelard wrote that Bernard of Clairvaux, on a long-awaited "holy visitation" to the Paraclete, had expressed surprise at the change. He justified the change on the grounds that as Matthew's Gospel was originally written in Hebrew — or so it was believed — the Matthaean version had greater authority than that given by Luke.[89] Abelard may not have had a clear idea of the meaning of *supersubstantialis* — which was a mistranslation of a rare Greek term, *epiousion*, probably used to translate an Aramaic idiom meaning *fresh* — but he defended the term on the grounds that it was more authentic.[90] Abelard repeated this justification in a small exposition of the Lord's Prayer and more briefly in a sermon to the Paraclete, in which he maintained that the Matthaean version was superior because it was delivered to the apostles, whereas according to Luke it was given to the crowds.[91] Whether the inspiration for this change came first from Abelard or Heloise, it was fully consistent with Heloise's desire for authenticity in the practice of religious life, articulated so forcefully in her third letter to Abelard, as well as with the general principles Abelard laid down in the prologue to *Sic et Non*.

Unlike Abelard, Bernard of Clairvaux never used the phrase *Hebraica veritas* in his writings. He preferred the mystical and allegorical interpretation of scripture to the concern with its literal meaning. Heloise's interest in the *Hebraica veritas* is also evident in her comments about liturgy as reported in the prefaces to the hymnal that Abelard composed for the benefit of her nuns, not all of which were actually implemented at the Paraclete. With a great show of erudition, drawn from Jerome's preface to his translation of the book of Psalms, Abelard explained that he composed what are called hymns in Greek but *tillim* in Hebrew.[92] Abelard emphasized that this zeal for returning to the *Hebraica veritas* was a particular interest of Heloise, who objected to the singing of hymns that had words frequently inappropriate for the time at which they were conventionally sung. Though the early Cistercians, under Stephen Harding, sought to preserve authenticity in the liturgy by only singing hymns thought to have been composed by St. Ambrose, Heloise wanted Abelard to compose hymns that were faithful to the authentic spirit of the Psalter. She had no qualms about asking Abelard for new hymns, many — though not all — of which she subsequently included in the liturgy of the Paraclete.

Conclusion

Evidence for the contact of both Abelard and Heloise with actual Jews is frustratingly slender. In the earliest version of his treatise on the Trinity, Abelard was more interested in showing how Jews have not understood the doctrine of the Trinity than in exploring the ground they share with philosophers. By between 1129 and 1132, when he wrote *Collationes* or dialogues of a philosopher with a Jew and a Christian, and perhaps those early sermons about circumcision, namely, Abelard started to explore in depth the significance of the Jewish law and its relationship to natural law as investigated by a philosopher. The first of its two dialogues provides him with an opportunity to reflect on the best sides of Jewish tradition as well as on its limitations — from the perspective of philosophy. Abelard developed these insights much more fully in his commentary on St. Paul's Epistle to the Romans, written during the 1130s, while he had resumed teaching in Paris. His emphasis on the essential rationality of human nature led him to consider that all humanity, whether Jewish or non-Jewish, has the capacity to devote itself to natural law as well as to the supreme good. Abelard distanced himself from those who condemned the Jews as Christ killers. Those who were unaware that they were killing the Son of God were not culpable of this deed. Whereas so many of his contemporaries engaged in Christian apologetic against Jews, Abelard wished to explore the common ground shared by Jews, philosophers, and Christians, namely the reflection on the supreme good and how it could be sought.

Abelard's growing interest in Hebrew tradition may have been deepened by Heloise, whom he claimed was unusually learned in Hebrew letters. *Problemata* shows that Heloise had a close interest in the Hebrew Bible, in particular in those passages that talked about women or questions of sin. A small hint that even as a young woman she may have already been steeped in knowledge of the Bible may be gleaned from the *Epistolae duorum amantium*, which, as I have argued elsewhere, is a record of their early correspondence, letter 27. The young woman in this exchange is not only well versed in the study of philosophy and the ideals of Cicero in particular, but she also makes far more regular allusion to images drawn from the Bible.[93] After a particularly sensuous letter from her lover, in which he asks her "to reveal what is hidden," she sends a cryptic message, offering him "the spirit of Bezalel, the strength of the three locks of hair, the beauty of the father of peace, the depth of Ididia." She expected Abelard to understand her wonderfully concise allusions to the range of Biblical virtues which she wanted him to emulate: the skill of Bezalel, a great craftsman inspired by God, the strength of Samson, the beauty of Absolom, and the wisdom of Solomon. This young woman is clearly fascinated by images in the Hebrew Bible.

As so often with Heloise, we have to be content with only the slightest of allusions about her interest in the Hebrew scriptures. She certainly was not interested in the rigors of a strictly literal interpretation of the Jewish law. The figure of the enlightened Jew that Abelard presents in the *Collationes* may be a fictional creation, but he echoes concerns raised by Heloise in her own insistence on the priority of ethical authenticity over against the hypocrisy of simply earning the epithet of being virtuous through carrying out formal precepts. She was more interested in the ideal of returning to the religious authenticity communicated by the *Hebraica veritas* than by specific precepts of the Law.

By the early 1140s, the tide was turning against the kind of tolerant philosophical discussion projected in the *Collationes*. The polemical treatise of Peter the Venerable, *Adversus Iudaeorum inveteratam duritiem*, was composed either immediately before or in the wake of the calling of the Second Crusade. The very title of that treatise conveys a different tone from that of a *Dialogus* or even a *Disputatio*, in which both parties were allowed to present their side of the story. During the 1130s, there was still no clearly established consensus about Christian attitudes toward Jews. Rebecca Moore puts forward strong arguments that Hugh of St. Victor, who often refers back to the *Hebraica veritas* of scripture, was familiar with Jewish midrash in his own notes on the Pentateuch.[94] Perhaps even more important is her observation that the authentic scriptural writings of Hugh of St. Victor share none of the hostile polemic about the Jews to be found in other commentaries from St. Victor, not in fact authored by Hugh. Her research establishes that within the school of St. Victor there was no consistent set of attitudes toward Jews, thus rendering more complex the picture of tolerant cooperation drawn by Smalley in work that focused on the contribution of Andrew of St. Victor.[95]

The *Ysagoge in theologiam*, authored by an Englishman called Odo, and dedicated to Gilbert Foliot, perhaps before he became abbot of Gloucester (1139–48), is remarkable for the extent of its quotation of key biblical passages in Hebrew but is quoted for polemical rather than irenic purposes: "Who does not see a Hebrew person being moved more by exhortation or discussion in Hebrew than by any other authority that is proclaimed?…Greatly therefore because this [Hebrew language] is the mother of all languages, so also the same Law and the prophets, namely the first foundations of theology were handed on, and translated by the Greeks and the Latins."[96] Although Landgraf edited the *Ysagoge* as part of the "School of Peter Abelard," this is a very different text from the *Sententie Parisienses*, a rough and apparently verbatim record of Abelard's theological sentences, or the *Commentarius Cantabrigiensis*, written up from Abelard's spoken lectures on the Pauline epistles. Even though the *Ysagoge* author does echo Abelard in declaring that both the Gentile philosophers and Catholic authors proclaimed a faith in God as a trinity, namely in the power, wisdom, and goodness of God, and does draw on Cicero and Macrobius for basic definitions of virtue, he gives little attention to philosophical authority.[97] On many issues, such as his definition of faith or on Christology, Odo steers firmly away from the ideas of Abelard. He is interested in quoting the Hebrew version of the prophets to persuade Jews of the truth of Christian revelation — a rather different goal from that of Abelard in the *Collationes*.

To engage in debate about whether or not Abelard is sympathetic or unsympathetic to Jews runs the risk of distorting the evident complexity of his attitudes. They cannot be reduced to a simple formula. Over the course of his later career, Abelard's ideas evolved. The comments he made in *Collationes* reflect his interest in exploring the common ground shared by the Jew, the philosopher, and the Christian. There was no single Christian attitude toward Jews in twelfth-century France. Though Abelard never doubted the superior truth of Christian revelation, the comments he made about Jews — both in the Bible and very occasionally in the present day — reveal that he was genuinely interested in what they had to say. He thought that many Jews outshone Christians in their zeal and love of education for its own sake rather than out of self-interest. His attitudes were unusual, however, within a clerical milieu, in which it was much more common to speak of the spiritual blindness of the Jews. They would not become as influential as those supported by Peter the Venerable in shaping Christian perception of Jews in the Latin West.

Endnotes

1. Peter Abelard, *Collationes* 15, ed. and trans. John Marenbon and Giovanni Orlandi (Oxford: Clarendon Press, 2001), 19–21.
2. Anna Sapir Abulafia, *Christians and Jews in the Twelfth-Century Renaissance* (London–New York: Routledge, 1995).
3. Peter von Moos, "Les *Collationes* d'Abélard et la 'question juive' au XIIe siècle," *Journal des savants* 2 (1999): 449–89.
4. The need to respect the complexity of these relationships is nicely underlined by John Van Engen in Signer and Van Engen, Introduction, 1–8.
5. Gérard Nahon, "From the *Rue aux Juifs* to the *Chemin du Roy*: The Classical Age of French Jewry, 1108–1223," in Signer and Van Engen, 311–39, esp. 314–15.

6. On the *vicus Iudaeorum* see Robert Bautier, "Paris au temps d'Abélard," in *Abelard en son temps*, ed. Jean Jolivet (Paris: Belles Lettres, 1981), 35. On the expulsion, see Robert Chazan, *Medieval Jewry in Northern France. A Political and Social History* (Baltimore–London: Johns Hopkins University Press, 1973), 64–76. See J. Monicat and J. Boussard, eds., *Recueil des actes de Philippe Auguste, roi de France*, 3 vols. (Paris: Imprimerie Nationale, 1966) I, no. 9, 115–16.

7. The *furnus* may have been under Christian control, however; according to Robert de Lasteyrie, ed., *Cartulaire générale de Paris* (Paris: Imprimerie nationale, 1887), no. 419, 365, from around 1160, Robert, son of Matthew of St. Merri was disputing control of the bakery. The prior of Notre Dame des Champs said that it had been given to his abbey by a woman named Teelina, her husband, Bartholomew, and her son, Henry. According to no. 184 (1119), confirmed in no. 258, 257 (1135) it belonged to St. Martin des Champs, but in 1140 Louis VII confirmed that it had been given by a certain Bartholomew to Notre Dame des Champs (no. 281, 272). In 1167 (no. 464, 393), William of Garland gave rent from a bakery in the *vicus Iudaeorum* to the Church of Saint Lazaire.

8. See Chazan, 63, and Jeremy Cohen, "A 1096 Complex? Constructing the First Crusade in Jewish Historical Memory, Medieval and Modern," in Signer and Van Engen, 9–26, as well as Chazan's contribution in this volume.

9. On the 1096 massacre at Rouen, see Guibert de Nogent, *Autobiographie* II, 5, ed. Edmond-Réné Labande (Paris: Belles Lettres, 1981), 246–48. Chazan emphasizes the relative stability of the Jewish communities in France during the twelfth century, unlike those in Germany, in Chazan, *Medieval Jewry*, 25–62. On the Jewish community at Rouen, including the discovery of its twelfth-century synagogue, restored after the massacre, see Norman Golb, *Les Juifs de Rouen au Moyen Age: portrait d'une culture oubliée* (Mont-Saint-Aignan: Publications de l'Université de Rouen, 1985).

10. See Jan M. Ziolkowski, "Put in a No-Man's-Land: Guibert of Nogent's Accusations against a Judaizing and Jew-Supporting Christian," in Signer and Van Engen, 110–22.

11. Suger, *Vie de Louis VI le Gros* 32, ed. Henri Waquet (Paris: Belles Lettres, 1964), 264. In their notes to the translation, Richard C. Cusimano and John Moorhead, *The Deeds of Louis the Fat* (Washington DC: Catholic University of America, 1984), 148–49, observe that there was a similar ceremony to welcome a newly elected pope in the City of Rome. On Suger's economic dependence on the Jews, see Aryeh Graboïs, "L'abbaye de Saint-Denis et les juifs sous l'abbatiat de Suger," *Annales* 24 (1969): 1187–95.

12. Chazan, *Medieval Jewry*, 43; Rigord's account is translated in Jacob Marcus, *The Jew in the Medieval World: A Source Book: 315–1791* (Cincinnati: Union of American Hebrew Congregations, 1938), 25–26; see H. François Delaborde, ed., *Gesta Philippi Augusti*, parts 6, 12–13, 15–16 Œuvres de Rigord et de Guillaume le Breton, historiens de Philippe-Auguste, Société de l'histoire de France 210 (Paris: Librairie Renouard, H. Loones, successeur, 1882), 1:15–29. See also William Chester Jordan, *The French Monarchy and the Jews: from Philip Augustus to the Last Capetians* (Philadelphia: University of Pennsylvania Press, 1989), 26–32.

13. Beryl Smalley, *The Study of the Bible in the Middle Ages* (Notre Dame, IN: University of Notre Dame Press, 1964), 77–80, 103–105; Aryeh Graboïs, "The *Hebraica Veritas* and Jewish-Christian Relations in the Twelfth Century," *Speculum* 50 (1975): 613–34.

14. Graboïs, "*Hebraica Veritas*," 617.

15. Stephen Harding, *Censura de aliquot locis bibliorum*, PL 166:1373–76.

16. St. Anselm, *Epistola de incarnatione Verbi*, in *Sancti Anselmi Opera*, 6 vols., ed. F. S. Schmitt (Edinburgh: Thomas Nelson, 1946–61), 1, 285; 2, 10; St. Anselm seems to be referring back to this comment of Roscelin when he refers to Jews and *pagani* in the *Cur Deus homo* 2, 22, ed. Schmitt, 2, 133; see Sapir Abulafia, *Christians and Jews*, 44–45.

17. *Dialogi contra Iudaeos*, PL 157, 527–672. For a full study of the work and a list of surviving manuscripts, see John Tolan, *Petrus Alfonsi and His Medieval Readers* (Gainesville: University Press of Florida, 1993), 12–41, 182–98.

18. *Disputatio cum Judaeo*, in *The Works of Gilbert Crispin, Abbot of Westminster*, ed. A. Sapir Abulafia and G. R. Evans, Auctores Britannici Medii Aevi 8 (London: Oxford University Press, 1986), 1–87; see Richard W. Southern, "St. Anselm and Gilbert Crispin, Abbot of Westminster," *Mediaeval and Renaissance Studies* 3 (1954): 78–115; Sapir Abulafia, *Christians and Jews*, 77–81.

19. Peter the Venerable, *Adversus Iudaeorum inveteratam duritiem*, ed. Y. Friedman, CCCM 58 (Turnhout: Brepols, 1985); Dominique Iogna-Prat, *Ordonner et exclure. Cluny et la société chrétienne face à l'hérésie, au judaïsme et à l'islam* (Paris: Aubier, 1998), 272–323, esp. 281–83.

20. Letter 130, Giles Constable, ed., *The Letters of Peter the Venerable*, 2 vols. (Cambridge, MA: Harvard University Press, 1967), vol. 1, 328.

21. Bernard, Letter 353 and 355, Jean Leclercq, ed., *Sancti Bernardi Opera*, 8 vols. (Rome: Editiones Cistercienses, 1955–77), vol. 8, 311–17, 320–22.

22. Ephraim of Bonn, *Sefer Zekhira*, in *The Jews and the Crusaders: the Hebrew Chronicles of the First and Ssecond Crusades*, ed. and trans. Shlomo Edelberg (Madison: University of Wisconsin Press, 1977), p. 122 ; see also Chazan, *Medieval Jewry*, 42.

23. *Concilium Lateranense III*, in *Conciliorum Oecumenicorum Decreta*, ed. Guiseppe Alberigo and others (Bologna: Istituto per le scienze religiose, 1973), 223–24.

24. Hicks, *Historia calamitatum*, 34.

25. *Theologia Summi boni* (hereafter *TSum*), I, 6–7, ed. E.-M. Buytaert and C. J. Mews, CCCM 13 (Turnhout: Brepols, 1987), 88–89.

26. *Dialogi contra Iudaeos*, PL 157, 608–12; Tolan, *Petrus Alfonsi*, 14; on Rashi's response to Christians, see also Michael Signer, "God's Love for Israel: Apologetic and Hermeneutical Strategies in Twelfth-Century Biblical Exegesis," in Signer and Van Engen, 123–49, esp. 129–30.

27. Rebecca Moore, *Jews and Christians in the Life and Thought of Hugh of St. Victor* (Atlanta, GA: Scholars Press, 1998), 82.

28. *TSum,* I, 63, 110.

29. Ibid., III, 67, 185–86.

30. *Theologia Christiana* (hereafter *TChr*), I, 46–53, ed. Buytaert, CCCM 12 (Turnhout: Brepols, 1969), 90–94.

31. *TChr,* I, 131–132, 128; cf. *TSum,* I, 62, 110.

32. I argue that the council took place in 1141 in Mews, "The Council of Sens (1141): Bernard, Abelard and the Fear of Social Upheaval," *Speculum* 77 (2002): 342–82. I first discussed the date of the *Collationes* in "On Dating the Works of Peter Abelard," *Archives d'histoire doctrinale et littéraire du moyen âge* 52 (1985): 73–134.

33. Marenbon-Orlandi, *Collationes* 78, 98.

34. Ibid., 76, 96, quoting the same texts of Augustine as in *TChr,* II, 117, without the additional material added in *TChr CT,* II, 117-a, 185, carried over into *Theologia Scholarium* (hereafter *TSch*), II, 19, ed. Buytaer and Mews, CCCM 13, 415.

35. *Expositio in Hexaemeron*, PL 178, 768B.

36. Marenbon, *Collationes*, Introduction, xxxvii. Thematic parallels between the *Collationes* and the *Historia calamitatum*, as well with early sermons for the Paraclete, make it perhaps more likely that the *Collationes* was written during these early years of the refoundation of the Paraclete, between 1129 and 1132, rather than the earlier date of around 1125 to 1126 suggested in Mews, "On Dating," 125. I am now more inclined to think that Abelard might have been able to use the situation of not teaching in the schools to compose a treatise more philosophical than scholastic in the manner of *TSch*.

37. Marenbon-Orlandi, *Collationes* 8, 12.

38. Ibid., 14, 16.

39. Ibid., 20, p. 24.

40. Ibid., 25, p. 34.

41. Ibid., 29–30, 38–40.

42. Ibid., 36, 44.

43. Ibid., 43, 52.

44. Ibid., 25, 32.

45. *TChr,* II, 21, 141, quoting Ovid, *Amores* 3.4.7.

46. Marenbon-Orlandi, *Collationes* 29, 40.

47. Ibid., 45, 54–56.

48. *Commentarius in Epistolam ad Romanos*, ed. Buytaert, CCCM 11 (Turnhout: Brepols, 1969), pp. 114–17.

49. Ibid., 118.

50. Ibid., 240–42.

51. *Scito teipsum*, ed. Rainer Ilgner, CCCM 190 (Turnhout: Brepols, 2001), 41: "Quid itaque mirum, si crucifigentes dominum ex illa iniusta actione, quamuis eos ignorancia excuset a culpa, penam, ut diximus, temporalem non irracionabiliter incurrere possent?" This is passage is also edited by David Luscombe, *Peter Abelard's Ethics* (Oxford: Clarendon Press, 1971), 62.

52. Ilgner, *Scito teipsum*, 44; Luscombe, *Peter Abelard's Ethics,* 66.

53. Artur Landgraf, ed., *Commentarius Cantabrigiensis in Epistolas Pauli e Schola Petri Abaelardi*, 4 vols. (Notre Dame, IN: University of Notre Dame Press, 1937–45). As the pages are numbered continuously, reference will only be to the page number.

54. Ibid., xi–xxxiii; Luscombe comments on this text, concluding that this author "allows us to approach very near to the actually spoken teaching of Abelard"; Luscombe, *The School of Peter Abelard* (Cambridge: Cambridge University Press, 1969), 145–53.

55. Landgraf, *Commentarius Cantabrigiensis*, 47: "Sed hos parum, immo nichil penitus dixisse dicimus."

56. *Philosophus* or *inquit* occurs in Landgraf, *Commentarius Cantabrigiensis,* I, [Romans] 65, 72, 74, 77, 81, 93, 94, 95, 97, 112, 122, 132, 144, 144, 163, 169, 175, 179–841, 190, 203, 21; [I Corinthians] 242, 244, 247; [II Corinthians] 287, 325, 328; [Galatians] 359, 366, 370; [Ephesians] 395, 396, 417, 430, 432, 244; [Philippians] 449; [Colossians] 483; [I Timothy] p. 561, 586; [II Timothy] p. 601; [Hebrews] 660, 662, 663, 682, 683, 692, 711, 721, 723, 724, 733, 734, 738, 746, 750, 756, 774, 781, 785, 787, 794, 802, 811, 816, 817, 825, 835, 846.

57. Landgraf, *Commentarius Cantabrigiensis,* 729.

58. Ibid., 455: "Quod parum attendunt illi, ut supra meminimus, qui de dextra domini pape contendunt, quis eorum dexter sedeat, nolentes reminisci honore invicem prevenientes." Ibid., p. 456: "Quod abbates non multum attendunt, qui potius amministrari quam amministrare veniunt ni monibus Christo contrarii."

59. Ibid., 454: "Unde, cum abatissa Pacliti persuaderet suis virginibus, ut sibi di culpis precaverent, dicens: Ecce, quia ego non solum morior in me ipso, si peccavero, sed et in singulis vestris mors mea imminet, si peccaveritis, pro Deo providete vobis et michi, ne in vobis moriar, bene una illarum respondens ait: Domina, etiamsi propter Deum non esset, saltem propter te in proposito nostro permaneremus. Ita et apostolus, ut etiam propter amorem suum perseverent in eo, quod erant, rogat." To make sense of Heloise's phrase, I propose reading a semi-colon after *si peccaveritis.*

60. Ibid., 460–61: "Veluti in preterito anno, cum maxima imminente fame pauperes per terram suam consul Theobaldus, qui et ipse plus quam decem milia pauperum procurabat cotidio, procurari preciperet et militibus suis et purgensibus numerum pauperum unicuique secundum suam facultatem assignaret. Multi in werra illa pauperum manutenenda contra famem dupplices erat, qui videlicet potius timore principis, ne sua amitterent, id faciebant, quam pura intentione propter Deum."

61. Ibid., xvi, reports that there was a severe famine in Eastern France from around 1139 to 1146, according to F. Curschmann, *Hungersnote im Mittelalter. Ein Beitrag zur deutschen Wirtschaftsgeschichte des 8–13 Jahrhunderts,* Leipziger Studien aus dem Gebiet der Geschichte VI.1 (Leipzig: B. G. Teubner, 1900), 138–43.

62. Suger emphasizes Theobald's selfishness and alliance to Stephen of Garlande, in Suger, *Vie* 31, 254. Landgraf, *Commentarius Cantabrigiensis,* xvi, observes that Peter the Chanter tells a story about Theobald's compassion in *Summa de sacramentis et animae consiliis* in Paris, BnF lat. 9593, f. 111v; see also Peter the Chanter, *Verbum abbreviatum* 107, PL 205, 290B.

63. Abelard speaks about Theobald's generosity to religious but notes that his gifts could be plundered from others, in Abelard, *Carmen ad Astralabium,* ed. Josepha Maria Anaïs Rubingh-Bosch (Groningen: J.M.A. Rubingh-Bosscher, 1987), l. 921–922: "Multa Theobaldus largitur religiosis / sed, si plura rapit, sunt data rapta minus." A much fuller version of the same exemplum about Count Theobald is attributed to Peter Abelard by Peter the Chanter, *Verbum abbreviatum* 46, PL 205, 146BC.

64. Landgraf, *Commentarius Cantabrigiensis,* 33.

65. Ibid., 35: "Quippe in puero idem contingit, cuius genitalia eque pulcrum est videre sicuti faciem illius; sed postquam ad annos venit et concupiscentiam sentit, et ipsum monstrare pudor detinet et alterum speculari, eo quod, quicquid ex illo membro nascitur, in peccato nasci recordamur."

66. Ibid., 76: "Est enim, ut beatus Jeronimus dicit, anima, quamdiu in infantili etate est, sine peccato, id est sine culpa." The reference is to Jerome, *Super Ezechielem*, quoted by Abelard in *Sic et Non* 108, 1; Landgraf, *Commentarius Cantabrigiensis*, 166.

67. Ibid., 36.

68. Ibid., 53–54.

69. Ibid., 65: "Judei vero a philosopho sepe requisiti nullatenus dicunt se istam bene-dictionem posse assignare in carnali Ysaac, per quem vel cuius semen gentes potius extirpate sunt quam benedictionem susceperint."

70. Ibid., 71: "Nec mireris, cum ebraice constructiones nimis sint distorte et defective, que omnino substantivo verbo carent."

71. Ibid., 93.

72. Ibid., 141–42: "Neminem autem apostolorum invenimus ministrasse illi preter mulieres, que ei ministrabant, quarum una, id est Maria Magdalena, unxit ei pedes. Sed modo abbates etiam nostri in mensa sedent nec exemplo Christi ministrant, imo eis splendide ministratur, qui omnia bonia terre comedunt et cotidie cibum mistera-tionis habere volunt."

73. Ibid., 182.

74. Ibid., 154: "Sed tamen Sarazeni vehementius illos odio habent et magnas violentias eis inferunt propter ilas videlicet veteres inimicitias, que inter illos orte fuerunt, quia gentes per istum populum exhereditate sunt. Christiani vero cum illis concordiam habent dispessante ecclesia, que neminem cogere vult, sed cum omnibus pacem habere."

75. Ibid., 434: "Imo 'educate in disciplina' etc. Hinc est, quod iudei nos multum possunt arguere, sicut beatus Jeronimus dicit super illum locum, ubi de Susanna dicitur: *Et parentes eius, cum essent iusti,. Erudierunt filiam suam secundum legem Moysi* [cf. Jerome, *In Danielem* [13, 3] 4, 13 line 702, CCSL 75A] quia christiani, si filios suos erudiunt, non faciunt propter Deum, sed propter lucrum, ut videlicet frater, si cleri-cus fuerit, iuvet patrem et matrem et alios fratres. Dicunt enim, quia clericus sine herede erit, et, quicquid habebit, nostrum erit et aliorum fratrum. Ei autem satis erit et nigra capa, in qua eat ad ecclesiam et suum superpellicium. Judei vero selo Dei et amore legis, quotquod habent filios, ad litteras ponunt, ut legem Dei unusquisque intelligat. De quibus, cum dicat apostolus: obsecratio mea pro illis ad Deum in salutem, supponit: perhibeo enim illis testimonium, quia magnum fervorem habent ni Deum, etsi non secundum scientiam. Judaeus enim, quantumcumque pauper, etiamsi decem haberet filios, omnes ad litteras mitteret non propter lucrum, sicut christiani, sed propter legem Dei intelligendam, et non solum filios, sed et filias." This passage is translated in part by Smalley, *Study of the Bible*, 78.

76. Abelard, Sermon 29, PL 178, 557A: "Hoc adhuc sacrarum litterarum zelo judaicus populus in ipsis etiam tenebris caecitatis suae plurimum fervens, non mediocriter nostram, id est Christianorum negligentiam accusat. Tanto quippe ardore legem amplectuntur, ut quislibet eorum quantumcumque pauperl quotquot habeat filios, neminem divinas litteras ignorare permittat."

77. Smits, Letter 9, 219–36; trans. Vera Morton with Jocelyn Wogan-Browne, *Guid-ance for Women in Twelfth-Century Convents* (Woodbridge, Suffolk: Boydell and Brewer, 2003), 121–38.

78. Abelard, Letter IX, p. 219, quoting Jerome, Letter 125, 11 (CSEL 56, 130): "Ama scienciam scripturarum et carnis uicia non amabis." In the Rule, Letter 8, ed. T. P. McLaughlin, "Abelard's Rule for Religious Women," *Mediaeval Studies* 18 (1956): 289 Abelard misquotes this as "Ama scientiam litterarum...". Heloise cites it correctly in her introductory letter to Abelard, a response to Letter 9, *Problemata*, PL 178, 678B.
79. Morton, Letter 9, 231, 133.
80. Letter 9, 135; my translation differs here from that of Morton, 135.
81. William Godell, *Chronicon*, cited from Paris, BNF lat. 4893, f. 56v), in Mews, CCCM 13, 291.
82. See the Chronicle of Tours, edited as an appendix by Peter Abelard, *Abelard and Heloise in Medieval Testimonies* (Glasgow: University of Glasgow Press, 1976), 51, reprinted in Dronke, *Intellectuals and Poets*; and Robert of Auxerre, *Chronicon* (ca. 1203), ed. Oswald Holder-Egger MGH SS 26 (1882), 235.
83. Peter the Venerable, Letter 115, 305: "Et quia hoc nomen Debora, ut tua nouit eruditio, lingua Hebraica apem designat, eris etiam in hoc et tu Debora, id est apis."
84. Jerome, *Liber interpretationis hebraicarum nominum*, ed. Paul de Lagarde, CCSL 72 (Turnhout: Brepols, 1959), 5: debbora apis siue eloquentia, or 32: debbora apis uel loquax; see also Jerome, *Commentarii in Ezechielem*, ed. F. Glorie, CCSL 75 (Turnhout: Brepols, 1965) l. 1356; Jerome receives the information from Origen.
85. *Problemata* 14, PL 178, 702C.
86. Heloise, *Problema* 35, PL 178, 717C.
87. PL 178, 718A.
88. On the disciples of Rashi, see Simon Schwarzfuchs, *Rachi de Troyes* (Paris: Albin Michel, 1991), 32–36; Schwarzfuchs, "La communauté juive de Troyes au XIe siècle," in *Rashi 1040–1990: Hommage à Ephraïm E. Urbach*, ed. Gabrielle Sed-Rajna (Paris: Cerf, 1993), 525–34.
89. Abelard, Letter 10, in *Peter Abelard: Letters IX–XIV*, ed. Edmé Smits (Groningen: Bouma's Boekhuis, 1983), 239–43.
90. David Wulstan explains the Semitic etymology of the term in a learned note, appended to Mews, "Liturgy and Identity at the Paraclete: Heloise, Abelard and the Evolution of Cistercian Reform," in *The Poetic and Musical Legacy of Heloise and Abelard*, ed. Marc Stewart and David Wulstan (Toronto–Westhumble, Surrey: The Institute of Mediaeval Music and The Plainsong and Mediaeval Music Society, 2003), 26 n. 46.
91. The commentary attributed to Abelard in PL 178, 611–18 is inauthentic. There is no reason to doubt Abelard's authorship of another *Expositio*, however, ed. Charles S. F. Burnett, "The 'Expositio orationis dominicae' Multorum legimus orationes," *Revue bénédictine* 95 (1985): 60–72; Sermon 14, PL 178, 490D; ed. Paola De Santis, *I Sermoni di Abelardo per le monache del Paracleto* (Leuven: Leuven University Press, 2002), 210.
92. *Hymnarius Paraclitensis*, Pref. Ed. Joseph Szovérffy, *Peter Abelard's Hymnarius Paraclitensis* (Albany, NY–Brookline, MA: Classical Folia Editions, 1975), 9. I translated the three prefaces to the Hymnal in Mews, "Liturgy and Identity at the Paraclete," 30–33. On 30, n. 69, Wulstan appends a note about the contraction *tillîm* of *tehillîm* as given by Jerome, *Praefatio in libro Psalmorum iuxta Hebraeos* in *Biblia sacra iuxta Vulgatam versionem*, ed. Bonifatius Fischer et al. (Stuttgart: Württembergische Bibelanstalt, 1975), 768.

93. Mews, *The Lost Love Letters of Heloise and Abelard. Perceptions of Dialogue in Twelfth-Century France* (New York: Palgrave, 1999), esp. 18, 138, with text and translation of the letter on pp. 212–13.

94. Moore, *Jews and Christians*, 77–93. These were first identified by Herman Hailperin, *Rashi and the Christian Scholars* (Pittsburgh, PA: University of Pittsburgh Press, 1963), 109.

95. Moore, *Jews and Christians*, 138.

96. *Ysagoge in theologiam*, ed. Landgraf, *Ecrits théologiques de l'école d'Abélard*, 127.

97. *Ysagoge* 3 and 1, ed. Landgraf, 56–57, 74. Its discussion of different virtues seems likely to be drawn from the *Moralium dogma philosophicorum*, PL 171, 1021B-1024B; this text was attributed to William of Conches by I. Holmberg, *Das Moralium dogma philosophorum des Guillaume de Conches* (Uppsala: Almqvist & Wiksells boktryckeri-a.-b., 1929). A marginal note in the manuscript of the *Ysagoge*, 65–66, was identified as coming from the *Moralium* by R.-A. Gauthier, *Les deux recensions du "Moralium dogma philosophorum,"* in *Revue du Moyen Âge latin* 9 (1953): 171–260, esp. 238–241. Though Gauthier questioned the attribution of the *Moralium* to William of Conches, it still seems likely to be a source for the *Ysagoge* rather than the other way around. On the debate about its authorship, see J. R. Williams, "The Quest for the Author of the *Moralium dogma philosophorum* (1931–1956)," in *Speculum* 32 (1957): 736–47. I am grateful to Riccardo Quinto for pointing out these issues to me.

7

Reason and Natural Law in the Disputational Writings of Peter Alfonsi, Peter Abelard, and Yehuda Halevi

Alex Novikoff

The early twelfth century was a period of great development in the genre of Christian–Jewish polemical writings partly as a result of a new direction in early twelfth-century thought.[2] The growth of cathedral schools, the use of private masters, the rise of the early universities, the translation of many Greek and Arabic texts into Latin (often by Jewish scholars in Spain and southern France), and the increased communication among intellectual communities across western Europe all contributed to the making of what is called the *twelfth-century renaissance*. Within this emerging renaissance, an increasing number of authors — mainly Christian — turned their attention to the differences between Christians and Jews seeking to provide convincing argumentation for the superiority of their own world view.

Some of the results of these convergences can be seen in the roles of reason and natural law in the *Dialogi* of Peter Alfonsi (c. 1110), the *Collationes* of Peter Abelard (c. 1127–1132), and the *Kuzari* of Yehuda Halevi (c. 1140). Although each of the three authors belonged to very different social and intellectual environments, their participation in the rapidly growing confrontation between Jews and Christians and between reason and revelation offers valuable glimpses into the argumentation of early twelfth-century Jewish–Christian disputation.

Alfonsi was born a Jew in Spain, possibly in the Aragonese region of Huesca, and was initially educated within a world of Judaeo-Arabic influence.[3] He converted to Christianity around 1106, following the Christian reconquest of Aragon, and eventually moved to England, where some believe he may have served at the court of Henry I. He is perhaps best known for his *Disciplina clericalis (Scholar's Guide)*, a collection of moral tales from Jewish and Muslim traditions that influenced such later poets as Geoffrey Chaucer and Giovanni Boccaccio. His

Dialogi is a disputation — literally a series of dialogues — staged between his former self, Moses, and his new identity, Peter, and serves, among other things, as an *apologia* for his conversion to Christianity. In this work Alfonsi is the first Latin Christian writer of the Middle Ages to make extensive and effective use of Hebrew and rabbinic sources in refuting Judaism. His direct influence in this arena of writing extends to Peter the Venerable and Joachim of Fiore, as well as many others, and his art of persuasion based on science and knowledge of Jewish and Muslim theology — and language — predates the attempts of a more famous thirteenth-century Spanish missionary: Raymond Llull.[4]

Abelard, the most celebrated of twelfth-century authors — and lovers — spent his lifetime teaching at various schools in and around Paris.[5] He produced many works, of which the *Collationes*, a series of two dialogues, the first between a philosopher and a Jew and the second between the same philosopher and a Christian, remains among the most enigmatic and perhaps the least understood.[6] Significantly, Abelard's composition is the first to introduce the character of a philosopher as the main interlocutor in two dialogues where the Jew and the Christian do not speak to each other directly. His distinction between positive justice and natural justice represents an important step in his evolving philosophy concerning natural law, and the *Collationes* seems to be the first instance in medieval political theory where positive justice is used as a term for human laws that are neither natural nor universal.[7]

Like Alfonsi, Halevi was born into and was educated within a Jewish community in Spain.[8] The political circumstances of twelfth-century Spain, coupled with a profound love of his religion and what he saw as his manifest destiny, caused Halevi to leave Spain for the Holy Land and to devote some twenty years of his life to composing his masterpiece, the *Kuzari*, which uses the true story of the Khazar kingdom's conversion to Judaism in the eighth century as the staging ground for his own dialogical defense of Judaism against representatives of Christianity, Islam, and philosophy.[9]

In each of these works, reason serves as a fundamentally important instrument for intellectual dispute. But this instrument proves to be a dangerous challenge to orthodox belief. Harmonizing the role of reason, natural law, and the authority of revelation is thus a challenge that confronts Alfonsi, a Jewish convert to Christianity; Abelard, a Christian; and Halevi, a Jew, and significantly shapes the intellectual content of their polemical works, each of which, importantly, takes the form of a dialogue or series of dialogues between characters.[10]

Reason

Alfonsi's *Dialogi* opens in a touching manner. In the prelude to the first chapter, Peter says that since tender childhood he has been friends with a certain Moses who has, over the years, been to him both a companion and a fellow student (*meus consocius fuerat et condiscipulus).*[11] Shocked and upset by the news that Peter has abandoned the old faith, Moses entreats Peter to explain to him his intention (*intentio*) and reason (*ratio*) behind this decision.[12] But Moses does not simply ask Peter to explain himself. He sets the objective of their investigation, saying,

> I both consider what you have done to be an error and I also cannot decide which [of two possible explanations for your leaving the faith] is the better. For this reason I ask you to drive away this stumbling block from my mind so that both of us may wander on the plane of alternate reason (*in alterne rationis campo discurramus*) until I arrive at finding out for sure whether your deed is just or unjust.[13]

Alfonsi chooses carefully the language with which Moses makes his pronouncement. The stumbling block preventing Moses from understanding Peter's choice to convert is an eloquent expression of the widely held belief that Jews are unable to see beyond a literal interpretation of their Law and the emphasis on reason as a criterion for arriving at the truth (i.e., a just deed or not) is well in line with Anselmian principles of investigation.[14] Moses follows by asking whether Peter does in fact accept the biblical Moses as a prophet of the Jewish people and whether he accepts the books of Moses as the Law of God, both of which Peter does. The scene is now set for the two characters to debate openly their ideas and their understandings of Judaism and Christianity, all on the plane of reason.

Alfonsi is similar to Anselm of Canterbury (1033–1109) in that he wishes to prove his arguments *sola ratione*.[15] However, the emphasis Alfonsi accords reason is slightly different from that of his predecessor. For Alfonsi there are two kinds of Christian truths: those that reason shows to be necessarily true, what many scholastics called *ratio necessaria*, and those that reason shows to be possible (*ratio conveniens*), the truth to which scriptural authority testifies.[16] Alfonsi's twofold understanding of Christian truth leads him to reject some of Anselm's arguments. He rejects, for example, the logical necessity of the Incarnation and presents a completely different argument to prove the existence of God. According to Alfonsi, there are three ways of knowing something: "to perceive by some corporeal sense, to recognize by necessary reason, or to discover through similitude with other things."[17] This last method serves to prove the existence of God, for just as one can deduce the existence of fire when one perceives smoke, Peter says, so can one deduce the existence of the Creator by perceiving the created. It should be noted that this argument has little to do with *sola ratione*; rather, it is based on what might offhandedly be labeled common sense, or at least what is deemed to be common sense by Alfonsi. Independent confirmation of Alfonsi's hypothesis is not needed because of the implied validity of the perceivable information. Concerning the existence of God, Peter and Moses are not in dispute. So it hardly matters how Peter demonstrates his argument, since he will not encounter any objection from the Jew.

The issue of reason takes on two principle guises in Alfonsi's *Dialogi*. In the first four chapters of the disputation Peter sets out to discredit the validity of Judaism, arguing that the Old Law has been supplanted by the New Law. A strong emphasis is placed on Jewish postbiblical literature, and especially the Talmudic homilies (*aggadot*). In the first chapter, Peter shows how Talmudic literature violates both reason and any defensible interpretation of the Old Testament. In doing this, Alfonsi calls in his scientific knowledge, disputing, for example, how rabbinic dicta can claim that God resides in the West if "the West" does not have an absolute, independent existence but varies according to an individual's frame of reference. Numerous *aggadot* are cited, which, as Alfonsi explains time and again, are absurd and therefore run contrary to reason. In chapter 2, however, Alfonsi changes somewhat his line of argument, citing Talmudic passages in support of his contention that Jews have, since the killing of Christ, ceased to be the pious people they once were. Moses apparently does not notice Peter's wavering treatment of the Talmud. On the contrary, by the end of the fourth dialogue, he is thoroughly convinced by Peter's use of reason: "Thus far you have explained most clearly — and demonstrated with rational arguments — how inane and defective is the faith of the Jews in every respect, how illogical and displeasing to God is their prayer, and why you withdrew from their faith; and you have shown me in what grievous error I still remain."[18]

The fifth chapter of the *Dialogi* contains the attack on Islam. Alfonsi, who was raised and educated in a society governed by Muslims, was certainly familiar with the Arabic language and customs, as well as the Islamic religion. Why did he not convert to Islam, Moses asks?[19] Peter's reply consists more of a defamation of the Muslim religion than an offering of the rational explanations of the shortcomings of Islam. Among the reasons for his rejection of Islam, Peter says, are the continual presence of pagan idolatry, the focus on the carnal in matters of doctrine and praxis, and because Muhammad was not a true prophet.

This brings us to Alfonsi's second use of reason, his defense of Christianity, which occupies the remainder of the work. In discussion of the Jewish tradition, both biblical interpretation and the *aggadot*, Alfonsi generally uses philosophy and science to discredit their teachings, indicating his belief that religious doctrine must be in accord with reason and the natural world. When Alfonsi turns to his defense of Christian doctrine, however, he does not state that the truth of Christianity relies on its accord with reason and science; he accepts it on faith.[20] However, because he is arguing with a nonbeliever, he must provide rational or scientific explanations for Christian doctrine, even if this cannot fully explain some of the more mysterious doctrines of Christianity, such as the Trinity. Nevertheless, Peter strongly asserts that Christian doctrine is not contradicted by reason.[21]

The issue of the Trinity poses further difficulty to Peter's logical arguments. Although biblical authority is a source for Peter's delicate explanations, reason will afford him what he believes to be an equally convincing method of argument.

In explaining the Trinity to Moses, Peter actually turns to philosophical arguments before he offers scriptural proof.[22] The basis of this rational proof is the definition of the Trinity in terms of personal attributes: *substantia* (Father), *sapientia* (Son), and *voluntas* (Holy Spirit).[23] It is clear that the separation of the persons of God, while maintaining His unity, is important to the development of his argument. Equally important is the already existing Jewish–Christian dialogue into which this plays. The question of the relation of attributes to God was not confined to Christian teachings; in fact, it was central to both medieval Islam and Judaism. The orthodox Muslim view stated that the attributes were real and eternal. Orthodox Muslims denied, however, that any of these attributes was a God, asserting that they were merely properties of God.[24] And the Jewish Mutakallimun (theologians influenced by the Kalâm), such as Saadya, al-Muqammiz (c. 900), and Qirqisani (a Karaite who lived in the first half of the tenth century), drew on this Muslim critique of attributes to argue that the reality of attributes compromised God's unity, simplicity, and incorporeality.[25] Following Christian doctrine and the concerns of anti-attributists, Moses asks Peter to prove that the attributes of wisdom and will are eternally with God. Peter responds by arguing that if these attributes have a beginning, either they were created by God or they created themselves. Since nothing can create itself, they must have been created by God.[26]

Saadya and al-Muqammiz had raised the question of whether attributes ascribed to God are the same as human attributes. They deny this because divine attributes are with God eternally, whereas human attributes are acquired and lost. Only human attributes, therefore, have real distinct existence apart from humans. Although Alfonsi does not cite this Jewish philosophical view — he hardly cites any sources — he must be well aware of them, for in taking this proof of the eternity of attributes — which Moses admits — he effectively uses the Jewish acceptance of the eternity of attributes to prove his Trinitarian doctrine. Of course there is a problem in this rational proof. Alfonsi is manipulating the Jewish argument, using the Jewish — and for that matter Muslim — acceptance of the eternity of God and his attributes to imply a Trinitarian understanding of God while neglecting the context of the Jewish and Muslim debate over the eternity of God's attributes, a debate that had to do, among other things, with the creation of the world *ex nihilo*, not the Triune God of Alfonsi's christological context. In effect, Alfonsi is arguing at cross-purposes with Jewish and Muslim logic, but because Moses offers little comprehensive rebuttal of Peter's deductions, Alfonsi appears to the reader to have a seemingly rational proof of the Trinity. Seeking further proof, Moses insists that Peter provide scriptural evidence as well. This is consistent with Alfonsi's general principle, common among Christian polemicists, which Jews hold rigidly and literally to their Law. Where reason is not able to convince them, scriptural proof will. This affords Peter an opportunity to discuss at length the Hebrew names for God.

Alfonsi's regard for reason shifts from his attack on Judaism to his defense of Christianity. In the first four chapters Alfonsi wishes to make it clear that all aspects of the Jewish tradition are contrary to reason. This constitutes Peter's successful, and original, attempt at convincing Moses why the continued observance of the Jewish Law is irrational and wrong. When addressing the doctrines of Christianity, Peter invokes the use of reason as an instrument for dispute, but this is only because, by his own words, he is arguing with an infidel. Acceptance of Christianity can be validated by faith and faith alone, even if, as Peter insists, nothing in Christian doctrine is contrary to reason.[27] For this reason Alfonsi concludes the *Dialogi* with Peter saying to Moses that if he will accept on faith what Christians accept on faith, he, too, will receive the divine illumination that will perfect his intellectual grasp of religious truth.[28] In other words, faith is an antecedent for comprehending Christianity's accord with reason. Thus, Alfonsi's use of reason may properly be compared to someone like Anselm of Canterbury, for like his contemporary Alfonsi affirms that Christianity does not contradict reason. He also follows Anselm's formula of faith seeking to understand (*fides quaerens intellectum*), taking in his defense of Christianity the position that a complete understanding of the religion can only come through faith. He goes further than Anselm, however, in using reason and science to demonstrate, mainly through Jewish postbiblical literature, that Judaism may be disproved *sola ratione*.

Abelard was first and foremost a teacher. His propensity for intellectual debate, in and out of the classroom, meant that argumentation and dialectic were at the forefront of his philosophy. In the *Collationes*, which is not one of his more influential works, there are two dialogues, each of which centers very much on the concept of reason and rational arguments. As in Alfonsi's *Dialogi*, reason plays a critical role in the opening discussion. The Philosopher and the Jew are the first to engage in debate. Demonstrating humility unseen in the *Dialogi*, Abelard's Jew begins his speech by warning the Philosopher of his possible philosophical shortcomings. The Jew beseeches the Philosopher not to "turn the intellectual incapacity of one little man into the shame of his whole race, nor find fault with a faith because of a person's deficiency."[29] The Philosopher politely replies, saying that his efforts are directed "to seeking for the truth, not to making a show of superiority." Although the latter claim is questionable, the debate at least sets out in a strictly intellectual and mutually tolerant manner. In response to the Philosopher's initial challenge of why the Jew and the Christian each adhere to their faiths, the Jew quickly invokes the value of reason. He agrees with the Philosopher in deploring, in adulthood, the adherence to faith based on a blind following of another's opinion. He insists that the passage from youth to an age of reason should, among Jews, mark a change in their conceptualization of their faith. "Now, my reasons for saying this," the Jew explains, "is that, although perhaps at first our attachment to our parents and family and the customs which we first knew brought us to this faith, it is reasoning [*ratio*] rather than opinion [*opinio*] which now keeps us in it."[30] Clearly, the Jew is a proponent of using reason to guide one's commitment to the faith. It remains to be seen what these reasonings are.

The Jew's explanation of Jewish commitment to the faith follows a somewhat fragmented logic. It can be summarized as follows. For generations, the Jews have followed a Law that most people, including Christians, agree was given to them by God. The Law cannot be shown to be wrong by reasoning, and, in addition, it is very fitting that he should have given such a Law to show his concern for his people. Supposing that God did not give this Law to Jews, it is still preferable to obey this Law since there is no harm in following some observances that have not in fact been commanded. Besides, given how much Jews suffer both at the hands of their oppressors and in daily life, it would be very cruel on the part of God not to reward the Jews.[31]

The Philosopher listens patiently to the Jew's lengthy exhortation on the malaise of Jewish life. For some, this might constitute evidence of Abelard's tolerant, or sympathetic, attitude toward Judaism. It would be more accurate to say that this sets up the Philosopher's explanation of how Jewish practice goes against reason. The only reward promised anywhere in the Old Testament, says the Philosopher, is earthly happiness, which the Jews now, by their own account, singularly fail to achieve. At this point the Philosopher cites several biblical passages showing Jewish failure to obey the Law. As a result, he puts it to the Jew that either they are not properly following the Law or that the one who gave them this Law is dishonest. These examples and deductions all form part of the Philosopher's earlier argument that Jewish obedience to their Law, the Law of the Old Testament, runs contrary to reason. What sense does it make, after all, for the Jews to continue following a Law that promises reward when the suffering they have endured for so long has gone unrewarded and, in any case, is a Law they can no longer fully observe?

The Jew states at the beginning of the dialogue that the arguments supporting the Jewish faith could be shown to be in accord with reason — reason that every Jew beyond the age of innocent childhood ought to be able to discern. But is the Jew's defense against the Philosopher's accusations really founded on reason? He begins his defense of Jewish Law with the somewhat shallow argument, "I cannot compel you to accept that it was given by God, yet you are not able to refute this."[32] He then supports his observances saying that since Jewish Law cannot be shown to be contrary to reason, there is therefore no imposing reason not to follow it. "Why need I risk a danger from which I am able to stay safe?"[33] Or, as he says later, "suppose these duties do not profit me, what harm will they do me, even if they are not commanded, since they are not forbidden?"[34] But these arguments do not demonstrate any rational justification for the observance of Jewish Law or, indeed, any positive use of reason. Rather, they are arguments out of default. Simply put, the Jew follows his Law out of lack of anything better. And in the mind of the Jew, diligent observance of the Law is given authority both by the Law's antiquity and by the general opinion among people. Confident in the reasons he has put forth, the Jew draws a stubborn conclusion: "Either, then, find something in this law to criticize or stop asking why we follow it."[35]

What, then, can we say about the Jew's use of reason? Certainly he begins in the right direction, willingly following the philosopher's lead that reason should alone (*sola ratione*) be the criterion for arguing their positions. But as the discussion unfolds, it becomes increasingly clear that the Jew fails in his attempt to engage in rational argumentation. Interestingly, this mirrors Abelard's explanation of Jewish intent. For just as the Jews were valiant in their desire to please God but wrong in their ultimate intent, so here the Jew is correct in his desire to argue on the plane of reason but ultimately is a failure in his attempt to demonstrate reason.

As adjudicator of the three disputants — the dialogues take the form of a dream vision — Abelard does not offer any judgment at the end of the first *collatio*. The Philosopher, on the other hand, does. He is brief, but to the point:

> My considered judgment of what has taken place in our debate is this. Even grant-ing that you were given your law as a gift from God, you cannot compel me on its authority to admit that I should submit to its burden, as if it were necessary to add anything to that law which Job prescribes for us through his own example or to that discipline of acting well which our philosophers left to their successors by setting out the virtues which suffice for happiness.[36]

It hardly matters, then, that Abelard indefinitely postpones his critique of the first debate. The Jew has argued his case, touchingly at times, but reason has proved to be a conceptual obstacle for him; the Philosopher is, from a reader's perspec-tive, quite right to move on to someone else as he searches for the rational path to virtue and happiness.[37] Although the greater part of the second *collatio* is taken up by an ethical discussion of the highest good and the greatest evil, it is worth briefly considering the place of reason in the discussion between the Philosopher and the Christian.

The Philosopher begins his debate with the Christian explaining that he had described Christians as "mad" at the beginning of the discussion just so as to pro-voke argument. (He made no such qualification about calling the Jews "stupid.") Indicating once again his limited faith in the Jews, the Philosopher states that, as the newer Law, more is to be expected of Christianity than of Judaism. He even praises Christianity for its power in having converted ancient philosophers who "relied greatly on rational arguments."[38] Why then, asks the Christian, "are you not moved to the faith by their example?" The Philosopher's response is perhaps the single most intriguing passage relating to Abelard's conception of Jews. Its importance demands close scrutiny:

> We do not yield to their authority in the sense that we fail to discuss rationally what they have said before we accept it. Otherwise we would cease to be philosophers — that is to say, if we put aside rational inquiry and made great use of arguments from authority, which are considered to require little skill and are entirely without

connection to the matter in hand, and are based on opinion rather than truth...If only you were able to convince your own people of what you are saying, so that you would show yourselves truly as logicians, armed with verbal reasoning, through what, as you say, is the highest wisdom, which you call in Greek the *logos* and in Latin the *verbum Dei* — and not put to me that commonly cited escape-clause for wretches provided by your Gregory when he said, "Faith lacks merit when human reason provides proof for it." Because the people you live among are incapable of sufficiently explaining the faith which they uphold, they immediately take up this statement of Gregory's as a consolation for their lack of skill.[39]

Abelard allows his Philosopher to express the full range of his philosophical implications. Having left the Jew behind, as it were, Abelard resolves to use the Christian, whom he has already identified as the more capable of the two law keepers, to provoke the Philosopher into an articulate critique of Christian thinking and contemporary attitudes toward authority. But it is more than just a critique. Building on arguments introduced in the first *collatio*, the Philosopher also outlines a model for a proper theological understanding, a model that centers on the relative positions of reason, authority, and philosophy. Reaching God — the Supreme Good — is, for the Philosopher, contingent on being able to (1) understand the faith through verbal reasoning and rational investigation and (2) explain to others the rational nature of this belief. Failure to rationalize the faith means failure to articulate its merit, and failure to articulate its merit equals a failure in the proper understanding of what it means to reach the Supreme Good.

Who wins this contest: the Philosopher or the Christian? The Christian defends the accusation that his coreligionists do not respect reason, stating that many things may seem to be in accord with reason when in fact they are not.[40] The Philosopher counters by saying that the same is true of authorities. He cites the many different religious sects as an example of what happens when diverging authorities are used and restates his earlier opinion that reason and not authorities ought to be one's guide. Now the Christian is ready to conclude. "Indeed," he says, "debate, both about texts and about views, makes itself a part of every discipline, and in every clash of disputation truth established by reasoning is more solid than the display of authority."[41] At last, the Christian is convinced. He continues to scorn the Philosopher's professed rejection of Holy Scripture, but for the first time he agrees that arguments based on reason are preferable to those founded on authority. From this moment on the discussion turns to the ethical questions relating to the highest good and how to achieve it. And even if the Christian succeeds in convincing the Philosopher on several points of ethics, there are, significantly, no further arguments that rest on a nonbiblical authority.

Abelard thus offers three versions of the exercise of reason in the *Collationes*. On the one hand, the Jew professes an appreciation and adherence to reasoned arguments but in fact fails to show any substance to his claims. On the other hand, the Christian is wary of reason and cautions against favoring reason over authority but ultimately proves that he is able to argue forcefully without resorting to authoritative statements and opinions. Bridging the divide between the followers of the two laws is the Philosopher. He is solely responsible for provoking his two opponents into a defense of their respective positions, and he ultimately challenges them to reexamine their ideas and their methods of argumentation. Indeed, the position of the Philosopher as intermediary sets Abelard's use of reason — and the structure of the dialogue — apart from Alfonsi, who chooses to use the Christian as the proponent of both rational philosophical inquiry and Christianity.

The *Kuzari* opens with the recounting of a dream in which an angel tells the king of the Khazars that although his intentions are pleasing to God, his actions are not. Unable to decipher this cryptic message, the king calls on representatives of different beliefs to interpret his dream. The Philosopher, who is the first to explain the dream and to present his doctrine to the king, is also first in raising the issue of rational conduct. His answer to the king consists mainly of a denial: a denial not only of the prophecies, dreams, and visions, which as he sees it are not of the essence of the highest perfection of man, but also of the relevance of any actions to the life of contemplation. From these theological assumptions the Philosopher is led to the conclusion that any would-be philosopher (i.e., the king who seeks his advice) has three paths from which to choose: (1) to be indifferent as to his religious, ethnic, or political group as well as his manner of worship; (2) to invent for himself a religion for the purpose of regulating his actions or worship as well as of his moral guidance and the guidance of his household and his city; and (3) to take as his religion the rational *nomoi* (laws) composed by the philosophers and to make purity of the soul his aim and purpose.[42] So what does the philosopher mean by these rational *nomoi*? Surely they go beyond the mere denial of dreams and visions given by the Philosopher. But they cannot be identical with the laws of nature, which bind every man regardless of nation or creed, nor can they be associated per se with the rational laws, whose elementary rules of social conduct apply to all forms of communities.[43] Nor do they constitute an outright rejection of the positive religions — Judaism, Christianity, and Islam — in favor of the religion of reason, for the Philosopher is quite clear in leaving the choice open. The rational *nomoi* of which the Philosopher speaks are part of a more specific intellectual quest that he alternatively defines as the religion of the philosophers.[44] They are neither obligatory nor scriptural, but, as Leo Strauss observed, "being emphatically 'rational,' they have been set up by the philosophers with a view to the unchanging needs of man as man; they are codes fixing the political or other conditions most favorable to the highest perfection of man."[45] And perfection of man, for the philosophers, entails the pursuit of "the true knowledge of all things, to the point where your intellect becomes active and no longer passive."[46] This latter statement is, as the language makes clear, a direct reference to Aristotle's concept of a passive and active intellect. Throughout the *Kuzari* these Aristotelian ideas are linked to the ideas of the Philosophers who, even after the Philosopher leaves the scene, provide stimulating counterargu-ments to the Rabbi's explanations of Jewish Law.[47] In fact, the philosopher does not impose his ideas on the king. He is asked for advice, and he gives it, stressing the intellectual and rational endeavors of the philosophical life and respecting, though not agreeing with, the beliefs and attitudes of the positive religions. It is in this spirit that the Philosopher concludes his dialogue with the king by stating that the "philosophers' religion" does not approve of, or command, the killing of other religions as such.[48]

The Philosopher's ideas seem reasonable, fulfilling, and tolerant. Why is the king not convinced? Very simply because they do not solve his problem: Namely, why he has been told that his intentions are desirable but his actions are not when he believes his actions are the product of his good intentions? In turning to the Christian and the Muslim, the king does not get any closer to a solution. Both speakers give succinct and rigid expositions of their religions, neither of which seem terribly rational or logical to the king. With the Christian the king is par-ticularly at odds. "Logic plays no part in your argument," he says, "if anything, logic dictates the exact opposite."[49]

When the Jew enters the scene, we already know something about the king's expectations. We know, for example, that the contemplative life of philosophical investigation is, by itself, unsatisfactory. We know that any solution to the king's problem must, contrary to the Philosopher, be able to distinguish among action, intent, and Divine wisdom. And any solution he hears must prove logically sus-tainable as well as spiritually fulfilling. From the first three conversations it is clear that the Philosopher, whose speech is longer than those of the Christian and the Muslim combined, provides the most thought-provoking and intriguing advice to the king. It is no surprise, then, that his arguments are the ones that provide the greatest challenge to the Rabbi. They continue to be cited by the king long after the Philosopher leaves, and the greater part of the Fourth Essay is devoted to the Rabbi's rebuttal of the Philosopher's ideas. So what precisely does the Rabbi have to say about the rational *nomoi*? At first glance, his attitude seems to be self-contradictory. In one passage he opposes the "rational religions," whereas in others he approves of them.[50] The ambiguity is not due to chance or carelessness but, as is often the case when it comes to Halevi's rhetorical agenda, to deliberate choice. Indeed, it reflects the author's wish, and struggle, to indicate a grave question.[51]

The Rabbi's remarks unfavorable to the rational *nomoi* occur in the First Essay, when the king is still skeptical of the Jewish religion. The favorable com-ments are given in the later essays where the king has, by that point, converted to Judaism. In other words, the Rabbi adopts an unfavorable stance toward the rational *nomoi*, whereas the king is still outside the Jewish community. Once he has converted and adopted the major precepts of Judaism, then the Rabbi speaks more favorably of these rational *nomoi*. The question at stake, therefore, concerns the circumstances and parameters for employing a rational approach. Used by a non-Jew it may be misleading and potentially dangerous. This is why the Rabbi, in the very beginning of his conversation with the king, cautions against the king's suggestion that religion ought to pursue truth and emulate the righteousness and wisdom of the Creator. He states, "What you are referring to is a religion arrived at through logic and analysis. But because it is arrived at through these means, it is subject to much ambiguity. That is why when you ask philosophers their opinion about religion, you find that they are unable to agree on one proper routine of conduct or on one philosophy."[52]

However, used within the boundaries of Judaism, a rational approach can be profitable. In a manner somewhat resembling Alfonsi's claim that nothing in Christianity contradicts reason, Halevi also vigorously defends the rationality of scripture: "The Torah never expects us to believe in things contradicted by evidence or proofs."[53] Later when the king suggests that Jews reject arriving at religion through proofs and "intellectual analysis," the Rabbi interjects, "never does the Torah write something that logic dictates as false."[54]

Halevi has a fundamental concern not just with articulating the precepts of Judaism but also with responding to the "religion of the philosophers" as well. But responding to the rational approaches and intellectual analysis of the philosophers is not something Halevi is able to do singularly or completely. He addresses the issue on several occasions — most notably in the Fourth Essay — and with varying degrees of success. The complication arises because of Halevi's own considerations of reason and rationality. What remains to be seen is what these considerations actually are and what their relation is to his refutation of philosophy.

Before the Rabbi actually uses the term "rational *nomoi*," he first makes clear the presence of man's rational faculty. In terms reminiscent of Aristotle — and Cicero — the Rabbi distinguishes between man's "intelligent behavior" and the behavior of "all other animals." "Man's higher intellect," he goes on, "demands of him more refined behavior, the establishment of civilizations, the exercising of social justice, and other forms of conduct and etiquette."[55] At this point the existence of an intellectual, or rational, faculty is solely associated with the formation of governments and states within society. It is practical reason only. Yet later on the Rabbi seems to call attention to two other examples of reason. There is, as we have already seen, the rational religion of the philosophers that leads to ambiguity, incoherence, and uncertainty. But there is also a rationalism of a different origin. In another passage concerning the intellectual quest for God, still in the First Essay, the Rabbi contrasts the right approach to God, based on divine knowledge proceeding from God, with the heretical approach of "using research, logic, and extrapolation, or by using what is written in the astrology books regarding harnessing spiritual influences or the making of talismans."[56] In this context criticism is again being leveled on the rational approach; only here, the Rabbi ascribes his criticisms not to philosophers but to astrologers and other types of superstitious people — people whom he goes so far as to call heretics. Thus, Halevi seems to admit two kinds of rational *nomoi*: one being the work of the philosophers, and the other being the work of heretics.[57]

Halevi's discussion of reason and rationality does not limit itself to attacks on philosophers and heretics. Indeed, Halevi's approval of reason and rational *nomoi* makes the concept such an intriguing aspect of his thought. Having led the king as well as the reader through the First Essay to believe that a rational and logical approach to religion is both dangerous and futile, the Rabbi goes on in the Second Essay to give a more compromising perspective on the relation between divine law and intellectual conduct. Answering the king's assumption that closeness to God comes about simply through humility, lowliness, and the like, the Rabbi responds, "These and others like them are the rational laws. They are prerequisites — inherently and sequentially — to the Divine Torah. One cannot maintain any community of people without these laws. Even a community of robbers cannot exist without equity amongst themselves; if not, their association could not continue."[58]

To the historian of political thought these last words evoke the remarks of Cicero and Augustine, who cited the example of a gang, or community, of robbers as the most basic form of human society.[59] Halevi seems to imply the same, suggesting that certain rational laws are bound to all forms of human communities. Indeed, they are necessary for receiving divine law, although of course this is not to say that all communities — much less a community of robbers — will actually receive the divine law. This statement, then, suggests a changed attitude toward rationalism. Not only does it readjust his stance on the acceptability of rationalism, for here it is clearly cited approvingly; it is also a departure from the traditional teachings of the *kalâm*. For whereas the *kalâm* terminology of revealed laws generally implies that the Divine Law as a whole consists of both rational and revealed laws, here the Rabbi considers the rational laws as preparatory to, and hence separable from, the Divine Law.[60] So even though both may originate from God, rational laws and revealed laws do not go hand in hand. What is more, these rational laws are part of a governing principle that applies, apparently, to all human societies, for even a gang of robbers cannot exist without such laws. In a sense this remark introduces into Halevi's thought the idea of natural law in so far as it is part of intellectual capabilities that are universal to mankind. So in setting rational laws as the preparatory, and necessary, stage for fulfillment of the divine commandments Halevi is distancing himself not only from the Aristotelian concept of a rapprochement with the Creator, which centers on the idea of the active intellect, but also from the philosophy of the Jewish Mutikallimun, who draw no distinction between a preliminary rational law and a subsequent divine law. Effectively, Halevi raises two new and critical issues in the debate with philosophy: the role of natural laws in human society and their effect on the morality of those societies — including, of course, Jewish society.

The critical role that reason plays in Alfonsi's *Dialogi*, Abelard's *Collationes*, and Halevi's *Kuzari* suggests a few general conclusions. For all three authors, reason and rational inquiry present themselves as a challenge. For Alfonsi the challenge is to demonstrate how Judaism runs contrary to reason and how reason upholds Christianity. This challenge is set, and overcome, by Peter and by Peter alone. Moses acts as a mere player, albeit an essential player, in an intellectual quest dictated by his adversary. For Abelard the challenge is whether a revealed religion, either Judaism or Christianity, is capable of adhering to the principle of rational investigation. The failure of the Jew lies not in a rejection of reason — for his principles of rational belief accord well with the Philosopher — but in his inability to prove his points and in his inability to rise above his carnality and his literal interpretation of the Law. His failure, however, is contrasted by the Christian's willingness, through some persuasion, to allow reason to serve as the intellectual helm in a philosophical discussion that can then proceed to more ethical questions, such as attaining the supreme good. With Halevi the challenge is a twofold confrontation between Aristotelian philosophy and Jewish Law on the one hand and rational laws and suprarational laws on the other. Having examined the first one, and partially the second, it is clear that an overall ambiguity exists in what Halevi approves and disapproves of in rational thinking. This ambiguity can partly be explained by the evolving relationship between the king and the Rabbi — the Rabbi modifies his stance on reason and rational inquiry once the king converts at the end of the First Essay — and partly by Halevi's struggle to situate himself between the doctrinally unbounded assertions of Aristotelianism and the Islamic rational approach of the *kalâm,* both of which Halevi sees as a threat to Judaism. In each of the three works a different perspective is taken toward reason, and in each work a different line of argumentation is being advanced in support of a concept that none of the authors is fully willing to give total liberty.

Natural Law

The previous section followed chronological order and examined Alfonsi first. On the question of natural law, however, Alfonsi's *Dialogi* offers much less material for investigation. Instead, it is more fitting to look first at Abelard and Halevi, each of whom deals directly with the issue, and then to consider Alfonsi.

Abelard begins the *Collationes* with a clear distinction among the beliefs of the three disputants. This distinction is presented in terms of laws: The Jew follows the Law of the Old Testament, the Christian follows the Law of the New Testament, and the Philosopher, who has no sacred texts, is "content" to follow natural law.[61] The Philosopher defines his understanding of natural law as follows:

> Natural law is the first law, I say, not just in time, but also by nature: for whatever is more simple is naturally prior to that which is more multiple. Now natural law, that is the knowledge of morals, which we call 'ethics' is made up just of moral

precepts, whereas the teaching of your laws [i.e. the Old and New Testaments] adds to them various commands to do with external signs, which seem entirely superfluous to us.[62]

The Philosopher has thus two main attractions to natural law. On the one hand, it precedes any of the sacred laws, thus endowing it with an air of primacy; on the other hand, it includes a dimension of morality to which neither of the scriptural laws adds anything. These two sides of natural law are an important prologue for the two discussions, or *collationes*, that follow. In fact, they seem to constitute an outline for what follows: It is the issue of primacy and universal applicability that forms the majority of the Philosopher's discussion with the Jew, and it is the issue of morality that constitutes the majority of the second *collatio*, where the philosopher and the Christian proceed to topics of ethics.

In the first dialogue the Philosopher aims to show the Jew how the Law of the Old Testament adds little of value to the Law he already follows. In addition to being naturally prior to the scriptural laws, the Philosopher points out that natural law is applicable to everyone, unlike the Law of the Old Testament, which is applicable only to the Jews. To prove his point about natural law, the Philosopher turns to Job and argues that his virtue did not lie in a specific observance of the Mosaic Law: "When Job himself explains to us the nature of justice through his own example, so that we can imitate it, he mentions nothing about the observances of the law, but only the observances of natural law, which natural reason urges on everyone."[63] Two points are worth noting about the Philosopher's arguments. First, the Philosopher uses examples from the Old Testament to disprove the efficacy of that very scripture. As has already been noted, the citations from the Old Testament are part of the Philosopher's agreement to only use texts on which both he and the Jew can agree. But in the instance of natural law, the Philosopher goes yet further and argues that the contents of the Old Testament are proof enough of its failure to supplant natural law. Second, the Philosopher is seen attempting to draw a distinction between reason and natural law. He argues that because natural law is the knowledge of morals instituted by God prior to any scriptural law, reason is man's ability — indeed his inclination — to grasp the truth of divine wisdom, independent of scriptural law.[64] All this suggests that the Jews' rejection of natural law in favor of their own law must therefore be contrary to both nature and reason.

The Jew does not let the Philosopher's accusations go unanswered. His answers, however, follow a rather unusual path. He does not offer, as he could have, one systematic interpretation of divine and natural law, separating the two from each other. Rather, he offers a series of arguments that justify the Jewish position, several of which have already been encountered. Responding to the Philosopher's claim that Jews no longer follow natural law, the Jew offers an answer based on the commandment — in Deuteronomy, Leviticus, and elsewhere

— to love God and to love one's neighbor. He collects several scriptural passages demonstrating the importance of loving God and says to the Philosopher,

> Reflect, therefore, I beg you, on the basis of these on how far the law extends the feeling of love both to people and to God, and you will realize that your law too, which you call *natural*, is included within ours: so that, even if all the other commandments were put aside, then for us just as for you those which concern perfect love would be enough for salvation... These added laws, it seems to me, are concerned not so much with what constitutes a holy way of life as with safeguarding it.[65]

Here, as well as most everywhere else, Abelard's Jew is struggling to find coherence in his objections. On the one hand he wishes to uphold the validity of Mosaic Law as a divine gift to the Jewish people, while also showing how it accords with reason; on the other hand he is seemingly forced into the conclusion, unconvincing to the Philosopher, that Jewish Law is useful, if for nothing else because it protects — rather than provides — the spiritual life. This is rather like his conclusion that Jews follow the Law of Moses out of lack of any better law. In instances like these Abelard may be said to lack any understanding either of Jewish spirituality or how Jews view the significance of their Law.[66]

The issue of natural law does not end with the conclusion of the first *collatio*. It is an issue with which the Philosopher and the Christian must come to terms if they are to discuss spirituality and morality at any length. Turning to the Christian in hope of a more reasoned mind who follows a more recent law,[67] the Philosopher is quick to invoke natural law, and also the Jews, in setting out his position. "In its concern with the rules of good behavior," he says, natural law "is especially suited to philosophers because, clearly, they use this law and follow reasoning — as your learned writer commented: 'The Jews seek signs and the Greeks look for wisdom.'"[68] In this, the Philosopher seems to side with Christian natural law interpretation; there are the Jews, who interpret everything literally and are only convinced by miraculous signs, and there are the Greeks, the pagan philosophers, who, like the Philosopher of the dialogue, use reason as a guide to interpreting the laws of nature. For the moment nothing is explicitly said about the Christian outlook. Faced with this scheme, the Christian cannot but agree that the search for wisdom is the better of the two approaches. However, he is not convinced that the Philosopher has it all right. Why, after all, does he remain a pagan when he is clearly aware of Christian doctrine? This leads the two disputants into an interesting discussion of another form of law: positive law (*ius positiva*). By this the Philosopher means what is not common to all people and is not innately graspable: It has either been laid down in writing or is based on custom. In making the distinction between universally applicable moral laws (natural law) and laws peculiar to particular places and times, Abelard clearly draws on *De inventione*, where Cicero distinguishes between *naturale ius* on the one hand and *ius* by custom or *ius* by law on the other. Abelard makes the distinction more clear, however, by calling positive law anything that is not natural law.[69] This distinction is not insignificant, for the Philosopher then takes positive law and, within it, distinguishes between positive justice (*iustitia positiva*) and natural justice (*iustitia naturale*), a distinction Abelard had already made in the *Theologia Christiana* some years earlier. But unlike his earlier use of these terms, which seems to echo Calcidius in his commentary on the *Timaeus*, this passage in the *Collationes* seems to be the first case where positive justice is used, as it then continued to be used in legal philosophy, as a term for human laws not natural and not universal.[70]

What does the Philosopher's discussion of natural law and positive law have to do with the Christian–Jewish debate? Quite a lot. The finer distinction made in the second *collatio*, in the presence of the Christian, differs markedly from the bare divisions of natural law versus Old Law offered in the first *collatio*. The divisions of justice that, in the second *collatio*, immediately precede the strictly ethical discussion of good and evil are nowhere to be found in the dialogue with the Jew. Why is this? Because, as was the case with reason, the Jew of the first *collatio* cannot rationalize beyond his affection for his law. He cannot distinguish sufficiently between natural law and his scriptural law; therefore, it would be pointless on the part of the Philosopher to attempt to introduce any further complications to a concept that the Jew is clearly unable to grasp. Thus, like reason, the understanding of natural law proves, among other things, to be a concept that distinguishes the irrational Jew from the increasingly competent Christian.[71] It is thus that the Philosopher answers the Christian's worries about reason, saying, "What you said about people sometimes going wrong in distinguishing and grasping reasonings is indeed true and evident. But this happens to those people who lack the skill of rational philosophy and lack discernment about arguments; as the Jews acknowledge themselves to be, asking for signs in place of arguments."[72] Without reason one cannot acknowledge natural law, and without first acknowledging natural law it is impossible to discuss ethics. This is a fundamental message of the *Collationes*.

We have already met, in part, Halevi's concept of rational laws and, accompanying it, the so-called law of reason. The term "rational *nomoi*" had a clear meaning so long as they were contrasted, as the Rabbi of the *Kuzari* says they should, with divinely revealed, or suprarational, laws. It ceases to be clear, however, if rational laws are to be distinguished from nonrevealed laws, such as civil and natural laws. Focusing attention on natural law will therefore not only elucidate Halevi's concept of this term; it will also help complete our understanding of all that is implied under the term "rational *nomoi*."

Natural law enters into the *Kuzari* in two very distinct contexts. On the one hand, it forms part of the Rabbi's didactic explanation of Judaism's unique customs and laws, and, on the other, it constitutes an important element in his refutation of the philosophic outlook. Not all of his statements accord with one another, but this must be seen as deriving from the overall ambiguity with which he treats philosophical concepts.[73] This chapter focuses on the aspects of natural law that are most pertinent to understanding the Rabbi's intellectual struggle between faith and reason. Concerning Jewish customs, Halevi is above all interested in explaining why Jewish Law is both valid and unlike other religious laws. The historical destiny of the Jewish people in the present — that is, their downtrodden status among the other nations — poses a fundamental problem. It cannot be ascribed to their failure to observe prescribed commandments since, according to the Rabbi, the Jews are even more meticulous in this than are other peoples, such as Muslims.[74] What is more, their hopes for the future are associated with nonnatural events, analogous to the miracle of the Exodus.[75] How, then, does one account for the possibility of miraculous events, both past and future, in spite of the present state of the Jewish people? Halevi responds to the problem by making recourse to a theory of the preordained harmony between the Torah and the laws of nature:

> The purpose of this text [the *aggadah*] is to reconcile nature with the Torah— according to the laws of nature, things occur naturally, while according to the Torah, things occur supernaturally. The reconciliation is that all supernatural phenomena were implanted within nature. They were part of God's original intent when he first created the laws of nature, and were therefore fixed within the nature of these things—during the six days of creation—to surface at the appropriate time.[76]

Laws of nature do not, for Halevi, exist independently of revealed law. Quite to the contrary, they are part of God's divine plan, and indeed they help distinguish the Jewish people from other peoples. As the Rabbi explains elsewhere, the entire world will be guided by these laws of nature, except for Jews.[77] The Rabbi makes it clear that through observance of God's commandments Jews may discover that worldly affairs "are governed by Something bigger than nature."[78]

It is evident that Halevi's own Judaic concept of the laws of nature, if it may be called that, is very much entangled in his reading of the Torah commandments as well as his concern to explain and to justify the unfavorable situation of the Jewish people vis-à-vis other religions and, let us not forget, the religion of the philosophers. This dual agenda may help explain why the Jews' unique status as the nation that received the Torah commandments constitutes their superior link with God on two independent levels: (1) their unique status as the only people obliged to perform the Torah commandments; and (2) their opportunity to observe the commandments as those who have been enjoined to do so and fulfill their duty. On the first basis, Israel's election does not depend on the actual observance of the commandments; on the second it does. These two points are crucial to Halevi's defense of Judaism (the "despised faith" alluded to in the title of the work): They explain the ability of Jews to survive in conditions of abasement; they give sense and reason to this humiliation, and they thereby open the door to hope for a better future.[79] They also explain the unique divine leadership of the Jewish people, and on the historical plane their reflection is that the Jews are exempt from the dominion of the laws of nature whatever lifestyle they lead.[80] According to Halevi, divine law is therefore meant to emphasize God's absolute sovereignty over all creation. This sovereignty has many manifestations and implies both nonreliance on the natural order of things and the capacity to instigate innovation and novelty suddenly rather than through a process.

Natural law, as distinct from the laws of nature, finds expression in Halevi's intellectual struggle over philosophy. For the purposes of this discussion it is wise to refer to natural law when discussing laws that only concern humans, distinguishing it from the laws of nature that govern the natural world. To understand Halevi's critique of philosophy it is first necessary to further understand some of the implications of the Philosopher. The Philosopher of the *Kuzari* is concerned with discovering the intentions that should occupy the background of human activity.[81] In his opinion, philosophers must intentionally distance themselves from their deeds. Thus, the Philosopher says to the king, "Once you have integrated this philosophy within yourself, you need not concern yourself with which specific dogma, set of rituals and other actions, choice of words or language that you will practice."[82] The Philosopher's reason for taking such a view is closely tied to a belief that certain customs follow a universal set of rules. The decimal system and the seven-day week, so the Philosopher believes, are shared by all humanity — not because they constitute anything that we might call natural laws but because they go back to some common beginning, agreement, and convention.[83] According to the Philosopher, it follows that the human intellect ought at the very least to be able to understand the rational rules of conduct, for they "have originated from human sources." What is more, knowledge of these rules of conduct, like the perception of truth in general, is a spontaneous activity of the human intellect working alone, with no outside help from an omnipotent deity. Obviously this poses a problem for Halevi, who outwardly acknowledges God's influence over human intellect and reason.[84] The Philosopher is convinced that the value of human action corresponds to the absence of obligatory material but the presence of universal rules of conduct. He also asserts that it is impossible to set rules of conduct that are appropriate to every concrete situation since the natural conditions in which human beings find themselves are not within the realm of the intellect.[85] Indeed, this is the core of what Halevi cannot accept from the Philosopher. He cannot accept the Philosopher's doctrine that the intellect achieves its goal independent of any outside agencies, nor can he accept the Philosopher's view of the essence of God, a God who is not the principle of hierarchical order.

Halevi's rejection of the Philosopher's ideas occupies an important position in the makeup of the *Kuzari*. But unlike the *Collationes*, where the Philosopher is clearly a proponent of natural law and the Jew is not, in the *Kuzari* no such radical distinction exists between the differing ideologies. In some passages the

Rabbi denounces the Philosopher's view of the laws of nature, whereas in other places he offers his own view on the issue. Concerning the topic of God's creation on Earth, for example, the Rabbi can only criticize what he sees as a competing world view: "Any entity [in the plant kingdom] that possesses these traits of growth, reproduction, and receiving nourishment, and at the same time lacks locomotion — such an entity is controlled by *nature*, according to the Philosophers. But the reality is that the blessed Creator controls plants, via a particular attribute [He implanted within them]."[86] But elsewhere, the Rabbi offers an alternative to the Philosopher's belief in a common human origin of religion. This is expressed in terms of a pre-Mosaic state of being that is cleverly disguised as a justification of the divine law of the Torah:

> This is how people were before the advent of Moses. With the exception of a few individuals, people were seduced by astrology and other natural forces. They wandered from religion to religion, from god to god, some even adhering to several gods. Eventually, they forgot the One Who conducts and manages these forces and Who placed them in the universe to benefit mankind. Instead these forces became a source of harm to man because of man's inadequate preparation [to receive influence] and his improper use of them. Ultimately, then, the only truly beneficial tool is the [Divine] Torah, and lack thereof causes harm.[87]

Although the Rabbi does not use the term *natural law* here to describe man's disorganized state in pre-Mosaic times, this is, effectively, an expression of Halevi's view of what constitutes the naturalistic, nonnormative, behavior of the human race — that is, human society before God's Law is revealed to his chosen people, the Jews. His avoidance of the term may, of course, be deliberate, not wanting to sound too much like the Philosopher who views natural forces as superior to divine forces in all circumstances. Of course the flipside of this statement is the implication that other peoples, adherents to religions other than Judaism, remain in an existence much akin to a state of nature. Halevi does not venture to expand on this, but some further implications about religion in general can be found in his discussion of laws and morality.

Natural law in the *Kuzari* also finds expression on the subject of morality, a subject that is as important to Halevi's thought and writings as ethics is to Abelard.[88] From the Rabbi's statements about divine laws and universal societies arises one basic question: Do duties toward God belong to the moral minimum required of any society however low?[89] The Rabbi's answer to this question cannot be established by reference to the seven Noahidic commandments for, as he suggests shortly after first mentioning the rational laws, the Noahidic commandments are "inherited" and hence are not merely rational.[90] To deny that religion is essential to society would be difficult for a man of Halevi's piety. On the other hand, to assert that it is would amount to ascribing some value even to the most abominable idolatrous religion: the proverbial gang of robbers or the lowest of communities.[91]

Yet when speaking of the most primitive communities, he mentions justice, goodness, and recognition of God's grace.[92] So, for Halevi, even the least developed community does partake in a certain level of morality. However, the Rabbi also distinguishes between governmental laws, which do not mention any duties toward God, and divine laws and psychic laws, which almost exclusively do deal with such duties. So where does one draw the line between morality and religion? Resolution of the issue involves a qualification of terms: Duties toward God do not belong to natural laws, for they are inspired by divine law, but certain natural laws, such as those only guaranteeing the preservation of human society, cannot be called rational since they are associated with governmental laws. In Halevi's terms natural laws are, in effect, no more than the indispensable and unchangeable minimum of morality required for the bare existence of society.[93] And, to answer our earlier question, duties toward God cannot constitute a universal principle applicable to any society no matter how low. They are distinguishable by the presence of a divine law that perfects the natural law and instills in society a morality greater than anything offered in society without a divine law.

Of the three texts studied here, Alfonsi's *Dialogi* poses the most problems for considering the question of natural law. For one, Alfonsi does not present a well-defined or even systematic description of natural law. He does not seem to consider natural law a separate criterion from reason in his theological and philosophical understanding of revealed religion. On the other hand, he is certainly better versed in Greek and Arabic science and philosophy than Abelard and certainly appreciated them more than Halevi. Indeed, his emphasis on science and the natural world is a distinguishing feature of the *Dialogi*.[94] It would only make sense, then, that Alfonsi derives from his sources an understanding of certain principles of nature. And he does, but these principles concern the scientific, and empirical, deductions from the natural world, not any laws governing human societies and customs. Is this surprising? Perhaps not. For though Alfonsi does invoke philosophy and reason in his attack on Judaism — and Islam — and in his defense of Christianity, there is no spokesperson for philosophy per se. The dialogues are between a Christian understanding of religion and a Jewish understanding of Jewish Law. Philosophy is a vehicle for building arguments, such as the ones encountered in connection with reason, not a scripture-neutral voice of intellectual contemplation. The implication, of course, is that natural law arises from a nonscriptural attempt to understand human customs and societies, something decidedly not the focus of Alfonsi's *Dialogi*.

The issue of natural law is expressed and treated differently by Abelard and Halevi and not at all by Alfonsi. Attempts to understand natural law in the *Collationes* constitute an insurmountable obstacle for the Jew and a philosophical challenge to the Christian. It serves to elicit the spiritual and logical weakness of Judaism but to stimulate the ethical vitality of Christianity. In the *Kuzari*, natural law is a concept handled by both the Philosopher, or the philosophical approach, and the Rabbi. The Rabbi rejects it when it threatens his cosmological beliefs, embraces it when it upholds his categorization of the natural world, and dodges the issue slightly when it does not accord so smoothly with his broader explanations of religion and morality. Alfonsi, the author who most invokes philosophy and science and makes frequent recourse to the rational ordering of the natural world, is conspicuously silent on the issue his contemporaries were so struggling to situate within the framework of their dialogues.

Conclusions: Intellectual Ferment or Religious Intolerance?

From the arguments of Alfonsi, Abelard, and Halevi there begins to emerge a picture of the broad-ranging approaches to a debate that includes not only Christians and Jews but Muslims and philosophers as well, or at least their ideas. The topics of reason and natural law are by no means the only two points for investigating the convergences and divergences among these three authors, but they do shed important light on their respective ideas, argumentations, and intellectual context. Their individual handlings of reason and natural law pertain not only to the Christian–Jewish debate; they also reveal a wealth of ideas concerning the relationship between man and God, individual and society, and, importantly, faith and reason — an issue that, it is now equally clear, is central to all three. In light of what is known about twelfth-century society and thought, and the way it is often approached by modern historians, it seems not unfair to ask whether their arguments demonstrate aspects of intellectual ferment or religious intolerance. In other words, do these texts belong to the intellectual renaissance so often evoked in discussion of the twelfth century, or do they manifest attitudes of prejudice, negative stereotypes, or even hatred?[95] An important clue in answering this question lies in the concern each author has in accounting for the position of Jews in contemporary society. For Alfonsi and Abelard the abject status of Jews is a reality that neither denies nor seeks to deny. Even Halevi, defending Jewish society, recognizes this. Where these authors differ is in what conclusions they draw. What is for Abelard evidence of the Jews' wrong intention in serving God is for Halevi an example of the prophetic experience between Jews and God that favorably distinguishes Jews from members of other confessions. The universal, natural laws that separate Abelard's Philosopher from his Jew are, for Halevi, nothing more than the indispensable and unchanging minimum of morality required for the bare existence of society. These and other issues discussed in the *Dialogi*, the *Collationes*, and the *Kuzari* unquestionably serve as a platform for intellectual dispute. Abelard's harsh portrayal of the Jew's use of reason and Alfonsi's firm denunciation of the irrationality of Moses's Jewish Law — and other rabbinic writings — do exhibit some very negative attitudes toward the Jewish faith. Halevi's confidence in his own religion not only provides him with an eloquent and detailed defense of Judaism but with a demonstration of its superiority over other competing world views.

Where, then, are these texts located within the social, religious, and historical contexts of twelfth-century Europe? Are they examples of intellectual ferment or religious intolerance? The answer, it seems, is something of both. The importance of the *Dialogi*, the *Collationes*, and the *Kuzari* can be felt both in their contributions to the expanding genre of polemical — and specifically dialogue — writings and in the increasing friction between Christians and Jews. In all three works there is evidence of both a novel approach to intellectual dispute and a concern to situate Jews and Judaism against the onslaught of a more rational alternative to Judaism.

Notes

1. This paper originated as a Cambridge M.Phil. dissertation under the supervision of Anna Sapir Abulafia, whom I wish to thank for all her assistance, wise counsel, and cheerful enthusiasm. I also wish to acknowledge the very helpful comments and criticisms I received from David Abulafia, Nicholas de Lange, John Marenbon, and Edward Peters at various stages along the way.

2. The study of Christian–Jewish polemics owes its beginnings to the work of A. L. Williams and especially Bernhard Blumenkranz, who was the first to offer a detailed study of Christian polemical writings in the early Middle Ages: Williams, *Adversus Judaeos: A Bird's-Eye View of Christian Apologiae until the Renaissance* (Cambridge, UK: Cambridge University Press, 1935); Blumenkranz, *Die Judenpredigt Augustins. Ein Beitrag zur Geschichte der jüdisch-christlichen Beziehungen in den ersten Jahrhunderten* (Basel: Helbing & Lichtenhahn, 1946); Blumenkranz, *Les Auteurs chrétiens latins du Moyen Age sur les Juifs et le Judaisme* (Paris: Mouton, 1963). Recent overviews of the subject include Gilbert Dahan, *Les Intellectuels chrétiens et les juifs au Moyen Age* (Paris: Editions du Cerf, 1990); Anna Sapir Abulafia, *Christians and Jews in the Twelfth-Century Renaissance* (London: Routledge, 1995); Samuel Krauss, *The Jewish–Christian Controversy from the Earliest Times to 1789, vol. 1: History,* ed. and rev. William Horbury (Tübingen: J.C.B. Mohr, 1995); Cohen. Also relevant for the twelfth century are the collected essays in Abulafia, *Christians and Jews in Dispute: Disputational Literature and the Rise of Anti-Judaism in the West, c. 1050–1150* (Aldershot: Variorum, 1998); Signer and Van Engen.

3. Further biographical details of Peter Alfonsi can be found in John Tolan, *Petrus Alfonsi and His Medieval Readers* (Gainesville: University Press of Florida, 1993), 3–11; Jeremy Cohen, "The Mentality of the Medieval Jewish Apostate: Peter Alfonsi, Hermann of Cologne, and Pablo Christiani," in *Jewish Apostasy in the Modern World,* ed. T. Endelman (New York: Holmes and Meier, 1987), 20–47; Horacio Santiago Otero, "Pedro Alfonso," *Biblioteca bíblica ibérica medieval* (Madrid: Consejo Superior de Investigaciones Científicas: Centro de Estudios Históricos, 1986), 250–58.

4. Cf. Cohen, 245–70. Alfonsi's influence on Joachim of Fiore has been documented by B. Hirsch-Reich, "Joachim von Fiore und das Judentum," in *Judentum im Mittelalter. Beiträge zum Christlisch-Jüdischen Gespräch*, ed. P. Wilpert (Berlin: de Gruyter, 1966), 228–63. See also Abulafia, "The Conquest of Jerusalem: Joachim of Fiore and the Jews," in *The Experience of Crusading: Defining the Crusader Kingdom*, ed. Marcus Bull and Norman Housley (Cambridge, UK: Cambridge University Press, 2002), 127–46. Alfonsi was answered later in the century by his fellow townsman Jacob b. Reuben of Huesca, whose great book *The Wars of the Lord* (c. 1170–1190) opened a succession of Jewish polemical works. For a survey and analysis of medieval Spanish Jewish polemic see Hanne Trautner-Kromann, *Shield and Sword: Jewish Polemics against Christianity and the Christians in France and Spain, 1100–1500* (Tübingen: Mohr, 1993), 123–90.

5. Most recently, see Constant J. Mews, *Abelard and Heloise* (Oxford: Oxford University Press, 2005). On Abelard's theology, see Jean Jolivet, *La théologie d'Abelard* (Paris: Editions du Cerf, 1997).

6. Cf. Mews, "Peter Abelard and the Enigma of the Dialogue," in *Beyond the Persecuting Society: Religious Toleration Before the Enlightenment*, ed. J. C. Laursen and C. J. Nederman (Philadelphia: University of Pennsylvania Press, 1998), 25–51. Perhaps the most disputed aspect of the *Collationes* (or *Dialogue of a Philosopher with a Jew and a Christian*, as it is sometimes called) is its date of composition. Although long believed to date to the end of the Abelard's life (c. 1141–42) on account of its seemingly unfinished second dialogue, Mews argues convincingly for an earlier date (possibly as early as c. 1125–27) on the basis that the work is not incomplete and corresponds to an earlier phase in Abelard's intellectual development. See Mews, "On Dating the Works of Peter Abelard," *Archives d'Histoire Doctrinale et Littéraire du Moyen Age* 52 (1985): 104–26. The date 1127–32 adopted here is after the *Collationes*'s most recent editors, John Marenbon and Giovanni Orlandi, who partially agree with Mews. For a fuller treatment of the historiography surrounding the dating of the work, see Marenbon's introduction in *Peter Abelard: Collationes*, ed. and trans. J. Marenbon and G. Orlandi (Oxford: Oxford University Press, 2001), xxvii–xxxii.

7. See Marenbon, "Abelard's Concept of Natural Law," in *Mensch und Natur im Mittelalter*, ed. A. Zimmermann (Berlin: de Gruyter, 1992), 609–21; Marenbon, *The Philosophy of Peter Abelard*, (Cambridge: Cambridge University Press, 1997), 267–70; Marenbon, "Abelard's Ethical Theory: Two Definitions from the Collationes," in *From Athens to Chartres: Neoplatonism and Medieval Thought: Studies in Honour of Edouard Jeaneau*, ed. H. Westra (Leiden: Brill, 1992), 301–14.

8. On the life of Halevi see Yitzhak Baer, *A History of the Jews in Christian Spain*, trans. L. Schoffman (Philadelphia: Jewish Publication Society of America, 1961), vol. 1, 67–77. Although slightly dated, the best biography in English remains Rudolf Kayser, *The Life and Times of Jehuda Halevi*, trans. Frank Gaynor (New York: Philosophical Library, 1949).

9. For many years it was believed that the story of the Khazar kingdom's conversion to Judaism was Halevi's own fabrication. Though the conversations presented in the *Kuzari* are surely the work of Halevi's imagination, considerable archaeological evidence — and two important documents —confirm the existence of the Khazar kingdom and the king's decision to convert his people to Judaism. The documents in question are a tenth-century exchange of letters between King Joseph and Rabbi

Hadai ibn Shaprut (a vizier to the Caliph Abd Al-Rahman III in Cordoba), describing how King Bulan called in different theologians and finally settled on Judaism. For further information on the Khazar kingdom, see Douglas Dunlop, *The History of the Jewish Khazars* (New York: Schocken Books, 1967); Peter B. Golden, *Khazar Studies: An Historico-philological Inquiry into the Origins of the Khazars* (Budapest: Akadémiai Kiadó, 1980); Kevin Brook, *The Jews of Khazaria* (Northvale, NJ: Jason Aronson, 1999). The letters between King Joseph and Rabbi Hasdai ibn Shaprut are translated in Yehuda Halevi, *The Kuzari: In Defense of the Despised Faith*, ed. and trans. N. Daniel Korobkin (Northvale, NJ: Jason Aronson, 1998), 341–57.

10. The fact that Alfonsi, Abelard, and Halevi each chose the literary form of a dialogue, or series of dialogues, to present their arguments should not go unappreciated. Indeed, it warrants special and detailed attention within the wider picture of medieval dialogue writing, twelfth-century thought, and the not-coincidental flourishing of the genre in the twelfth century, a subject currently the focus of my research but for reasons of space are not included in this chapter.

11. *Dialogi contra Iudaeos*, PL 157: col. 537. The only published modern edition of the work is contained in a Spanish translation, *Diálogo contra los judios*, ed. Klaus-Peter Mieth and trans. Esperanza Ducay (Huesca: Instituto de Estudios Altoaragoneses, 1996). The numerous typographical errors, however, prevent the edition from being a serious improvement over the *Patrologia Latina*.

12. One notes that it is Moses who approaches Peter for answers and not the other way around, as is typical of most disputational writings for this period.

13. *Dialogi*, col. 538.

14. Christian accusations of Jewish blindness have been well documented in the writings of Abulafia and Cohen.

15. Anselm's approach to proving his points *sola ratione* occurs principally in his most major oeuvre, *Cur Deus Homo*, a speculative work on divine nature that is also set in the framework of a dialogue with his student, Boso. Despite the reference to Jews in *Cur Deus Homo*, Abulafia challenges Anselm's participation in and immediate contribution to the Jewish–Christian debate, arguing instead that the phrase *sola ratione* refers to pagans alone, not to Jews. See Abulafia, "St. Anselm and Those Outside the Church," in *Faith and Unity: Christian Political Experience, Studies On Church History 6,* ed. D. Loades and Katherine Walsh (Oxford: Published for the Ecclesiastical History Society by B. Blackwell, 1990), 11–37. See also Amos Funkenstein, *Perceptions of Jewish History* (Berkeley: University of California Press, 1993), 178–81. For an alternate interpretation of Anselm's participation in the Jewish–Christian debate and what is intended by the phrase *sola ratione*, see Cohen, 175–79.

16. Tolan, *Petrus Alfonsi*, 34.

17. *Dialogi*, col. 555.

18. Ibid., col. 597.

19. Ibid., col. 597.

20. Ibid., col. 617.

21. Ibid., col. 617. Cf. Anselm, "Cur Deus Homo," in *Anselm of Canterbury,* vol. 3, trans. Jasper Hopkins and Herbert Richardson (Toronto: E. Mellen Press, 1975), I.1.

22. *Dialogi*, col. 606.

23. The definition of the Trinity by attributes originated in the Eastern Church, where the persons corresponded to essence, wisdom, and life. John Scotus Eriugena introduced this Eastern doctrine into the West in the ninth century, but his teaching was condemned. Abelard, in his *Theologia Christiana*, also proposed an attributist Trinitarian doctrine, which identified the Father as power (*potentia*), the Son as Wisdom (*sapientia*), and the Holy Spirit as goodness (*benignitas*), but this doctrine was similarly condemned at the Council of Sens in 1140.

24. Harry Wolfson, *The Philosophy of the Kalam* (Cambridge, MA: Harvard University Press, 1976), 236.

25. Daniel Lasker, *Jewish Philosophical Polemics against Christianity in the Middle Ages* (New York: Ktav Publishing House, 1977), 51–60; See also Colette Sirat, *A History of Jewish Philosophy in the Middle Ages* (Cambridge, UK: Cambridge University Press, 1985), especially chapters 2–4.

26. *Dialogi*, col. 607.

27. Alfonsi's logic seems to be this: Christianity does not require a justification by reason alone, since acceptance must come on faith. However, Christianity can be shown to accord with reason on the basis that there is nothing in the faith that contradicts reason. Since Alfonsi is arguing with an infidel this is what he aims to demonstrate. Conversely, Moses ought to abandon Judaism since it can be shown to contradict reason.

28. *Dialogi*, col. 672.

29. *Collationes*, p. 13.

30. Ibid., 15.

31. Ibid., 17–23.

32. Ibid., 15.

33. Ibid., 17.

34. Ibid., 19.

35. Ibid.

36. Ibid., 75–77.

37. Cf. Hans Liebeschütz, "The Significance of Judaism in Peter Abaelard's *Dialogus*," *Journal of Jewish Studies* 12 (1961): 7–8.

38. *Collationes*, 87.

39. Ibid., 89–91.

40. Ibid., 91–93.

41. Ibid., 89–91.

42. *Kuzari*, I.1, 5. The translation offered by Korobkin actually reads "intellectually stimulating rituals." This is taken from ibn Tibon's Hebrew translation of the Arabic original. Here I am following Leo Strauss, who gives "rational *nomoi*" as a translation from the Arabic. Strauss, "The Law of Reason in the *Kuzari*," in *Persecution and the Art of Writing*, ed. Strauss (Glencoe, IL: Free Press, 1952), 114. In a forthcoming translation of the *Kuzari* by B. Kogan and L. Berman for the Yale Judaica Series, Srauss gives a slight variation for that same phrase: "intellectual *nomoi* [that is, the laws]." Selections of this forthcoming translation have already appeared in Daniel H. Frank, Oliver Leaman, and Charles Henry Manekin, eds., *The Jewish Philosophy Reader* (London: Routledge, 2000), 203–214, 206.

43. The distinction between laws of nature and rational (or natural) laws is a fine one. An attempt to separate the two from each other is offered in the following chapter.

44. *Kuzari*, I.3, 7.

45. Strauss, "Law of Reason," 116.

46. *Kuzari*, I.1, 5.

47. H. Davidson, "The Active Intellect in the Cuzari and Halevi's Theory of Causality," *Revue des études juives* 131 (1972): 351–96. See also Harry Wolfson, "The Platonic, Aristotelian and Stoic Theories of Creation in Halevi and Maimonides," in *Studies in the History of Philosophy and Religion*, vol. 1, ed. Wolfson (Cambridge, MA: Harvard University Press, 1977), 234–49.

48. *Kuzari*, I.3, 7.

49. Ibid., I.5, 9.

50. He opposes them in I.81, 28. He approves of them in II.48, p. 94, III.7, p. 134, and V.19, 228–9.

51. Cf. Strauss, "Law of Reason," 118.

52. *Kuzari*, I.13, 12.

53. Ibid., I.67, 23.

54. Ibid., I.88, 33.

55. Ibid., I.35, 16.

56. Ibid., I.79, 26.

57. For a more adequate understanding of the relation between the rational *nomoi* of the philosophers and the rational *nomoi* of heretics and superstitious people, recourse should be had to Maimonides's *Guide to the Perplexed*. According to Maimonides, the Sabeans were a people of extreme ignorance and as remote from philosophy as possible. They were also given to many sorts of superstitious practices, yet, despite this, there existed "*nomoi* of the Sabeans," which were closely related to their "religion" and their superstitious habits represented forms of "political guidance." And so, as Maimonides points out, their willingness to assert the reality of the most strange things led to their belief in the eternity of the world, which in turn meant that they essentially agreed with the philosophers over the adherents of revealed religions. Maimonides, *Guide of the Perplexed,* ed. and Chaim Rabin (Indianapolis: Hackett Publishing Co., 1995), III.29, 175–80; Strauss, "Law of Reason," 124–25.

58. *Kuzari*, II.48, 94.

59. Cf. Cicero, *De officiis*, II.11; Cicero, *De republica*, III.14, III.24; Augustine, *De civitate dei*, IV.4.

60. Strauss, "Law of Reason," 128, n. 105.

61. *Collationes*, 3–9.

62. Ibid., 9. This forms part of the Philosopher's opening remarks to the Jew.

63. Ibid., 33.

64. Confusion arises in understanding how Abelard distinguishes between natural law, or what he defines as knowledge of morals instituted by God prior to scriptural law, and ethics, or what he earlier defined as the pursuit of the highest good. The distinction seems to be this: Natural law refers to morals that precede scriptural law, and ethics refers to morals founded on scriptural law.

65. *Collationes*, 55.

66. Cf. Abulafia, "*Intentio Recta an Erronea?* Peter Abelard's Views on Judaism and the Jews," in *Medieval Studies in Honour of Avrom Saltman*, ed. Bat-Sheva Albert et al. (Ramat Gan, Israel: Bar-Illan University Press, 1995), 28–30. According to Abulafia it is primarily Abelard's conception of the Christian faith and his philosophy that accounts for him being blind to Jewish spirituality. To this we may add his ideas of natural law, which the Philosopher is able to distinguish from scriptural law but the Jew is not.

67. *Collationes*, 79–81.
68. Ibid., 87, citing I Corinthians 1:22.
69. Marenbon, "Introduction," in *Collationes*, lxxviii.
70. Ibid., lxxix. See also Stefan Kuttner, "Sur les origines du term 'droit positif,'" *Revue historique du droit francais et étranger* 4e série 15 (1936): 728–40.
71. It is not inappropriate to describe the Christian as increasingly competent since the Philosopher's initial speeches set the tone and the parameters for the rest of the dialogue. It is only once the Philosopher articulates his points that the Christian succeeds in joining ranks with him on an intellectual level.
72. *Collationes*, 95.
73. Yochanan Silman, in his recent interpretation of Halevi, posits an overall theory that the *Kuzari* attests to a gradual evolution in Halevi's thought, moving from a position of moderate Aristotelianism to antiphilosophic Jewish piety. See Silman, *Philosopher and Prophet: Judah Halevi, the Kuzari, and the Evolution of His Thought*, trans. Lenn Schramm (Albany: State University of New York Press, 1995).
74. *Kuzari*, III.8–9, 135.
75. Ibid., III.11, 136–44.
76. Ibid., III.73, 197.
77. Ibid., I.109, 48.
78. Ibid.
79. Cf. ibid., II.32, 88–89.
80. However, as the Rabbi reminds us, the concrete destiny of the Jewish people does depend on their way of life. Ibid., I.109, 47–50.
81. In this the Philosopher seems to support the statement of the angel: namely, that understanding the relation between intention and action is the only important thing concerning the pursuit of proper living.
82. *Kuzari*, I.1, 5.
83. Ibid., I.57, 20. These ideas are retold by the Rabbi, who is presenting the Philosopher's arguments to then disprove them.
84. Cf. ibid., II.50, 96: "The Torah did not leave the details of the services up to the individual; everything was carefully prescribed. This is because man is incapable of determining what is necessary to rectify the faculties of the soul and body, or what measure of rest or activity is necessary…"
85. Silman, *Philosopher and Prophet*, 80.
86. *Kuzari,* V.10, 268.
87. Ibid., I.79, 27.
88. Given that for Abelard ethics entails the understanding and pursuit of morality, it seems safe to conclude that, in fact, both authors have a basic preoccupation with further grasping the moral values of their respective religion.
89. The relevance of this question is that an answer in the affirmative would seem to imply that duties toward God are grounded in a universal principle suggestive of natural law.
90. *Kuzari*, I.81, 28; I.83, 28–30. Strauss, "Law of Reason," 128, n. 107.
91. Strauss, "Law of Reason," 130.
92. *Kuzari*, II.48, 94.
93. Strauss, "Law of Reason," 132.
94. Tolan, *Petrus Alfonsi*, 103–7.
95. On this second approach to twelfth-century history, I am thinking particularly of the work of Gavin Langmuir.

8

The Jews in the *Golden Legend*

Thomas Renna

Why are there Jews in the lives of the saints? Though the image of the Jews in twelfth- and thirteenth-century Christian literature has been studied from many points of view, this role has barely been noticed in modern scholarship. Was there a hagiographical perspective on the Jews? Was the Jew simply a rhetorical *topos* or an actual reflection of attitudes toward the Jews at the time the *lives* were written? The concern in this chapter is with the function of the Jews within the genre of saints' lives, in particular in the most influential anthology of such *vitae*, the *Golden Legend* of the mid-thirteenth century.

Prior to the twelfth century, references to Jews in the lives of the saints are infrequent. The *vitae* show no interest in the *adversus Judaeus* tradition and the warnings to Christians not to adopt Jewish practices such as magic. They almost never distinguish between present-day Jews and biblical Jews, whether Old or New Testament. Patristic and early medieval commonplaces appear, as in the "cruel Jews,"[1] the "hatred of the Jews,"[2] "night of night,"[3] and "per ipsum Iudaeorum increpat turbam."[4] There are occasional references to Jewish converts.[5] All these casual references to Jews lack theological interpretation, as in Augustine's argument that the Jews must survive until the end of time because they give witness, by their scriptures, to the truth of the Christian faith.[6] The Jews should continue to observe the Torah, according to Augustine, and should continue as a protected people. Christians should not hinder the Jews in their faithfulness to their ancestral customs. It need not be surprising that stereotypes about the Jews had not penetrated much into saints' lives, given the occasional tension in the late Roman Empire between Christians and Jews caused by imperial legislation, Christian polemics, proselytizing among pagans by both Christians and Jews, attempts by Christians and Jews to convert each other, and Judaizing by Christians. Patristic commonplaces were slow in becoming *exempla* for pulpit sermons. The Jews stand on the edges of hagiographical writing, of little interest to those who exalted their Christian heroes. It could be argued that in some places, such as England, actual contacts influenced at least a few lives of the saints.[7]

After 1100 the Jews figure more prominently in Christian sources, particularly in scriptural exegesis,[8] sermons, liturgy, and anti-Jewish tracts. Modern scholars sharply disagree on how much of this interest in the Jews was the result of actual contact with Jews, such as in business transactions, of the attacks on Jewish communities during the First Crusade, of the Christian–Jewish open debates, particularly in Spain, or of popular antagonism against Jews sparked by incidents such as the blood libel accusations.[9] Whatever the role of contemporary Jews in the formation of Christian attitudes toward them, it was perhaps inevitable that Jews would appear in saints' lives, the number of which increased in the twelfth and thirteenth centuries. At the least, one might expect biblical Jews to be marshaled in *vitae* and sermons as types of behavior to avoid.

One story was particularly influential in vivifying the heritage of the Jews who denied the Messiahship of Jesus at the time of his crucifixion: the discovery of the True Cross. The legend was to enjoy a prominent place in the liturgy, literature, and art — witness Piero della Francesca's frescoes in Arezzo — of the High Middle Ages.[10] The legend is revealing about attitudes toward the Jews because of the biblical and patristic association with the Jews and the Cross and also with Helena, the mother of Constantine. In the medieval retelling of the legend the role of the Jew who reveals the Cross becomes increasingly central to the tale. This Jew was no less than the personification of the Jewish people. The fate of the story of the True Cross in saints' lives serves as an index of hagiographical attitudes toward the Jews.

Sometime during 350 to 450 CE three versions of the legend of the discovery of the True Cross originated and circulated. In the legend of Helena, mother of Constantine, three crosses were found with the assistance of Marcarius, bishop of Jerusalem.[11] She had the Church of the Holy Sepulcher built over the site. Constantine made a horse's bridle out of the nails. The Protonike legend links the discovery of the Cross to the founding of the church at Edessa. Protonike, a convert from Rome, went to Jerusalem in search of the Cross, and contact with the True Cross brought Protonike's daughter back to life.

The third version of the legend, the Judas Kyriakos, is by far the most influential in the Western understanding of the discovery of the Cross.[12] In this story the role of Helena is eclipsed by Judas Kyriakos, who emerges as the key figure. When Helena arrived in Jerusalem she summoned the leading Jewish experts in the Law and berated them for not accepting Jesus as the Messiah.[13] Then one of them, Judas, told the story of his grandfather, who told of how the discovery of the True Cross would effectively abolish the Law and the kingdom of the Jews and would assure the victory of the Christians. When Helena threatened to burn the legal experts if they did not reveal the location of the Cross, they relented and handed over Judas, who hesitated to show her the place. To compel him to reveal the location of the Cross, Helena threw Judas into a well for seven days, after which time he agreed to lead her to the place where the Cross was buried. After Judas prayed that God might reveal this place, he began to dig and quickly found three crosses. To determine which of the three was the cross of Jesus, a corpse was brought to the crosses; the raising of the dead man identified the True Cross. When a demon was cast out of a possessed person, Satan complained that the "second Judas" threatened to undo the betrayal of the first Judas. Astounded by the faith of Judas, Helena put the Cross in a silver casket and had Judas baptized and entrusted to the bishop. Pope Eusebius then made him bishop of Jerusalem, with the new name of Cyriacus. Not content with just the cross, Helena searched for the holy nails, with which "the Jews" had crucified Jesus. When Cyriacus prayed for their discovery, a flash of light from heaven revealed where they were. This miracle caused many Jews to convert to Christ. Helena had the nails made into the bit of Constantine's horse so that he might conquer all his enemies to put an end to all war. Helena had expelled from Jerusalem any Jews who refused to accept the faith. Cyriacus's intercessory prayers drove out the demons and cured many who were sick. Helena ordered all believers to commemorate the finding of the cross every year for all time.

It is clear that in this revised version of the original Helena legend the role of the new figure, Judas, becomes pivotal. The Cross somehow became the story of the Jews, who are generally portrayed as obstinate in their reluctance to accept Christ as the Messiah. For the Jews the Cross seemed incompatible with the Messiah they had come to expect. There is considerable disagreement among modern scholars as to the reasons why the discovery of the Cross story was incorporated into a stock *adversus Judaeos* tract.[14] Though the arguments in favor of the use of force against the Jews were certainly present and even with implicit warnings against Judaizing, the primary purpose of the revised tale is likely to have been to exhort Jews in Palestine and elsewhere to convert to the Christian faith.[15] But why this sermonette in the context of the Holy Cross? Because in the mind of the compilers of the story, the Cross contains the entire mystery of salvation; the cross is also the chief obstacle to the conversion of the Jews.

From the point of view of the later hagiographical rendering of the True Cross, the important element in the Cyriacus legend is the role of Judas, the convert from Judaism — clearly intended to be the representative of all Jews, and a counterpoint to the betrayer Judas Iscariot. Important elements from the legend include the miracles produced by the power of the Cross, the miracle effected by Judas to discover the Cross in the first place, the salutary effects the miracles have on the Jews present, and the perfect sanctity of the now transformed Judas. It seems odd, nevertheless, that the Western liturgy did not make more use of the legend about Judas and the True Cross.[16] One way the legend of the finding of the cross survived was its connection with Pope Sylvester I, who cured Constantine of leprosy and became associated with the famous forgery, the Donation of Constantine.[17] In the Western liturgy the discovery of the physical cross was much less important than what it symbolized: the redemption of humankind. Very early in the liturgy the cross was integrated in public and private prayer and was intimately connected with baptism and the Eucharist.[18] Particularly influential in the Middle Ages were the striking images used by Augustine, such as the cross as mousetrap, which emphasizes the cross as the sign of Christ's compassion and humility, a sign humans were to imitate.[19] The cross, furthermore, became increasingly important in the West as a symbol of Christ's triumph over sin, death, and Satan.[20] More important, however, than the liturgy in the transmission of the story were the sermons,[21] which preachers used to explore the homiletic possibilities of this ancient theme of conversion. Certainly the sermons were what formed the link with saints' lives in the twelfth and thirteenth centuries.

It must be emphasized that anti-Jewish themes intensified in many types of literature before the thirteenth century. Traditional patristic and early medieval stereotypes can be found in the lives of the saints. The monk Aelfric of Eysnham (c. 955–c. 1020) collected homilies — in the collection *Lives of the Saints* — which exhibit anti-Jewish motives.[22] The Jews are accused of being carnal by nature, killing Christ, and being spiritually blind. Interestingly, Aelfric repeated Augustine's assertions about the Jews' important role in the history of salvation: They will be converted before the Second Coming. The people of the new covenant have replaced those of the old covenant. In his sermon on the exaltation of the Holy Cross[23] Judas and the Jews conspired to hide the Cross as a way of continuing the persecution of the Christians. Many of these anti-Jewish themes can found in French literature a century later.[24] Blame for the Passion of Christ often falls on the Jews, not on the Roman authorities. Following the appearance of the blood libel accusations[25] there are more references to the power of the Eucharist to effect conversions to Christianity. The Jew in these *exempla* is often a rhetorical set piece intended to deepen the faith of Christian readers and listeners. When Jews attempt to abuse a cross, they are often converted by the miracle that follows, such as an outpouring of blood. The emphasis in these stories is not on the perfidy of the Jews but on the power of God to effect conversions.[26] The Christian listener is thus exhorted to trust in God. These conversion themes increased considerably in the thirteenth century with the renewed papal directives to clerics to preach and to hear confessions. The penitential homily was the inevitable result.

With regard to the Jews and the Cross they were portrayed both negatively and positively. Negative portrayals emerged because the Cross represented the major obstacle to the conversion of the Jews, who would not accept Christ as the Messiah and *a fortiori* as a crucified Messiah. This theme receives increased attention afterward with the spread of apocalyptic expectations and the accompanying belief that the Jews must be converted before the end time. They were shown positively because of the power of the Cross to convert Jews and thereby to hasten the fulfillment of God's salvific plan. It must be stressed that the saints' lives in the

Golden Legend were compiled, revised, and composed at a time when anti-Jewish motifs were prominent in art, polemic literature, sermons, and secular and ecclesiastical legislation, not to mention attacks on the Talmud and concerted attempts to convert Jews. As one would expect, then, the traditional anti-Jewish *topoi* become incorporated into the literary requirements of the hagiographical genre.

The saints' lives of the thirteenth century must be viewed in the context of the "growth of a Christo-centric piety with increased emphasis on the humanity of Christ."[27] The new interest in "Christ's humanity led to an intense hunger to know the details of his earthly life,...especially his suffering and death." One result of this new piety was the "increased attention paid to those who were perceived to be Christ's enemies during his life on earth, namely the Jews."[28] In the Passion narratives the Jews are often portrayed as the cause of Christ's torments. Jews seek to reenact the Crucifixion "through the infliction of wounds upon images of Christ."[29] The literal reading of the Passion was given close attention. With this intense interest in seeking to identify with Christ crucified and his sufferings, it is understandable that those who were allegedly responsible — as in much of the received tradition — would be seen negatively. If the stress is on penitential conversion, those who will not convert will be seen as outsiders. Thus, the *Golden Legend* was composed at a time of heightened hostility toward the Jews. Much of this antagonism was, to be sure, directed against biblical Jews. But living Jews were sometimes targeted, as can be seen in the legal restrictions on the Jews' movement, commerce, contacts with Christians, as well as the obligatory sermons aimed at Jewish conversion, and the public debates. Jews were sometimes associated with heretics, infidels, demons, and witches.

Though many of the allusions to Jews in the *Golden Legend* are conventional, the tone of these commonplaces is subdued and shows "noticeable restraint."[30] Certain themes predominate. In the *vita* of St. Nicholas of Bari, a Jew accepts baptism after seeing a dead man raised to life by the intercession of the saint.[31] Another Jew made a statue of St. Nicholas but smashed it when Nicholas failed to protect his house from thieves.[32] After Nicholas threatened the thieves for "beating" him, the Jew converted to Christ on hearing of the robbers' vision. In the tale of St. Stephen, the first martyr, the Jews, jealous of Stephen's power to perform miracles, tried to discredit him by argument, false witnesses, and torture.[33] Stephen accused the Jews of being stiff-necked and of refusing to accept their own prophets of old. He attempted but failed to convert his accusers by shame, fear, and love. Citing the *Glossa Ordinaria* and St. Augustine, Jacobus's retelling of the first martyr emphasizes not the Jews' hatred of Stephen but his Christ-like behavior and the miracles performed after his death.[34]

A prelude in the *Golden Legend* to the *Inventio Crucis* is the lengthy account of Saint Sylvester, who cured Constantine of leprosy.[35] Jacobus seems not to have noticed the inconsistencies between his account of Helena and his narrative about her in the "Exultation of the Cross." In the Sylvester story the twelve Jewish doctors present their case against the Christians one by one. But the issue is decided not by verbal discourse but by a contest, reminiscent of the prophet Daniel, between wonder workers over who can bring a dead bull back from death and who can tame a ferocious dragon.[36] Since Sylvester wins on both counts, Helena, the Jews, the pagans, and the bystanders are converted to the faith. The story ends on a hagiographical note typical of the *Golden Legend*: the clergy are exhorted to be worthy pastors of the faithful. Thus, the learned Jews in the tale are not the object of attack but are merely the occasion that brings out the miracle-working sanctity of Sylvester. Also, Jacobus of the Order of Preachers seems to be gently mocking his scholastic contemporaries who naively believe they can convert Jews and infidels by reason alone.[37] In the end the very hagiographical solution of divine intervention produces the desired result.

Certainly anti-Jewish commonplaces abound in the *Golden Legend*. In the "Epiphany" the Jews knew the place where Christ was to be born yet took no trouble to find it.[38] The "impious Jews" beat up the apostle Barnabas and burned Eusebius out of fear that the latter would release him.[39] Repeating a well-known tale in the High Middle Ages, the account of the Assumption of the Virgin tells of a Jewish father who threw his son into a furnace for going to church and receiving Holy Communion.[40] But the Virgin Mary saved the boy, whereupon the local Christians threw the father into the furnace. In the "Life of Bartholomew" a demon in hell says that the Jews crucified Christ "thinking that they could put an end to him by death."[41] In "Saints Simon and Jude, Apostles" the Jews murmur against Jesus and plot to kill him.[42]

Nowhere in the *Golden Legend* are the Jews more prominent than in the entries about the Cross. In the *Golden Legend*'s version of the exaltation of the Holy Cross a Jew stabs an image of Christ in the Church of St. Sophia in Constantinople.[43] When blood pours out of the image and splatters him, he becomes terrified and flees. When a Christian outside, seeing the blood, accuses the Jew of having committed murder, the Jew immediately converts to the Christian faith, so astounded is he by this miracle of the outpouring of blood. This account of the Cross in the *Golden Legend* continues with another story about a Jew who inadvertently kept a picture of Christ in his house.[44] When the local Jews were informed of the picture, they threw the man out of his house and trampled the image and "renewed upon it all the indignities of the Lord's passion. When they thrust a lance into the image of his body, a copious flow of blood and water issued from it and they filled a vase that they held under it."[45] They took the blood to their synagogues, and all the sick anointed with it were cured. The Jews told the bishop about these events and thereupon accepted the faith and baptism. It turns out that the picture of Christ was eventually taken out of Jerusalem to the kingdom of Agrippa, where the Jews were then turning their synagogues into churches. Jacobus de Voragine added that the power of the Cross is such that even in later centuries, many non-Christians, including Jews, continued to be converted by the miraculous effects of the Cross. A certain Jew made the sign of the cross to protect him while he was inside a pagan temple. After this sign drove away the evil spirits, the Jew accepted baptism by the local bishop.[46]

The finding of the Holy Cross in the *Golden Legend* largely follows the revised Helena legend.[47] The role of Judas, however, is somewhat magnified. What was originally a variant of an *adversus Judaeos* composite of a Helena legend and an anti-Jewish tract becomes a sort of saint's life, the saint being the Jew who converted to Christianity. Judas here clearly symbolizes the totality of the Jewish people, the counterpoise to Judas the betrayer. To indicate the change to saint-hood, Judas's name is changed to Quiriacus. The anti-Jewish harangue of Helena gets lost in the edifying story of Bishop Quiriacus, who is martyred because he discovered the True Cross. Thus, the story is another example of the power of the Cross. The bishop is the occasion of the conversion of Jews to the Christian faith. Nowhere else in the *Golden Legend* does a Jew become so integrated into a conventional life of a saint. Even the devil admits that Quiriacus is making converts and that soon he, the devil, will be expelled from his realm.[48] Judas not only ceases to be a Jew but has been transformed into the model Christian. Lest the reader forget that this entire episode about Judas is about the power of the Cross, Jacobus noted that Emperor Julian the Apostate put Quiriacus to death precisely because the bishop interfered with his campaign "to destroy the cross."[49] It is doubtful that Jacobus directed this story of Judas specifically at the actual Jews of his day. More likely, the story of the Cross was intended for Christian preachers, including Dominicans, who were to exhort Christians to improve their lives. It is these Christian preachers, moreover, who would bring the gospel to the Jews. What causes conversions, according to Jacobus, is not verbal argument, however, but the example of holy Christians and their miraculous intercessory powers. The received anti-Jewish tradition is largely absorbed into the lives of the saints. It might be added that another motive of Jacobus in narrating the story of the True Cross was to urge Christians to observe the liturgical commemorations of feasts relating to the discovery of the Cross.

On the basis on these stories about the True Cross, can we conclude that the author of the *Golden Legend* expected all Jews to be eventually converted to the Christian faith? Did Jacobus classify Jews as a single group of "the Jews," reminiscent of the Fourth Gospel, in the patristic image of the biblical hard-hearted Jews who refused to accept Jesus as the Messiah? Did Jacobus believe that most or at least some the Jews were capable of being saved? It would seem *prima facie* that at least some Jews will not accept Jesus, even when proof is presented from their own scriptures. The Jewish leaders' resistance to the arguments of the first martyr Stephen concerning the Mosaic Law is one notable example of this reluctance. Yet when the stories of the Cross are considered as a whole along with the other references to Jews throughout the *Golden Legend*, the overwhelming impression is that the Jews are prepared to be converted, if not by rational argument then at least by the authority of miracles. Some Jewish leaders might be hostile, but clearly most Jews are amenable to the faith. This notion of some Jews as more inclined to convert was in fact common among the schoolmen of the thirteenth century. Thomas Aquinas distinguished three personality types among the Israelites: the obstinate, the ordinary, and the excellent — with the latter category being those for whom the ritual commandments functioned as mystical signs, whereas the "moral precepts assured them that their actions were upright."[50] Aquinas was very much aware of the difference between the Jews of the Old Testament and the Jews of the first century. He clearly distinguished between the elite (*majores* or *principes* or *sapientes*) and ordinary Jews at the time of Christ.[51] He usually associated this elite with the Pharisees,[52] although there was a tendency among some early medieval Bible commentators to identify the Jews with the Pharisees.[53] It has been plausibly argued that many Christians in the twelfth and thirteenth centuries were suspicious of Jewish converts, as if the latter somehow remained Jewish even after their conversion.[54] But in the *Golden Legend* the Jews who accept the Christian faith are invariably sincere in their conversion. There is no suggestion that the converts retained an attachment to their ancestral beliefs, culture, and blood ties. Judaism is treated strictly as a religion. Indeed, some, like Judas, became archetypical Christians. Though the historian can never be certain, it would seem that Jacobus's occasional anti-Jewish stereotypes were not intended to attack Jews — whether thirteenth century, first century, or under the Old Law — but to imply that the Jews are disposed to convert to the Christian faith. The old dispensation, Jacobus seems to be saying, was close to disappearing within the new dispensation. Finally, it is possible that Jacobus was influenced by the widespread belief that the Jews must be converted in the final stages of human history.[55]

Does the *Golden Legend* indicate a new attitude toward the Jews, or at least a view that was out of step with Jacobus's contemporaries? Not really, although the anti-Jewish polemic is certainly understated in the *Golden Legend*. Nor does this collection tell the historian anything about attitudes toward the Jews in mid-thirteenth century Europe, except perhaps in the author's conviction that Christians should preach to Jews and that the latter are receptive to conversion — a view not always shared at the time. Possibly Jacobus and some of his mendicant colleagues believed that the end times were approaching, and that Christians must intensify their efforts to convert the Jews to hasten the fulfillment of the divine plan. But there is nothing explicit about this view in the *Golden Legend*. At the least, Jacobus seems convinced that the Jews should be converted and that they are willing to listen. It might be noted that many of the Jews in the lives are contemporaries of the saint being discussed in addition to the biblical Jews of old. The patristic early medieval penchant to classify biblical Jews and all Jews since then as the Jews is considerably diminished in the *Golden Legend*.

The *Golden Legend*, as well as saints' lives in general prior to this work, is probably not a major source for Christian attitudes toward the Jews in the thirteenth century. But the legend's treatment of Jews reveals much about contemporary hagiography. Here the Jews are not simply *exempla* in sermon-like stories intended to edify readers and listeners. But the Jews to some extent have been integrated into the figure of the Christian saint, particularly in the legends about the True Cross. The patristic vision of the church as having two complementary parts, the Church of the Gentiles and the Church of the Circumcision, which would be reunited before the Second Coming of Christ, finds its hagiographical expression in the *vitae* of the saints. More precisely, one half of the church universal (the two halves are symbolized by Bethlehem and the celestial Jerusalem in apse mosaics in Italy, particularly in Rome) loses its identity and merges into the Church of Bethlehem. But the primary hagiographical function of this use of anti-Jewish commonplaces is not to convert the Jew, but rather to convert the Christians, that is, to exhort them to take their faith more seriously. God offers models of sanctity from everywhere, even from the Old Law. Strangely enough, this blending of the old and new dispensations in the *Golden Legend* appears in the context of an increased polemic against the Jews. The lives of the saints sought to restore the balance with moderation and quiet conviction.

Notes

1. Iudeos saevos, in Ursinus episcopus Biturigensis; Acta Sanctorum (AA.SS), Nov. IV, Dies 9, col. 109C. I used the AA.SS data base (Proquest) at the University of Michigan under the keywords: iudeos, judeus, iudaeus, iudaeorum, iudaei, and variants.
2. AA.SS, Nov. III, Dies 5, De SS. Zacharia et Elisabeth Parentibus S. Iohannis Baptistae., c. 2, 4: Fama communior: Zachariam, col. 11B.
3. "Unde bene per prophetam dicitur: 'Dies diei eructat verbum, et nox nocti incidat scientam.' Quasi dicat: "Dies diei,' hoc est, christianus christiano, 'et nox nocti,' hoc est, Iudaeus Iudae." Nov II Pars I, Dies 4, De SS. Agricola et Vitali Martyribus Bononiae. Epistula S. Ambrosio attributa de Martyrio SS. Agricolae et Vitalis, col. 248A; Nov II Pars I, Dies 4, col. 277. The "perfidious Jews," a patristic commonplace, seldom occurs in thirteenth-century saints' lives. See Venerabilis Virgo Ida de Lovanio, Sanctimonialis Ordinis Cisterciensis, Liber I, C. II Contra diaboli tentationes Christi passio assumpta. Penitentiae; Apr. II, Dies 13; cf. Oct IX, Dies 22, S. Nunilo soror, Oscae in Hispania, col. 838D.
4. AA.SS, Nov IV, Dies 10, De Sanctis Tryphone. VIII. Passio SS. Tryphonis et Respicii A. Theodorico Monacho, col. 370C. Julian the Apostate is an "alter-Judas"; Nov III, Dies 6, De Sancto Leonardo Confessore. I. Vita et Miracula S. Leonardi, col. 164C: "Non hic imperator christianus, sed haereticus vesanus, Iulianus apostata, alter Iudas, Iudaeorum compar, qui pacem simulans bellum concitat, in fratres sicarius, in Christum Herodes cruentissimus..."
5. AA.SS, Apr. IX, De SS. Iudaeis, ad fidem conversis, Marrtyibus Leontinis in Sicilia, col. 810; Apr. I, Dies 9, col. 819A. Nov IV, Dies 10, De S. Martyrinao seu Mari De Beth-Sahde Martyre, col. 442DF (the well-known story of the Jewish leper).

6. Michael Signer, "Jews and Judaism," in *Augustine Through the Ages: An Encyclopedia,* ed. Allan D. Fitzgerald (Cambridge, UK: William B. Eerdmans, 1999), 470–74; Gedaliahu Stroumsa, "From Anti-Judaism to Anti-Semitism in Early Christianity in 'Contra Iudaeos,'" in *Ancient and Medieval Polemics Between Christians and Jews,* ed. Ora Limor and Gedaliahu Stroumsa (Tübingen: J.C.B. Mohr, 1996), 1–26; Paula Fredriksen, "Excaecati Occulta Justitia Dei: Augustine on Jews and Judaism," *Journal of Early Christian Studies* 3 (1995): 299–324; Pier Bori, "The Church's Attitude Towards the Jews: An Analysis of Augustine's 'Adversus Iudaeos,'" in *Miscellanea Historiae Ecclesiasticae* VI, 1 *Bibliotheque de la Revue d'Histoire Ecclesiastique* 67 (Brussels: Editions Nauwelaerts, 1983), 301–11; Lisa Untereseher, "The Mark of Cain and the Jews: Augustine's Theology of Jews," *Augustinian Studies* 33 (2002): 99–121; Marcel Dubois, "Jews, Judaism and Israel in the Theology of Saint Augustine: How He Links the Jewish People and the Land of Zion," *Immanuel* 22–23 (1989): 162–214.

7. See Andrew Scheil, "Anti-Judaism in Aelfric's *Lives of Saints,*" *Anglo-Saxon England* 28 (1999): 65–86.

8. See Signer, "The *Glossa Ordinaria* and the Transmission of Medieval Anti-Judaism," in *A Distinct Voice: Medieval Studies in Honor of Leonard E. Boyle, O.P.,* ed. Jaqueline Brown and William P. Stoneman (Notre Dame, IN: University of Notre Dame Press, 1997), 591–605; Jeremy Cohen, "The Jews as the Killers of Christ in the Latin Tradition: From Augustine to the Friars," *Traditio* 39 (1983): 1–27. Personally I think Cohen overstates the alleged newness of the anti-Jewish polemic in the thirteenth century, as he also does in Cohen, *The Friars and the Jews: The Evolution of Medieval Anti-Judaism* (Ithaca, NY: Cornell University Press, 1982).

9. The bibliography on this question of Christian–Jewish contacts in the twelfth century is immense. A good place to start is John van Engen, "Introduction," in Signer and van Engen; Gilbert Dahan, *The Christian Polemic Against the Jews in the Middle Ages,* trans. Jody Gladding (Notre Dame, IN: University of Notre Dame Press, 1998), chap. 3 — as the title indicates, this study focuses on the polemical literature. See also David Berger, "Mission to the Jews and Jewish–Christian Contacts in the Polemical Literature of the High Middle Ages," *American Historical Review* 91 (1986): 576–91.

10. See E. D. Hunt, *Holy Land Pilgrimage in the Later Roman Empire, AD 312–460* (Oxford: Clarendon Press, 1982), chap. 2; Joseph Vogt, "Helena Augusta: das Kreuz und die Juden. Fragen um die Mutter Constantins des Grossen," *Saeculum: Jahrbuch für Universalgeschichte* 27 (1976): 211–22; H. Drake, "Eusebius on the True Cross," *Journal of Ecclesiastical History* 36 (1985): 1–22; Han J. W. and Jan W. Drijvers, *The Finding of the True Cross: The Judas Kyriakos Legend in Syriac,* Corpus Scriptorum Christianorum Orientalium 565, Subsidia 93 (Louvain: In Aedibus Peeters, 1997); Jan W. Drijvers, *Helena Augusta: The Mother of Constantine the Great and Her Finding of the True Cross,* rev. ed., Dutch thesis as *Helena Augusta: Waarheid en Legende* (University of Groningen, 1989. Leiden/New York/Copenhagen/Cologne: E. J. Brill 1992), esp. final chap.; fundamental, and the most relevant for our purposes here, is Stephan Borgehammar, *How the Holy Cross Was Found: From Event to Medieval Legend,* Bibliotheca Theologiae Practicae 47 (Stockholm: Almquist & Wiksell International, 1991).

11. Drijvers and Drijvers, *Finding of the True Cross,* 13–14.

12. Ibid., 20–29; Borgehammar, *How the Holy Cross Was Found,* chaps. 8, 9.

13. The best Latin edition and translations are in Borgehammar as "Inventio sanctae crucis A" in the appendix to *How the Holy Cross Was Found*, 255–302.

14. See Stefan Heid, "Der Ursprung der Helenalegende im Pilgerbetrieb Jerusalems," *Jahrbuch für Antike und Christentum* 32 (1989): 41–71; Drijvers, *Helena Augusta*, 187–231; Amnon Linder, "Ecclesia and Synagoga in the Medieval Myth of Constantine the Great," *Revue belge de philologie d'histoire* 54 (1976): 1019–60; Günter Stemberger, *Juden und Christen im Heiligen Land. Palästine unter Konstantin und Theodosius* (Münich: C. H. Beck, 1987), 251; Borgehammar, *How the Holy Cross Was Found*, 161–73.

15. This is the view offered by Drijvers and Drijvers, *Finding of the True Cross*, 28–29, an interpretation I find plausible.

16. See Borgehammar, *How the Holy Cross Was Found*, 189–94.

17. See *Inventio Crucis* C in Borgehammar, appendix, 294–302.

18. See Nathan D. Mitchell, "Washed Away by the Blood of God," in *The Cross in Christian Tradition: From Paul to Bonaventure,* ed. Elizabeth A. Dreyer (New York: Paulist Press, 2000), 51–71; Mitchell, "The Cross that Spoke," in ibid., 72–92. See also Peter J. Gorday, "Becoming Truly Human: Origen's Theology of the Cross," in ibid., 93–125; Gorday, "The Martyr's Cross: Origen and Redemption," in ibid., 126–46 on Origen's understanding of the cross as a sign of martyrdom and the expression of the virtue of faith.

19. See John Cavadini, "'The Tree of Silly Fruit': Images of the Cross in St. Augustine," in Dreyer, *Cross in Christian Tradition*, 147–68; Cavadini, "Jesus' Death is Real: An Augustinian Spirituality of the Cross," in ibid., 169–91.

20. See Gerardus Reijners, *The Terminology of the Holy Cross in Early Christian Literature* Graecitas Christianorum primaeva 2 (Nijmegen: Dekker & Van de Vegt, 1965), 192–93; Borgehammar, *How the Holy Cross Was Found*, 192–94; Celia Chazelle, *The Crucified God in the Carolingian Era: Theology and Art of Christ's Passion* (Cambridge, UK: Cambridge University Press, 2001), 99–131.

21. See Borgehammar, *How the Holy Cross Was Found*, 191–92. Sermons on feast days of saints often retold the legend associated with the saint. Numerous examples of anti-Jewish motifs in sermons in Joan Young Gregg, *Devils, Women, and Jews: Reflections of the Other in Medieval Sermon Stories*, SUNY Series in Medieval Studies, ed. Paul Szarmach (Albany: State University of New York Press, 1997), chap. 4.

22. See Borgehammar, *How the Holy Cross Was Found*, 191–92; Scheil, "Anti-Judaism."

23. Scheil, "Anti-Judaism," 69–70.

24. See Maureen Boulton, "Anti-Jewish Attitudes in Twelfth-Century French Literature," in Signer and Van Engen, 234–54.

25. See articles on the legend in Britain in Alan Dundes, ed., *The Blood Libel Legend* (Madison: University of Wisconsin Press, 1991); Miri Rubin, *Gentiles Tales: The Narrative Assault on Late Medieval Jews* (New Haven, CT: Yale University Press, 1999), chaps. 1, 2.

26. Numerous examples in Jacques Le Goff, "Le Juif dans les *exempla* médiévaux: le cas de *l'Alphabetum Narrationum*," in *Pour Léon Poliakov: le racisme mythes et sciences,* ed. Maurice Olender (Brussels: Editions Complexe, 1981), 209–20; Gregg, *Devils, Women, and Jews*, chap. 4. See also Valerie I. J. Flint, "Anti-Jewish Literature and Attitudes in the Twelfth Century," *Journal of Jewish Studies* 37 (1986):

39–57, 183–205; Gilbert Dahan, *Les intellectuels chrétiens et les juifs au moyen âge* (Paris: Editions du Cerf, 1990); David Berger, "The Attitude of St. Bernard of Clairvaux toward the Jews," *Proceedings of the American Academy for Jewish Research* 40 (1974): 89–108 (perhaps overstates Bernard's "hatred" of the Jews and its effects on later attitudes toward the Jews); Cohen, "'Witnesses of Our Redemption:' The Jews in the Crusading Theology of Bernard of Clairvaux," in *Medieval Studies in Honour of Avrom Saltman*, Bar-Ilan Studies in History 4 (Ramat-Gan: Bar-Ilan University Press, 1995), 67–81.

27. Thomas H. Bestul, *Texts of the Passion: Latin Devotional Literature and Medieval Society* (Philadelphia: University of Pennsylvania Press, 1996), 71 (chap. 3); this entire chapter deals with the representation of the Jews in the Passion narratives. See also Dahan, "Saint Bonaventure et les juifs," *Archivum Franciscanum Historicum* 77 (1984): 369–405.

28. Bestul, *Texts of the Passion*, 71.

29. Ellen M. Ross, *The Grief of God: Images of the Suffering Jesus in Late Medieval England* (New York: Oxford University Press, 1997), 20, 74.

30. Sherry L. Reames, *The Legenda aurea: A Reexamination of Its Paradoxical History* (Madison: University of Wisconsin Press, 1985), 262, n. 9. I completely agree with Reames's assessment. Even to say "anti-Jewish" would be to exaggerate the role of the Jews in the *Golden Legend*.

31. Jacobus de Voragine, *The Golden Legend: Readings on the Saints*, trans. W. G. Ryan (Princeton, NJ: Princeton University Press, 1993), vol. 1, chap. 3, St. Nicholas, 25–27; G. P. Maggioni, ed., Iacopo da Varazze, *Legenda Aurea* (Florence: SISMEL Edizioni Del Galluzzo, 1998), vol. 1, 44.

32. de Voragine, *Golden Legend*, I, 26; Maggioni, *Legenda Aurea*, I, 45.

33. de Voragine, *Golden Legend*, I, 45–50; Maggioni *Legenda Aurea*, I, 78–86.

34. de Voragine, *Golden Legend*, I, 48–50; Maggioni *Legenda Aurea*, I, 83–86.

35. de Voragine, *Golden Legend*, I, 62–71; Maggioni *Legenda Aurea*, I, 108–19.

36. de Voragine, *Golden Legend*, I, 70; Maggioni *Legenda Aurea*, I, 117–19.

37. For a discussion of Jacobus's conservative nature see Reames, *Legenda Aurea*, chap. 6.

38. de Voragine, *Golden Legend*, I, 79; Maggioni, *Legenda Aurea*, I, 132–35.

39. de Voragine, *Golden Legend*, I, 321; Maggioni, *Legenda Aurea*, I, 527.

40. de Voragine, *Golden Legend*, II, 87; Maggioni, *Legenda Aurea*, II, 796.

41. de Voragine, *Golden Legend*, II, 111; Maggioni, *Legenda Aurea*, II, 833.

42. de Voragine, *Golden Legend*, II, 261; Maggioni, *Legenda Aurea*, II, 1080.

43. de Voragine, *Golden Legend*, II, 170–71; Maggioni, *Legenda Aurea*, II, 933–34. The details about King Chosroës and Heraclius became immortalized in the fresco cycle by Piero della Francesca.

44. de Voragine, *Golden Legend*, II, 171–72; Maggioni, *Legenda Aurea*, II, 934–35.

45. de Voragine, *Golden Legend*, II, 171; Maggioni, *Legenda Aurea*, II, 935.

46. de Voragine, *Golden Legend*, II, 172; Maggioni, *Legenda Aurea*, II, 936.

47. de Voragine, *Golden Legend*, I, 277–84; Maggioni, *Legenda Aurea*, I, 459–70.

48. de Voragine, *Golden Legend*, I, 282; Maggioni, *Legenda Aurea*, I, 467.

49. de Voragine, *Golden Legend*, I, 283; Maggioni, *Legenda Aurea*, I, 469. For good measure, the story of the finding of the Holy Cross concludes with the tale of the Christian notary who vanquished demons by the sign of the cross, thereby displaying the power of the cross. Julian the Apostate learned the power of the cross when

he was a child, although he employed the power to drive out demons by having recourse to magic; de Voragine, *Golden Legend*, I, 129 (Saint Julian); Maggioni, *Legenda Aurea*, I, 215.

50. John Y. B. Hood, *Aquinas and the Jews* (Philadelphia: University of Pennsylvania Press, 1995), 42. This is the best study of Aquinas and the Jews in any language. See also Alexander Broadie, "Medieval Jewry Through the Eyes of Aquinas," in *Aquinas and the Problems of His Time*, ed. Gérard Verbeke and Daniel Verhelst (Louvain: Louvain University Press, 1976), 57–69; Bernhard Blumenkranz, "Augustin et les juifs; Augustin et le judaisme," *Recherches Augustiniennes* 1 (1958): 225–41; Hans Liebeschütz, "Judaism and Jewry in the Social Doctrine of Thomas Aquinas," *Journal of Jewish Studies* 12 (1961): 57–81; Beryl Smalley, "William of Auvergne, John of La Rochelle, and Thomas Aquinas on the Old Law," in *St. Thomas Aquinas Commemorative Studies*, ed. Armand Mauer et al. (Toronto: Pontifical Institute for Mediaeval Studies 1974), 11–71.

51. See Hood, *Aquinas and the Jews*, 64. A century earlier Abelard argued that the philosophers were closer to the natural law than were the Jews; Liebeschütz, "The Significance of Judaism in Peter Abelard's *Dialogus*," *Journal of Jewish Studies* 12 (1961): 1–18; Maurice De Gandillac, "Juif et judéité dans le 'Dialogue' d'Abélard," in Olender, *Pour Léon Poliakov: le racisme*, 385–401.

52. Ibid.

53. See Jonathan Elukin, "Judaism: From Heresy to Pharisee in Early Medieval Christian Literature," *Traditio* 57 (2002): 49–66. This study treats the period prior to the twelfth century.

54. See Elukin, "From Jew to Christian? Conversion and Immutability in Medieval Europe," in *Varieties of Religious Conversion in the Middle Ages,* ed. James Muldoon (Gainesville: University Press of Florida, 1997), 171–89; Elukin, "The Discovery of the Self: Jews and Conversion in the Twelfth Century," in Signer and Van Engen, 63–76; Elukin, "The Eternal Jew in Medieval Europe" (Ph.D. diss., Princeton University, 1993). Christians were suspicious of Jewish converts in part because in fact many converts returned to Judaism, particularly those who were coerced into baptism. See Alfred Haverkamp, "Baptised Jews in German Lands during the Twelfth Century," in Signer and Van Engen, 255–310.

55. This whole subject of apocalyptic influence on the *Golden Legend* has been little studied. For a provocative study of Honorius see Cohen, "*Synagoga conversa*: Honorius Augustodunensis, the Song of Songs, and Christianity's 'Eschatological Jew,'" *Speculum* 79 (2004): 309–40. See also Robert E. Lerner, "Millennialism," in *The Encyclopedia of Apocalypticism, vol. 2: Apocalypticism in Western History and Culture,* ed. Bernard McGinn et al. (New York: Continuum, 1999), 326–60; Lerner, *The Feast of Abraham: Medieval Millenarians and the Jews* (Philadelphia: University of Pennsylvania Press, 2001); Andrew C. Gow, *The Red Jews; Antisemitism in an Apocalyptic Age, 1200–1600*, Studies in Medieval and Reformation Thought 55 (Leiden: E. J. Brill, 1995). The conversion of the Jews before the last days was a major theme in Joachite apocalyptic expectations. See Beatrice Hirsch-Reich, "Joachim von Fiore und das Judentum," in *Judentum im Mittelalter: Beiträge zum christlich-jüdischen Gespräch*, ed. Paul Wilpert, Miscellanea Mediaevalia 4 (Berlin: de Gruyter, 1966), 228–63. For Hildegard and the Jews see Angela Carlevaris,

"Sie kamen zu ihr, um sie zu befragen: Hildegard und die Juden," in *Hildegard von Bingen in ihrem historischen Umfeld*, ed. Alfred Haverkamp (Mainz: P. von Zabern, 2000), 117–29.

9

Anti-Jewish Attitudes in Anglo-Norman Religious Texts
Twelfth and Thirteenth Centuries

Maureen Boulton

The first chapter of the history of the Jews in England was brief, beginning with their arrival in the wake of William's conquest and ending with their expulsion by Edward I in 1290. Though their residency during these two centuries was often peaceful and prosperous, it was also punctuated by periodic violent attacks of increasing frequency, and the final half century is a catalogue of extortion and legal attack by the crown. This story is well known in its outlines,[1] and a recent collection of essays nuances the picture of the economic and legal status of English Jews.[2] Paralleling the economic causes of resentment of the Jews in medieval England was a strong current of anti-Jewish sentiment that found expression in a variety of literary sources. Anthony Bale provides an overview of fictional portrayals of Judaism in Latin sources up to 1290, mainly chronicles and exempla. Much less known are the portraits of Jews in twelfth- and thirteenth-century Anglo-Norman religious texts. These are particularly important because they circulated among the social and political elites of medieval England and thus both formed and reflected the anti-Jewish attitudes that culminated in the outrages inflicted on Jewish communities in 1190 (King's Lynn, Norwich, and York), 1215 (London), 1234 (Norwich), 1239 (London), and 1255 (Lincoln).[3] This essay examines a group of religious texts that were either composed or copied in England in the twelfth and thirteenth centuries. One of the oldest of these is the *Jeu d'Adam*, the earliest surviving French play, whereas the most recent is a poem commemorating an accusation of ritual murder in Lincoln. Other works are Anglo-Norman translations of Latin texts like *Transitus Beate Virginae*, the *Gospel of Nicodemus* (*Gesta Pilati* and *Descensus ad Infernos*), and *Cura Sanitatis Tiberii*; although they did not break new ground in their anti-Jewish sentiments, they were important vehicles for extending these attitudes beyond clerical circles.

If it is difficult to establish any more than a relative chronology for these works, nevertheless a hardening of attitudes is clearly discernible between the earliest and the latest texts: In the middle of the twelfth century, Jews of the time of Christ were criticized for their failure to recognize him. A century later, it was English Jews of the mid-thirteenth century who were portrayed as not only blind but also violent and deserving of the harshest punishment.

Wace was a Norman cleric best known for his invention of Arthur's round table in his *Roman de Brut*, but he began his literary career around 1140 with a life of the Blessed Virgin titled the *Conception nostre dame*.[4] Although it may have been written on the Continent, two of the eighteen manuscripts were written in England in the thirteenth century, whereas the earliest copy (Tours, Bibliothèque municipale, 927) was made from an English exemplar by a scribe from southern France in the second quarter of the thirteenth century.[5] The first section of the poem, which recounts a miracle leading to the establishment of the Feast of the Conception of the Virgin, is English in origin. Wace (vv. 1–178) retells the story of Helsin, abbot of Ramsey, who was saved from a storm at sea by an angel during the reign of William the Conqueror. The remaining sections of the poem deal with the birth, childhood, marriage (vv. 179–1110), and assumption (vv. 1293–1810) of the Virgin, with a digression tracing her relatives through the three marriages of her mother, Anna (vv. 1111–1292).

The part of the poem dealing with Mary's parents and her childhood is set completely in a Jewish milieu, a fact barely acknowledged by Wace. Joachim and Anna exhibit exemplary piety, giving generously both to the poor and to the temple. The first event in the story occurs in the context of their observance of a feast "que Jüeu suelent celebrer" (v. 220: that Jews customarily celebrate). This is the sole occurrence of the word *Jew* in this part of the poem and the only overt recognition that the characters are, in fact, Jewish. The opening incident, in which Joachim is turned away from the temple because his childlessness is seen as a sign of God's disfavor, embodies a latent form of anti-Jewish bias. The confrontation (vv. 233–280) between the pious Joachim and the priest Isachar portrays the official representative of the Jewish religion as judgmental and condemning. The text also shows him to be wrong, for soon thereafter an angel appears to Joachim and announces the birth of Mary citing Isaac, Joseph, Samuel, and Samson as precedents for a child born to elderly parents (vv. 337–64).[6] When the angel makes a similar announcement to Anna, it is likewise set in the context of the barrenness of Sarah and Rachel (vv. 515–20).[7] Although not developed explicitly, the message of this encounter is that the Jewish leaders fail to recognize signs consistent with the events of their own history.

In the Assumption section, where the events take place after the death of Christ, the hostility toward the Jews is much more overt. At the beginning of the account, Mary fears (vv. 1407–14) that when she dies the Jews will burn her body, simply because she was the mother of a person they condemned. Her fears seem about to materialize when, hearing the singing of the funeral procession, a leader of the Jews urges his companions:

> Venez o mei e si pernun
> La biere o tut le cors ardun.
> Ço est la mere al sozduitor
> Par qui nos fumes en error.
> Toz les aposteles occiun
> Que nul mais vivre n'en laissun. (1635–40)
> (Come with me and let us take
> the coffin and burn it with the body.
> It is the mother of the deceiver
> By whom we were alarmed.
> Let's kill all the apostles,
> And leave none of them alive.)

There are verbal echoes ("cors ardun," "sozduitor") between this passage and the earlier one spoken by Mary, but though Wace took the first passage from his source, he significantly altered the Jew's speech. In the Latin *Transitus*, the Jew expresses only dismay at the large crowd that has gone to watch Mary's funeral procession, and although he does actually attempt to overturn the coffin he does not refer to it in his speech.[8] The change from third-person narrative to direct discourse for the passage makes it more vivid and its message is much more hostile. Wace replaced the impetuous action of a single individual with a Jewish leader who foments an organized and murderous attack. The last two lines, showing the Jew trying to instigate the extermination of his enemies, are Wace's invention.

As the narrative continues, Wace alters his source by describing how the attackers are struck blind, a feature mentioned briefly at the end of the Latin account. Thereafter, the French version is generally close to its source in this section, and the main changes are small omissions. When the leader of the group tries to overturn Mary's coffin, his hands wither and remain attached to the coffin. He asks Peter's help but is told that a cure cannot be effected without belief in Jesus Christ. He declares his belief, and his cure is effected in two stages: His hands are immediately reattached but remain withered until he kisses the coffin. After his conversion and cure, Peter gives him a palm branch to use in curing his followers. The new convert then urges conversion on the others, who are cured when they confess their belief. It is clear in both the Latin and the French texts that these conversions, offensive in the extreme to a Jewish reader, were seen in a positive light by the authors, and probably by their Christian audiences.

Wace's poem is an interesting example of a kind of unintentional anti-Jewishness. His aim was to write a pious tale, to show his literary skill (which is considerable), and to gain patronage, in which he was successful. The negative portrayal of Jews is mainly derived from his source, and the instance cited previously where he intensified his source is characteristic of the liberties he took with the original. Although Wace was almost certainly motivated by a writer's concern for style, he nevertheless felt free to embellish the wickedness of a Jewish character in his pursuit of verve.

The *Jeu d'Adam* or *Ordo representacionis Adae* was probably composed in the middle of the twelfth century. The only surviving copy is found in the same manuscript (Tours, Bibl. mun., 927) that contains the earliest copy of Wace's poem. Linguistic evidence in the play suggests that the southern French scribe was working from an exemplar written in England, probably between 1146 and 1174.[9] The play as a whole is markedly bilingual. Its first two sections are punctuated with liturgical pieces taken from different liturgical offices and sung by a choir. In the third section, which portrays a series of Old Testament prophets, each character begins his speech with a scriptural quotation in Latin. Although the Latin texts would probably not have been understood by the laypeople in the audience, their presence lends an air of liturgical authority to the words of the play. The message of the play is thus reinforced by the language of the official church. That message is the sinfulness of mankind, as portrayed by the fall of Adam and Eve in the opening section. This theme is reiterated in the second section showing Cain's murder of Abel, but the slaughter of the just by the unjust also announces typologically the death of the Savior. The messianic theme of the play is made explicit in the series of prophecies presented in the final section.

Whatever its dramatic strengths — and they are considerable — the *Jeu d'Adam* betrays overtly anti-Jewish attitudes, particularly in the prophet section.[10] Although one would scarcely expect to find the Jewish community among the audience of a Christian play presented either within or in front of a church, the third section of the play opens with a Latin invocation addressed to Jews: "Vos inquam, convenio, o Judei" (l. 1283: To you I speak, you it is I invoke, oh Jews),[11] a phrase borrowed from the text set as the lesson for the Matins of Christmas, the sermon *Contra Iudaeos Paganos et Arianos* of Pseudo-Augustine.[12] Though this polemical antisemitic tirade is the major source of this portion of the work, the playwright departed freely from it to shape a message that stresses the themes of redemption and the harrowing of hell as well as of the Incarnation.[13] Like its sources, the tenor of this section is strongly anti-Jewish.

The format of the play at this point is highly aggressive. It presents ten figures from Jewish history, all — except the pagan king Nebuchadnezzar — Jewish patriarchs or prophets. The series begins with Abraham and includes Moses, Aaron, David, Solomon, Balaam, Daniel, Habakkuk, Jeremiah, and Isaiah (who speaks twice), but not one of the group is ever identified as Jewish. Taken as a group, the series represents an outline of Jewish history. The Latin texts that they quote come from the Old Testament, but both the prophets and their texts are appropriated by the Christian dramatist and assimilated to the Christian message. As each figure takes the stage in turn, he reproaches the Jews for failing to understand the message of the scriptural prophecies. In this way, the major figures of Jewish history turn on the Jews, who thus lose both their history and their scriptures.

At one point, the playwright has inscribed a Jewish response into the text of the play. Just after Isaiah's first prophecy, a character labeled *Judeus* erupts to dispute with the prophet:

> Tunc exurget quidam de sinagoga disputans cum Isaia, et dicit ei:
> Ore me respon, sire Ysaïe!
> Est ço fablë ou prophecie?
> Quë est iço que tu as dit?
> Truvas le tu? Ou est escrit?
> Tu as dormi, tu le sonjas!
> Est ço a certes ou a gas? (1505–10)

> [Then shall rise up a certain man from the Synagogue, disputing with Isaiah, and he says to him:

> Now, lord Isaiah, give me answer!
> Is this a prophecy, or fable?
> What is this, that thou hast said?
> Art thou a poet? Where is't written?
> Why, thou has dreamed it in thy sleeping!
> Speak'st thou in mochery or truth? (p. 61)]

By questioning the prophet in this way, the Jew is portrayed as ignorant of his own scriptures. As the scene makes clear, however, the ignorance of the Jew is not something capable of remedy. Isaiah tells the Jew bluntly that he is "sick from wickedness" (1535) and "from error" (1540) and that he will never be cured (902, 904). The final insult of the play occurs in the last passage, taken from the book of Daniel and spoken by Nebuchadnezzar. The pagan king describes the three young (Jewish) men in fire:

> Chantouent un vers si bel
> Sembloit li angle fuissent del ciel
> Cum jo men regart, si vi le quartz,
> Chi lor fasoit mult grant solaz.
> Les chieres avoient tant resplendisant
> Sembloient le filz de Deu puissant. (1593–98)
> [They sang a hymn so fair, methought
> that angels had descended here.
> And as they sang, I saw the fourth,
> who gave great comfort to them there;
> his face resplendent was; he seemed[14]
> the Son of God, omnipotent.] (p. 65)

The biblical incident, which recorded God's protective intervention on behalf of the Jews, is recast in messianic terms. Whereas in the Bible the king is confounded, the play presents him as recognizing the power of God, a recognition from which the Jew in the play is explicitly excluded.

The cumulative effect of the play is to present an abridgement of Jewish history that not only excludes the Jews but also shows them willfully refusing to cooperate with the saving grace of God. Their refusal is twofold: In addition to their historic rejection of Jesus Christ, the figure of Judeus dramatizes the obdurate refusal of contemporary, twelfth-century English Jews.[15]

An even stronger presentation of the Jewish refusal of Christ's message is found in the biblical epic written by Herman de Valenciennes toward the end of the twelfth century.[16] Strictly speaking, Herman's *Roman de Dieu et de sa mere* is continental rather than insular in origin, but it is nevertheless significant in the present context because it circulated widely in England during the twelfth and thirteenth centuries. Fully nineteen of the thirty-six surviving manuscripts were copied by English scribes. These include the two oldest, both from the late twelfth century, and fourteen others from the thirteenth century, whereas the remainder were made after the period of concern in the present essay.[17] Herman's work, also referred to as his *Bible*, is cast in the epic form of a *chanson de geste* and has sections devoted to the Old Testament and to the life of Christ and the Blessed Virgin.

In the portrayal of Jewish characters, there is a marked contrast between the two parts of Herman's poem.[18] Abraham and his descendants are presented as heroic figures but are identified simply as the people or the lineage of Joseph. The patriarchs and the prophets are seen not as the founders of the Jewish people but as the ancestors of Christians. Herman thus appropriates Jewish history for his own very different purposes. The Jews are only identified as such during their wanderings in the desert, when they question Moses and worship the golden calf. In such negative contexts, Herman is able to assert "Signor, icil Gïu si furent molt felon" (2273: Lords, these Jews were very treacherous).

The theme of Jewish infidelity and ingratitude to God is developed overtly in the New Testament section. Early in the Passion narrative, Herman explains the hostility of the Jewish leaders to Jesus as a willful refusal to recognize the signs of his status and as ingratitude for his good deeds:

> Molt par furent felon et de molt povre sens
> Molt servoient deables, pas n'en estoient lent,
> Plus erent venimex que n'en est .i. serpanz,
> Molt orent male entente, molt orent mal porpens.
> Cil estoit de lor loi et estoit lor paranz.
> As sors rendi oïe et as dervez le sens,
> Lieprex sana assez qui estoient puanz
> Et d'yaue refist vin, miex valu que pimenz;

> Les morz resuscita, bel doctrina les genz.
> De nul que il sanast ne prist ne or ne argent. (5326–35)
> [They were most treacherous and of little sense,
> They served the devil and were not slow to do it.
> They were more poisonous than a snake,
> They had wicked goals and evil intentions.
> He was of their law and one of their own.
> He gave hearing to the deaf and reason to the mad;
> He cured the stinking lepers
> And out of water made wine worth more than spiced balm.
> He raised the dead, and taught the people well;
> From none that he healed did he take gold or silver.]

Herman then tries to demonstrate that these failings are simply a continuation of their infidelities throughout history. In a passage of six laisses (5338–5412) summarizing Jewish history — the flight from Egypt, crossing the Red Sea, the wandering in the desert, the story of David and Goliath — Herman repeatedly stresses the faithlessness of the Jews, who are described as "toz jors et cuvert et felon" (5350: always underhanded and treacherous), "chaitif" and "de povre sens" (5391: wretched, of little sense), "mescreant et dou lin au deable" (5404: unbelieving and of the devil's lineage). They willfully failed to recognize Jesus despite the clear indications of their prophets:

> Il troevent en lor livres, — ice n'est mie fable —
> Par la bouche au profete, qui dist parole estable,
> Que, qant icil naistroit qui feroit le miracle,
> Ja puis ne seroit jorz lor ointure durable... (5406–09)
> [They find in their books — this is not a fable —
> From the mouth of the prophets, who speak reliable words,
> That, when he was born who would perform the miracle,
> Their law would endure no longer.]

According to this view, the Jewish prophets both anticipated and welcomed the coming of Christ. They are thus aligned with the Christians who have appropriated their writings, which in turn become part of the evidence against the Jewish position.

In such a setting, the Passion narrative that Herman recounts is no longer a single instance of violent unbelief but is the culminating event in a long series of rejections of God's will. Since medieval Jews notably refused to accept Jesus as the Messiah, Herman's audience was led to see their Jewish neighbors not simply as members of another religious tradition but also as rebels against divine providence and as willful rejecters of salvation.

Of all of the accounts of the Passion available to a French-speaking medieval audience, the *Gospel of Nicodemus* was the most popular, with three poetic and five prose translations composed in French between the end of the twelfth and fifteenth centuries.[19] Two of these — a translation in verse and a short anonymous version in prose, both based closely on the A version of the Latin text — circulated in England before the end of the thirteenth century.[20] The poem by Chrétien — not to be identified with Chrétien de Troyes — survives in two English manuscripts of the thirteenth century, and Madeleine Blaess identified two copies, now lost, in the Abbey of Augustinian canons of Leicester.[21] The short anonymous prose version of *Evangile de Nicodème* identified by the editor as the "Tradition A" falls into the period presently discussed.[22] This text is essentially an Anglo-Norman version transmitted in six copies, four of them dating to the thirteenth century.[23] One possible explanation for the popularity of the apocryphon in England was increasing interest in the cult of Joseph of Arimathea, who was seen as the apostle of Britain.[24]

Like their source, the translations fall into three parts: the trial, the Crucifixion, and the descent into hell. The Latin text has been described as being in combat with the Jewish faith, and all of these translations follow their Latin source quite closely, if not always accurately.[25] As a result they all include its most blatantly anti-Jewish elements, specifically those that portray Pilate in a favorable light and heighten the treachery of the Jewish leaders.[26] Pilate orders his messenger to treat Jesus politely (Prose: "amiablement"; Chrétien: "Tut belement e par raisun/ Si ne lui feites si ben nun," Fairly and reasonably, do nothing but good to him.[27]). He reproaches the Jewish leaders for lying to him.[28] In a passage reminiscent of Herman de Valenciennes, Pilate tells the Jews that they have always opposed their God:

> Toz jorz fustez gent estrivose et cuntrarious[e] a cels qui por vos furent. Respundirent li gieu: "Qui fu por nos?" Pilate dist: "Vostre Deu, qui vos delivra del dur servage de Egypte, si vos mena par la mer si cumme par terre seche; et el desert vos put de manne et eve vos dona de la piere; et lei vos dona par Moÿsen. Et en totes manieres li fustes cuntrarieus…[Ford, p. 46, ll. 234–240]
>
> [You were always a combative and troublesome people towards those who were for you. The Jews replied, "Who was for us?" Pilate said: "Your God, who delivered you from hard servitude in Egypt, who led you through the sea as through dry land; and in the desert he fed you with manna and gave you water from the rock; and he gave you law through Moses. And in every way you were troublesome to him…]

Like Herman de Valenciennes, the translators of the *Gesta Pilati* appropriated Jewish scriptures for their own ends, in this instance to place their hostility to Jesus in the context of a long history of resisting the beneficent will of God. Putting such a reproach in the mouth of the complicitous Pilate only intensified the insult.

The third section of the text is a vivid account of Christ's descent into hell to liberate the souls of the just who have been excluded from paradise:

Dunc estendi nostre Seignor sa main, si dist: "Venez a mei, toz mes fiz, qui avez ma ymage et ma figure et qui par le fust deveé et par le deable fustes dampnez a mort. Ore venquez par le fust de la croiz et deable et mort!" [Ford, 56, ll. 723–6]

[Then our Lord stretched out his hand and said: "Come to me, all my sons, who have my image and my face and who were condemned to death by the forbidden wood and by the devil. Now you conquer both the devil and death by the wood of the cross.]

The report is provided by two eyewitnesses, Leucius and Carinus, the sons of Simeon, and describes the arrival of Christ and his encounters with prophets and patriarchs, including David, Isaiah, Habakkuk, Micah, Enoch, and Elijah, as well as the good thief Dismas, who appears carrying a cross. Once again, associating Hebrew prophets with the saving mission of Jesus Christ appropriates the Jewish scriptures to Christian purposes. When the prophets of the Jews are welcomed by Christ, his opponents are shown to be enemies of their own tradition.

Both Anglo-Norman translations end with the final chapter of the Latin text, in which Pilate sends a written report of the events to the emperor, erroneously identified as Claudius.[29] Perhaps a later addition to the narrative, Pilate's account of the death and resurrection of Jesus is consistent with the rest of the text in its shifting of blame from the Romans to the Jews but diminishes Pilate's role even further. He does not mention his own fear but in a clearly revisionist version of the incident claims to have been deceived and misled by Jewish lies:

> E cum li plusurs des Judeus
> Creirent ben k'il esteit Deus
> Li prince et li meistre kil virent
> Encontre furent, sil hairent;
> Cil le pristrent, sil me baillérent
> E sil batirent e liérent;
> Sur lui mentirent par envie
> E distrent ke par sorcerie
> Ovrout, e enchantére esteit,
> E encuntre lur lei feseit;
> Tels choses fit e viola
> Lur sabat e pas nel garda.
> Ço k'il me distrent ben crei
> E les paroles ke j'oi:
> Si lur livrai a turmenter
> E a lur volunté pener.   [Paris and Bos, 67, vv. 2137–52]

[And since some of the Jews believed that he (Jesus) was God, the princes and the masters who saw him were against him, and hated him. They took him and turned him over to me, and beat him and bound him. Out of envy they lied about him and said that he worked by sorcery and was a magician and acted against their law. He did such things and violated their sabbath and did not keep it. I believed what they told me, and the words that I heard, so I delivered him to them to torment and to punish according to their will.]

The letter continues by reporting Christ's resurrection and the attempts of the priests to buy the silence of the Roman soldiers guarding the tomb. The addendum effectively casts the announcement of Christ's death and resurrection in an official form and shows the effect of the evidence on a witness to the events. In this version of the events, Pilate represents himself as a believer, reporting the truth (v. 2179) and denouncing the "felunie" (v. 2108) of the Jewish leaders.[30]

The spectacle of pious Jews like Nicodemus and Joseph of Arimathea bearing witness to Christ's resurrection saving power (in the Descent section) can only have had the effect of making unconverted Jews seem obdurate and hostile in their rejection of the Christian message. Though such an image might not necessarily lead to violence against contemporary Jews, the *Gospel of Nicodemus* was often associated with another text that explicitly celebrated violence against their ancestors: the *Vengeance Nostre Seigneur.*

Five of the six Anglo-Norman copies of the Anglo-Norman prose version of *Evangile de Nicodème* also contain as a conclusion a version of the *Vengeance* that is actually a translation of the *Cura Sanitatis Tiberii.*[31] In this text, a deputy of the ailing Roman emperor arrives in Jerusalem shortly after the resurrection, seeking Jesus in the hope that he will effect a cure. Pilate once again tries to shift responsibility to the Jews. His prevarications are exposed, however, and he is arrested and exiled. The only violence in the account occurs at the end. Once restored to health, the emperor is baptized and orders his council to follow suit; those who refuse "[il] fist turmenter de deverz turmenz e tresqu'a la mort pener, pur çoe qu'il ne voldrei[e]nt Jhesu Crist aurrer" [Ford, p. 64, ll. 167–8: he had them tortured with various torments to the point of death, because they would not adore Jesus Christ.]

In contrast to the much more violent continental narratives of the destruction of Jerusalem, the Anglo-Norman text inflicts no punishment on the Jewish leaders who instigated the Crucifixion.[32] Nevertheless, the account clearly approves torture and death as fitting for those who refuse to embrace Christianity, a group that obviously includes the Jews.

The *Life of Little St. Hugh of Lincoln* moves from the realm of biblical and pseudo-biblical fiction to putative historical reality in an incident that illustrates the practical effect of the attitudes embodied in the apocryphal narratives. The Anglo-Norman poem recounts an instance of ritual murder imputed to the Jews of Lincoln in 1255. The body of a boy who had been missing for a month was discovered in a well and was buried in a shrine in the cathedral. The Jews of the city were accused of murder, and on the basis of a confession by one of their number nineteen people were executed by order of the king. Among the records of this incident are three chronicles accounts and a series of poems or ballads in Anglo-Norman, Middle Scots, and Middle English.[33]

The Anglo-Norman poem in 92 octosyllabic quatrains is the earliest of the series and survives in a single copy (Paris, Bibliothèque Nationale de France, fr. 902) written very close to the event, since Henry III (d. 1272) is referred to as living (v. 50).[34] According to the poem, the boy was abducted by a certain Peitevin and then was sold by a Jew named Jopin for thirty "deners" to Agim or Agon. After this transaction, however, the Jews of the city participated in the crucifixion of the boy in a manner consciously modeled on Christ's passion (cf. vv. 84, 107). When he was dead, they cut out his heart and ate it (vv. 125–8). The boy is portrayed as a martyr whose soul is escorted to heaven by angels (vv. 133–6). No explanation, other than sheer wickedness, is suggested in the text. Although the corpse was buried deeply, the murderers found it exposed the next day and put it in a privy. When the body emerged yet again, it was carried outside the city and placed in a well after the wounds had been sealed with wax. When the body was found once more, its wounds were seen to resemble those of Christ (v. 265), and it was duly buried in the cathedral. Lincoln's Jews, having been betrayed, were then arrested, and Jopin confessed (vv. 311–44) before the king. The poem ends with the execution of Jopin, who was condemned by a council of Jews.

The Anglo-Norman poem contains more local detail than any other account. The abductor it names, Peitevin, was actually a prominent Jew in Lincoln.[35] The Jewish quarter of Lincoln is identified as "Dernestal" (v. 6), and the site of the execution "Canevic" (v. 366) refers to a hill outside the city.[36] Given these references, it is probable that the poem reflects the version of the story current in Lincoln.

Gavin Langmuir argues the essential implausibility of the account and indeed of the incident itself.[37] The Anglo-Norman poem embellishes the narrative of ritual murder with repugnant details. It asserts that the child's heart was cut out and eaten by his killers. Thus, the Jews of Lincoln were not only killers and insulters of Christ but also cannibals. When the corpse defied concealment, throwing it into a privy seems a wanton and repulsive desecration. The case against the Jews, as presented in the poem, is implausibly strengthened by several factors: a Jewish convert prosecuted the case, the perpetrators freely confessed the crime, and a council of Jews condemned the wrong-doers. In this rendering, the criminal is punished not by his Christian neighbors or by the king but by his own people. The reported punishment, confined to a single person, seems mild in the circumstances. The whole account, then, plays down some aspects of the incident and exaggerates others to underline the gratuitous cruelty of the Jews and to stress the restraint of the Christians.

Though the poem's departures from truth and even from probability are obvious, the inflammatory aspects of the account are particularly telling in the context of anti-Jewish attitudes. What was implicit in the apocryphal narratives discussed earlier is made explicit in this text. The essential link between ancient Palestinian

Jews and the medieval Jews of England is established in the clearest possible way by the allusions to Christ's passion and the sacrilegious crucifixion of the child. Both are guilty of the same crime, and it is only an accident of chronology that the English Jews were not present at the death of Christ. Thus, attacks on medieval Jews could be justified as belated punishment of the killers of Christ. The addition of other repulsive crimes — cannibalism and desecration — never associated with the enemies of Jesus may be explained as extra incentive for provoking attacks on a group who, after all, had coexisted peaceably with their neighbors. The effectiveness of such demonization has been demonstrated too often in the twentieth century to require further explanation.

Notes

1. Roth traces this history into the nineteenth century. Henry G. Richardson, *The English Jewry under the Angevin Kings* (London: Methuen, 1960). For a corrective, see Gavin I. Langmuir, "The Jews in Angevin England" *Traditio* 19 (1963): 183–244.
2. Patricia Skinner, ed., *The Jews in Medieval Britain. Historical, Literary and Archaeological Perspectives* (Woodbridge, Suffolk: Boydell Press, 2003).
3. See Roth, 21, 23–25, 36, 53, 55–57.
4. See Geneviève Hasenohr and Michel Zink, eds., *Dictionnaire des Lettres Françaises: Le Moyen Age*, 2d. ed. (Paris: Fayard, 1992), 1498–99; Ruth J. Dean with the collaboration of Maureen Boulton, *Anglo-Norman Literature: A Guide to Texts and Manuscripts* (Occasional Publications Series 3; London: Anglo-Norman Text Society, 1999), no. 489.
5. William Ray Ashford, ed., *The Conception de Nostre Dame de Wace* (Chicago: Private Edition, 1933), pxii–xvi on date; xxii–xxiv on language of the Tours manuscript; see also n. 6. The other two Anglo-Norman manuscripts contain only fragments of the text: Oxford, University College, 100 (vv. 1129–1810); London, British Library, Cotton Vittellius A.X (vv. 1129–1203). In addition, the Benedictine Abbey in Peterborough owned a volume, now lost, with the "Concepcio S. Marie cum assumpcione" that may indicate Wace's poem; see Madeleine Blaess, "Manuscrits français dans les monastères anglais," *Romania* 94 (1973): 321–58, esp. 344. References are to Ashford's edition; translations are my own.
6. In this passage Wace implies that Abraham and Jacob had no other children, apparently unaware of — or else overlooking — the testimony of Genesis 16 and 25 (i.e., Abraham's sons by Hagar and by Keturah), and 29, 31–30, 24 (i.e., Jacob's children by Leah, Bilhah, Zilpah, and Rachel).
7. The reference to the barrenness of Rachel may be explained by Genesis 30:1, where she complains of having no children; the birth of her son Joseph is recounted later (30:23–24) in the same chapter.
8. The source of this section is the *Transitus* B text attributed to Pseudo-Melito, printed by Constantin von Tischendorf, *Apocalypses Apocrypha: Mosis: Esdras: Pauli Iohannis* (Leipzig: Mendelssohn, 1866), 124–36. See J. K. Elliott, *New Testament Apocrypha* (Oxford: Clarendon Press 1993), 691–723; the text is translated on 708–14.

9. The best edition is by Willem Noomen, *Le Jeu d'Adam (Ordo representacionis Ade)* (Paris: CFMA, 1971); the edition by Wolfgang van Emden, *Le Jeu d'Adam* (British Rencesvals Publ. 1; Edinburgh: Société Rencesvals, 1996) is accompanied by a useful discussion and facing-page translation. For discussions of the language, see the editions by Karl Grass, *Das Adamsspiel: Anglonormannisches Mysterium des XII. Jahrhunderts*, 2d ed. (Halle a. S.: M. Niemeyer, 1907), xxxviii–lxxv; Paul Studer, *Le Mystère d'Adam: An Anglo-Norman Drama of the Twelfth Century* (Manchester: University Press, 1918), xxxiv–li. See also Van Emden, *Le Jeu d'Adam*, vii–viii; Hasenohr and Zink, *Dictionnaire des Lettres*, 863; Dean and Boulton, *Anglo-Norman Literature*, no. 716.

10. On the literary qualities of the *Jeu*, see Noomen, "Le Jeu d'Adam, étude descriptive et analytique," *Romania* 89 (1968): 145–93; Tony Hunt, "The Unity of the Play of Adam (Ordo Representacions Ade)," *Romania* 96 (1975): 368–88, 497–527; Lynette Muir, *Liturgy and Drama in the Anglo-Norman Adam*, Medium Aevum Monographs, n.s. 3 (Oxford: Blackwell, 1973).

11. Quotations are taken from Noomen, *Le Jeu*; translations are taken from van Emden, *Le Jeu*, 52–53.

12. For the text of the sermon, see Karl Young, *The Drama of the Medieval Church*, 2 vols. (Oxford: Oxford University Press, 1933), 2, ch. 21, 125–71.

13. Of the eleven prophetic passages, five are taken from the Pseudo-Augustinian sermon; two are unique to the *Jeu d'Adam*; in two other cases, the author substituted a different quotation for the one used in the sermon; three others are not found in the sermon and were probably taken from liturgical plays in Latin: see van Emden, *Le Jeu*, xii–xvi.

14. The translation in van Emden, *Le Jeu*, reflects emendations in lines 943–44: "La chiere avoit tant resplendisant/ Sembloit..."

15. Cf. Michael Jones, "'The Place of the Jews': Anti-Judaism and Theatricality in Medieval Culture," *Exemplaria* 12 (2000): 327–58, which discusses mainly English texts.

16. On the date, see André de Mandach, "A Quand remonte la Bible de Herman de Valenciennes," *Mémoires du Cercle archéologieque et historique de Valenciennes* 9 (1976): 53–69, who proposed the period 1188 to 1195 as the probable date of composition.

17. For a list of the insular manuscripts with details of contents, see Dean and Boulton, *Anglo-Norman Literature*, no. 485; for other manuscripts, see Ina Spiele, ed., *Li Romanz de Dieu et de sa mere d'Herman de Valenciennes*, Publications romanes de l'Université de Leyde 21 (Leiden: Presse Universitaire de Leyde, 1975), 144–54. Quotations are from Spiele's edition; translations are mine.

18. For a fuller discussion, see Boulton, "Anti-Jewish Attitudes in Twelfth-Century French Literature," in Signer and Van Engen, 234–54.

19. On the various French versions, see Richard O'Gorman, "The *Gospel of Nicodemus* in the Vernacular Literature of Medieval France," in *The Medieval Gospel of Nicodemus: Texts, Intertexts, and Contexts in Western Europe*, Medieval & Renaissance Texts & Studies 158, ed. Zbigniew Izydorczyk (Tempe: University of Arizona Press, 1997), 103–31.

20. See Izydorczyk, "The *Evangelium Nicodemi* in the Latin Middle Ages," in Izydorczyk, *Medieval Gospel*, 43–101 on the different Latin versions. The A version has been edited according to the oldest manuscript by H. C. Kim, ed., *The Gospel of*

Nicodemus (Toronto: PIMS, 1973). Also useful is Rémi Gounelle and Izydorczyk, *L'Evangile de Nicodème ou les Acetes faits sous Ponce Pilate (récension latine A)* (Turnholt: Brepols, 1997), Introduction, 17–119.

21. Dean and Boulton, *Anglo-Norman Literature,* no. 500; Blaess, "Manuscrits français," 356–57. The other verse translation, described by O'Gorman as "doggerel" and "confused" (ibid., 106) is preserved in a single manuscript from the end of the thirteenth century (London: Lambeth Palace, 522). The verse translations were edited by Gaston Paris and Alphonse Bos, *Trois version rimées de l'Evangile de Nicodème par Chrétien, André de Coutances et un anonyme...* (Paris: Firmin Didot, 1885), 1–69, 137–212.

22. Alvin E. Ford, ed., *L'Evangile de Nicodème: Les Versions courtes en ancien français et en prose,* Publications romanes et françaises, 125 (Geneva: Droz, 1973). He edits the A Version from Paris, B.N. fr. 19525 with variants from London, Brit. Libr., Harley 2253, Egerton 2710, and Cambridge, Emmanuel College, 106. Two additional manuscripts (London, British Library, Egerton 613 and Aberystwyth, National Library of Wales, 5028C), unknown to the editor, are listed in Dean and Boulton, *Anglo-Norman Literature,* no. 497. The text of Egerton 2710 was published by Bengt Lindström, ed., *The Late Middle English Version of the Gospel of Nicodemus Edited from the British Museum MS. Harley 149,* Acta Universitatis Upsaliensis: Studia Anglistica Upsaliensia, 18 (Uppsala: Almquist & Wiksell, 1974) as the source of the Middle English text.

23. According to reviewers, the continental copies of the text differ from it sufficiently to constitute a separate version: see the reviews of this work by R. O'Gorman, *Cahiers de Civilisation Médiévale* 19 (1976): 59–61; and C. R. Sneddon, *French Studies* 31 (1977): 441–42.

24. O'Gorman, *"Gospel of Nicodemus,"* 112; Valerie M. Lagorio, "The Evolving Legend of St. Joseph of Glastonbury," *Speculum* 46 (1971): 209–31.

25. Gounelle and Izydorczyk, *L'Evangile de Nicodème,* 71: "L'auteur de *l'Evangile de Nicodème* est en débat avec le judaïsme." See Paris and Bos, *Trois version rimées,* xiii–xvi on the inaccuracies of Chrétien's translation.

26. See, for example, Ford, *L'Evangile de Nicodème,* 120, 236, 424.

27. Ibid., 41, l. 24; Paris and Bos, *Trois version rimées,* 4, vv. 97–98.

28. Prose: Ford, *L'Evangile de Nicodème,* 43, l. 97; Paris and Bos, *Trois version rimées,* 9, v. 265.

29. Paris and Bos, *Trois version rimées,* 66–68, vv. 2091–2180; the letter is not included in Ford, *L'Evangile de Nicodème*; see Dean and Boulton, *Anglo-Norman Literature,* no. 498: all but one of the manuscripts of *L'Evangile de Nicodème* include the letter.

30. Gonnelle and Izydorczyk, *L'Evangile de Nicodème,* 95, 209–11, n. 217.

31. Ford, ed., *La Vengeance de Nostre-Seigneur: The Old and Middle French Prose Versions,* Texts and Studies 115 (Toronto: Pontifical Institute of Mediaeval Studies, 1993), Family D, 52–64.

32. See Ford, *Vengeance de Nostre-Seigneur* for other versions.

33. See Francisque Michel, *Hugues de Lincoln: recueil de ballades anglo-normandes* (Paris: Silvestre, 1834) for editions of all of these as well as the Latin account of the incident by Matthew Paris. On the event and associated texts, see Langmuir, "The Knight's Tale and Young Hugh of Lincoln," *Speculum* 47 (1972): 459–82.

34. On the Anglo-Norman poem, see Dean and Boulton, *Anglo-Norman Literature,* no. 531.

35. See Langmuir, "Knight's Tale," 466.
36. Michel, *Hugues de Lincoln,* 60–63, n. 2, n. 27.
37. Langmuir, "Knight's Tale."

10

Henry II, William of Newburgh, and the Development of English Anti-Judaism

John D. Hosler

"The blood of Jews was poured out like [that of] cattle": So reads the *Chronicle of Melrose* in a reference to the outbreak of anti-Jewish violence in York on March 16, 1190.[1] It was the endgame of months of rioting, sparked initially by attacks against the London Jews at the coronation of Richard I of England (1189–1199) on September 3, 1189. What followed was widespread anti-Jewish fervor, and by March 1190 attacks on Jews had occurred in Norwich, Stamford, Bury-St. Edmunds, Colchester, Thetford, Osplinge, and Lincoln, culminating most famously at York with the mass suicide of the Jews within Clifford Castle.[2] Although anti-Jewish violence was not uncommon on the continent, the calamitous fury leveled against the Jews in England[3] was somewhat unprecedented in the twelfth century. Its development owed much to the crusading fervor in the period between the Second and Third Crusades, as *crucesignati* and their relations found commonalities between the struggle for the Holy Land and their own locales.[4] Jews, like Muslims, were perceived as a viable threat to the church, but because they lived within English borders Jews were easier targets for abuse. Besides the crusading mentality, other elements were instrumental, as Robert Stacey neatly summarizes: "Behind the massacres of 1189–90 in England there thus lay a complicated mixture of anti-Jewish prejudice and hostility: of sadism, greed, carnival and riot; of economic resentment and regional hostility; of political rivalry; and of protest against the crown's relationship to Jews and Jewish moneylending."[5]

The memory of twelfth-century English Jews has endured throughout the frequent references to Jewish policies in contemporary medieval evidence, much of which was collected and translated by Joseph Jacobs in 1977.[6] Insofar as Jacobs's compilation remains a fragmentary record of assorted financial receipts, chronicle excerpts, and legal notices, it offers only a glimpse of the complex nature of anti-Judaism in English society.[7] Clearly there were strong anti-Jewish sentiments in Angevin England, but the reader quickly becomes aware that many policies, especially those stemming from the royal court, appear to have been somewhat favorable, if not outright sympathetic, of Jewish interests and traditions. We have, then, a muddled picture in which Jews enjoyed liberties on the one hand and suffered disparate abuse on the other.

A more contextual glimpse of Anglo–Jewish relations in the latter half of the twelfth century is found in the writings of the Augustinian canon William of Newburgh, one of the period's most engaging chroniclers. Living in Yorkshire, William spent a great deal of time composing his *Historia Rerum Anglicarum*, an account that constitutes a major piece of evidence for Henry II and Richard I's reigns.[8] The chronicle ends in 1198, presumably with the death of its author.[9] William has received much good press from both historical and literary scholars alike. He has been applauded for his critical historical eye (earning him the title Father of Historical Criticism), for his knowledge of Latin and contemporary theology, as well as for his storytelling skills.[10] One conspicuous feature of William's writing is, as Antonia Grandsen notes, his "judicious impartiality."[11] Although he was not a chronicler in the strictest sense, William wrote chronologically but often paused to add detail, typically rendering thoughtful judgments attempting to render up Christian lessons when possible.[12] As regards the Jews in England and the York massacre of March 1190 in particular, William was more verbose than any of his peers and has thus attracted the attention of numerous scholars of both English and Jewish history. Richard B. Dobson's characterization of the author bears repeating: "William of Newburgh's treatment of the York riots shows him at his very considerable best: well-informed and emotionally involved, he was yet sufficiently detached from the atrocities to provide a comparatively impartial and well-balanced if sometimes over-calculated story."[13]

William was not pleased that Jewish blood was spilled: Grandsen argues that he was indignant of the riots' violation of law and order as well as the massacre, which he deplored on humanitarian grounds.[14] Yet William was no impartial witness, and a study of his narrative reveals that William was also not a friend of the Jews. Nancy Partner reminds us that he "cannot be expected to have regarded the Jews with sympathy or understanding," but there is little doubt that his view was shaped not only by the events in York but also by general English attitudes toward the Jewry.[15] The bulk of scholarly attention has focused on William's narrative of the riots of 1189 to 1190; however, independent of those events, the *Historia Rerum Anglicarum* is also an encapsulation of a host of anti-Jewish attitudes pervasive in late twelfth-century English society before the succession of Richard and in the reign of his father, Henry II (1154–1189), in particular. This study seeks to locate events during Henry II's tenure that served to promote English anti-Judaism in popular circles as well as within such intellectual discourses on the Jews as offered by William of Newburgh.

The reign of Henry II has been called the "Golden Age in early Anglo-Jewish history," in which, "with the exception of occasional financial oppression, the Jews enjoyed the widest liberty."[16] There is some merit to this notion. Henry extended the charter of protection created by his grandfather Henry I (1100–1135), which gave Jews limited jurisdictional power over their own affairs. No copy of this charter has survived, but chronicler Roger of Howden provides some of the document's features:

> Be it also known, that all Jews, wheresoever they are in the kingdom, are to be under the tutelage and lawful protection of the king; and no one of them can serve under any rich man without the king's leave; for the Jews and all their property belong to the king. And if any person shall lay hands on them or their money, the king is to demand restitution thereof, if he so pleases, as of his own.[17]

The charter of protection extended over Normandy as well, where Jews were considered a sort of sub-bourgeoisie.[18] Outside of situations in which they might infringe upon public order, Jews could discipline their own under the auspices of Talmudic Law and not the Justices in Eyre.[19] Henry II granted the Jews several separate burial grounds to offer an alternative to the common graves outside of London.[20] The office of archpriest of the Jews was instituted during Henry's reign, and Jews were permitted to conduct business in a newly created Jewish branch of the Exchequer.[21] Payments were made from the royal treasury to Jewish scribes in Rouen, and although Jews did not govern their own communes there, during Henry's tenure they were free from all Angevin customs and tolls.[22] Under such conditions many Jews in Henry's domains were able to amass substantial wealth. Aaron of Lincoln, for example, had more liquid assets in 1185 than anyone in England and lent money to at least nine Cistercian abbeys as well as to the cathedrals of Lincoln and Peterborough.[23] In addition, a deed of William of Tottenham to the Jewess Avigaia of London reveals that repayment of Jewish loans was a precise process that included assurances for the lender in instances of nonpayment.[24] Increasing Jewish prosperity prompted the English nobility to rely heavily on usury to fund various activities. Between 1158 and 1163, Knight Richard of Anesty contracted several loans from Jews at Cambridge to cover his legal expenses, often receiving new loans before satisfying the old.[25] Richard Fitz Gilbert's expedition to Ireland in August 1170 was financed in part by the Jew Josce of Gloucester.[26] King Henry began contracting Jewish loans in 1157, three years after his coronation, and by 1165 he was heavily in debt, repaying over £2,000 to Isaac, son of Rabbi Josce, and Aaron of Lincoln between 1165 and 1166 alone.[27] In 1177, a consortium of several Jews banded together to loan Henry £3,000 in a single payment.[28] Usury allowed many Jews to enjoy private, intellectual lives, and during Henry's reign some of the most prominent Jewish scholars of the day visited England.[29]

Such enormous wealth had its drawbacks, as did the close connection between the English crown and the Jewish population. Its use of the Jewish financial resources alerted the royal court to a fundraising opportunity, an advantage that English kings were quick to exploit.[30] Direct taxation was one method of acquiring additional funds. Henry II often levied taxes against the English Jewry, beginning with the collection for his 1159 Toulouse expedition and concluding with the more famous Saladin Tithe on personal property in 1188.[31] To the latter, the monk Gervase of Canterbury reports that Jews contributed £60,000, compared to £70,000 collected from non-Jews, a substantial amount for a minority population.[32] More recent study indicates that Gervase's figures are off the mark, but Jews did pay at least £12,000 to the Saladin Tithe over a period of two years.[33] Apart from taxation, the crown found other methods of extracting funds from the Jewish populace. One legal measure, the mandate that usurers relinquished their property to the crown upon their death, was quite favorable to Henry. In 1185, hearing of the death of the wealthy Aaron of Lincoln, the king set about seizing the Jew's funds. Aaron's personal wealth was shipped to France in February 1187 but was unexpectedly lost when the ship sank during its journey from Shoreham to Dieppe. Aaron's personal loans were then collected in benefit of the court, and the Exchequer spent five years collecting nearly £15,000 from his English, Breton, and Scottish debtors.[34] Henry was not the only person to benefit from such favorable royal policies; as queen, Eleanor of Aquitaine could expect a 1 percent share from every legal judgment against the Jews.[35] Later policies would declare increased leeway for Christian debtors: In 1215, for example, the eleventh clause of the Magna Carta cemented the already established tradition that permitted widows of those indebted to Jews to retain their dowries and refuse to repay outstanding loans.[36] Thus was the propagation of Jewish usury a very profitable enterprise for Henry and his successors, not to mention the various knights and nobility that contracted enormous loans with which to conduct their affairs.[37]

Politically, the economic prosperity of some English Jews in the twelfth century led to mounting suspicions on the part of the public. The frequent and sizable Jewish loans to Henry II and his nobles were interpreted as contributing to a burgeoning Jewish influence over the court, and anti-Jewish commentary increased. In his treatise on the frivolities of courtiers, John of Salisbury associated Jews with flatterers and warned of their power, large numbers, and devious cunning that could conquer even kings and princes.[38] It is not known whether John had Henry in mind as he wrote; however, Henry's initial Jewish loan contracts were in 1157, the same period in which John was writing the *Policraticus*, which was finished in fall 1159.[39] John was not alone in his sentiment. Roger Asterby of Lincolnshire demanded that Henry, for the peace of his realms and the happiness of his rule, expel the Jews from his realm and go on crusade; as is shown in this chapter, the link between English Jews and the Holy Land was an important concept for intellectuals of the time.[40] In terms of royal policy, the 1181 Assize of Arms has been identified as tangible evidence of declining Jewish rights. This feudal document was specific to England, and other versions had been issued by Henry on the Continent. The Assize of Arms dictated the standard military equipment each man ought to possess, based on his present financial and legal condition, and it prohibited Jews from owning *hauberks*. The Assize, Hyamson argues, forced the disarming of the Jews, rendered them defenseless, and prepared the way for the later massacres during the reign of Richard I.[41] In this case the evidence may be overstated, but England was clearly moving toward the increased restriction of Jewish practices and activities during the reign of Henry II. A more concrete written political response is woven throughout William of Newburgh's *Historia Rerum Anglicarum* in a bevy of contemporaneous anti-Jewish sentiment, much of it stemming from the increase in Jewish prosperity under Henry. The king's financial dealings with the English Jewry, that nation "perfidious and hostile to Christians," had made the Jews proud and insolent.[42] The Jews were the enemies of the Truth and hateful to all men.[43] In particular, he cites the London riots in 1189 as a sign that God was with Richard I and that the enemies of Christians would be laid low as the Jews had been.[44] To William, therefore, the suspicions that had coalesced during the reign of Henry II and that escalated in the midst of Saladin's capture of Jerusalem in October 1187 had transformed into righteous, and justifiable, indignation under the king's eldest son.

Given the burgeoning resentment of Jews in England in the later twelfth century, William of Newburgh was not alone in his sentiment, especially in clerical circles. Ecclesiastical allowances of usury were far less tolerant than those of the crown, and the church did its best to restrict the practice of moneylending. The Second Lateran Council of 1139 condemned usury on the grounds of both the Old and New Testaments. Bernard of Clairvaux and Peter Lombard both rejected the practice, with Peter associating usury with fraud, rapine, and theft, all violations of the seventh commandment.[45] More direct papal actions coincided with the increase in Jewish prosperity during Henry II's reign. Of the eight decrees of the Council of Tours of 1163, the fifth canon condemns usury as *manifestius damnatas* and threatens any clerk who has entered into a usurious contract with the loss of ecclesiastical office.[46] Among the three sources for these canons at Tours is none other than William, the only Englishman to provide such information.[47] Pope Alexander III (1159–1181) widely prohibited credit sales and other types of dubious transactions,[48] and in 1179, the Third Lateran Council stripped from usurers their rights to the Eucharist and a Christian burial. Clergy presiding over the burial of a nonrepentant usurer were immediately suspended.[49] Anyone accepting the word of a Jew over that of a Christian in a legal court was anathematized, Christians could not live in Jewish households, Jews could not employ Christian servants, and only through baptism could Jews guarantee their own property against disinheritance or confiscation.[50]

In England, the trepidations of the church regarding the involvement of its members in usurious contracts were reasonably justified, for clerical involvement in the practice was a persistent problem in the later twelfth century. Policies against usury were borne from concerns over economic practicalities as well as theology. Aaron of Lincoln's customers included Guy Rufus, bishop of Bangor, and Robert de Chesney, bishop of Lincoln, as well as the abbot of Westminster and the prior of the Knights Hospitaller.[51] According to John of Salisbury, the abbot-elect Clarembald of St. Augustine's Abbey, Canterbury, was heavily indebted to both Jewish and Christian usurers.[52] When the abbey's financial burden rose to an untenable height in 1179 — the same year as Lateran III, no less — Alexander III exhorted Henry II to protect the abbey in its business affairs with the Canterbury Jews.[53] For his part, Henry resurrected an old statute of Edward the Confessor (1042–1066) in 1180, declaring usury "the root of all vices," and in the *Dialogus de Scaccario* Richard Fitz Nigel called the practice degenerative, with its practitioners deserving to have all revenues confiscated by the crown.[54] Such decrees sought to prevent the sort of rapid spread of Christian involvement in and practice of usury that, in some quarters of the Continent, was outpacing Jewish moneylending.[55] Yet in England Henry II's reliance on Jewish loans, not royal edicts, kept the practice of Christian usury somewhat checked. In the process, Jewish economic freedom, such that it was, was extended during his reign. This seems to fall into accord with Kenneth Stow's argument that the legal and constitutional status of the Jews — not the policies of the church —governed Jewish life in the Middle Ages.[56] Moreover, despite the economic difficulties between Christians and Jews, social relations between the two groups, at least in Canterbury, remained relatively friendly on the whole.[57]

Such friendly relations did not prevent burgeoning fear among England's Christian population, however, and trepidations about usury were accompanied by other, more sinister charges against the Jews. Three allegations in particular constituted the core of medieval anti-Judaism: ritual crucifixion, ritual cannibalism, and desecration of the consecrated host.[58] In England, the most notable of these was the allegation of ritual crucifixion, initiated by the much touted, but historically suspect, murder of the boy William of Norwich by Jews in 1144.[59] The notoriety of this story ensured that news of later, similar events in England spread rapidly and encouraged great anger. During the reign of Henry II, Jews were suspected of murdering three Christian children in separate incidents at Gloucester in 1168, Bury-St. Edmunds in 1181, and Bristol in 1183.[60] It appears that the Jews remained relatively safe in these cases, due to Henry's charter of protection, but the rumors did little to ease Christian fears.[61] Similar incidents from abroad added to the sentiment, with the first charge of ritual crucifixion in the twelfth century arising in Paris in 1163.[62] The natural successor of the suspicion of ritual murder was a reprise of the more traditional refrain that the Jews were the condemners and executioners of Jesus Christ.[63] Earlier in the twelfth century, Anselm of

Canterbury and Abelard had each proposed particular theological analyses of the trial under Pontius Pilate that absolved the Jews in some measure.[64] Yet if later English writers were aware of such nuanced explanations they certainly did not adopt them. Peter of Blois offers a complex biblical assessment of Jewish culpability in the matter, and John of Salisbury indicts the Jews for the death of Christ and reminds the Canterbury monk Ralph of Arundel that Christ accused the Jews of killing him without just cause.[65] The occasional rumors of child crucifixion, borne out in such frightening descriptions as Christian boys bleeding on a cross, only stirred this particular pot anew. In the context of burgeoning animosity against the Jews, additional incidents of supposed Jewish aggression against the body of Christ, either in the desecration of the Blessed Host or through attacks on Christian clergy, were contextualized into a unified and negative perception of the Jews that allowed room for retribution on the part of the wronged.[66] For example, Henry II's court satirist Walter Map claims to have witnessed a Jew attack a procession of clerics in Paris, where they seized one from their number, and cast him into a cesspool. Louis VII of France (1137–1180) ordered the Jew to be burned at the stake as a result.[67] Somewhat detached in perspective, Map notes that such incidents were trifles but still notable enough to relate in his modest writings; it is worth pondering whether or not Map based his comment in quantitative or qualitative terms.[68]

In the midst of the various accounts of Jewish violence, the *Historia Rerum Anglicarum* of William of Newburgh offers the most comprehensive discussion of how the Jewish murder of Christ affects the church and world at large. After prefacing his analysis by declaring that the Jews killed Christ, William then proceeds not through invectives but by outlining the historical implications of the event in theological terms. Thus, the Jews suffer a most just punishment for their crime: the condemnation of living in a perpetual state of subservience among the Christian population. His sentiment resembles the canons ratified at the Third Lateran Council, in the sense that they prohibit Jews from employing Christians and cast doubt on rights of inheritance. Because William is one of the chief English sources for Lateran III, he may well have incorporated its contents into his theory.[69] He goes well beyond the legalistic council canons, however, by illustrating a history of the Holy Land that excludes the Jews from God's divine plan. This aside, found in Book Three, Chapter Fifteen, of the *Historia Rerum Anglicarum*, was composed at a time following the news of Saladin's capture of Jerusalem in 1187. In England, the event inspired many to assume the cross: Henry II became *crucesignatus* in January 1188 and provided substantial funding for crusading efforts.[70] Much of the aforementioned Saladin Tithe was drawn from the English Jewry, a tax to which William alludes.[71] After discussing Saladin at some length, William offers his lengthy, personal aside on the matter of Holy Land, which is in essence a complex justification of the default Christian right, as well as an obligation, to the Promised Land of Canaan.

The central feature in William of Newburgh's digression is his contention that the land of Abraham belongs only to the righteous. Canaan was originally a gift to the Old Testament Jews, but it was by no means an absolute or irretrievable; God could take the land back should they be unable to maintain their adherence to his commands. What follows this preamble is a lengthy tale of God's rapprochement in regard to the Jews. Abraham's descendants took their rightful possession of Canaan but later lost their right to the land by killing Christ; the Jews were subsequently exiled from Judea. Here, then, emerges a direct connection between late twelfth-century charges of Christ-killing and William's interpretation of the Old Testament. The stripping of the Jewish privileges in the Holy Land coincides with the Christ-killing accusations rampant in the later twelfth century. John of Salisbury, notably, prosecutes a similar position in a letter to Peter the Scribe. John hints that the Jews were conspirers against the saving grace of Christ: "The Jews, as you recall, slew Christ, so as not to lose home and people; and in the act, lost both, as they deserved."[72] His comments likely resonated with the Canterbury religious, who owed substantial debts to the local Jewish community.[73] It is William, however, who develops this view more fully by suggesting that the dislocation of the Jews presaged the adoption of the Holy Land by the early Christians, to whom the dialogue now turns.

William of Newburgh specifically names the Roman emperors Vespasian and Titus as the "ministers of Divine justice" over Jews living in the colony of Judea in 70, but it was left to future, and Christian, emperors to restore God's covenant in the Holy Land.[74] More than two centuries later, following Constantine the Great's Edict of Milan, Christians worshipped in public amid the Jews and pagans in the city of Jerusalem. Righteous Christians, for years forced by persecutions into hiding, now supplanted the Jews as God's chosen people, not just physically but also symbolically because the temple destroyed by Titus was superseded by the Church of the Holy Sepulchre, which was dedicated in 335.[75] William dubs these Christians in Jerusalem "the true seed of Abraham," another dispossession of Jewish spiritual inheritance.[76] The narrative continues. The Christians, having been awarded control over the land, then rendered themselves unworthy of God's reward through their many sins, invariably becoming the victims of Saracen military might. In other words, inheritance of the Holy Land depended not on race or creed but on the virtue and vice of those given the honor of its governance.[77] Thus, the connection is made between Canaan, understood by William as now the heritage of Christianity, and the need for a general crusading effort of restoration. With the Third Crusade on his mind, William suggests that further military efforts might return the east to its rightful, Christian successors who will rule the land justly.[78] Here the digression ends, and William returns to the chronology of his history at large.

This particular interpretation of the physical and spiritual inheritance of the Holy Land is not unique to William of Newburgh. In particular, the destruction of the Temple and the role of Rome as the tool of divine retribution were important subjects in the early Middle Ages, with Gregory the Great establishing a celebration for the event that was reintroduced into the liturgical calendar in 740.[79] By the twelfth century, several men had written at length about the vengeance of God delivered through Vespasian and Titus, most notably Otto of Freising (d. 1158) and Peter of Blois (d. 1212).[80] Following the Battle of Hattin in 1187 in particular, the failure of Western forces to preserve Outremer was generally viewed as a religious crisis. One response was a system of prayers for the Christians in the Holy Land, the so-called *Jerusalem Liturgy*, which is found in two English chronicles on which William relied for his information.[81] These documents list only the required prayers for the liturgy, however, and it is William who departs from their strict evidentiary method by combining the contemporary loss of the Holy Land, the acquisition of Canaan by Christians, and the role of the Jews into a single, coherent spiritual history. Yet the digression in the *Historia Rerum Anglicarum* is fixated on an earthly, geographical center; William does not consign Jews to eternal flames for their sins but sketches their punishment in purely physical terms, the loss of a homeland. As M. J. Kennedy illustrates through study of William's *Commentary on the Song of Songs*, his perspective on Jewish culpability as regards the Crucifixion of Christ and the loss of Jerusalem does not, theologically, abolish the idea of their salvation; moreover, he posits the Virgin Mary as their benefactor who has forgotten that their ancestors killed her son.[82]

William of Newburgh's discourse on the Holy Land is neither original nor all encompassing, but it is an interesting integration of twelfth-century English anti-Jewish sentiments. William considered Henry II a great friend of the Jew and thus tied their prosperity, and continuing perfidy, to the royal court. The privileges extended to the English Jewry stood in opposition to William's world view and the council canons he had recorded: How could Jews be given greater freedom in England when they had reneged on their original covenant with God in the Promised Land? With both royal and ecclesiastical Jewish policies on his mind, William incorporates English anti-Judaism into a theological justification of the destruction of the Temple and Christendom's right to be called Abraham's seed. William's answer to the problem is also couched in economic terms: Jewish gains in England were offset by the Christian habitation in the Holy Land. This, essentially, was English anti-Judaism in the later twelfth century. The mounting discontent during Henry's reign, borne from frustrations over Jewish prosperity, a sense of duty to a crucified Lord, the multitude of debts owed by crusaders to Jewish financiers, and other assorted elements culminated in outright violence soon after the king's death.[83] No advocate of bloodshed, William nonetheless hoped for the repentance and conversion of the Jews.[84] Considering his views on Jewish earthly culpability, his ultimate solution for the perfidious Jew, "itaque Judæi inter Christianos debent quidem pro utilitate nostra vivere, sed pro sua iniquitate servire," fits snugly into the general attitude held by king and commoner alike:

The English Jewry, whatever its economic or legal status, remained subservient to Christians in both a practical and theological sense.[85]

Notes

1. Alan O. Anderson, ed. and trans., *Early Sources of Scottish History: A.D. 500 to 1286* (Edinburgh: University of Edinburgh Press, 1922), 323.
2. For the events at York, see Richard B. Dobson, *The Jews of Medieval York and the Massacre of March 1190* (York: St. Anthony's Press, 1974), 24–28, for a brief timeline of the anti-Jewish riots.
3. No Jewish communities existed in Scotland, Ireland, or Wales prior to 1290; see John Gillingham, *The English in the Twelfth Century: Imperialism, National Identity and Political Values* (Suffolk: Boydell, 2000), 12.
4. The crusading fervor was probably not, however, the single cause of the tension; see Kenneth Stow, "Conversion, Apostasy, and Apprehensiveness: Emicho of Flonheim and the Fear of the Jews in the Twelfth Century," *Speculum* 76 no. 4 (October 2001): 929.
5. Robert C. Stacey, "Crusades, Martyrdoms, and the Jews of Norman England, 1096–1190," in *Juden und Christen zur Zeit der Kreuzzüge,* ed. Alfred Haverkamp (Sigmaringen: Jan Thorbecke Verlag, 1999), 250. Moore, 31–32, argues that the crusades propagated but did not cause anti-Judaism.
6. See Joseph Jacobs, ed., *The Jews of Angevin England: Documents and Records* (New York: Gordon Press, 1977).
7. I employ the term *anti-Judaism* in preference to *anti-Semitism* for two reasons. First, the medieval English suspicions of and attacks against Jews stem from religious, not biological, prejudices. Though these attitudes provide much of the irrational basis for post-Darwinian anti-Jewish attitudes, they are not its complete foundation. Attitudes in the Middle Ages, then, provide but a portion of the totalizing, modern concept of *anti-Semitism.* Given the radical move to biological explanations in the nineteenth century, *anti-Judaism* is a useful term in the study of a developing but not yet fully developed, premodern, anti-Jewish sentiment. Second, I disagree with Robert Chazan that *anti-Judaism* is too flaccid a term; if employed rigorously in contextual, historical analyses, it effectively indicates hatred of the Jewish religion and its practitioners and not just a sense of normal, interreligious rivalry; see Chazan, *Medieval Stereotypes and Modern Antisemitism* (Berkeley: University of California Press, 1997), 125–29. Moreover, *anti-Judaism* does not seek to differentiate between magnitudes of varying anti-Jewish attitudes and actions; rather, it is a lexical differential between historical prejudices.
8. The present study employs the Latin edition: Richard Howlett, ed., *Historia Rerum Anglicarum* [hereafter *HRA*], *Chronicles of the Reigns of Stephen, Henry II, and Richard I,* 4 vols., Rolls Series 82 (London: Longman, 1884–89). Other editions include the older Latin source, Hans C. Hamilton, ed. *HRA Willelmi Parvi,* 2 vols. (London: Sumptibus Societatis, 1856); and English translation of Joseph Stevenson, ed. and trans., *Church Historians of England,* vol. 3 (London: Seeleys, 1856) and of P. G. Walsh and M. J. Kennedy, ed. and trans., *William of Newburgh: the History of English Affairs, Book 1* (Warminster, Wiltshire: Aris & Phillips, 1988).

9. Antonia Grandsen, *Historical Writing in England, c. 550 to c. 1307* (Ithaca, NY: Cornell University Press, 1974), 263. Specific studies of William are limited in number, but see Kate Norgate, "The Date of Composition of William of Newburgh's History," *English Historical Review* [hereafter *EHR*] 19 (1904): 288–97; H. E. Salter, "William of Newburgh," *EHR* 22 (1907): 510–14; and in response to Salter, C. N. L. Brooke, "Short Notices," *EHR* 77 (1962): 554. The only single-volume treatment of William is the brief Rudolf Jahncke, *Guilelmus Neubrigensis: ein Pragmatischer Geschichtsschreiber des Zwölften Jahrhunderts* (Bonn: A. Marcus and E. Weber, 1912).

10. Grandsen, *Historical Writing*, 264–8. For William's literary skills, see Bruce Dickins, "A Yorkshire Chronicler," *Transactions of the Yorkshire Dialect Society* 5 (1934): 15–26. For his criticism, see Monika Otter, *Inventiones: Fiction and Referentiality in Twelfth-Century English Historical Writing* (Chapel Hill: University of North Carolina Press, 1996), 95–96; Nancy F. Partner, *Serious Entertainments: the Writing of History in Twelfth-Century England* (Chicago: University of Chicago Press, 1977), 62–66. William was the only historian to criticize Geoffrey of Monmouth's *Historia Regum Brittanie* prior to Polydore Vergil (1470–1555). For his theology, see his exposition on the Canticle of Mary: John C. Gorman, ed., *William of Newburgh's Explanatio Sacri Epithalamii in Matrem Sponsi* (Fribourg: University Press, 1960).

11. Grandsen, *Historical Writing*, 265.

12. Partner, *Serious Entertainments*, 58.

13. Dobson, *Jews of Medieval York,* 24. For William's narrative on the event, see *HRA*, I, 317–22.

14. Grandsen, *Historical Writing*, 265. See also Kennedy, "'Faith in the One God Flowed over You from the Jews, the Sons of the Patriarchs and the Prophets': William of Newburgh's Writings on Anti-Jewish Violence," *Anglo-Norman Studies* 25 (2002): 146–47.

15. Partner, *Serious Entertainments*, 226.

16. Albert M. Hyamson, *A History of the Jews in England* (London: Chatto & Windus, 1908), 31.

17. Roger de Hoveden, *Chronica*, ed. William Stubbs, 4 vols. Rolls Series 51 (London: Longman, 1868), II, 231; the translation is from Henry T. Riley, trans., *The Annals of Roger de Hoveden*, 2 vols. (New York: AMS Press, 1968), I, 553. The law ensured that Jewries had a unique and distinct legal status from other communities in England; see Henry S. Q. Henriques, *The Jews and the English Law* (Clifton, NJ: A. M. Kelley, 1974), 53.

18. Norman Golb, *The Jews in Medieval Normandy* (Cambridge, UK: Cambridge University Press, 1998), 353.

19. Roth, 11. Kings John (1199–1216) and Henry III (1216–1272) extended the charter of protection, but the oversight of the crown served simultaneously to weaken the power of Jewish institutions. Representative of this is the divorce case of David of Oxford and his wife, Muriel, in 1242. Three rabbis — Mosse of London, Aaron of Canterbury, and Jacob of Oxford — found in favor of David but demanded that he offer his wife some sort of restitution. The nature of this sentence is unknown but was probably financial; in any event, he refused, the rabbis threatened excommunication, and David appealed to Henry III for satisfaction. The crown forced the Beth Din to withdraw its sentence, and David walked away satisfied. On the incident,

see Cecil Roth, ed., *Anglo-Jewish Letters* (London: Soncino Press, 1938), 12–13; Michael Adler, *Jews of Medieval England* (London: Printed and published for The Jewish Historical Society of England, 1939), 29.

20. Roger de Hoveden, *Chronica*, II, 137. The first of these sites was at Oxford; see the discussion in D'Blossiers Tovey, *Anglia Judaica*, ed. Elizabeth Pearl (London: Weidenfeld and Nicolson in association with M. Green, 1990), 13.

21. On the Jewish *Exchequer*, see briefly Henry G. Richardson, *The English Jewry under Angevin Kings* (London: Methuen, 1960), 176; and, in extensive detail, C. Gross, "The Exchequer of the Jews of England in the Middle Ages," in *Papers Read at the Anglo-Jewish Historical Exhibition* (London: Office of the *Jewish Chronicle, 1888*), 170–230.

22. Golb, *Jews in Medieval Normandy*, 350–53.

23. Roth, 15.

24. John Horace Round, ed., *Ancient Charters Royal and Private, Prior to A.D. 1200* (London: Printed by Wyman & Sons, 1888), 82–84.

25. For Anesty's precise accounting of his debts, see Jacobs, *Jews of Angevin England*, 38–42. For an analysis of the same, see Joseph Shatzmiller, *Shylock Reconsidered: Jews, Moneylending, and Medieval Society* (Berkeley: University of California Press, 1990), 78–79.

26. Jacobs, *Jews of Angevin England*, 51–2. Jacobs argues that were it not for the loans from Josce to Fitz Gilbert ("Strongbow") the Irish expedition would not have been feasible; see also Marie T. Flanagan, "Strongbow, Henry II and Anglo-Norman Intervention in Ireland," in *War and Government in the Middle Ages: Essays in Honour of J. O. Prestwich*, ed. John Gillingham and J. C. Holt (Woodbridge: Boydell, 1984), 77–9.

27. Richardson, *English Jewry,* 60–61. See also Emilie Amt, *The Accession of Henry II in England: Royal Government Restored, 1149–1159* (Woodbridge: Boydell, 1993), 101. Henry was willing to borrow funds from Christian moneylenders as well, but he appears to have relied almost entirely on Jews after 1164; see Graeme J. White, *Restoration and Reform, 1153–1165: Recovery from Civil War in England* (Cambridge, UK: Cambridge University Press, 2000), 133.

28. Richard Mortimer, *Angevin England, 1154–1258* (Oxford: Blackwell, 1994), 49.

29. Frank Barlow, *The Feudal Kingdom of England, 1042–1216*, 5th ed. (London: Longman, 1999), 269.

30. Chazan, *Medieval Stereotypes*, 114.

31. For the amounts taken from the Jews from 1155 to 1159; see Amt, *Accession of Henry II*, 189–94. For the text of the Saladin Tithe, see William Stubbs, ed., *Select Charters and other Illustrations of English Constitutional History*, 8th ed. (Oxford: Clarendon Press, 1900), 159–60.

32. Gervase of Canterbury, *The Chronicle of the Reigns of Stephen, Henry II, and Richard I*, ed. William Stubbs, 2 vols., Rolls Series 73 (London: Longman and Co., 1879), I, 422.

33. Hyamson, *History of the Jews*, 29, adopts the exaggerated numbers, which are questioned by Christopher Tyerman, *England and the Crusades, 1095–1588* (Chicago: University of Chicago Press, 1988), 79.

34. Jacobs, *Jews of Angevin England,* xiv–xv. For the shipwreck, see William Stubbs, ed., *Gesta Regis Henrici Secundi*, 2 vols., Rolls Series 49 (London: Longmans, Gree, Reader, and Dyer, 1867), II, 5; Roth, 15–16.

35. Arthur Hughes, C. G. Crump, and C. Johnson, eds., *Dialogus de Scaccario* (Oxford: Clarendon Press, 1902), xxvi, 157.

36. Holt, *Magna Carta*, 2d ed. (Cambridge, UK: Cambridge University Press, 1992), 452–55. For a brief discussion on widows in the 1100s, see Barlow, *Feudal Kingdom*, 215.

37. As an example, Henry could release his subjects from their financial commitments, as evidenced by a charter drawn at Cheltenham in 1187 that absolves a certain Roger of his Jewish debts; see R. W. Eyton, *Court, Household, and Itinerary of Henry II* (London: Taylor and Company, 1878), 276.

38. John of Salisbury, *Frivolities of Courtiers and Footprints of Philosophers* [*Policraticus*], ed. and trans. John B. Pike (Minneapolis: University of Minnesota Press, 1938), III, 13, 198–99.

39. This date is evidenced by his dedication of the book to Thomas Becket; see *Policraticus*, i: 17, 10–11.

40. W. L. Warren, *Henry II* (Berkeley: University of California Press, 1973), 382–83. The complaint is recorded by Giraldus Cambrensis, *De Principis Instructione Liber*, ed. George F. Warner, Rolls Series 21 (London: Longman, 1891), III, 186.

41. Hyamson, *History of the Jews*, 34. The evidence to this point is rather sketchy. The Assize denied possession of a hauberk or "aubergel" to Jews, that is to say, defensive clothing, but weaponry such as lances, headpieces of iron, helmets, and shields are not mentioned, and Jews may have retained some capability in this regard. For the text of the Assize in English, see David C. Douglas and George W. Greenaway, eds., *English Historical Documents* (London: Eyre and Spottiswoode, 1953), II, 416–17; in Latin, see Stubbs, *Select Charters,* 153–56.

42. *HRA*, I, 280: "Gentem perfidam et Christianis inimicam, Judæos scilicet fœnerantes, propter largiora quæ ex eorum percipiebat fœnerationibus commoda, plus justo fovit: in tantum ut in Christianos protervi et cervicosi existerent, plurimaque eis gravamina irrogarent."

43. Ibid., 294: "Caventes enim iidem hostes veritatis ne forte habita sub rege priore felicitas minus eis arrideret sub novo, ejus decentissime honoranda primordia et favorem non disparem amplitudine munerum redimendum duxerunt."

44. Ibid., 298: "Quid enim aptius portendit, si quid portendit, quod regiæ consecrationis ejus diem pariter et locum blasphemæ gentis nobilitavit exitium, quod in ipso regni ejus exordio hostes Christianæ fidei cœperunt juxta eum cadere et infimari?"

45. The scriptural justification was Deuteronomy 24:20–21, and, by the Second Lateran Council, Luke 6:35; see generally Benjamin N. Nelson, *The Idea of Usury* (Princeton, NJ: Princeton University Press, 1949), 5–10. For the central figures in the debate, see John T. Noonan, *The Scholastic Analysis of Usury* (Cambridge, MA: Harvard University Press, 1957), 42–44; Cohen, 224–25.

46. *HRA*, I, 137.

47. Robert Sommerville, *Pope Alexander III and the Council of Tours* (Berkeley: University of California Press, 1977), 39–40.

48. Noonan, *Scholastic Analysis*, 19.

49. The canons of the Third Lateran Council are provided in *HRA*, I, 206–23 and by Gervase of Canterbury, *Chronicle,* I, 278–92. For a study of the council, see Jean Longère, ed., *Le Troisième Concile de Latran (1179): Sa place dans l'histoire* (Paris: Etudes augustiniennes, 1982).

50. Marshall W. Baldwin, *Alexander III and the Twelfth Century* (New York: New-man Press, 1968), 198–99. Alexander ordered Richard, archbishop of Canterbury, to enforce the ban on Jews employing Christian servants, perhaps demonstrating the seriousness of the papacy on this particular issue; see Shlomo Simonsohn, *The Apostolic See and the Jews, Documents: 492–1404* (Toronto: Pontifical Institute of Mediaeval Studies, 1988), no. 56, 57.

51. Roth, 16. Such dealings of churchmen in usurious affairs could become rather involved. A Jewish deed from late in Henry II's reign shows the monks of Biddles-den, Buckinghamshire, accepting lands and a mill as payment for helping a man erase his debt to an Oxford Jewess; Israel Abrahams and H. P. Stokes, *Starrs and Jewish Charters Preserved in the British Museum* (Cambridge, UK: Cambridge University Press, 1930), no. 1207.

52. W. J. Millor and C. N. L. Brooke, eds., *The Letters of John of Salisbury, Volume Two: The Later Letters (1163–1180)* (Oxford: Clarendon Press, 1979), no. 322. Other English abbeys fell into debt with Jews as well; see, for example, the case of Bury-St. Edmunds as depicted in Jacobs, *Jews of Angevin England*, 59–62.

53. Adler, *Jews of Medieval England*, 51–52. Specifically, Alexander requested that Henry not press the abbot to repay his loans; see Simonsohn, *Apostolic See and the Jews*, no. 58. Such dealings of churchmen in usurious affairs could become rather involved. On Anglo–Jewish relations in Canterbury in 1188–1189, see Gervase of Canterbury, *Chronicle*, I, 405; Everett U. Crosby, *Bishop and Chapter in Twelfth-Century England* (Cambridge, UK: Cambridge University Press, 1994), 97–98.

54. de Hoveden, *Chronica*, II, 237; *Dialogus de Scaccario*, XIII, 146.

55. Nelson, *Idea of Usury*, 17.

56. Stow, 4.

57. William Urry, *Canterbury under the Angevin Kings* (London: Athlone Press, 1967), 117.

58. Robert Stacey, "From Ritual Crucifixion to Host Desecration: Jews and the Body of Christ," *Jewish History* 12 no. 1 (1998): 14.

59. For the earliest account of the incident, see Michael Swanton, ed., *The Anglo-Saxon Chronicles* (London: Phoenix, 2000), 265. Some notable studies of the event include, in brief, Roth, 9; and, in more detail, John M. McCulloh, "Jewish Ritual Murder: William of Norwich, Thomas of Monmouth, and the Early Dissemination of the Myth," *Speculum* 72 (1997): 698–740 and Jeremy Cohen, "The Flow of Blood in Medieval Norwich," *Speculum* 79:1 (2004): 26–65. No verdict was issued in the case of William of Norwich, as the Jews were legally under the protection of King Stephen and could not be tried in an ecclesiastical court; Crosby, *Bishop and Chapter,* 190.

60. William D. Rubinstein, *A History of the Jews in the English Speaking World: Great Britain* (New York: St. Martin's Press, 1996), 38–39.

61. Henry's supremacy over the clergy on Jewish matters was unexceptional. At the council of Westminster in October 1163, Henry declared jurisdiction over clerks accused of major crimes as well, the result being the famous dispute with Thomas Becket. For a documentary overview of the legal developments, see Douglas and Greenaway, *English Historical Documents*, 713–34.

62. Stacey, "Host Desecration," 23. On the French incidents, see William C. Jordan, *The French Monarchy and the Jews: From Philip Augustus to the Last Capetians* (Philadelphia: University of Pennsylvania Press, 1989), 18–20.

63. The so-called "blood curse" is found in Matthew 27:20–26.

64. Anselm minimized the guilt of the Sanhedrin, and Abelard absolved it completely; Cohen, 288. See in general Cohen, "The Jews as the Killers of Christ in the Latin Tradition, from Augustine to the Friars," *Traditio* 39 (1983): 1–27; Moore, 34–39.

65. Anna S. Abulafia, "Twelfth-Century Christian Expectations of Jewish Conversion: a Case Study of Peter of Blois," *Aschkenas* 8 no. 1 (1998): 63–64; Millor and Brooke, *Letters of John of Salisbury*, no. 246; Salisbury quotes in this regard John 10:32. Although different attitudes toward Jewish culpability existed, one notable custom in eleventh-century Toulouse was the *colaphus Judeo*, a ritual slap to the face, which was administered to Jews annually, perhaps as a punishment for their role in Christ's crucifixion; see Michael Frassetto, "Heretics and Jews in the Writings of Ademar of Chabannes and the Origins of Medieval Anti-Semitism," *Church History* 71 (March 2002): 9.

66. As Stacey, "Host Desecration," 11, notes, "Christians were in no doubt that Jews were the enemies of the body of Christ."

67. The case of Louis VII is a study in contrasts. During the Second Crusade, Louis VII annulled the interest owed to Jews by crusaders; see Stacey, "Jews of Norman England," 241. Under consideration then is not only Map's account but also the petition of Louis to disregard Canon 13 of Lateran III, a request denied by Alexander III; see Simonsohn, *Apostolic See and the Jews*, no. 59. The Jews were expelled from the Ile de France by Louis's son Philip Augustus, but to only a limited degree; see Jordan, *French Monarchy and the Jews*, 3–5.

68. Walter Map, *De Nugis Curialium*, ed. and trans. M. R. James (Oxford: Clarendon Press, 1983), V, 5, 453–55.

69. *HRA*, I, 316–17: "Quippe eadem Christianæ utilitatis ratione perfidious Judæus Domini Christi crucifixor inter Christianos vivere sinitur…"

70. Henry had promised with Louis VII to go on crusade on September 21, 1177, but the oath was never fulfilled; see de Hoveden, *Chronica*, II, 144, for their sworn oath at Ivry.

71. See Hans E. Mayer, "Henry II and the Holy Land," *EHR* 97 (1982): 721–39, and especially Tyerman, *England and the Crusades*, 36–56. For William's short notice, see *HRA*, I, 247.

72. Millor and Brooke, *Letters of John of Salisbury*, no. 300; John also alludes to the Jews' conspiring nature in II, no. 250. Peter the Scribe worked in both the chancery of Henry II and at the priory of Canterbury.

73. See n. 52.

74. *HRA*, I, 253: "Quas stamen postmodum, eo quod non cognoverint tempus visitationis suæ, sed detestabili vesania proprium peremerunt Redemptorem, eadem terra, jam in ea patratis divinis mysteriis inclita, severiori judicio nunquam revocandas evomuit, Romanis imperatoribus Vespasiano et Tito divinæ animadversionis ministris." Vespasian celebrated a triumph in Rome for his Judean wars, and Titus, his son, led the five-month siege and subsequent sack of Jerusalem in 70 A.D.; see the respective accounts of Suetonius, Joseph Gavorse, ed. and trans., *The Lives of the Twelve Caesers* (New York: Modern Library, 1931), VIII, 328, 338–39.

75. "Jerusalem," in *The Oxford Classical Dictionary*, ed. Simon Hornblower and Antony Spawforth (Oxford: Oxford University Press, 1996), 795.

76. *HRA*, I, 253: "Tunc enim Terra Sancta, pio ejusdem principis studio, a gentilium rit-
    uum sordibus emundata, data est in hereditatem et possessionem vero semini Abrahæ,
    id est, Christianis; a quibus et possessa est annis multis usque post tempora beati
    Gregorii."
77. Partner, *Serious Entertainments*, 106.
78. Paradoxically, the tax levied on Jewish moneylenders helped to finance the Third
    Crusade, which William hoped would regain Christendom's adopted birthright.
79. Amnon Linder, "Jews and Judaism in the Eyes of Christian Thinkers of the Middle
    Ages: The Destruction of Jerusalem in Medieval Christian Liturgy," in *Witness to
    Witchcraft*, 115–17.
80. Abulafia, "A Case Study of Peter of Blois," 54, 65–66. William of Newburgh's
    account predates that of his contemporary Peter of Blois, however, for Peter's invec-
    tive was probably not composed until 1196, two years after William's death.
81. As noted in Linder, "Destruction of Jerusalem," 120–21. The chronicle entries are
    from Stubbs, *Gesta Regis Henrici Secundi*, II, 53–54; de Hoveden, *Chronica*, II,
    359–60; William's reliance on these two works of Howden is demonstrated in John
    Gillingham, "Two Yorkshire Historians Compared: Roger of Howden and William
    of Newburgh," *Haskins Society Journal* 12 (2002): 20, 25–26.
82. Kennedy, "William of Newburgh's Writings," 150–51. For the text of the *Commen-
    tary*, see n. 10.
83. Stacey, "Jews of Norman England," 242–43.
84. Kennedy, "William of Newburgh's Writings," 151.
85. *HRA*, I, 317.

11

Jewish Witness, Forced Conversion, and Island Living
John Duns Scotus on Jews and Judaism

Nancy L. Turner

John Duns Scotus was one of the most influential theologians of the late Middle Ages. His arguments concerning the Immaculate Conception were influential on Catholic doctrine from the fourteenth century forward, and his writings concerning salvation and beatitude came to form a cornerstone of Catholic teachings until modern times. His teachings on the univocity of the concept of being and his distinction between intuitive and abstractive cognition were so influential that within two decades of his death in 1308, his doctrines had attracted a strong following among thinkers and students in both Paris and Oxford; indeed, even during Scotus's lifetime, students at Oxford who espoused his method and doctrine were already identified as *Scotists* by their fellow students. By the middle of the fourteenth century, Scotus's teachings on a wide range of subjects were frequently cited by theologians in Italy and the German universities as well, and by the late fifteenth century Franciscan studia had come to treat the texts of Scotus as their fundamental authority.[1]

Among the teachings of Scotus that are less well known among modern historians but that were frequently cited by thinkers throughout the fourteenth century were his views on the licitness of forcibly converting Jewish adults and children to Christianity. As this chapter demonstrates, Scotus's arguments in support of the forcible conversion of unwilling Jews were exceptionally harsh, even extreme, in a century that saw many hostile attitudes toward Jews. Perhaps some of Scotus's unusually negative attitudes toward Jews can be explained by noting a few of the cultural and social influences that may have been at work on him during his childhood and young adult life. Scotus came of age in England in the two decades before the expulsion of Jews from that realm in 1290. He was born in either 1265 or 1266, the son of Scottish farmers, on an estate in extreme southeastern Scotland. John entered the Franciscan order as a teenager and was ordained into the priesthood in 1291 in Northampton, England. He studied at Cambridge and Oxford in the years between 1291 and 1293 and at Paris sometime in the years between 1293 and 1297. Scotus delivered his commentary on Lombard's *Sentences* a first time at Cambridge between 1297 and 1300 and a second time at Oxford between 1300 and 1301. He was then sent by his order to teach at the University of Paris in 1302 where he lectured on Lombard's *Sentences* for the next three years. In 1305 Scotus obtained his doctorate in theology at Paris, where he continued to teach until 1307. In this year, he was transferred by his order to Cologne, teaching there as principal reader until his death just one year later in 1308.[2]

In the decades leading up to the expulsion of Jews from the realm of England, its inhabitants displayed exceptionally negative attitudes and behavior toward Jews in comparison with many Christian communities on the Continent. In the 1140s the English were among the first communities to apply the ritual murder libel to Jews — that is, to accuse Jews of murdering Christian children, frequently by crucifixion, and in some cases of using their blood to perform gruesome religious rituals.[3] The ritual murder libel appeared in other countries across Europe, but it did not occur as frequently in France or Germany as it did in England. Indeed, one of the most infamous cases of the ritual murder libel in the Middle Ages — the death of young Hugh of Lincoln,[4] a story with enough potency to inspire Geoffrey Chaucer to base his "Prioress's Tale" on it more than a hundred years later — took place in 1255, only ten years before Scotus's birth. Furthermore, Northampton, where Scotus studied for the priesthood and was ordained, recorded a case of executing Jews on the charge of crucifying a Christian boy in 1279,[5] just a decade before Scotus lived in that community.

Yet, as is demonstrated here, although fourteenth-century thinkers were familiar with Scotus's stance advocating the forcible conversion of Jews, this is by no means the only context in which Scotus discusses Jews or Judaism in his works. Rather, Scotus devotes several distinctions in his *Sentences* commentary to a discussion of the sacramental character of circumcision and to a comparison of the laws of the Old and New Testament. In his teachings on circumcision and Old Testament Law, Scotus generally supports standard Christian teachings on these issues; echoing the pronouncements of Augustine[6] and of later thinkers such as Peter Lombard and Thomas Aquinas,[7] Scotus expresses great respect for the rites and ceremonies of the Old Law and continually emphasizes the value of these rites for what he sees as their prefiguration of Christian ceremonies and of the coming of Christ. His respect for the Old Law does not translate, however, into a respect for the Jews themselves. Indeed, he depicts even Old Testament Jews as selfish, primitive, and stubborn.

Following standard Christian doctrine, Scotus acknowledges that Judaism was the rightful religious tradition established by God before the coming of Christ and one worthy of respect from Christians. He states quite baldly at one point, "The Old Law was not bad, as idolatry is, and therefore ought not suddenly be repealed...The synagogue ought to have been buried with honor, so as to show it to have been good for its time."[8] Scotus argues forcefully in support of his belief in God's intention for all those who had followed the Old Law (before the New Law was instituted) to merit grace and be blessed for their devotion and that circumcision is the Old Testament rite most blessed by God, thus possessing the greatest potency. He cites Bede's pronouncement that circumcision was the Old Testament's counterpart to baptism and thus that it "performed the same aid of being a saving cure that baptism became accustomed to perform in a time of grace."[9]

Indeed, Scotus makes clear his belief that many precepts of the Old Law, before the coming of Christ, had many of the same strengths and legitimacy as the New Law would eventually possess and that God intended the faithful under the Old Law to be blessed and rewarded for their faithfulness. As he explains, "God at no time left a group of humans without a necessary cure to reach salvation, especially those to whom he gave the Law."[10] Scotus declares that this necessary cure was circumcision, and he reasons that such a cure necessarily had the power to remove original sin because "they could not attain salvation without the removal of original sin."[11] Like Bede and Aquinas,[12] Scotus argues that circumcision did not just remove original sin in its recipients; it also conferred grace. He acknowledges that whether circumcision had the power to confer grace as well as delete sin is a complex question and states that this issue must be considered in terms of both God's absolute power and God's ordained power. He declares that in terms of God's absolute power, "God can remove original sin (*culpa*), without conferring grace."[13] However, according to Scotus, in terms of God's ordained power, "it is not possible to remove original guilt, nor any other mortal sin, without an infusion of grace."[14] He adds that God "frees no one, nor thus can he free one from guilt, unless he gives grace to him."[15] On this point, Scotus asserts his disagreement with some thinkers[16] who argue that because circumcision was instituted for the purpose of removing original sin, and thus would confer grace only as a consequence, grace was not conferred with circumcision.[17] Scotus takes a much more positive view of circumcision's power and pronounces that grace was principally intended in circumcision. He explains that according to right reason, God more chiefly intends perfection than simple removal of defect; thus, God intended the positive perfection of grace with circumcision, not just the removal of the defect of original sin.[18]

Scotus, however, does not limit his acknowledgment of the potency of the Old Law to circumcision. He explains that other ceremonies of the Old Testament also conferred grace on their practitioners. He mentions the rites of cleansing that the Jews practiced, such as the cleansing from the touch of the dead, the cleansing from the touch of leprosy, and numerous sacrifices and offerings to God. He acknowledges that these rites cannot be considered sacraments in the strict sense because they did not confer grace by virtue of the work worked (*ex virtute operis operati*), the standard description and definition of the workings of the Christian sacraments.[19] Yet according to Scotus, "nevertheless grace was conferred in these through the means of merit."[20]

He supports this stance by referring to acts that "pertained to the performance (*cultum*) of worship for the time in which God wanted thus to be worshipped"; he declares that these acts were proper, blessed acts, intended by God to be performed. Scotus emphasizes the inviolability of the Old Law with his reference to Matthew 23:2, with which he makes the point that the precepts of even the (in Christ's eyes) hypocritical Pharisees must be followed because they "sit on Moses' seat."[21] Therefore, in Scotus's view, any religious acts done out of love for God, as the rites of the ancients Jews were done, merited grace. He comments on Abraham's circumcision, "I understand nothing was conferred to him inside through the means of the sacrament or by the virtue of the work worked (*virtute operis operati*); but I believe that it was conferred to him through the means of merit, or by virtue of the work being worked (*virtute operis operantis*)." He then supports this position by stating, "I believe that the act of circumcising himself out of obedience to God, and his proceeding [to do so] out of love (*caritas*), was meritorious for [Abraham], just as, indeed, the sacrifice of Isaac [would have been]."[22]

Scotus then concludes by again referring to those arguing that because many of the religious rites of the Old Law were not sacraments in the strict sense those who performed them could not merit grace. Scotus expresses his disagreement with this position with the statement, "This, indeed, seems very, very cruel, namely, that something that would be done out of love and obedience, observing a command of God [and its doer] would not [thereby] merit." Scotus continues, "It seems irrationally said that God gave someone a command, not wishing the person observing that command to merit to the extent that the person observed it out of love and obedience…therefore, Jews, out of love, observing sacraments not strictly pronounced as such, merited grace."[23]

Scotus does declare, however, that the powers of circumcision are limited when compared to those of baptism. He presents Bede's argument that circumcision did not reveal to its recipient the entrance to heaven, as baptism does. Scotus argues, however, that this inability of circumcision was not a result of a defect in it but simply was because circumcision was performed in the period before the entrance to heaven had been revealed to anyone through the act of Christ's passion and death. He adds that, in fact, "the entrance had not lain open to those [who were] baptized [and died] before the passion."[24]

Yet in a departure from the traditional Christian viewpoint, Scotus argues that the Old Law was a system proper and blessed not only in the period before the passion of Christ but for several generations afterward as well. Indeed, Scotus, unlike Aquinas,[25] argues that the blessed status of the rites of the Old Law did not suddenly come to an end with the death of Christ but rather that it was acceptable for Jews to continue to follow the Old Law for an extended time after the passion of Christ. In fact, he argues that the precepts of the Old Law are never explicitly pronounced illicit in the course of the New Testament and insists that, as a result, one can only infer that they became so. On the issue of circumcision specifically, Scotus holds that although circumcision was eventually rendered useless and mortally sinful, it is not stated explicitly anywhere in the scriptures exactly when it became illicit according to the New Law. In support of his argument on this point, he points to the fact that Paul and the other apostles continued to practice many of the rites of the Old Law even after baptism and the other rites of the New Law had become widespread practices.

Scotus explains why it was acceptable and even necessary to continue to follow the precepts of the Old Law after the coming of Christ: "No one is held to some divine precept unless it has been promulgated to them by someone suitable and authentic [for example, a prophet]." Scotus reasons that because circumcision had been authentically promulgated by God, its practice should not have been abandoned by Jews until it was properly replaced by a clearly authentic promulgation of baptism.[26] Scotus never questions that baptism eventually replaced circumcision absolutely, but he argues that the process of annulling circumcision and replacing it with baptism was long and complex. He declares that from the time of the Passion up to the time of the preaching of the Gospel, circumcision still held in full force because "there was no other certain new remedy given to them [yet] because it had not been announced."[27] Scotus explains that up until the time that the various Jewish communities heard the new promulgation concerning baptism, they were still required to circumcise their children "because in no way was it obvious to them that circumcision had been revoked."[28] Scotus then argues that even after the Gospel had begun to be preached, practicing the Old Law rite of circumcision remained acceptable because Paul himself continued to follow the Old Law. Citing the passage in Acts 1:2–7, in which Paul followed the Old Law by going to the temple and offering a sacrifice for himself, Scotus states that with such an act, "by Paul himself, the observation of the Law in converted Jews was approved. And Paul himself among all Christians executed the work of the Law."[29]

Scotus is careful to make it clear that circumcision did not remain meritorious and proper among all persons everywhere after Christ's Passion, and he makes a distinction between the observance of circumcision among gentile converts and Jewish converts to Christianity. He notes that beginning with the preaching after Pentecost, gentile converts were not allowed to be circumcised or to practice the Old Law. However, in Scotus's opinion, it was still clearly licit for converted Jews to do both. Thus, on the issue of whether first-century Jews were immediately cut off from God's grace with the coming of Christ, Scotus declares,

> If you ask when circumcision was simply illicit for converted Jews, I respond that
> we do not have that time [stated] in any scripture because the historical scripture
> did not cover the Church beyond the fifth year of Nero's reign, namely, no more
> than thirty years beyond the passion of Christ; and all that time the converted Jews
> observed the law.

He continues,

> Nor do I believe that this was abandoned among the Jews who converted all the
> way up to the destruction of Jerusalem or up to the dispersion of the Jews among
> the nations. Then perhaps the [Jewish converts] conformed themselves to gentiles,
> among whom they were dispersed, and thus little by little the observance [of the
> Old Law] ceased among them."[30]

Scotus argues, then, that it was not with Christ's death that the Old Law was
annulled, because the New Law could not take effect until it had been properly
promulgated. According to this standard, then, the New Law could not replace
and annul the Old Law until the Gospel was widely preached, which, as Scotus
notes, took decades. He explains that the requirement of baptism for some people
took place "the month after Pentecost, and for others a year after and for others
ten years after, and so on as it was preached to them."[31]

In support of this assertion of the licitness of the Old Law for decades after Christ's
Passion, Scotus refers to the controversy that arose during the ministries of Paul and
Peter over whether Paul was justified in rebuking Peter for withdrawing from Gentiles
during his preaching and openly observing the Old Law among prospective Jewish
converts (Galatians 2:11). Many theologians had insisted that Peter was censurable in
this instance for slavishly observing the Old Law to avoid offending Jews whom he
hoped to convert. Scotus disagrees with previous thinkers, most notably Augustine,
on this point and argues that although Peter was censurable for this behavior, "it could
not be said that he was censurable because he observed the Law."[32]

Scotus maintains that the Old Law clearly remained in force because even
after this incident, Paul followed the Old Law by circumcising Timothy and four
years afterward obeyed the Law again by purifying himself in the temple. According to Scotus, Peter did deserve rebuke for his behavior during this incident, but
not for observing the Law; rather, his doings were reprehensible for other reasons:
because he deliberately separated himself from the Gentiles for the sake of the
Jews, because he did not act out what was in his heart concerning circumcision
and the Old Law, and because he did not do what he knew was right out of fear
of the Jewish response.[33] In emphasizing that Peter did not deserve censure for
observing the law, Scotus later states, "in observing the Law in Jerusalem, however, Peter did not sin, because it was proper for a Jew, among Jews, to observe
the Law then."[34]

Scotus further supports his stance on the legitimacy of the Old Law for an
extended period after the Passion of Christ by taking issue with the standard

interpretation of Christ's pronouncement on the cross: "It is consummated" (John 19:30). Theologians from Bede to Aquinas had insisted that Christ was referring to the Old Law in this passage and that with this pronouncement the Old Law was brought to an end. Scotus argues, however, that this statement does not refer to the ancient Law but rather to "those things which were written about the son of man." He quotes Luke 18:31 in support of this position: "Behold, we are going up to Jerusalem and everything that is written of the son of Man by the prophets will be accomplished." Scotus contends that if this statement is taken as a reference to the Old Law, "it ought to be understood thus: it is accomplished as a cause, for the death of Christ was the cause of the confirmation of the [New] Law of the Gospel; but the latter was not confirmed as necessary to be observed before the public preaching of it, which did not begin during the Passion, but at the Pentecost."[35]

Yet despite the great respect Scotus expresses for circumcision and the Old Law, and despite his repeated declarations that the Old Law retained its legitimacy and power for decades after the death of Christ, it is quite clear that Scotus's respect for the Old Testament Law does not extend to the Old Testament Jews. According to Scotus, the Old Law should be respected and revered because it came from God; the Old Testament Jews, however, in Scotus's eyes, were a violent, primitive, and selfish people. Any respect he expresses for Old Testament Jews stems solely from the fact that they were devoted worshippers of God and followers of Old Testament Law. So, for instance, as previously remarked, Scotus says that Abraham merited grace from the act of circumcision because he did it "out of obedience to God." He does not express respect for Old Testament Jews in any context in which their devotion to the Law is not the central focus.

Indeed, Scotus generally depicts the Jewish populace of the Old Testament as backward and lacking in insight or intelligence. He explains that God felt it necessary to instruct and even dictate to the Jewish people an understanding about His unity that should have been evident to them through natural reason. As Scotus explains, "The Jewish people were uncivilized and prone to idolatry; therefore they needed to be instructed about the unity of God through laws, even though this could have been demonstrated through natural reason."[36] Indeed, in a passage discussing Christ's suffering on the cross, Scotus makes a clear distinction between the Old Law and the Jews who followed it. He declares that the Law was not to blame for the errors of the Jews but rather that the Jews were at fault for the excessive and slavish way they chose to interpret the Law. He refers in one passage to "how they were weakened by the inordinate and distorted affection for their law." He argues that their distorted interpretation of the law led "to many evils," among them allowing a sheep or cow to be retrieved from a well during the Sabbath but not permitting a sick human being to be attended to on his or her day of rest. He emphasizes that the Jews, not the Law, needed correction and adds that Christ "wanted to call the Jews back from their errors through his works and sermons... because the truth had to be taught to the Jews."[37] Scotus's purpose in this passage seems to be more to illustrate the Jews' overly literal behavior and excessive legalism than to point out flaws in the Old Law.

Scotus's argument that the Old Law was noble and laudable for its time but that that time had passed is reenforced by his repeated — but by no means unique — reference to the imagery in the New Testament (Hebrews 10:1; Colossians 12:17) of the Old Law as "but a shadow of the good things to come instead of the true form of these realities." Drawing on this imagery, as Christian thinkers had done dating back to the church fathers, Scotus states that the ceremonies of the Old Law were valuable because they prefigured "the truth" of the New Law; however, he explains, the many ceremonies of the Old Testament no longer have a meaning in themselves "because the shadow passed and the truth advanced."[38]

In Scotus's mind, the Old Law's ceremonies retain significance and sanctity in the post-biblical world only in what they signify concerning Christ and the Christian sacraments that followed — that is, in what they prefigured about the future offerings of Christ. Scotus says of the many ceremonies and offerings of the Old Testament, "All of those purifications signified purification from sin. The offerings prefigured the completed offering of Christ; and the acts of worship prefigured faith, hope, and charity toward God."[39] By reiterating that Christian law is the law of truth that has perfected the incomplete, only half-realized practices of the Old Law — "the shadow" — Scotus emphasizes that the Old Law has run its course and no longer serves any useful purpose in the form in which it was presented in the Old Testament.

Indeed, Scotus frequently reiterates his belief that the New Law is superior to the Old Law. Scotus contends that the New Law supersedes or replaces the Old Law, not only because the New Law completely realized the Old Testament's rites and beliefs but also because observance of many of the Old Laws was flawed or clumsy and because their practitioners could only have benefited by their replacement. Scotus points to the "harshness of the ceremonies of the Old Law"[40] as evidence of how the New Law improved on the previous system. He interestingly, and not a little surprisingly, cites Maimonides's *Misneh Torah* in support of his claim that the Old Law ceremonies were harsher than those of the New Law.[41] Scotus states, "Rabbi Moses counts more than 600 precepts to which they were all held, certain ones of which were very difficult." To illustrate his point, he then lists three precepts of Old Testament law: the requirement that every Jewish male must present himself in Jerusalem three times a year, "no matter how far distant"; a precept requiring Jews "to be free for two years from the gathering of income/fruit"; and "many others, such as not touching a corpse or not eating or drinking after hauling a corpse without cleansing"[42] — all precepts Scotus judges and assumes his readers will also judge to be unreasonable and excessive. Scotus juxtaposes these more than 600 requirements of the Old Law with the "few and clear rites of the sacraments" of the New Law. He points out that the New Law comprises only seven sacraments and that these seven "are not all necessary for all Christians."[43]

Scotus, utilizing Aquinas's division of the Old Law into the three categories of moral precepts, ceremonial precepts, and judicial precepts, compares the moral precepts of the two laws.[44] Scotus maintains that "moral laws are the same as then, but more explicit." With respect to judicial laws, Scotus asserts that Christ presented no new judicial laws because, under the New Law, which "is more gentle and humane," it was not proper to have judicial laws. He cites St. Paul's criticism of the fractiousness of the ancient Jews in 1 Corinthians 6:7: "For it is a defect in you, that you have law suits at all among you. Why not accept an injury? Why not suffer fraud?"[45]

In his conclusion on this issue Scotus expresses some harsh sentiments about the Old Law. He characterizes the Old Law as one burdened by a "multitude of ceremonies and judicial laws" that ultimately do not benefit the practitioners but "only weigh [them] down."[46] He concludes that the New Law is superior, and ultimately easier to follow, because it is a law of love, whereas the Old Law is "a law of fear" — and love, according to Scotus, "if it were looked for in all things, makes all burdens light." He includes in this passage the declaration that God exhibits many more loving acts to Christians than Jews.[47]

Clearly the Subtle Doctor considers the Old Law to be a system that was useful and blessed in the period before the Passion of Christ but one that was nonetheless flawed and incomplete. The Old Testament Jews merited grace when they followed its precepts, but they were also weighed down by its excessive ceremonies and rules. Even when they followed its precepts with exactitude and devotion, the Old Law did not confer on them the grace necessary to obtain eternal life, nor did it free their hearts properly to love God. Furthermore, the Jews as a people were burdened by a primitive, fractious, and literal-minded character, which was redeemed and made respectable only when the Jews followed the precepts of the Law.

Thus, Scotus believes that the Old Law and the Jews who followed it in the period before the Passion of Christ — and, indeed, for several generations afterward — deserve respect and were rightly rewarded by God for the loyalty and devotion they displayed. Although Scotus argues that it was proper and laudable that they continued to follow the Old Law until it had officially been replaced, he plainly believes that Jewish teachings and beliefs lost all validity and usefulness in the centuries after Christ's death. Scotus clearly believes that, as a result, the post-biblical Jews were unreasonable, stubborn, and selfish for not acknowledging and accepting the New Law when it was finally presented to them.

For Scotus implies that Jews knew that their special pact with God was a temporary one, the purpose of which was to prefigure and to prepare the way for the eventual New Law. He argues that God conferred grace on Old Testament Jews because the passion of Christ "was foreseen by them themselves, and was believed in advance by other faithful, as it was to be performed."[48] The implication of such a stance is, of course, that the Jews should have been ready for and receptive to the preaching of the gospel and the New Law — after all, they knew it was coming and were proud to be paving the way for it.

Scotus's respect for Old Testament law but hostility toward the Jews for their refusal to join the larger fold of Christianity by renouncing, according to Scotus, their antiquated and limited pact with God becomes especially evident in a segment of his discussion on the superiority of New Testament sacraments. In one passage, Scotus declares that God created Christianity as a universal religion that would unite and encompass all of humankind. The Old Law, however, according to Scotus, had a much more limited purpose and focus. Scotus states, "God chose only the Jewish people for the law of Moses, but for the New Law [he chose] the whole world."[49] Scotus thus implies that part of God's intention with the arrival of Christ and the New Law was to broaden the scope of his covenant with the Jews to include everyone. He states several folios later, "There was some future sign of a pact between God and the whole human race; and it was better for the seed of Abraham to cross over to the common pact than to remain under the sign of a special pact. [This is] because it is better to be a part in the whole, for which it would simply be better, than to be distinct from the rest of the part, so that in some way or other it would be good for themselves and bad for others."[50] Here, Scotus clearly criticizes the Jews for refusing to give up their "special pact" and to join the larger fold. By asserting that the Jews feel they benefit from clinging to their special pact, Scotus suggests that the Jews refused to accept Christianity out of selfishness and anger over their reduced status under the New Law.

Even more telling in determining Scotus's attitude toward the Jews than his pronouncements on the value of the Old Law versus the New Law is Scotus's stance on whether the Jews recognized Christ's true nature once he had arrived and thus were capable of, and culpable for, the crime of deicide. Scotus enters the fray concerning the issue of whether the Jews were aware of Christ's divinity when they demanded the Romans crucify him when, in Book Three, Distinction 20 of his *Sentences* commentary, he discusses the issue of whether Christ's passion was necessary to save humankind. In this context he makes clear his opinion on the character and mindset of the first-century Jews by taking issue with Anselm of Canterbury's argument in *Cur Deus Homo* that "no person could ever desire, at least knowingly, to kill God."[51] Scotus responds to Anselm's argument with the simple and ominous statement, "This, I do not believe, but I believe that even if they had known him to be God by [the] union [of Son and Father in God], still they would have been able to have killed him."

It is significant to note that in discussing the killers of Christ in this passage, neither Scotus nor Anselm explicitly names the Jews as those responsible but instead use the generic phrase "those who killed Christ" (*occidentes Christum*).[52] It is likely that both Scotus and Anselm were conscious of the ambiguity in this reference, for beginning with Ambrosiaster in the fourth century, theologians routinely addressed and discussed the question of exactly who could be considered culpable for Christ's death. A central point in the discussion is the question of exactly to whom Paul was referring in 1 Corinthians 2:8 when he mentions that certain "princes of the world" were ignorant of the divine nature of Christ and thus were not guilty of conscious deicide. Ambrosiaster in the fourth century argued that *princes* in this context could only mean the demons, not the Jews and not the Romans. Ambrosiaster argued that the Jews were aware of "the impiety of their actions," but he affirmed the Jews' ignorance of Jesus' divinity.[53] Along the same lines, thinkers such as Augustine and Ambrose argued that what the Jews had done to Christ was evil, but they also contended that the Jews' actions were a result of their ignorance concerning His true nature.[54] Peter Abelard argues similarly in *Ethics* that the Jews killed Christ out of ignorance, leading him to further assert that as a result their crucifixion of Christ could not be considered a true sin.[55]

This attitude began to change, however, in the twelfth century. By the time of the compilation of the *Glossa Ordinaria* on the Bible in the early twelfth century, theologians had begun to argue that the leaders of the Jews — not, however, the masses of uneducated Jews — had indeed realized that Jesus was the Messiah but had failed to recognize his divinity.[56] Though the *Glossa* ultimately adhered to the school of thought that included the Jews among the ignorant princes, its writers added a subtle but important element to this whole argument by making a distinction between the knowledge, and thus culpability, of the Jewish leaders (*majores*) and that of the uneducated Jewish masses (*minores*). The *Glossa* argued that the Jewish masses were completely ignorant of Jesus' true nature, but though ignorant of Jesus' divinity their leaders recognized him as the Messiah promised in their Law.

Some twelfth-century theologians, such as Peter Comestor, adopted the argument that limited Jewish ignorance to the uneducated masses and contended that only the leaders were aware of his messiahship; nevertheless, the argument in support of general Jewish ignorance still held sway among many theologians of the late twelfth and early thirteenth centuries. Alexander of Hales and Albertus Magnus argued that the Jewish leaders recognized that Jesus was a holy man but were unaware of the magnitude of their crime in killing him. Bonaventure and Hugh of St. Cher both developed harsher arguments concerning the knowledge and intention of the Jewish leaders yet still concluded that the Jews were ultimately ignorant of Jesus' divinity.[57]

Thomas Aquinas took a much harsher stance with regard to the Jews' knowledge of their crime. Aquinas refused to concede that all first-century Jews were free of the sin of deicide and resorted to the same strategy found in the *Glossa* of dividing the Jewish community at the time of Christ's death into two groups and assigning a different level of guilt to each group. In the article in Part Three of his

Summa, Aquinas states quite explicitly, "a distinction must be drawn between the Jews who were educated and those who were not."[58] He then pronounces, "The educated, who were called their rulers, knew, as did the demons, that Jesus was the Messiah promised in the Law."[59] Significantly, however, with this stance separating the first-century Jews into two categories, Aquinas stops short of viewing or declaring all members of the Jewish community guilty of the conscious crime of deicide.

Scotus does not discuss the issue of the Jews' knowledge of Jesus' nature in as much depth as Aquinas did, nor as Peter Auriol,[60] a near contemporary of Scotus, later did. Aquinas devotes an entire question to this issue, and Peter Auriol expands on it for many paragraphs, the Subtle Doctor discusses the issue quite briefly and only in the context of the redemptive power of Christ's Passion. In this context he very briefly and baldly states that he disagrees with Anselm's pronouncement that the killers of Christ could not have knowingly killed him. Scotus was obviously aware of the argument distinguishing between the knowledge and culpability of the leaders of the Jews and that of the mass of their uneducated followers. He makes use of such a distinction himself in Book Four of his *Sentences* commentary in his discussion of the licitness of Peter's behavior when preaching to the Jews. At this juncture, Scotus cites Matthew 15:14 in which Christ criticizes the Pharisees for following the rules of ritual purity too literally. He explains that Christ states that it remains acceptable to disobey the laws of ritual purity when necessary, even though it would offend Jews, "because there was not therein any cause of offense to the perfect [*perfectis*], nor to the lesser ones [*parvulis*], but only to the Pharisees."[61] In Book Three, question 40, of his *Sentences* commentary where Scotus compares the harshness of the Old Law to that of the New Law, he again singles out the Pharisees from the general Jewish populace and refers to the less educated Jewish people as "the simple ones" (*simplices*).[62]

Although Scotus differentiates among the various groups of Jews in these two contexts, he does not choose to make such a distinction in the context of discussing the Jews' ignorance of Christ's divinity. Instead, with a simplicity and straightforwardness from which even Aquinas shies, Scotus presents the Jewish people as one homogeneous body, declaring in the context of addressing the identity of those "princes of the world" whom Paul had declared were ignorant of Christ's nature: "[The Apostle] was not speaking of the Jews, but about the princes of the world, namely, about the demons."[63] Scotus's view of the character of the first-century Jews soon becomes more evident in the comment in which he states that he believes the Jews — all Jews, not just their leaders — were capable of killing a man whom they knew to be God. He declares, "I believe that, even if they had known him to be God by union, still they would have been able to have killed him."[64] Thus, if elsewhere Scotus argues that the Jews of the Old Testament were backward, primitive, and violent, redeemed only by their devotion to the Law, he here adds to their flaws a willingness to kill the Son of God, the religious figure for whose arrival they had knowingly and consciously paved the way. In his discussion concerning the redeeming power of Christ's Passion, Scotus depicts the Jews as evil and spiteful people, capable, if not actually guilty, of wantonly killing their God.

Perhaps this image of Jews as unreasonable, self-serving people, unwilling voluntarily to join the larger fold and capable of knowingly killing their God allows Scotus to feel justified in arguing for the forcible conversion of all Jews. On this issue, Scotus's stance was not fully in accord with the tenets of the Christian church and its practices. It had been the clear and standard Christian position from the time of Augustine that, with respect to adults, only a person who voluntarily accepted baptism was able to receive its benefits.[65] By the thirteenth century, Aquinas was able to devote dozens of folio pages to the nuances of what comprised a valid baptism but was also able to cite and support many impressive arguments against the forced baptism of non-Christians. He addresses the issue directly in his discussion of whether "infidels ought to be compelled to believe." Embedded in his discussion of apostates and heretics, Aquinas declares, "Among unbelievers there are some who have never received the faith, such as heathens and Jews. These are by no means to be compelled, for belief is voluntary."[66] He repeats these same sentiments in his more specific discussion of what constitutes a licit baptism. In this context he makes the simple and unnuanced pronouncement, "Therefore, the will or the intention of receiving the sacrament is required on the part of the one being baptized." He then pronounces in conclusion, with little discussion, "an adult who lacked the intention of receiving baptism should be rebaptized."[67]

Yet in the same century when Aquinas was making such straightforward declarations against forced baptism, the conception and definition of what constituted the voluntary acceptance of baptism had begun to develop ominous loopholes. In 1201 Pope Innocent III, responding to general consensus and practice, pronounced that if anyone who was being baptized against his or her will ceased objecting at any point during the baptizing process, this could be interpreted as an expression of conditional willingness or consent, even though, strictly speaking, the individual was not truly willing.[68] Scotus expresses his agreement with the papal pronouncement on this point and even contributes a further justification and explanation for it. As does Aquinas, Scotus devotes an entire question to the issue of "whether someone who does not consent can receive the effect of baptism."[69] After much discussion, Scotus states, "If someone does not consent, but only by not wanting (*tantum negative*), I say that he receives the sacrament if he consents virtually." To support this argument he states that God does not obligate a human being to do the impossible or to do something that for his position in life is "very, very difficult." Scotus explains that due to the weakness of the human will it is very difficult for any person to fully assent to follow God's will. But, according to Scotus, God understands this and is content with whatever level of assent an individual is able to give. The result of this is that God "in accepting baptism, does not oblige humans to be undistracted."[70] Of course, this position is quite charitable to a sinful, eager, would-be Christian desiring absolution in baptism, but it takes on threatening implications for unwilling non-Christians forced to accept baptism. According to Scotus's argument, if an individual consents to baptism out of fear or a desire to escape injury or death, God considers this conditional acceptance sufficient to make the baptism valid.

Scotus also directly addresses the question of whether a person who feigns consent receives the effect of baptism. He explains that by "feigning consent" he means "those who present on the exterior that which is different from what they have on the interior.[71] After some discussion, he declares that such individuals may show themselves to be disposed to receiving grace "and nevertheless not be disposed on the inside, either because they do not have the right faith, or because they are suffering from some mortal sin."[72] In this context, Scotus bluntly states, "in no way does such an individual receive grace."[73] This position worries Scotus somewhat, however, because, according to basic Christian doctrine, baptism cannot be repeated, with the result that the path to salvation would be barred to such individuals because they could not be rebaptized if they should change their minds and sincerely desire baptism. Later thinkers solve this problem by arguing that a feigned baptism would simply not be considered valid in any form and such individuals could and should be re-baptized if they later change their minds and sincerely desire to accept baptism.[74] Scotus, however, states, "such an individual cannot be re-baptized."[75] He chooses to resolve the problem then by asserting that such individuals could receive grace and thus salvation by sincerely repenting their sins or feigned consent, in which case they would not need to receive baptism again, implying that the first, involuntary baptism conferred a limited but nonetheless lasting effect.

In the course of this discussion of the elements of an effective baptism, Scotus deals at some length with the question of whether the children of Jews should be baptized against the will of their parents, an issue that seems to have developed a practical application for the first time in the 1260s. Solomon Grayzel found a papal bull he conjectures was produced by Pope Clement IV between 1265 and 1286 that directly responds to the actions of a certain bishop on this point. In this bull, the pope orders the bishop to return a Jewish child who had been abducted by Christian authorities to her parents. Among the reasons the pope gives for his mandate is that "not to return the child would give some critics an opening for maligning the Church."[76] Aquinas presents in his *Summa Theologiae* a slightly less down-to-earth argument against the baptism of Jewish children without the consent of their parents. Aquinas argues that according to natural law, Jewish children are the property of their parents and thus may not be removed from their parents or baptized against the wishes of their parents.[77] Scotus responds to this contention with the elaborate argument that though private persons cannot baptize Jewish children against the will of their parents, a public person, in the form of the prince under whose dominion the parents live, may rightfully do so. According to Scotus, a hierarchy exists in the cosmos with God at the top and secular princes in an intermediary position below God but above private persons. If a conflict arises between these powers, the higher one must prevail over the lower one; as a result, the prince, occupying an intermediary position, is obligated to serve his highest lord, God, in the way that would be the most beneficial to that lord.[78] According to Scotus's argument then, the prince has the right, even the duty, to override parental rights and fulfill God's desire to have all people baptized into the Christian faith.[79]

Some scholars argue that Scotus's development of this unusually harsh stance in favor of the forced conversion of Jews, for which he has become infamous,[80] is simply a byproduct of Scotus's general theory of salvation in which he holds that God does not require even willing Christians to accept baptism with all their heart and soul.[81] Yet Scotus's general teachings on salvation do not and cannot explain or justify Scotus's extreme position in favor of the forcible baptism of all Jews. For Scotus at this point goes even further and makes the radical argument that Jewish adults should also be forcibly baptized. He supports this stance with the contention that even if forcibly converted adult Jews do not remain faithful to the Christian religion, nevertheless their children, if educated in the faith, will become faithful by the third or fourth generation. He also insists that even if these adult Jews are not faithful to Christianity, less evil results from preventing Jews from observing their laws than from allowing them to practice their religion with impunity.[82]

With this radical position encouraging the forced conversion of Jewish adults as well as Jewish children, Scotus is not only at odds with the directives of numerous popes and theologians against such conversions; he is also arguing in opposition to the centuries-old doctrine of Jewish witness.[83] This doctrine, developed by Augustine and reiterated by nearly every major Christian thinker from the fifth century on, asserts that Jews play a necessary, even vital function in God's plan for human salvation and Christian faith; thus, Jews must not be killed or converted by Christians but rather be protected and preserved within a larger Christian society. Augustine explains in his *De civitate Dei*[84] that God had a clear purpose in allowing Jews to continue to live and practice their faith after the arrival of Christ; namely, their observance and thus preservation of the teachings of the Old Testament provide testimony to the truth of the prophecies concerning Christ. To support this argument, he points out the injunction contained in Psalms 59:11: "Slay them not, lest at any time they forget your law; scatter them in your might."[85]

In addition to the concept of Jewish witness, theologians throughout the early and High Middle Ages had routinely drawn on the pronouncement of St. Paul in Romans 9:27 to justify a continued Jewish presence within Christian society. In this passage, Paul cites the prophecy of Isaiah (Isaiah 10:22) that a remnant of Israel must be present at the Second Coming. Scotus is obviously aware of this declaration by Paul since he cites it explicitly in his discussion on this point.[86] Thus, Scotus clearly faces a dilemma on the issue of whether it is licit to forcibly convert Jews. On the one hand, he argues that the forced conversion of all Jews would be of benefit to both Jews and Christians. On the other hand, both the New and Old Testaments, as well as the doctrine of Jewish witness, require that a remnant of Jews be allowed to exist within Christendom until the Final Days. What, then, is Scotus's solution? While technically staying within the boundaries of orthodox Christian teaching, Scotus chooses to distort the biblical command that a remnant of Jews must be present at the Second Coming.[87] With an almost breathtaking literalism, Scotus suggests that a handful of Jews (*aliquos paucos*) be taken and placed on an island somewhere (*aliqua insula*) and there be allowed to go on practicing their faith.[88] Apparently, as far as Scotus is concerned, allowing a few Jews to live sequestered on an island is all that is required of a Christian society to fulfill God's command requiring the continued existence of Jews.[89]

There are many possible explanations for Scotus's extreme call for a nearly Jew-free society achieved by the means of the forced conversion of Jews. We know already that Scotus was not the only resident of England to feel that a Jewish presence was unwelcome and ultimately not necessary, since, as stated earlier, England's King Edward I expelled all Jews from his territory in 1290. One could speculate that perhaps because Scotus did not personally experience anything detrimental as a result of the absence of Jews in the British Isles, he determined that all of Christendom would do fine without them.[90] Indeed, many other writers, artists, and theologians living in England during the hundred years after the Jewish expulsion of 1290 depicted Jews in extremely harsh terms as well.[91] Perhaps this negative portrayal of Jews in the fourteenth century by contemporary English Christians was the result of the shared need by the inhabitants of England to justify the lack of Jews on their island by convincing themselves that this "other" was dangerous and contemptible and thus deserved removal from their society.[92]

One could argue as well that Scotus's negative portrayal of Jewish character may have evolved out of the exasperation he shared with many Christian clergy of the late thirteenth century over the Jews' continued refusal to accept Christianity despite the intense conversion efforts that had been directed at them, and Muslims, for more than a century.[93] As the end of the thirteenth century approached and few Jews or Muslims had converted, many popes, theologians, and secular rulers, in addition to Scotus, reacted with anger and frustration at what they saw as the stubborn unreasonableness of the Jews for refusing to accept what Christians believed to be logically demonstrable Christian doctrines.[94] Along these same lines, many modern scholars have argued that much of this more intense hostility on the part of religious thinkers toward Jews was the result of a growing emphasis in the thirteenth century on achieving an all-encompassing religious unity throughout Christendom. As Jeremy Cohen argues, by the thirteenth century "all of society came to be viewed as an organic unity, whose *raison d'etre* consisted of striving for and ultimately realizing the perfect unity of Christ on earth."[95] Scotus's insistence that it would simply be better for Jews to join "the whole" rather than to be "distinct from the rest," certainly seems to be an expression of this sentiment[96] and would explain his intense antagonism to their refusal to join the Christian faith.

Finally, Scotus's sentiments supporting the near eradication of contemporary Jews by means of their forced conversion were undoubtedly intensified and perhaps even the result of the Christian "discovery" of the Talmud in the thirteenth century. Christian thinkers had been aware since the fourth century of the existence of the Talmud, but well into the High Middle Ages Christian scholars had viewed the Talmud as simply a tool used by Jewish thinkers to analyze the Hebrew scriptures. Christian leaders' perception of the Talmud changed, however, in the thirteenth century with the actions of Nicholas Donin of La Rochelle, a Jewish convert to Christianity. Based on motivations that remain unclear, in 1236 Donin drew up a list of 35 charges against the Talmud and presented them to Pope Gregory IX. Donin claimed, among other things, that the Talmud licensed theft, religious intolerance, even murder, and contained direct attacks on the church.[97] Donin further argued that the Talmud contained blasphemies and expressed an intense hostility to Christianity. Based on Donin's report and analysis, Gregory, echoing Donin, proclaimed that the Talmud "contained matter so abusive and so unacceptable that it arouses shame in those who mention it and horror in those who hear it."[98] He pronounced that Talmudic Judaism was a perverse and deliberate deviation on the part of the Jews from the religion of the Old Testament, rendering the Talmud and its Jewish users a dangerous and corruptive element within Christian society. Gregory thus directed the kings of France, England, Spain, and Portugal to confiscate all of the books of the Jews in 1240, and after a lengthy postponement to allow a formal inquisitional process to take place an estimated 10,000 to 12,000 volumes of the Talmud were burned at the stake in Paris in 1242.[99]

In the next decade, Pope Innocent IV takes up Gregory's attack against the Talmud and castigates the Jews for abandoning their proper belief in the Old Testament in favor of the Talmud's "heresies." He charges that in their use of the Talmud, contemporary Jews "throw away and despise the Law of Moses and the prophets, and follow some tradition of their elders." He includes among these traditions "blasphemies," "abusive errors, and unheard-of follies."[100] The declaration by these Christian leaders that post-biblical Jews had deviated from the teachings entrusted to them by God posed a serious threat to the doctrine of Jewish witness. If the reason for allowing the Jews to exist within a Christian society was so that they might serve as a reminder of the truths contained in the writings of the Old Testament, once Jews were perceived by Christian leaders to no longer be living according to the precepts of the Old Testament their purpose in society and thus their protected status was no longer defensible.

Clearly, this contention that the Jewish witness to the truths of the Old Testament was no longer in effect is what motivates Scotus to argue that it is reasonable to call for the forcible conversion of all but a tiny number of Jews. Because of the Jews' willingness to consult the "blasphemous" Talmud to find religious inspiration, their status as pristine witnesses to the teachings of the Old Testament was no longer valid. As a result, according to Scotus, the justification for the Jews' right to live within Christendom was no longer applicable, and their forced conversion to Christianity was fully justifiable. With the teachings of John Duns Scotus on Jews and Judaism then, we see clear signs of a weakening in the effectiveness of the doctrine of Jewish witness to protect European Jews from calls by secular and religious leaders to eliminate them from Christian society and the beginning of a disintegration of a Christian doctrine that had served to create a place within Christendom for Jews for nearly a millennium.

Notes

1. Several works treat Scotus's influence on his contemporaries and on later medieval thinkers; see, among others, Etienne Gilson, *History of Christian Philosophy in the Middle Ages* (New York: Random House, 1955), 454–71; Efrem Bettoni, *Duns Scotus: The Basic Principles of His Philosophy*, trans. Bernardine Bonansea (Washington, DC: Catholic University Press of America, 1961). For a lucid discussion of the importance and influence of Scotus's doctrines concerning the univocity of being, and intuitive and abstractive cognition, along with excellent bibliographies of the primary and secondary literature on these issues see Stephen D. Dumont, "Theology as a Science and Duns Scotus's Distinction between Intuitive and Abstractive Cognition," *Speculum* 64 (1989): 579–97; Dumont, "The Univocity of the Concept of Being in the Fourteenth Century: John Duns Scotus and William of Alnwick," *Mediaeval Studies* 49 (1987): 1–75; Dumont, "The Univocity of the Concept of Being in the Fourteenth Century: II: The De Ente of Peter Thomae," *Mediaeval Studies* 50 (1988): 186–256.
2. Allan Wolter, *Philosophical Writings: John Duns Scotus, A Selection* (Indianapolis: Bobbs-Merrill, 1962), ix–xvii. See also Bettoni, *Duns Scotus,* 1–7; Charles Balic, "The Life and Works of John Duns Scotus," in *John Duns Scotus, 1265–1965,* ed. John K. Ryan and Bernardino M. Bonansea (Washington, DC: Catholic University of America Press, 1965), 1–27; A. G. Little, "Chronological Notes on the Life of Duns Scotus," *English Historical Review* 47 (1932): 568–82; Richard Cross, *Duns Scotus* (Oxford: Oxford University Press, 1999), 3–5.
3. Indeed, until recently, the English were considered to have been the originators of the ritual murder libel; however, John McCulloh persuasively argues that the libel first appeared not in England but in Germany at the time of the Second Crusade; McCulloh, "Jewish Ritual Murder: William of Norwich, Thomas of Monmouth, and the Early Dissemination of the Myth," *Speculum* 72 (1997): 698–740. For the development and spread of the ritual murder libel in England, see Gavin I. Langmuir, "Thomas of Monmouth: Detector of Ritual Murder," *Speculum* 59 (1984): 820–46.

4. See Langmuir, "The Knight's Tale of Young Hugh of Lincoln," *Speculum* 47 (1972): 459–82.

5. Roth, 78.

6. Bernhard Blumenkranz, *Die Judenpredigt Augustins* (Basel: Helbing & Lichten-hahn, 1946); Paula Fredriksen, "Divine Justice and Human Freedom: Augustine on Jews and Judaism, 392–398," in *Witness to Witchcraft*, 29–54; for an excellent overview of Augustine's teachings on the doctrine of Jewish witness, see Cohen, 23–65.

7. For an analysis of the teachings of Peter Lombard on Jews and Judaism, see Nancy L. Turner, "'An Attack on the Acknowledged Truth': French, English and German Theologians on the Jews in the Fourteenth Century" (Ph.D. diss., University of Iowa, 1996), 18–28. For an excellent study of Thomas Aquinas's writings on Jews and Judaism, see, among others, John Y. B. Hood, *Aquinas and the Jews* (Philadelphia: University of Pennsylvania Press, 1995).

8. *In Sententias*, 4, d. 3, q. 4, in Luke Wadding, ed., *Joannis Duns Scotus Opera Omnia* (Paris: Vives, 1891–95), Vives XVI 343b: "quia lex vetus non erat mala, sicut est idololatria, et ideo non debuit subito repelli, in hoc enim fuisset repulsa quasi mala. Sed debuit Synagoga cum honore sepeliri, ut ostenderetur fuisse bona pro tempore suo." All English translations of Latin passages from Scotus's works throughout the article are mine.

9. Ibid., 4, d. 1, q. 6, Vives XVI 196b: "Item Beda super illud Lucae 2: Postquam consummati sunt dies octo. 'Idem salutiferae curationis auxilium Circumcisio in lege agebat, quod Baptismus tempore gratiae agere consuevit.'"

10. Ibid., 4, d. 1, q. 6, Vives XVI 209b: "quia Deus nullo tempore reliquit genus humanum sine remedio necessario ad salutem, maxime illos, quibus ipse legem dedit."

11. Ibid., 4, d. 1, q. 6, Vives XVI 209b: "Non possunt autem attingere ad salutem sine deletione originalis culpae."

12. *Summa Theologiae*, 3.70.4.

13. *In Sententias*, 4, d. 1, q. 6, Vives XVI 209b: "Concedo ergo conclusiones ultimarum rationum, quod de potentia absoluta posset Deus dimittere culpam originalem, non conferendo gratiam."

14. Ibid., 4, d. 1, q. 6, Vives XVI 220a: "Quoad hoc teneo quod non est possibile de potentia orinata, culpam originalem, nec aliquam aliam mortalem dimitti sine infusione gratiae."

15. Ibid., 4, d. 1, q. 6, Vives XVI 220a: "et ideo nullum liberat, nec sic liberare potest a culpa, nisi cui dat gratiam."

16. For an enumeration and discussion of the views of "alii" see the sixteenth-century editors' commentary on this passage of Scotus's work in Vives XVI, 224–26.

17. *In Sententias*, 4, d. 1, q. 6, Vives XVI 220a: "Alii dicunt, quod principaliter instituta fuit propter dimissionem originalis, ex consequenti autem ad gratiam conferendam; et pro tanto dicitur non conferre gratiam, quia non ex principali institutione, sed concomitanter."

18. Ibid., 4, d. 1, q. 6, Vives XVI 220a: "Addo etiam contra secundam opinionem, quod principaliter intenditur gratia in Circumcisione, quod probo, quia agens secundum rectam rationem, principalius intendit perfectionem, quam carentiam defectus, sive imperfectionis, quia non intendit illam carentiam, misi propter perfectionem. Deus

ergo in instituendo Circumcisionem (cum sit agens secundum rectam rationem) principalius intendit perfectionem positivam, puta gratiam quam carentiam imperfectionis, id est, peccati originalis."

19. Ibid., 4, d. 1, q. 6, Vives XVI 221b–222a: "ergo Judaei ex charitate observantes Sacramenta improprie dicta, meruerunt gratiam, vel augmentum eius, si eam jam habebant, sed non propter hoc illa erant proprie Sacramenta. Sacramentum enim ex virtute operis operati confert gratiam."

20. Ibid., 4, d. 1, q. 6, Vives XVI 221b: "Erant etiam ibi Sacramenta improprie dicta, alia ab istis, tamen plus accidentia ad perfectionem, cuiusmodi erant oblationes hostiarum; haec enim pertinebant ad cultum latriae pro tempore, in quo Deus voluit sic coli; haec et illa, scilicet purgationes et sacrificia sive oblationes, dicebantur caeremoniae et improprie Sacramenta. Et de istis concedo, quod non causabant gratiam tanquam signa efficacia respectu gratiae, eo modo quo expositum est in definitione Sacramenti, sed tamen in illis conferebatur gratia per modum meriti."

21. Ibid., 4, d. 3, q. 4, Vives XVI 344a: "quia dicitur Matth. 13 'Super cathedram Moysi sederunt,' etc."

22. Ibid., 4, d. 1, q. 6, Vives XVI 222b: "et intelligo, nihil ei intus contulit per modum Sacramenti, sive virtute operis operati; sed credo, quod ei contulerit per modum meriti, sive virtute operis operantis, quia credo, quod actus circumcidendi se ex obedientia Dei, et ex charitate procedens, ei fuit meritoris, sicut et immolatio Isaac."

23. Ibid., 4, d. 1, q. 6, Vives XVI, 221b: "Hoc enim videtur nimis durum, scilicet quod aliquia ex charitate et et obedientia sit servans Dei praeceptum, et non mereatur. Hoc etiam videtur irrationabiliter dictum, quod Deus alicui dederit praeceptum, nolens observantem praeceptum mereri, quantumcumque ex charitate et obedientia observaret...ergo Judaei ex charitate observantes Sacramenta improprie dicta, meruerunt gratiam."

24. Ibid., 4, d. 1, q. 6, Vives XVI, 228a: "Ad tertium de apertione januae, dico, quod non fuit defectus Circumcisionis, quod non aperuit januam, sed quia cucurrit tempore, quo pretium non fuit solutum, nam post solutum pretium, potuit alicui aperiri janua, qui non fuisset baptizatus, sed solum circumcisus, et in gratia; baptizato vero defuncto ante passionem, non patuisset janua pro tunc."

25. *Summa Theologiae*, 1a2ae.103.3. For an analysis of Aquinas's stance on the efficacy of circumcision and Old Testament rites, see Turner, "Attack on the Acknowledged Truth," 37–42.

26. *In Sententias*, 4, d. 3, q. 4, Vives XVI 343a: "Ex quo dicto accipio istam propositionem, quod nullus tenetur ad aliquod praeceptum divinum, nisi per aliquem idoneum et authenticum sibi promulgetur. . . . illud autem positivum quod praecessit de Circumcisione, non debuit statim dimitti, ex quo certum fuit, quod a Deo fuerat institutum, nisi etiam certitudo fieret illud secundum fuisse datum a Deo; haec autem certitudo de secundo non poterat haberi sine promulgatione authentica."

27. Ibid., 4, d. 3, q. 4, Vives XVI 346b: "Item, nunquam fuit homo relictus sine remedio certo, et de quo non esset certus, quod erat remedium certum; sed in illo tempore post passionem, ante publicationem, nullum fuit aliud certum novum remedium datum eis, quia nec publicatum."

28. Ibid., 4, d. 3, q. 4, Vives XVI 346b: "Item, post mortem Christi usque ad promulgationis tempus, Judaei tenebantur circumcidere parvulos suos, quia nullo modo constabat eis de revocatione Circumcisionis."

29. Ibid., 4, d. 3, q. 4, Vives XVI 347a: "et in ipso Paulo, et in Judaeis conversis approbatur observatio legis; et ipse Paulus ibidem inter tot Christianos opus legis implevit."

30. Ibid., 4, d. 3, q. 4, Vives XVI 369a: "Et si quaeras, quando fuit Circumcisio simpliciter illicita, etiam Judaeis conversis? Respondeo, quod tempus illud non habemus in Scriptura aliqua, quia historica Scriptura non perducit Ecclesiam ultra quintum annum Neronis, scilicet, non ultra trigesimum annum a passione Christi, et toto illo tempore etiam Judaei conversi observabant legem, quod hoc fuerit omissum usque ad eversionem Jerusalem, sive ad dispersionem Judaeorum cum Gentibus, inter Judaeos conversos; tunc enim forte conformabant se Gentibus, inter quas erant dispersi, et sic paulatim cessavit etiam apud eos observatio." In fact, Scotus holds that the only explicit evidence we have that the Old Law was officially superseded is a promulgation by Innocent III declaring it heretical to practice the Old Law and the law of the Gospels together: Ibid., 369a-b: "Vel potest aliter dici, quod Deus per Apostolos, vel successores eorum, determinato tempore, simpliciter prohibuit legalia servari, licet de hoc non habeamus in Scriptura, quia historia Scripturae non datur, vel durat usque ad illud tempus. Istud autem est probabile, quia Ecclesia tenet, quod haeresis est dicere legalia currere cum lege Evangelica, ut habetur Extrav. de Baptismo et eius effectu, c. Majores, ubi dicit Innocentius: 'Absit ut in illam damnatam haeresim incidamus, quae perperam affirmabat legem cum Evangelio, et Circumcisionem cum Baptismo servandum.'"

31. Ibid., 4, d. 3, q. 4, Vives XVI 357a: "et quibusdam incepit tempus secundum ad mensem post Pentecosten, et aliquibus ad annum, aliquibus ad decem annos, et sic deinceps, sicut eis praedicabatur."

32. Ibid., 4, d. 3, q. 4, Vives XVI 367a: "non enim potest dici, quod tunc reprehensibilis erat, quia servabat tunc legem nam post illud factum, etiam Paulus circumcidit Timotheum."

33. Ibid., 4, d. 3, q. 4, Vives XVI 368a: "Primum enim poterat dici reprehensibile, quia 'ad quamcumque Ecclesiam veneris, illi te conformes,' ait Ambrosius Augustino; ergo reprehensibile fuit in Ecclesia Gentium, non conformare se modo eorum vivendi, vel quia in hoc dabat occasionem Gentibus servandi legem, vel quia ostendens facto illud esse necessarium, vel saltem necessarium ad hoc ut conversi ex Judaeis vellent communicare cum eis, et saepe inferiores facerent aliqua difficilia, ne excludentur a communione superiorum…Secundum etiam potest intelligi, vel quia simulabat, non reputans hoc corde esse faciendum, quod fecit in opera…dici reprehensibile, quia non utebatur auctoritate Praelati. Cum enim esset superior illis nuntiis Jacobi, magis debebat ipse veritatem constanter tenere in opere, et eos adducere ad rectitudinem suam, quam propter timorem eorum flecti ad illud, quod erat eis placitum, vel magis acceptum."

34. Ibid., 4, d. 3, q. 4, Vives XVI 368b-369a: "Petrus autem in Jerosolyma servans legem, non peccavit, quia licuit Judaeo, et inter Judaeos legem servare tunc."

35. Ibid., 4, d. 3, q. 4, Vives XVI 369b: "Ad illud Joan. 19. 'Consummatum est,' dico quod hoc intelligur de his, quae scripta sunt de filio hominis, juxta illud Lucae 18, 'Ecce ascendimus Jerosolymam, et consummabuntur omnia quae scripta sunt per Prophetas de filio hominis.' Vel si illud referatur ad antiquam legem, sic debet intelligi: Consummatum est in causa, nam mors Christi causa erat confirmationis legis Evangelicae; sed illa non fuit confirmata tanquam necessaria ad observandum, ante praedicationem eius publicam, quae non incepit in passione, sed in Pentecoste."

36. Ibid., 1, d. 2, q. 3, Vives VIII 499a: "Dico quod populus Judaicus fuit rudis et pronus ad idololatriam, ideo indiguit instrui per leges de unitate Dei, licet per rationem naturalem poterat demonstrari." Also see Jacob Guttmann, "Die Beziehungen des Johannes Duns Scotus zum Judenthum," *Monatschrift für Geschichte und Wissenschaft des Judentums* 38 (1894): 26–39.

37. *In Sententias*, 3, d. 20, Vives XIV 737b–738a: "vidit enim mala Judaeorum, quae fecerant, et quomodo inordinata affectione et distorta afficiebantur ad legem suam, nec permittebant homines curari in Sabbato, et tamen extrahebant ovem vel bovem de puteo in Sabbato, et multa alia (Mat. 12 et Marci 4. Lucae 6 et Joan. 7 et 9). Christus igitur volens eos ab errore illo revocare, per opera et sermones, maluit mori quam tacere, quia tunc erat veritas dicenda Judaeis."

38. Ibid., 3, d. 20, Vives XIV 737b–738a: "Caeremonialia autem non manent in se, sed in suis significatis, quia umbra transiit, et veritas successit. Scotus also utilizes this imagery earlier in this question: "Debuit etiam istud Sacramentum esse evidens in significatione, quia ista est lex veritatis evacuans umbram."

39. Ibid., 3, d. 20, Vives XIV 370a-370b: "Omnes enim illae purificationes significabant purificationem a peccato, et illae oblationes figurabant oblationem perfectam Christi, et actus quosdam latriae, fidei, spei et charitatis in Deum."

40. Ibid., 3, d. 40, q. 1, Vives XV 1085a: "sed haec gravitas non aequiparatur gravitati caeremonialium legis veteris."

41. For the frequent citing of Maimonides by thirteenth-century Christian thinkers see Guttmann, *Die Scholastik des Dreizehnten Jahrhunderts in ihren Beziehungen zum Judenthum und zur Jüdischen Literatur* (Breslau: M. & H. Marcus, 1902).

42. *In Sententias*, 3, d. 40, q. 1, Vives XV 1085b: "Rabbi Moyses enumeravit plus quam sexcenta praecepta, ad quae omnia tenebantur illi; quorum quaedam erant valde difficilia, puta quod omne masculinum ter in anno praesentaretur in Jerusalem, quantumcumque distarent; et septimum annum colere, propter quod oportebat eos duobus annis vacare a collectione fructuum, et multa alia, sicut de non tangendo morticinum, vel de non comedendo vel bibendo post tractum mortui sine baptismo."

43. Scotus explains that baptism is necessary for all Christians, as is penance after a lapse into mortal sin. He points out, however, that not everyone is called to orders, nor is everyone required to marry. Moreover, confirmation, the Eucharist, and extreme unction "are easy enough," he contends. He contends that of all the sacraments, confession is the most difficult, but the confessor can make it easier; Ibid., 3, d. 40, q. 1, Vives XV 1086a: "Lex autem nova secundum Augustinum ibidem, paucis et manifestis Sacramentorum ritibus contenta est; non enim habet, nisi septem Sacramenta, quae etiam omnia non sunt omnibus Christianis necessaria. Non enim omnes matrimonium contrahunt, sed necessarius est Baptismus, et post Baptismum in peccatum mortale recidivando Poenitentia, ita quod difficilius, quod est in Ecclesia, videtur esse Confessio. Difficile enim videtur alicui peccata sua privata, soli Deo et sibi nota revelare alicui homini; sed ibi apposita sunt remedia, ita quod propter revelationem talem non oportet timere confessionem; obligatur enim audiens ad maximum sigillum secreti. Alia Sacramenta a Baptismo et Poenitentia forte non sunt necessaria, aut si sunt, sunt satis facilia, puta Confirmatio, Eucharistia, Extrema unctio."

44. For a brief but useful discussion of Aquinas's categories, see Cohen, 376–77.

45. *In Sententias,* 3, d. 40, q. 1, Vives XV 1085a: "In lege autem nova moralia sunt eadem quae tunc, sed magis explicata. Caeremoni sunt multo pauciora et leviora, quae imposita sunt per Christum. Judicialia nulla sunt posita per Christum, sed magis est lex militatis et humanitatis, in qua non oportet habere judicialia, juxta illud 1. Cor. 6. 'Jam quidem omnino delictum est in vobis, quod judicia habetis inter vos. Quare non magis injuriam accepistis, quare non magis fraudem patimini.'"

46. Ibid., 3, d. 40, q. 1, Vives XV 1096b: "Ad primum concedo quod si lex nova contineat omnia moralia, quae lex vetus, et addat alia, vel saltem addat aliquam explicationem aliquorum, ad quae forte ipse non tenebantur, quod quantum ad hoc est gravior; tamen hoc non tantum gravat, sicut ex alia parte gravat caeremonialium multitudo, et judicialium."

47. Ibid., 3, d. 40, q. 1, Vives XV 1097a: "multi enim actus dilectionis Dei immediate magis explicantur Christianis quam Judaeis. Nec mirum, quia illa dicitur esse lex timoris, haec autem amoris; amor autem et praecipue finis, si ille quaeratur in omnibus, facit omnia onera levia."

48. Ibid., 4, d. 2, q. 1, Vives XVI 247b: "et etiam respectu gratiae collatae antiquis Patribus, tamen majorem efficaciam habet respectu nostrorum Sacramentorum et gratiae nunc conferendae, quam tunc; quia juste obsequium exhibitum ad bonum majus acceptatur, quam praevisum. Trinitas autem nunc confert tanquam propter passionem Christi exhibitam, etiam a nobis creditam, ut exhibitam; tunc autem contulit, ut propter eam a seipso praevisam, et ab aliis fidelibus praecreditam, ut exhibendam."

49. Ibid., 4, d. 3, q. 6, Vives XVI, 334b: "quia Deus ad legem Moysi elegit unum populum tantum, sed ad novam legem totum mundum."

50. Ibid., 4, d. 3, q. 6, Vives XVI, 370b–371a: "tamen futurum erat aliquod signum foederis, inter Deum et totum genus humanum; et melius erat semini Abrahae transire in illud foedus commune, quam remanere sub igno foederis specialis, quia melius est partem esse in toto, cui simpliciter bene sit, quam esse distinctum a caeteris partibus, ut sibi aliqualiter bene sit, et aliis male."

51. See discussion of Anselm's stance in Cohen, 173–79.

52. *In Sententias,* 3, d. 20. q. 1 Vives XIV 732b: "Praeterea, perpassionem Christi non potuerunt redimi occidentes Christum; igitur nec genus humanum."

53. For a useful survey of Christian thinkers' positions on the Jews' knowledge of Christ's divinity, see Jeremy Cohen, "The Jews as the Killers of Christ in the Latin Tradition from Augustine to the Friars," *Traditio* 39 (1983): 1–27.

54. Ibid., 8–10.

55. Peter Abelard, *Ethics,* D. E. Luscombe, ed. and trans. (Oxford: Clarendon Press, 1971), chap. 13, 14. For more on Abelard's writings on the Jews' culpability for Christ's death, see Robert Blomme, *La doctrine du péché dans les ecoles théologiques de la première moitié du XIIe siècle* (Louvain: Publications Universitaires de Louvain, 1958), 147–54.

56. Cohen, "Jews as Killers," 13–14.

57. Ibid., 13–19.

58. 3, 37, 5.

59. Ibid., 71.

60. For an analysis of the teachings of the fourteenth-century French Franciscan Peter Auriol on the character and sins of the first-century Jews, see Turner, "Jews and Judaism in Peter Auriol's *Sentences* Commentary," in *Friars and Jews in the Middle Ages and Renaissance,* ed. Steven McMichael and Susan Myers (Leiden: Brill, 2004), 81–98.

61. *In Sententias,* 4, d. 3, q. 4, Vives XVI 386a–b: "Nec potest excusari Petrus, quod hoc faceret propter scandalum Judaeorum vitandum, quia non erat ibi materia scandali perfectis, neque parvulis, sed tantum Pharisaeis."

62. Ibid., 3, d. 40, q. 1, Vives XV 1085a: "ita enim docuerunt Pharisaei simplices de populo."

63. Ibid., 3, d. 20, q. 1, Vives XIV 739a: "Et quod Apostolus dicit: 'Quod si cognovissent, nunquam Dominum gloriae crucifixissent,' (1 Cor. 2) loquitur non de Judaeis, sed de principibus mundi, scilicet de daemonibus."

64. Ibid., 3, d. 20, q. 1, Vives XIV 739a: "Ad aliud dico, quod peccatum occidentium Christum potuit redimi, tamen Anselmus dicit 15 capt. 2 <Cur Deus Homo>, quod non potuerunt eum scienter occidisse, hoc tamen non credo, sed credo quod licet scivissent eum Deum per unionem, adhuc potuissent eum occidisse; et si hoc fecissent, adhuc eorum peccatum fuisset remediabile per passionem Christi, quia plus dilexit Deus illam passionem acceptando quam odisset eorum malum."

65. Henri Krop, "Duns Scotus and the Jews: Scholastic Theology and Enforced Conversion in the Thirteenth Century," *Nederlands Archief voor Kerkgeschiedenis* 69 (1989): 169; Solomon Grayzel, "Confessions of a Medieval Jewish Convert," *Historica Judaica* 27 (1955): 90–91.

66. *ST* 2a2ae.

67. *ST* 3.68.7.

68. Grayzel, *Church and the Jews,* 15; Grayzel, "Confessions of a Medieval Jewish Convert," 92.

69. *In Sententias,* 4, d. 4, q. 4, 416a: "Utrum non consentiens possit recipere effectum Baptismi?"

70. Ibid., 4, d. 4, q. 4, 416a–b: "Si autem non consentiat tantum negative, dico quod recipit Sacramentum, si consensit virtualiter, quia noluit Deus obligare hominem ad impossibile, vel secundum statum huiuh vitae, nimis difficile. Nunc autem non distrahi nimis vidteru difficile homini pro statu, quia secundum Agustinum 3. de liber arbit. 'Non est in voluntate nostra, quin visis tangamur'; ergo noluit Deus salutem hominis ponere in ista conditione, 'si non distrahatur.' Nec ergo voluit obligare eum, quod in suscipiendo baptismum, non distraheretur; et ita est universaliter in aliis Sacramentis."

71. Ibid., 4, d. 4, q. 5, 425b: "fictus dicitur, qui aliud preatendit exterius, aliud habet interius."

72. Ibid., 4, d. 4, q. 5, 426a: "Alio modo potest aliquis esse fictus, ostendendo se esse dispositum ad recipicendum Sacramentum, et tamen non est dispositus interius, vel quia non habet rectam fidem, vel quia habet aliquod peccatum morale tunc in actu, vel praeteritum."

73. Ibid., 4, d. 4, q. 5, 426b: "nullo modo recipit gratiam."

74. See the pronouncements to this effect by the late fourteenth-century thinkers James of Eltville and Pierre d'Ailly in Turner, "Attack on the Acknowledged Truth," 218–19, 238–39.

75. *In Sententias,* 4, d. 4, q. 5, 426b: "Respondeo, rebaptizari non potest, quia Deus instituit Baptismum initerabilem."

76. Grayzel, "Popes, Jews, and Inquisition: from 'Sicut' to 'Turbato,'" in *Essays on the Occasion of the Seventieth Anniversary of the Dropsie University,* ed. A. I. Katsh (Philadelphia: Dropsie University, 1979), 160–61.

77. *ST* 2a2ae.10.12.

78. *In Sententias,* 4, d. 4, q. 9, Vives XVI 487b: "Sicut ergo Imperator deberet sententiare aliquem obedire debere Proconsuli, contempto praecepto Curatoris, id est, inferioris Proconsule, si contradiceret Proconsuli, ita etiam, si essent sub eodem dominio ordinata, scilicet, quod aliquis esset servus Titii, et Titius Petri, magis deberet Imperator cogere servum servire Petro, quia superior est Titio quam Titio, si Titius vellet uti servo illo contra dominium Petri; ergo maxime debet Princeps zelare pro dominio servando supremi Domini, scilicet Dei, et per consequens non solum licet, sed debet Princeps auferre parvulos a dominio parentum volentium eos educare contra cultum Dei, qui est supremus et honestissimus dominus, et debet eos applicare cultui divino."

79. Scotus's contention on this point was undoubtedly an outgrowth of the common tenet of "Jewish serfdom," which accorded a status to Jews that approximated that of being the private property of the king in whose territory they dwelled. Recent scholars such as J. A. Watt point out that the day-to-day, practical implications of the concept of Jewish serfdom were so nebulous that it is almost impossible to generalize concerning them; however, much evidence exists that legal laymen, such as Scotus, routinely viewed Jews as being the actual property of the "public person" or king under whom they lived, rendering Jews' children the property of the king as well. Watt, "The Jews, the Law, and the Church: the Concept of Jewish Serfdom in Thirteenth-Century England," in *The Church and Sovereignty, c. 590–1918,* ed. Diana Wood (Oxford: Basil Blackwell, 1991), 153–72. There are numerous studies on the status of Jews as royal serfs in the Middle Ages. See, among others, James Parkes, *The Jew in the Medieval Community* (New York: Hermon Press, 1976); Langmuir, "'Judei Nostri' and the Beginning of Capetian Legislation," *Traditio* 16 (1960): 203–39; Guido Kisch, *The Jews in Medieval Germany: A Study of Their Legal and Social Status* (New York: Ktav Publishing House, 1970).

80. Willehad Paul Eckert, "Theologie und Rechsprechung hinsichtlich der Juden im 13.Jh," in *Aquinas and Problems of His Time,* ed. Gerard Verbeke and D. Verhelst (Louvain: Leuven University Press, 1976), 81–82; Guttmann, "Die Beziehungen des Duns Scotus," 30–31.

81. Krop, "Duns Scotus and the Jews: Scholastic Theology and Enforced Conversion in the Thirteenth Century," *Nederlands Archief voor Kergeschiedenis* 69 (1989): 170, explains Scotus's teachings: "Sinful man is not able to choose for God with all his heart. Hence, God is content with less. He does not require that man should assent fully to the bond with God brought about in baptism." Krop directly cites Scotus's teachings: "God does not want to make our salvation dependent on the condition that we do not will other things (si non distraheretur). So, in accepting baptism, he did not oblige man to be undistracted. Generally this applies to all sacraments." *In Sententias,* 4 d. 6, q. 4, Vives XVI, 420b; Krop's central purpose with this article is, in essence, to support his argument that Scotus's teachings condoning and encouraging the forcible baptism of Jewish children and adults should not be construed as extreme or exceptional. Krop argues that Scotus's views on the forced conversion of Jews are simply the logical byproduct of his teachings on salvation and on the proper relationship between secular and ecclesiastical powers. See Krop, "Duns

Scotus and the Jews," 171–75. He bolsters his position that Scotus's hostile teachings on the Jews are purely the outcome of the larger conclusions Scotus reaches concerning the relationship between earthly and spiritual powers in Book 4, distinction 6 with the clearly false contention that "this question with the Latin title: 'utrum parvuli Judaeorum et infidelium sint invitis parentibus baptizandi,' constitutes the only text by Duns Scotus in which the Jews are discussed."

82. *In Sententias,* 4 d. 6, q. 4, Vives XVI, 489a: "Immo quod plus est, crederem religiose fieri si ipsi parentes cogerentur minis et terroribus ad suscipiendum Baptismum, et ad conservandum postea susceptum, quia esto quod ipsi non essent vere fideles in animo, tamen minus malum esset eis, non posse impune legem suam illicitam servare, quam posse eam libere servare. Item filii eorum, si bene educarentur in tertia et quarta progenie, essent vere fideles." The argument Scotus presents here is intimated, although not as explicitly stated, by Gregory the Great in a letter he wrote to a deacon in 594; see Cohen, 77.

83. Cohen's *Living Letters of the Law* is a masterful description of the history of how the doctrine of Jewish witness was accepted and incorporated into Christian policy concerning the proper treatment of Jews in the fifth through the thirteenth centuries. For more on the doctrine of Jewish witness see also Robert E. Lerner, *The Feast of Saint Abraham: Medieval Millenarians and the Jews,* (Philadelphia: University of Pennsylvania Press, 2001), 23-24.

84. Augustine, *De civitate Dei* 18.46, CCSL 48: 644–45.

85. Cohen, 33.

86. *In Sententias,* 4, d. 4, q. 9, Vives XVI 489b: "Et si dicas quod secundum prophetiam Isaiae, quam recitat Paulus Rom 9:27, 'Reliquiae Israel convertentur in fine'; et ideo Judaeos non oportet cogere totaliter ad Baptismum suscipiendum et relinquendum legem suam."

87. It is ironic, given the Christian condemnation of Jewish literalism, that Scotus chooses to follow the letter of Christian teaching concerning the preservation of the Jews on this issue but arguably ignores its spirit.

88. *In Sententias,* 4, d. 4, q. 9, Vives XVI 489b: "Et si dicas, quod visa destructione Antichristi, illi qui sibi adhaeserant, convertentur, dico pro tam paucis, et sic tarde convertendis, non oporteret tot Judaeos, in tot partibus mundi, tantis temporibus sustinere in lege sua persistere, quia finalis fructus de eis Ecclesiae est, et erit modicus. Unde sufficeret aliquos paucos in aliqua insula sequestratos permitti legem suam servare, de quibus tandem illa prophetia Isaiae impleretur." Scotus seems blind to the irony that he had been born, raised, and educated on the island of Great Britain — an island that would conceivably have served quite adequately as a location where his handful of Jews could have been sequestered. One suspects, however, that this is not the island Scotus had in mind.

89. Fortunately for the Jewish community of the late Middle Ages, Scotus's rather extreme pronouncements in favor of forcible conversion were noted but not adopted by thinkers who followed him. For instance, the French theologian Peter Auriol discusses the Subtle Doctor's argument calling for the forcible baptism of Jewish children at length but ultimately pronounces in favor of Aquinas's argument that Jewish children are, according to natural law, the possession of their parents and cannot be removed from the parents and baptized; see Turner, "Jews and Judaism," 81–98. Much later in the fourteenth century, the French theologian Pierre d'Ailly

(d. 1420) presents Scotus's argument that public persons may remove children from their Jewish parents to have them baptized but chooses not to make his own pronouncement on the issue; see Turner, "Attack on the Acknowledged Truth," 238.

90. For an analysis of how the lack of a Jewish presence in England influenced other Christian thinkers and writers in the late Middle Ages, see Denise L. Despres, "Mary of the Eucharist: Cultic Anti-Judaism in Some Fourteenth-Century English Devotional Manuscripts," in *Witness to Witchcraft*, 388–89.

91. See, for instance, more than a dozen essays on the negative portrayal of Jews in fourteenth-century England in Sheila Delany, ed., *Chaucer and the Jews: Sources, Contexts, Meanings* (New York: Routledge, 2002).

92. See Sylvia Tomasch's arguments to this effect in Tomasch, "Postcolonial Chaucer and the Virtual Jew," in ibid., 69–85.

93. See Robert I. Burns, "Christian–Islamic Confrontation in the West: The Thirteenth-Century Dream of Conversion," *American Historical Review* 76 (1971): 1386–1434; Robert C. Stacey, "The Conversion of Jews to Christianity in Thirteenth-Century England," *Speculum* 67 (1992): 267–73.

94. See, for instance, Robert Chazan, *Daggers of Faith: Thirteenth-Century Christian Missionizing and Jewish Response* (Los Angeles: University of California Press, 1989), 180–81.

95. Cohen, *Friars and the Jews,* 248.

96. See ibid., 256.

97. Ibid., 71.

98. As quoted in ibid., 66.

99. Ibid., 62–63.

100. Ibid., 67.

Contributors

Maureen Boulton, professor of French at the University of Notre Dame, has edited the Old French *Evangile de l'Enfance* (Pontifical Institute of Medieval Studies, 1984) and a related text in Anglo-Norman, *Enfaunces de Jesu Crist* (Anglo-Norman Text Society, 1985), and published a study of lyric quotations in thirteenth- and fourteenth-century romances, *The Song in the Story* (University of Pennyslvania Press, 1993). She collaborated with Ruth J. Dean on *Anglo-Norman Literature: A Guide to Texts and Manuscripts* (Anglo-Norman Text Society, 1999). She is currently working on translations of Anglo-Norman texts of popular piety for the series The French of England and a study of apocryphal lives of Christ in Old and Middle French titled *Pious Fictions.*

Daniel F. Callahan, professor of history at the University of Delaware, received his Ph.D. in 1968 from the University of Wisconsin, Madison, where his major professor was David Herlihy. He has published articles on tenth- and eleventh-century spirituality, with a concentration on the writings of Ademar of Chabannes. His most recent pieces include "The Cult of St. Michael the Archangel and 'The Terrors of the Year 1000,'" in *The Apocalyptic Year: Religious Expectations and Social Change, ca. 950–1050,* edited by R. Landes and D. Van Meter (Oxford University Press, 2002). He is currently working on the book *The Making of a Millennial Pilgrim: Jerusalem and the Cross in the Life and Writings of Ademar of Chabannes.*

Michael Frassetto is an independent scholar and adjunct instructor at the University of Delaware. He has earned degrees from LaSalle University (B.A.), Michigan State University (M.A.), and the University of Delaware (Ph.D.). He is the editor of *Heresy and the Persecuting Society in the Middle Ages* (Brill, 2006); *Medieval Purity and Piety: Essays on Medieval Clerical Celibacy and Religious Reform* (Garland Publishing, 1998); *The Year 1000* (Palgrave/MacMillan, 2002) and coeditor, with David Blanks, of *Western Views of Islam in Medieval and Early Modern Europe: Perception of Other* (St. Martin's Press, 1999).

Matthew Gabriele is assistant professor and coordinator of medieval and Renaissance studies in the Department of Interdisciplinary Studies at Virginia Tech. A recent graduate of the University of California, Berkeley, he has published articles on the emperor Otto III and the Oxford *Chanson de Roland*. His current project focuses on the legend of Charlemagne and the origins of the First Crusade.

John D. Hosler was educated at Iowa State University and the University of Delaware, where he was awarded his Ph.D. in 2005. He is now assistant professor of British history at Morgan State University in Baltimore, Maryland. A specialist in Anglo-Norman and Angevin England, he has contributed to the *Haskins Society Journal* and the *Journal of Medieval Military History*.

Phyllis G. Jestice is associate professor of history and department chair, University of Southern Mississippi. She is the author of *Wayward Monks and the Religious Revolution of the Eleventh Century* (Brill, 1997) and numerous articles on medieval religion and history. She has also translated several works and is the editor of *Holy People of the World: A Cross-Cultural Encyclopedia* and *Encyclopedia of Irish Spirituality* (ABC-CLIO, 2004).

Constant J. Mews is associate professor in the School of Historical Studies, Monash University (Australia), where he is director of the Centre for Studies in Religion and Theology. He specializes in the religious and intellectual history of medieval Europe, with particular attention to the twelfth century. His publications include *The Lost Love Letters of Heloise and Abelard: Perceptions of Dialogue in Twelfth-Century France* (St. Martin's Press, 1999) and *Abelard and Heloise* (Oxford University Press, 2004) in the Great Medieval Thinkers series.

Alex Novikoff has taught classes in medieval history at the University of Pennsylvania and Temple University and Western civilization at St. Joseph's University and Franklin College in Lugano, Switzerland. He has published articles on medieval intellectual history and historiography in *Medieval Encounters*, in the *Haskins Society Journal* and *Pensiero Politico Medievale*. He is currently completing a translation of Jean-Claude Schmitt's *La Conversion d'Hermann Le Juif: Autobiography, Histoire et Fiction* for the University of Pennsylvania Press.

Thomas Renna is professor of history at Saginaw Valley State University, Michigan. He received his Ph.D. in medieval history from Brown University and has published several books, including *Jerusalem in Medieval Thought, 400–1300* and *The West in the Middle Ages* (E. Mellen Press, 2002), and over 100 scholarly articles on intellectual history of the Middle Ages and the Renaissance. He has also lectured on Jerusalem throughout the United States, Europe, and Israel.

Patricia Skinner is reader in medieval history at the University of Southampton. She is the author of *Family Power in Southern Italy: the Duchy of Gaeta and its Neighbours c. 850–1100* (Cambridge University Press, 1995), *Health and Medicine in Early Medieval Southern Italy* (Brill, 1997), and, most recently, *Women in Medieval Italian Society, c. 500–1200* (Longman, 2001). She is editor of *Jews in Medieval Britain* and has recently published on Jewish topics in *Past and Present* and *Early Medieval Europe.*

Nancy L. Turner is associate professor of history at the University of Wisconsin, Platteville. Her research focuses on Christian theologians' writings on non-Christians in the High and late Middle Ages, and she has published several articles on theologians' attitudes toward Jews and Judaism in the late Middle Ages. In addition to investigating theological issues, her research includes an examination of interactions between Christian and non-Christian thinkers in the areas of medieval science and astronomy.

Index

.